# CAPTAIN ELLIOT AND THE FOUNDING OF HONG KONG

In memory of my father
Charles Bursey
1916 – 1984

# CAPTAIN ELLIOT AND THE FOUNDING OF HONG KONG

## PEARL OF THE ORIENT

Jon Bursey

PEN & SWORD
HISTORY

First published in Great Britain in 2018
by Pen and Sword History
An imprint of
Pen & Sword Books Limited
47 Church Street,
Barnsley,
South Yorkshire
S70 2AS

Copyright © Jon Bursey, 2018

ISBN: 978 1 52672 256 0

The right of Jon Bursey to be identified as Author of this work has been asserted by him in accordance with the Copyright, Designs and Patents Act 1988.

A CIP catalogue record for this book is available from the British Library

A         l

Pri                                          ial

Pen & Sw                                    s of Atlas,
Archaeolog                          n, History,
Maritime, N                         nsport, True
Crime, Air Wo                     ember When,
Seaforth Put                      ocal History,
Wharncli                          White Owl.

For a complete list of Pen & Sword titles please contact
PEN & SWORD BOOKS LIMITED
47 Church Street, Barnsley, South Yorkshire, S70 2AS,
United Kingdom
E-mail: enquiries@pen-and-sword.co.uk
Website: www.pen-and-sword.co.uk

# Contents

# Acknowledgements

With apologies for any omissions, I offer my warmest thanks to all who have assisted me with the project.

The staff of the following libraries and institutions have been unfailingly helpful: the UK National Archives, Kew; the National Library of Scotland, Edinburgh; the London School of Economics; the University of Durham; the University of Hong Kong; the University of Cambridge; the Institute of Historical Research, University of London; the British Library, London; Birkbeck, University of London; the National Maritime Museum, Greenwich; the National Portrait Gallery, London; the London Library; the South West Heritage Centre, Exeter; Exmouth Museum and Exmouth Library.

Specific enquiries have been very helpfully answered, or access granted to sources, by Martin Barrow, Matheson and Co. Ltd.; Ken Brown, Archivist at Reading School; Dr Patrick Conner, Martyn Gregory Gallery; Richard Dabb, National Army Museum; Hugh Elliot, Queensland, Australia; Colin Fox, Friends of St Helena; Karla Ingemann, Records Officer, Bermuda Archives; and Keith Searle, Online Parish Clerk for Withycombe.

My thanks are due to my family and to former colleagues and other friends who have provided advice, encouragement, references, and practical help. They include Professor Dame Glynis Breakwell; Peter Bursey; Roger Clayton; Dr Ellie Clewlow; Ian Dixon; Diana Driscoll; Dr Shane Guy; Alasdair Meldrum; Eleanor Moore; Michael Niblock; Dr John Thomas; and Professor Vernon Trafford. My daughters and sons-in-law have been generous in accommodating me for my work in London. Above all, I am indebted to my wife Rowena for her interest, patience and constructive criticism, which have been invaluable and have sustained me throughout.

This brief expression of gratitude would not be complete without reference to my former colleagues the late Professors Kenneth Bourne and Michael Leifer, whose supportive and interested comments first sowed the seed, and to Claire Hopkins, Karyn Burnham and Janet Brookes at Pen and Sword for guiding me through the final stages.

Any remaining errors and infelicities in the text are entirely my own responsibility.

JB

# Author's Note

The events which shaped the establishment of Hong Kong as a colony have been the subject of numerous studies. Many have written about the First Anglo-Chinese War, usually referred to as the Opium War, over several decades and from different standpoints. In reading those accounts I have been struck, as have others, both by the crucial nature of Elliot's role and by the comparative lack of recognition accorded him subsequently as a person and for his work. I have sought in this book to describe his life and the challenges that faced him, and to set them in historical context.

I have consulted the only two works hitherto specifically about Elliot, Clagette Blake's 1960 biography *Charles Elliot RN 1801 – 1875: A Servant of Britain Overseas* and, especially, Susanna Hoe's and Derek Roebuck's 1999 study, reprinted in 2009, *The Taking of Hong Kong: Charles and Clara Elliot in China Waters*. Blake's book has the Texas period of Elliot's life as its main focus, though giving almost as much attention to his time in China. Hoe's and Roebuck's work concentrates on the China years and makes extensive use of personal correspondence from the collection of Minto family papers. I too have drawn heavily on those documents, and I owe a special debt to *The Taking of Hong Kong* for pointing me to them. Much has been written covering Elliot's role in China, less concerning his activities in Texas, and very little about the rest of his life. It has been my intention to cover the whole of Elliot's career as thoroughly as sources permit.

On the text:
For the sake of authenticity I have reproduced spelling, punctuation and syntax from sources as they appear in the original, odd though they may sometimes seem, including the apparently random use of capital letters. Elliot's own usage is often idiosyncratic but the meaning is always clear where it matters. His handwriting is notoriously difficult to read, but I have had the benefit of the work of others (especially Hoe and Roebuck) in deciphering much of it, for which I am duly grateful.

Except in a few cases where Anglicisation is more appropriate to the narrative, for example Hong Kong and Canton, pinyin Romanisation has been used for Chinese proper names.

Where sums of money are mentioned, illustrative present-day values are also usually noted, but as a rule of thumb mid-nineteenth century figures should be multiplied by 110 to give approximate real-terms worth for 2015.

# Maps

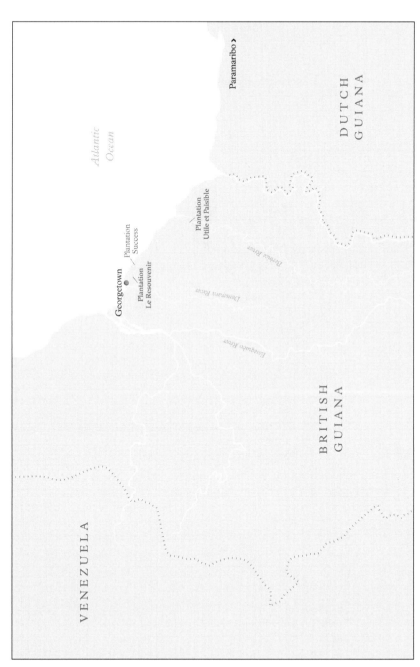

Northern British Guiana.

Pearl River Delta.

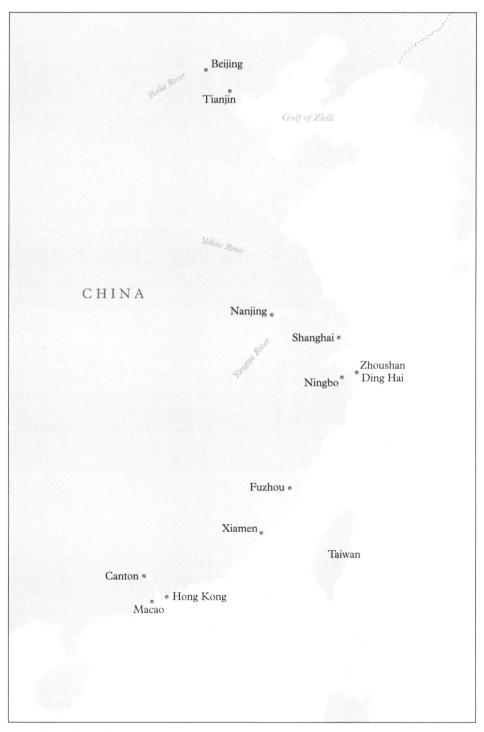

East China Coast

LOUISIANA

New Orleans

Mississippi R.

Gulf of
Mexico

Sabine R.

REPUBLIC
OF TEXAS

Washington

Galveston

Brazos R.

Houston

Austin

San Antonio

MEXICO

Republic of Texas

# List of Illustrations

1. Captain Charles Elliot c.1855 while Governor of Trinidad
   Photo. courtesy of the Governor of Trinidad and Tobago c.1953, from Clagette Blake, *Charles Elliot RN* (Cleaver-Hume, London 1960).
2. Minto House, Hawick, c.1910
   Historic Environment Scotland.
3. Rt. Hon. Hugh Elliot
   The Bodleian Libraries, University of Oxford.
4. Reading School and Playground, 1816
   Edmund Havell
   By kind permission of the Old Redingensians Association.
5. Bombardment of Algiers, 1816
   Thomas Luny
   Private Collection (Copyright), Royal Exchange Art Gallery at Cork Street, London/Bridgeman Images.
6. HMS *Minden* off Scilly, 1842
   Lieutenant Humphrey J. Julian
   Copyright National Maritime Museum, London.
7. Slave ship captured by boats of the Royal Navy, 1824
   Image Reference Magasin8, as shown on www.slaveryimages.org, compiled by Jerome
   Handler and Michael Tuite, and sponsored by the Virginia Foundation for the Humanities and the University of Virginia Library.
8. Emma, Lady Hislop (née Elliot)
   Thomas Charles Wageman
   Courtesy of Private Collection.
9. Georgetown Harbour, British Guiana c.1850
   Courtesy of Private Collection.
10. Henry John Temple, third Viscount Palmerston, 1844–45
    John Partridge
    Copyright National Portrait Gallery, London.
11. Howqua
    Lamqua
    Pictures from History/Bridgeman Images.
12. William Jardine
    Thomas Goff Lupton, after George Chinnery, 1830s
    Copyright National Portrait Gallery, London.

# Prologue

Relatively few people have heard of Captain Charles Elliot. Of those who have, most have probably done so because of his part in the founding of modern Hong Kong. While Governors, Colonial Secretaries and even junior officials are commemorated in eponymous streets and institutions, there is hardly any public recognition of Elliot in Hong Kong today. Glenealy, a steep ravine between Robinson Road and Wyndham Street on Hong Kong island, was formerly known as Elliot's Vale, and there is a government map book reference to an Elliot Crescent near the Roman Catholic Cathedral (though no evidence on the ground).[1] Elsewhere in the world there are a few other isolated reminders, such as a school in Bermuda and a small coastal town in South Australia.

This is neither a 'rags to riches' nor an 'obscurity to fame' story. Elliot was in many respects a man of his time; born into an ancient Scottish border family some of whose members had already achieved fame (or in an earlier, more turbulent age, notoriety). He had some distinguished contemporary relations, and he did not at that time stand out as an exceptional figure for someone of his background. In his early career, in the Royal Navy, and in his later career, as a colonial governor, Elliot was working in established organisational structures where expectations of him were, on the whole, clear and he could usually see the way forward. His mid-career years, taken up with his British Guiana, China, and Texas assignments, were on the other hand often nearer the other end of the spectrum, with less clarity both about his roles and about the policies which governed them. Some degree of uncertainty was inevitable; the three posts he held had each been established in response to particular, and problematic, local circumstances, and in Guiana and China his predecessors' performances had been less than impressive. These appointments were especially challenging.

Charles Elliot died in 1875. The seventy-four years of his life had seen huge changes in Britain, Europe and the wider world. Britain, which was reaping the commercial rewards of the industrial revolution, had through enterprise, philanthropy and military superiority attained a position of global pre-eminence.

For most of Elliot's life the dominant political figure in British foreign policy was Henry John Temple, third Viscount Palmerston (1784–1865) who as Secretary at War (1809–28), Foreign Secretary (1830–34, 1835–41, 1846–51) and Prime Minister (1855–58, 1859–65) played a major role in the projection of British power abroad. Palmerston's part in the Elliot story is important for the points at which the two men interacted directly during Elliot's China years (1834–1841), although for much of that time Palmerston was preoccupied with foreign policy issues closer to home, in Europe and the middle East.

In pursuing their overseas objectives Palmerston and mid-nineteenth-century British governments were confident in the knowledge that the Royal Navy, whose power and effectiveness had reached a peak in the protracted wars with France from 1793 to 1815, could generally be relied on to administer enforcement when required. From a peacetime complement in the eighteenth century of between 20,000 and 40,000, naval manpower at the height of the Napoleonic Wars totalled around 150,000. During the several decades of relative peace which followed, often known as the Pax Britannica, and with the gradual replacement of sail by steam-driven vessels, the size of the navy reduced. Britain nevertheless remained the world's leading maritime power.

Advances in ship design and the introduction of steam led to major improvements in communications. Voyages to far-flung parts of the world became significantly faster, having a direct effect on the execution of the British government's policies by its servants overseas. Between the 1830s and the 1860s average mail times to the Americas and Southeast Asia more than halved (though to Asia that reduction was also due to the introduction of the overland route between the Mediterranean and the Red Sea).

As better communication made imperial officials more readily accountable to government, legislation at home was making government – and Parliament – more accountable to the people. The Great Reform Act of 1832, which extended the franchise to all men in the towns and eliminated a number of undemocratic institutions such as the 'rotten boroughs', paved the way for further electoral reform and the eventual establishment of universal suffrage in the next century.

Humanitarian pressure groups were active alongside the movements for political and social change; chief amongst these was the campaign to abolish the slave trade throughout the British Empire. The campaigners achieved their aim after twenty years in the Act of 1807, and it became an important role of the Royal Navy thereafter to police the seas in enforcement of the legislation. By 1838 slavery had formally ended in all British overseas territories.

The impetus for political change was one consequence of the substantial movement of labour from the countryside to the towns, and of the resulting pressure groups and other organisations established to ameliorate the living conditions of the urban poor. The population of the towns and cities did not grow solely because of migration from rural areas, though; the population of the country as a whole grew dramatically in the first half of the nineteenth century, and to support this growth Britain needed the proceeds of trade.

The loose association of ever-changing formal and informal spheres of British influence which came to be known as the British Empire constituted a flexible framework in which commercial enterprises sought, with varying degrees of success, to develop and extend the trading opportunities they had established. The old saying that 'trade follows the flag' was rarely true. Though they had government support in principle, the companies formed in the seventeenth century in England, Holland, Portugal and France to pursue commerce in the East were essentially private ventures. It was nearly always the case that the flag followed trade.

The English East India Company, formed in 1600, came during the eighteenth century to dominate British trading activities not only in the East Indies but, more importantly, in India and China. Its monopoly, and by the start of the nineteenth century its indebtedness, had become matters of concern to the British government, which through legislation in 1813 and 1833 partially and then fully opened up to competition the areas in which it operated. It was Palmerston who in 1858, after what was known as the Indian Mutiny, presided over the transfer of responsibility for India from the East India Company to the British Crown.

With the exception of some five months in 1834–35 when the post was held by the Duke of Wellington, the only British Foreign Secretary apart from Palmerston during Elliot's mid-career period was the Earl of Aberdeen, who held office in Peel's Tory government from 1841 to 1846. It was to Aberdeen that Elliot was responsible for the execution of government policy while he was in Texas; it had been Palmerston from whom he had taken instructions in China, and the Secretary of State for War and the Colonies, Viscount Goderich, through the Governor, Sir Benjamin D'Urban, while in British Guiana. In Elliot's later years as a colonial governor there were thirteen different Secretaries of State, and in his naval career he served under at least nine different captains; but his reputation in history owes much, for better or worse, to his interaction with senior figures in England from his assignments in Guiana, China, and Texas.

# PART ONE

# Chapter One

# Forbears, Father and Family

When Charles Elliot was born on 15 August 1801, his father Hugh was 49, well over half way through a career in which he distinguished himself as a soldier and a diplomat. The Elliot clan was well-known in the Scottish Borders and in the upper echelons of British society and had already produced a number of accomplished lawyers, statesmen, diplomats, sailors, and poets.

In earlier, more turbulent, times the Elliots had become prominent for rather different reasons. A late nineteenth century chronicler of the clan's beginnings in the border country says that it was at the start of the sixteenth century that they began to feature with increasing frequency, 'chiefly at first in the criminal records, and later in the letters of the English border officers … Like their neighbours the Armstrongs, they were not only one of the most powerful, but also one of the most lawless and unruly of the Border clans'.[1]

The first Sir Gilbert Elliot (c. 1650–1718), great-grandfather of Hugh) made his money in the law, having established a substantial practice as an advocate by the time he was knighted in 1692. His wealth enabled him to purchase three Border estates in 1696 and 1697, and in 1703 he bought Minto, mid-way between modern day Jedburgh and Hawick, which he made his principal seat.[2] It remained the family home of the Minto Elliots almost continuously for the next nearly three hundred years.[3] Sir Gilbert had in 1700 become a baronet; the title passed on his death to his elder son (c.1693–1766), also named Gilbert and also an advocate. Like his father, the second baronet adopted the judicial title Lord Minto, served for a time as Member of Parliament (MP) for Roxburghshire, and became a senior figure in the Scottish legal system. He and his wife Helen Steuart had nine children, including Gilbert (1722–77), who in due course became the third baronet. This was Charles Elliot's grandfather, a prominent politician and scholar who served as an MP for twenty-four years[4] and, among other offices, as a Lord of the Admiralty and Treasurer of the navy.

Hugh Elliot was the second of Sir Gilbert's sons. Of his siblings, five brothers and two sisters, Hugh was closest to his elder brother, Gilbert. The two boys were tutored at home until 1764 when on advice given by their father's friend, the philosopher David Hume, they travelled to Paris to attend the *Pension Militaire* at Fontainebleau. After two years there the brothers returned to Britain, attending the Universities of Edinburgh and Oxford. Their ways then parted. Gilbert embarked on further study at Lincoln's Inn, while in 1770 Hugh went back to France, to the Military

Academy at Metz, in anticipation of the military career to which he had provisionally been committed as a boy.[5]

Many years later Hugh Elliot's granddaughter Emma (Nina), Countess of Minto, wrote a biography of him.[6] An admirer of Charles Elliot, Sir Henry Taylor, commented to Charles that

> In talking to N[ina] three weeks ago of your father as he appears in her book, she said to me what I had been saying once and again to others, that you were the person in whom he seemed to be reproduced, and that the resemblance was constantly coming out.[7,8]

Nina was born just six years before Hugh Elliot's death and her view of him, and hence of the likeness between him and her uncle Charles, will have been based largely on the perceptions of others (though it may be nonetheless valid for that) and on the record of what he did; Taylor on the other hand had almost certainly been at least acquainted with him and was a close friend of Charles. In Hugh Elliot's personal and professional life can be seen indications of the characteristics that would be passed on to his children and particularly – if Nina and Taylor are to be believed – to his son Charles.

The first setback in Hugh Elliot's career came early. The practice of purchasing military commissions had since the late seventeenth century become a widespread method of officer entry to the army, and during the eighteenth century it became commonplace also for commissions to be bought for children. Hugh had been granted a commission in the Guards when he was ten, but notwithstanding his military education, it was not confirmed.[9] There were however other options. Military experience of a full and direct kind could be had not by merely enlisting in an army but by joining a war. Hugh Elliot accordingly launched himself straightaway into active service by signing on as a volunteer with the Russian forces in their 1768–74 conflict with the Turks. Though his time as a soldier was brief, Elliot by all accounts distinguished himself in the 1773 campaign, earning praise from the Russian commander, General P.A. Rumyantsev, for displaying 'a truly British courage'.[10]

Military experience, even if short as in Elliot's case, was often a precursor for a diplomatic career, and at what may seem the very early age of 22 Hugh Elliot was given his first diplomatic appointment, as Envoy-Extraordinary to the Elector of Bavaria in Munich. There was no requirement for aspiring diplomats to receive any special training, and willingness to serve abroad was seen as an important attribute.[11] Except for two years (1790–92) in which he worked unofficially as a special agent (see below), Hugh Elliot undertook formal diplomatic assignments for a total of thirty-two years, from 1774 to 1806. From Munich he was posted to Berlin (1777–82), Copenhagen (1783–89), Dresden (1792–1802), and Naples (1803–06).

The Berlin appointment, Envoy-Extraordinary to the Prussian King Frederick the Great, was an important one in the light of Prussia's role as a major European power. During his tenure, however, Elliot was reprimanded by the British government for encouraging the theft of papers from visiting American agents, an incident which would prove to be one of several blots on his copybook in his diplomatic career. It was symptomatic of an impulsive, maverick streak, a characteristic which, according to his granddaughter, his brother-in-law William Eden described as 'a predominancy of Hotspur vivacity'.[12] He could nevertheless also be calculating and charming; the French General Comte Roger de Damas, who knew Elliot in Naples, wrote

> I often saw Elliot, the English Minister, an extremely pleasant and attractive man, with an active but ill-regulated mind, and always with two aims in view: the service of his government, and his own advancement. If there be two ways of attaining his desire he will always choose the one with the more conspicuous effects. He is keenly imaginative, insincere, unscrupulous and unprincipled: in short he is as dangerous in public affairs as he is amusing in society. Every man in office should fear him, and deal cautiously with him; while a man who takes an interest in affairs and is free for the moment but may be employed for the future should conciliate him, distrust him, and study him – but will certainly enjoy meeting him.[13]

Despite his inclination to the unorthodox, or perhaps because of it, Hugh Elliot achieved some notable successes as a diplomat. The negatives continued to build, however. In 1779 he had married, after eloping with her, the young Prussian heiress Charlotte von Kraut, but the marriage was soon in trouble. She did not go with her husband to Copenhagen; reports reached Elliot there of her continuing infidelity, and in 1783 he divorced her. That was an unusual thing to do at that time, but not as startling as his earlier challenging of a suspected lover – a cousin of Charlotte – to a duel. Elliot was not seriously wounded, but the incident was much talked about in diplomatic circles and is likely to have done significant damage to his reputation. There was one child of the marriage, a daughter, Isabella, born in 1781.

It was probably during his time in Denmark that Hugh Elliot married again. We know little about Margaret Lewis Jones, Charles Elliot's mother.[14] In her biography of Hugh, Nina mentions her in describing a visit to Dresden in 1799 by his brother Gilbert, now the first Earl of Minto: 'Some years had passed since the brothers had met, and in the interval Hugh Elliot had married a beautiful girl of humble birth, but whose personal qualities justified his choice'.[15] Lord Minto himself, writing to his wife, was more effusive: 'She is very handsome – her face and head remarkably pretty, in so much that the celebrated Virgin of

Raphael in the gallery, one of the finest pictures I ever saw, is her exact portrait....'[16] As well as being beautiful Margaret was to prove a loyal wife. She died in 1819, aged 49, having borne nine children.

Following his time in Copenhagen Hugh Elliot had three years to wait before his next posting, but the interval was constructively spent. Then as now governments made use of unofficial agents to influence, cajole and persuade in circumstances in which the formalities of diplomatic exchange would have been disadvantageous or otherwise inappropriate. In the constitutional uncertainty of immediate post-revolution France no decision-making machinery had yet been established for authority to take the country to war; the matter became urgent in 1790 when conflict threatened to break out between Britain and Spain over Nootka Sound, a disputed trading post off Vancouver Island, and Spain called on France to commit itself in support. British attempts to prevent such a commitment were made through formal diplomatic channels, but they were not considered sufficient. Two men, William Miles and then Hugh Elliot, were sent to France to make unofficial contact with members of the new National Constituent Assembly, who included Elliot's old friend and fellow student, the Comte de Mirabeau. Their work was successful. Importantly, the British Ambassador to France was fully aware and supportive of what was being done. Perhaps with examples of Hugh Elliot's past unpredictability in mind, the Prime Minister, Pitt, had cautioned him specifically that,

> whatever confidential communications may take place with the Diplomatic Committee [of the Assembly] for the sake of bringing them to promote our views, no ostensible intercourse can be admitted but through the medium of accredited Ministers or the Secretary of State for Foreign Affairs, and that in the name of the King.[17]

Elliot will have found his mission to France temperamentally more to his liking than his years in Copenhagen. He was subject there to bouts of gloom and despondency; like other diplomats posted to northern Europe, he found the climate and environment depressing, writing to Pitt in 1788 of 'this dismal abode' and of '...a chilling Danish fog, when the distinction between air and water seems to be lost and I only acknowledge my own existence by the intenseness of rheumatic complaints'.[18,19] British diplomats abroad were also inclined to complain about their salaries, which were often found to be inadequate; Hugh Elliot had himself accumulated a critical level of debt while he was at Munich, prompting him to take a period of leave in Switzerland in 1775.

Not all Elliot's communications to his political masters were about pay and conditions; he wrote on several occasions of various aspects of current procedure and practice in the diplomatic world which he found unsatisfactory. These included the engagement of locals or other foreigners as staff in key support roles, and a lack of awareness in Britain of the potential impact abroad of 'invective against foreign princes.... In England where that species of writing is as usual to us as our daily bread it is scarcely remarked, here the shoe pinches and a tight shoe upon a gouty foot is apt to raise ill humour.'[20] Highly pertinent observations such as this were evidence of a broad approach to his work, of his not confining himself to issues of the moment, but they were also indicative of a willingness to speak out as forcefully and as frequently as he thought necessary.

The ten years spent in Dresden were Hugh Elliot's longest assignment. He was Envoy-Extraordinary to the court of the Elector of Saxony, but this was not a key appointment and was to signal the plateauing of his career in diplomacy (though not of service to the crown). Uneventful though the decade was for him professionally, family life was full, five (possibly six) of his children with Margaret being born during these years.[21]

Of his siblings, Charles Elliot became closest to his sister Emma (1794–1866), who, on 30 October 1823, married Lieutenant General Sir Thomas Hislop, thirty years her senior. In the same church on the same day in London the eldest of Hugh and Margaret Elliot's sons, Captain (later Lieutenant Colonel) Henry Elliot, Royal Engineers, was also married, to the heiress Margaret Masterton; the officiating priest was their brother, the Rev. Gilbert Elliot (1800–91). Charles's other elder brother, Edward (Ned) (1796–1866), who was to meet up with him unexpectedly many years later, joined the Indian Civil Service. Dates of birth and death are incomplete for Charles's sisters Harriet (died 1845) and Caroline (Carrie). His two younger brothers were (Hugh) Maximilian (1802–26), who died after only one year of marriage, and Sir (Thomas) Frederick (1808–80), a distinguished civil servant who played a key role in managing the process of emigration to the colonies. For Hugh Elliot the rapid expansion of his family was yet another strain on his finances, about which he had many times sought assistance both from the government and from his bank (Coutts). Writing to his brother the first earl in 1802 he complained,

> Had I enjoyed for only three years out of the thirty I have served, the same advantages which have been conferred upon many of my juniors, I should at present have been free from encumbrance. As it is, my situation with a wife and nine children under my roof is not to be described, and is indeed a miserable conclusion of thirty years' struggle against the inadequacy of my salary[22]

If Hugh Elliot's professional life in Dresden had been relatively quiet, that was to change in Naples. His two immediate predecessors as English Ambassador, Sir William Drummond and Sir Arthur Paget, had each served for very short periods; they had succeeded Sir William Hamilton, who had been in post from 1764 to 1800. During most of Hamilton's tenure the Kingdom of Naples had enjoyed a relatively stable period under the rule of the Bourbon King Ferdinand IV, but Ferdinand's unsuccessful military opposition to Napoleon and the French revolutionaries resulted in his fleeing to Sicily. Though he was allowed to return, France's position was further strengthened in 1806 by the installation of Napoleon's brother Joseph as King of Naples. Against the backdrop of the turbulence which led up to this, Hugh Elliot did not distinguish himself. He sought to act as commander-in-chief of the recently arrived British force by instructing its commanding officer, the veteran General Sir James Henry Craig, first not to leave Naples and then to defend Naples and its associated territories. Elliot was reportedly under the influence of the Queen, a friend of Lady Hamilton and sister of Marie Antoinette; he was 'enchanted by that *femme fatale* of European monarchy, Maria Carolina.'[23] Craig nevertheless departed with his army to Sicily, and Hugh Elliot was recalled to London. There seems little doubt that his overbearing conduct was responsible for the termination of the Naples posting, but the more important consequence was that the recall marked the end of his diplomatic career.[24]

Hugh Elliot and his family had been back in England two years when the question of his next appointment arose. It was not straightforward and took some time to settle; he was uncharacteristically caught in a spell of indecision, writing to his sister-in-law Lady Minto:

> I am still in the greatest possible dilemma.... Within this last week Ministers have proposed to me to return to Sicily and I am to give my answer Sunday next. Innumerable delicate circumstances of a private and public nature concur to render the choice between the West Indies and Sicily exceedingly difficult.[25]

The nature of the 'delicate circumstances' can only be guessed at, but they are likely at least to have included anxiety about the effect of further relocation on family life. From correspondence two months later it seems that his mind may have been made up for him. He wrote, 'I ... have now learnt ... that my destination is finally determined upon, and that I am to proceed with as little delay as possible to Barbadoes'.[26] In the event, Hugh Elliot's next posting was not Barbados but the Leeward Islands, to which he travelled two years later, in 1810, to assume the Governorship of the colony. He did so with very considerable reluctance. Writing to his brother from Madeira, he was contemplating resigning as soon as he decently could:

> I am now upon my voyage to Antigua separated from every individual of my family, without the intention of remaining

there, as I understand from all quarters that the situation of Governor is quite untenable on account of its expense. Circumstances have however rendered it indispensable for me to go there before I relinquish it, and to ascertain upon the spot the impossibility of living there upon the actual income of my office. Mrs Elliot and my children are left in England with my home salary.[27]

In the West Indies the unhappiness arising from his loneliness was reinforced by his experience of slavery. A number of individual instances of ill-treatment, on which as Governor Hugh Elliot was called to adjudicate, confirmed him as an abolitionist. According to the Countess of Minto he wrote to his wife about one case of extreme cruelty in which he had upheld the sentence imposed on a plantation owner: 'God grant that this severe example may teach others in the West Indies to dread a similar fate, should they forget that slaves are their fellow-creatures, and their lives are protected by the laws both of England and the colonies'.[28] Like his father, Charles Elliot too was to develop an abiding hostility to slavery.

When Hugh Elliot returned to England in 1813 at the end of his Governorship his next (and final) assignment followed without delay. He was appointed Governor of the province of Madras (modern-day Chennai) and took up his post the following year. Charles's elder sister Emma's future husband, Sir Thomas Hislop, was commander-in-chief at Fort St George, Madras, for a six-year period which coincided almost exactly with Hugh Elliot's tenure as Governor. It is not clear which of Elliot's children went with him to India, but it seems that Charles was not among them. After Madras, Hugh Elliot spent ten years in retirement in England, sadly without his wife Margaret who had died shortly before he returned home. He died in December 1830.

It is easy to exaggerate the extent to which Charles Elliot resembled his father. The similarities between the two were nevertheless striking, both in their innate characteristics and in the way in which they reacted to particular situations. Hugh Elliot was a more colourful, unconventional man than his son; but despite being known for unorthodox behaviour, he was generally held in high esteem, a reputation which grew over time after his death. On a personal level he was remembered for a ready wit, which he was willing to deploy freely; the story was told of an exchange between Elliot and Frederick the Great:

It was he [Elliot] who, when the King of Prussia commented tartly on the expression of gratitude to God which accompanied the official account of Sir Eyre Coote's victory over Hyder Ali "Je ne savais pas que la Providence fut de vos allies", replied "Le seul, Sire, que nous ne payons pas".[29]

In 1898, nearly seventy years after Hugh Elliot's death, the former Prime Minister, Lord Rosebery, gave a farewell speech for a number of Old Etonians taking up posts overseas. They included the fourth Earl of Minto, Hugh Elliot's great-grandson, who was departing to become Governor General of Canada. Rosebery said:

> Lord Minto comes of a governing family – indeed at one time it was thought to be too governing a family. Under former auspices it was felt that the Elliots bulked too largely in the administration of the nation. At any rate, whether it was so or not, it was achieved by their merits, and there has been a Viceroy Lord Minto already. There have been innumerable distinguished members of the family in the last century, and there has also been a person, I think, distinguished above all others – that Hugh Elliot who defeated Frederick the Great in repartee at the very summit of his reputation, and went through every adventure that a diplomatist can experience.[30]

# Chapter Two

# Minor to Midshipman

L ittle detail is available to allow any revealing insights into Charles Elliot's childhood. The Countess of Minto's biography of Hugh Elliot reports on his brother the earl's impressions of Hugh and Margaret's children in Dresden, describing a scene of domestic harmony and contentment: 'I have, since I have seen Hugh's wife and beautiful children, better hope of his happiness than I ever had before ... two of the children are so like the cherubs looking up [in the Raphael painting – see Note 16, Chapter One] that I told Hugh it was a family picture'.[1] Lady Minto, Hugh's sister-in-law, wrote in the same vein: 'I admire Mrs. Elliot and the children to the utmost.... The children are really charming'[2]

To take up his post in Naples Hugh Elliot sailed with Nelson from Portsmouth in the frigate *Maidstone*, disembarking on 15 June 1803. From an irritated letter shortly afterwards to the Foreign Secretary, regretting the haste of his new posting, it is apparent that his family were not with him:

> I shall not allow myself to dwell upon the sacrifices I have made of private interest or feeling, by relinquishing the prospect I had entertained of settling my private affairs at Dresden, of joining my numerous family and bringing them with me to Naples, since I trust that from this painful disappointment, the King's service may ultimately reap considerable benefit.[3]

Where Charles and the other members of Hugh Elliot's family were while he was in Naples is not clear; Blake indicates that Charles, at least, was being tutored in England.[4] A long letter – essentially about salary – by Hugh to the Foreign Secretary from Palermo in 1806, shortly before leaving for home, may suggest otherwise:

> I appeal to your equity ... earnestly entreating that my salary may be continued to me until my arrival in England. His Majesty will be pleased to take under his consideration the impossibility of my diminishing my expenditure until time shall be afforded to me to have dismissed my numerous retinue and dependants in this country, and also to obtain an asylum for myself and family of ten children in England.[5]

By March 1808 it seems that most of the family – if not Hugh himself – were settled. It was from 8 Portland Place, London, that Hugh's letter to his sister-in-law about the uncertainty of his next appointment was written. Charles was a boy of 8 when his father left the family behind to take up his post as Governor of the Leeward Islands. On his way to Antigua, Hugh Elliot wrote to his brother from Madeira telling him of the circumstances and progress of each of his children. He expressed pride and hope about Charles: 'My sixth and seventh sons, Gilbert and Charles, are in their tenth and ninth years, are both fine, and are at Dr. Valpy's School, where they will receive a more classical education than has fallen to the lot of their elder brothers.'[6] He had good cause to be optimistic about the boys' educational prospects; the school in Reading, Berkshire, of which Dr Richard Valpy had been Headmaster since 1781, had experienced mixed fortunes since its foundation in 1125 and reconstitution in 1486, but had now established a wide reputation as one of the leading schools of the day. The credit for this renaissance is generally attributed to Valpy himself, an energetic and eccentric classicist who was a renowned disciplinarian and vigorous promoter of the School's interests. By 1791, when he had been in post just ten years, he had increased the number of pupils from twenty-three to one hundred and twenty and used his own funds to build new teaching accommodation.[7] The regime for pupils at Reading Grammar School was demanding but tempered with a kindly humour, especially on the part of Dr Valpy. A detailed, light-hearted, description of life at the School when Gilbert and Charles Elliot attended was later provided by a near contemporary of the Elliot boys whose time there overlapped with them.[8] Valpy was the dominant figure, and classical quotations and allusions abounded. Gilbert and Charles were visited at school by their elder brother Ned, aged 18, who wrote shortly afterwards to their sister Emma in Madras. It was clear that there were no anxieties concerning Gilbert, but that Charles's future was uncertain:

> At 2 o'clock I left London for Reading to see my brothers. I found them very well and in much better spirits than I expected. We talked of nothing else but you all, and the happiness we were to feel at the expiration of the three years when we were all to go out together. I stayed with them the following day and had a very long conversation with the Dr. [Valpy] about Gilbert. He is very sanguine about him, says that he is very clever indeed and regrets very much his not going to the University ... I am confident that Gilbert will do well in whatever profession he chooses for himself ... About Charles it will not be quite so easy to settle, by what Lord Melgund says. I should not wonder if he was to go into the Navy, but Lord Minto will do what is proper for him, in the course of next Vacation. Mrs. Valpy is very fond of them both and behaves very well to them. I have written to them both since I was there but have had no answer.[9]

The classical education at Reading will have stood Gilbert in good stead for his subsequent clerical career, but since Charles left aged 14, it will not have had such an impact on him; and for a naval career, in any case, that did not particularly matter.

Charles's wish to join the Royal Navy was met with only cautious enthusiasm by his father. He surmised – correctly – that with the victory at Waterloo the previous year the long period of war with France was at last coming to an end, and – less correctly – that this would mean years of inactivity for the navy and an unfulfilling career for his son.[10] Writing to his nephew the second Earl Minto from Madras in 1816 he reported that:

> Charles's profession is found and I hope for the best. I have thanked both Anna Maria and Ann Carnegie for the interest they took in deciding this point according to Charles's own inclination. It puzzles me however to form any confidence of what his lot will be if peace is as firmly established as I think it now must be.[11,12]

There were essentially two ways in which those aspiring to officer status could enter the Royal Navy. In 1729, during the tenure of Admiral of the Fleet George Byng, first Viscount Torrington, as First Lord of the Admiralty, a Royal Naval Academy was established at Portsmouth. The number of cadets there was initially limited to forty, each attending for three years, the Academy's aim being to provide its students with practical and theoretical training in preparation for a career at sea. The other, long-established, method of entry was based on patronage and influence. The families of intending officers were expected to support their young men financially both during their initial one to three years as volunteers and for the five to seven years as midshipmen. The funds supplied for this purpose, however, were made over not to the individuals but to their ships' captains, who then allocated the money as they thought fit. This was a significant income opportunity for the captains; graduates of the Academy tended not to come from the wealthiest families, so it was perhaps not surprising that for this reason, among others, the patronage route remained the dominant form of recruitment to the Service.[13]

Charles Elliot's family was well placed to secure for him the necessary start to his naval career, having provided over the preceding fifty years a number of distinguished naval officers. In March 1815 the young Charles enlisted initially, in accordance with common practice for someone of his age and background, as a volunteer (first class). He was posted to the Mediterranean to serve under Captain Thomas Briggs in HMS *Leviathan*, a 74-gun line-of-battle ship which had played an important role at Trafalgar but which now, after twenty-five years, was nearing the end of her active life.[14,15] When *Leviathan* was withdrawn from active service in 1816 to become a convict ship, Charles Elliot was advanced to midshipman in HMS *Minden*, also to be deployed in the Mediterranean and also a third-rate 74-gun ship of the line.

Lighter than the larger first-rates (at least 100 guns) and second-rates (at least 90 guns), but with heavier armament than the smaller frigates and sloops, the 74s had proved an effective combination of firepower and manoeuvrability and had been crucial to British naval successes in the Napoleonic Wars. For a newly arrived volunteer or midshipman, serving in such a vessel was usually to experience a sharp contrast with the relative comfort of his previous life; in third-rate ships their berths were on the lowest deck above the hold, with little air or light. A recent account describes their diet:

> Midshipmen and boys, regardless of social rank, generally ate the same fare as seamen and warrant officers. Salt beef and pork, ships' biscuit, cheese, pease porridge, potable soup, and the occasional fresh vegetable, all washed down with a gallon of small beer or a pint of grog each day made it a harsh transition for the palates of well-bred boys accustomed to fine food and wine.[16]

The number of midshipmen and volunteers differed from ship to ship, but they were always a small minority of the total complement. Fully manned British third-rates had crews of some 600 to 700 men, sometimes more, of whom typically around only twenty were midshipmen and volunteers (first class).[17] To the crush of officers and seamen and to difficult living conditions were added demanding duties; these were many and varied, but

> Standard responsibilities included such tasks as running aloft to supervise seamen in setting, reefing, or furling sail; supervising sub-divisions [of the divisions under the authority of the lieutenants] at small arms training; attending to the swift transition of the watch; maintaining the ship's safety by constantly checking for naked lights and lanterns below decks; witnessing visits to the purser's, steward's, or boatswain's store rooms; and casting the log line in order to determine the speed and, when in soundings, the position of the ship.[18]

If his service in *Leviathan* was a stark introduction to life in the navy, Charles Elliot's time in the *Minden* was something approaching the full experience. Under the captaincy of William Paterson, *Minden* was one of a combined force of British and Dutch ships which bombarded Algiers in August 1816. The scourge of piracy had long been a problem for the world's maritime trading nations, and particularly, because of its major share of sea commerce, for Britain. During the recent years of war between the European powers and in America, which had left the navies of these countries with very little capacity for any other activity, pirates in the Mediterranean, in the Indian Ocean, and in the Caribbean had operated with relative impunity.

The continuing major threat posed by Moorish pirates sailing from the Barbary Coast, principally out of Tripoli, Tunis and Algiers, was the taking of slaves from coastal regions throughout the Mediterranean and further afield, including England and Ireland. Attempts, including two under Admiral Lord Exmouth, had been made earlier to halt their depredations, but none of these had had any lasting impact. The raiding of Mediterranean coasts, shipping, and sometimes inland areas as well, to capture, transport and enslave local inhabitants had been practised by pirates based along the Barbary Coast since at least the start of the sixteenth century. The number of slaves taken in this way was not comparable with that of the Atlantic slave trade, but was far from insignificant; it has been estimated that the figure for the period between 1530 and 1780 was around one million, possibly more.[19]

HMS *Minden* was a relatively new vessel. Launched in 1810 at Bombay (Mumbai), she had the distinction of being the first British ship of the line to be constructed outside Britain – at greater cost than at a home dockyard – and was built of the more durable teak instead of oak.[20] The command of the expeditionary force to Algiers was again given to Exmouth.

It is not clear exactly when Charles Elliot joined the *Minden*. The force of nineteen warships, including three 74s of which the *Minden* was one, sailed from Plymouth on 28 July, and while still in the English Channel, *Minden* was sent on ahead to Gibraltar to prepare for the arrival of the main fleet. The British force reached Gibraltar on 9 August, when it was rejoined by the *Minden* and combined with six Dutch ships for the voyage to Algiers. Two days later than planned, because of unfavourable winds, the fleet set sail from Gibraltar on 14 August. Some 200 miles from their destination it was joined from Algiers by the 18-gun sloop HMS *Prometheus*, which had been sent in advance by Exmouth to Algiers. There her captain, Commander William Dashwood, had pleaded with the ruler, the Dey, to release the Consul and several of *Prometheus*'s crew who had been seized and imprisoned, but without success.

Intelligence brought by Dashwood confirmed Exmouth's earlier information about the strength of local forces and fortifications. The Dey had at his disposal some 40,000 men; around thirty to forty gun and mortar boats, five 24- to 30-gun corvettes and four 44-gun frigates; and shore batteries mounting at least 1,000 guns.[21] Against this, the British and Dutch fleet had a total of some 950 guns including 632 cannon of which, as has been pointed out elsewhere, half would be on the wrong side of the ships in an engagement.[22]

Exmouth's reputation was generally high as he contemplated the forthcoming battle, but he had his critics. There had been very mixed results from his two earlier attempts to bring the pirates to heel, and many felt that the force he now had with him was inadequate for the task. The relative firepower of the opposing sides suggested that in theory that was true, but what Exmouth did have, from his previous forays, was detailed knowledge of the coastal waters around Algiers and of its harbour. His plan was to approach out of range of most of the Algerian guns and then for his five largest ships – his flagship *Queen Charlotte* (100 guns), *Impregnable* (98) and the three 74s (*Albion, Minden,* and *Superb*) – to anchor in line roughly parallel with the mole enclosing the harbour and bombard the over two hundred guns of the main defensive battery positioned along it. Concurrently *Leander* (50) would take up position outside the harbour entrance and bring her fire to bear on the ships inside, herself protected from guns along the adjacent shore by the 40-gun frigates *Severn* and *Glasgow*.

Doubtless without any expectation or hope of a positive response, but because he thought convention required it, Exmouth sent a message to the Dey early on 27 July via Lieutenant Samuel Burgess setting out the British demands. Chief of these was the release of Christian slaves. No response was received from the Dey within the two hours he had promised, and after a further half an hour *Queen Charlotte* advanced to take up position 50yds from the mole. The bombardment that followed was triggered by two or three shots from several Algerian guns, and lasted for more than seven hours. It was by all accounts ferocious; the firepower of the British and Dutch ships wrecked the main Algerian gun emplacements and set much of the town ablaze. The American Consul gives a vivid account of the action:

> The cannonade endures with a fury which can only be comprehended from practical experience; shells and rockets fly over and by my house like hail. The fire is returned with constancy from several batteries situated at the north-west of the town and from four heavy guns directly below my windows.... At half-past seven, the shipping in the port is on fire.... The upper part of my house appears to be destroyed, several shells having fallen onto it, whole rooms are knocked to atoms.[23]

At about ten o'clock in the evening Exmouth called a halt to the attack and the fleet withdrew out of range of the Algerian guns. The demands were presented again early the following morning, and this time they were accepted.

After some negotiation over 1,000 Christian slaves were released, reparations were made for previous slave-taking to Naples and Sardinia, the British consul was reinstated, and peace was made by the Dey with the Netherlands. In Britain the expedition was judged a great success. Exmouth's reputation rose, earlier reservations about his abilities being set aside; as a midshipman in the *Queen Charlotte* loyally wrote in a letter home: 'I hope Lord Exmouth has proved that he is a degree better than the Mediterranean waterman which some people were pleased to call him.'[24]

Positive though all this seemed at the time, events over the succeeding years were for the European powers depressingly like the aftermaths of past attempts to solve the problem of Barbary Coast piracy. The corsairs regrouped and resumed their activities; the Dey of Algiers was killed in a coup a few months after the Battle, but it was not until the French occupation of Algeria from 1830 that the pirates there were finally overcome. Nor had the conduct of the Battle of Algiers itself gone quite as planned. From HMS *Minden*, before the action started, Midshipman Elliot will have seen the flagship come to anchor in close range of the main Algerian batteries. Behind *Minden* in line astern was the *Albion*, and on her starboard quarter HMS *Impregnable*. These positions were less than ideal; they did not follow the contour of the mole evenly, so that while the *Queen Charlotte* was close in, the ships behind her were progressively further out and less able to bring effective fire to bear. *Impregnable*, particularly, was not only unable to make a full contribution to the attack but was also in a highly vulnerable position. The casualty figures for the British ships reflected their deployment in the battle: overall, British losses were 128 killed and 690 wounded, of which the majority were accounted for by the out-of-position *Impregnable* and by the two vessels involved in the heaviest fighting, *Queen Charlotte* and *Leander*.[25]

Charles Elliot's participation in the Battle of Algiers at the age of 15 was a dramatic experience for him. The *Minden* played a valuable role in the action, even though she was not in the fiercest of the encounters (her casualties were seven killed and thirty-seven wounded), and she stayed in position after the main disengagement for some three hours to provide suppressive fire.[26] On 3 September the fleet set sail from Algiers for Gibraltar, whence it would return to England – except, perhaps, for the *Minden*, which was reported on 1 November at Gibraltar to be preparing to sail for Madras (Chennai) two weeks later.[27] From 1816 until 1820 Midshipman Elliot was to serve in the East Indies, where the commander-in-chief was Rear Admiral Sir Richard King, a highly experienced officer who had been one of Nelson's captains at Trafalgar.

Despite the dramatic reduction in men and in ships on active service being undertaken in the Royal Navy following the ending of the Napoleonic threat, much work was still to be done, not least against piracy, not only in the Mediterranean but also throughout the Indian Ocean region. The Honourable East India Company had done much to assist the Royal Navy but little impact had been made. European shipping continued to be vulnerable from pirates based along the Coromandel and Malabar coasts of southern India and, especially, from those operating out of the Persian Gulf. The origins and extent of Indian Ocean piracy have been much discussed, but there seems little doubt that it became much more widespread once European countries began expanding their trading expeditions to East Asia. Indian merchants, and after a time the rulers of coastal territories on the Indian sub-continent, resented the imposition first by the Portuguese and then by others of systems of maritime control. Inevitably such resentment led to conflict, the European powers attempting to quell what they saw as piratical interference with legitimate trade, and indigenous Indians seeking to resist encroachment on their maritime sphere of influence by foreigners whom they regarded, in turn, as pirates.[28] Recent military successes in India against the Kingdom of Mysore and the Maratha Confederacy enabled the British in 1818 to focus their attention on the Persian Gulf, in particular on the Qawasim pirates based at Ras-al-Khyma, west of the Strait of Hormuz and north-east of present day Dubai.

With news of the defeat of Napoleon orders had been given for the reduction of the number of ships in the East Indies Squadron of the Royal Navy. Nevertheless, the main naval base and dockyard at Trincomalee on the east coast of Ceylon (Sri Lanka) continued to be fully maintained. An example of the importance of Trincomalee to the British at this time is the estimated expenditure on personnel at her ten overseas dockyards for the four years from 1817; Trincomalee was responsible for around a fifth of the total, only Quebec taking more.[29,30] The strength of the East Indies Squadron during this period was usually twelve to fourteen vessels. Headed by HMS *Minden*, which became Sir Richard King's flagship, and the 50-gun frigate HMS *Liverpool*, the ships on the station typically consisted of four or five fifth-rates (36 to 46 guns), four sixth-rates (20 to 24) and two or three brig-sloops (18).[31] One of their functions, making use of port facilities at Bombay (Mumbai), Colombo and Madras (Chennai), as well as Trincomalee, was to support the military, which they had done to good effect. From the British viewpoint their most significant operation at this time, however, was the successful attack in December 1819 on Ras-al-Khyma, in which Royal Naval support comprised the *Liverpool*, the sixth-rate HMS *Eden* (24) and the brig-sloop HMS *Curlew*.

HMS *Minden* was elsewhere. On 18 August 1819 she had arrived from Bombay at Trincomalee, her main base, where she is recorded as having been berthed during the late summer and autumn of 1817 and into 1818.[32,33] In contrast to his experience in the Mediterranean, it seems that Charles Elliot saw little, if any, action during his time on the East Indies station. It is highly probable, though, that he met up with his family in Madras, where his father Hugh was Governor.[34] Such a meeting or meetings could have taken place either shortly after the *Minden*'s arrival on the station from Gibraltar in 1816, or following a visit by *Minden* in 1818, when she is recorded on 30 March as 'Returned to Trincomalee having conveyed the 15 Regiment of native Infantry from Madras to Colombo'.[35] It will have been the last time Charles saw his mother, who died in India on 1 March 1819. An obituary notice paid her due respect and mentioned her funeral:

> Mar. 1
> At Madras, the wife of the Rt.Hon. Hugh Elliot, Governor of Madras. She was universally esteemed; and while her death was a severe affliction to her own family, it excited general regret in the settlement.... The Right Rev. the Lord Bishop of Calcutta arrived at Madras on the 2 of March, and was thus accidentally enabled to celebrate the funeral obsequies of Mrs. Elliot.[36]

Later in 1819 Hugh Elliot wrote to his nephew, Lord Minto, 'Charles who must always vociferate his joke, good or bad, says it is a great pity that Edward always <u>cuts in last</u>, alluding, I suppose, to the age and other circumstances of the fair ladies who attract his brother's notice.'[37,38] As well as possibly helping to locate Charles at this time, his father's comment is an explicit observation of sibling rivalry between Charles and his elder (by five years) brother Ned; he insisted on being heard, and disliked being deprived by Ned of having the last word.

Having completed her deployment with the East Indies squadron, HMS *Minden* returned home in 1820. For Mr Midshipman Elliot there now followed two short postings on the Home Station. The first of these was under Lieutenant Commander John Reeve in the cutter HMS *Starling* (10 guns) with a complement of fewer than ninety men. As if to ensure his exposure to yet more contrast in a short space of time, he was then assigned from one of the smallest categories of armed vessel in the Royal Navy to the largest, HMS *Queen Charlotte*, a 100-gun first-rate ship-of-the-line. The *Queen Charlotte*, Exmouth's flagship at Algiers, was now the flagship at Portsmouth of Admiral Sir James Hawkins-Whitshed.

Charles Elliot's time on the Home Station gave him an opportunity to visit Minto House, the family seat in Scotland. His family was important to him, and after several years' absence he was determined to make the most of this period in Britain – which he doubtless knew might be brief – to renew contact with his relatives. Lord Minto received a letter from his uncle Hugh, now returned from Madras, at the end of 1820. Not for the first time, Hugh Elliot was short of money:

> This will be delivered to you by Charles. When he expressed his anxious wish to pay you a visit at Minto, I consented to it, upon the presumption that 3 or 4 guineas would have sufficed to go and the same to come back. But soon I found this trip will cost more than twenty guineas. As however I had consented in the first instance I do not like to disappoint him in a project upon which he had set his heart. I have given him ten guineas, and I shall be much obliged if you will advance to him whatever may be necessary for his return before the end of January at which time he is to join his ship at Portsmouth.[39]

In June 1821 Sir Robert Mends was appointed commodore and commander-in-chief of the West African Squadron, sailing on 20 November that year for Sierra Leone in the 42-gun fifth-rate frigate HMS *Iphigenia*.[40] Midshipman Elliot also joined the *Iphigenia*, one of a total complement of 264 men. The Preventive Squadron, as it was known, was not one of the more favoured postings for navy personnel. Its role was to enforce the prohibition on the transportation of slaves in the Atlantic, as required by the 1807 Act for the Abolition of the Slave Trade. The work was relentless, dangerous, unglamorous, and a constant risk to health. Having served for a short time in *Iphigenia*, Charles Elliot was transferred to a smaller ship in the squadron, the sixth-rate 20-gun *Myrmidon*. After another few months, in June 1822, he was promoted lieutenant.

# Chapter Three

# Commission to Captain

Since 1677 formal progression to the commissioned officer rank of lieutenant in the Royal Navy had been dependent on passing an examination. Samuel Pepys, then Secretary for the navy, had sponsored the measure, which required candidates to show competence in seamanship and navigation; they also had to be aged at least 20, and to have completed at least three years at sea. The examination did much to help raise levels of competence, as had been hoped, but the prospect of sitting it had the effect of limiting the number of men seeking promotion. It was not, in any case, an unavoidable hurdle on the route to lieutenancy; with the necessary patronage and influence exercised on their behalf aspiring midshipmen could still progress without taking it. The examination and the presence on some ships of schoolmasters, as they were known, were the more formal elements in what were essentially informal arrangements.[1] This was in large part because of those who, contrary to the advocates of the examination system, saw practical experience, the acquisition and development of leadership skills and the building of character as more important than instruction in technicalities. Many of the adherents to this traditional view were highly placed: 'There is no place superior to the quarterdeck of a British man of war', King William IV is said to have remarked, 'for the education of a gentleman.'[2]

There is nothing in the sources to suggest that Charles Elliot sat the examination. It seems unlikely that he would have done so, given his background and the standing of his family. His promotion to lieutenant after seven years' service was almost as fast as it could have been, given the normal pre-requisite of a minimum of six years at sea; among those progressing at least to commander the average period of service from entry to lieutenant at that time was nine to ten years, and for some men it was considerably more.[3]

The Preventive Squadron of which Lieutenant Elliot was a member had been formed only recently, in 1819. The Napoleonic Wars had demanded a level of ships and manpower which left very few resources for other purposes, however desirable, but the need for significant naval intervention on the west coast of Africa had in any case not become apparent until it was clear that the 1807 Act would not suffice to stop the capture of Africans and their transportation across the Atlantic. For the first few years after formal abolition the law was more honoured in the breach than the observance; the legislation was silent on many of the consequences of abolition, such as what to do with liberated slaves. British slave traders found ways of circumventing the new requirements with relative ease; investing their ships with the flags and crews of other nations was a common tactic.[4] Further complications arose from British attempts to police the activities of other nations which had abolished slave trading, notably the United States. A modest step forward was taken with a bilateral agreement in 1811 between Britain and Portugal, the earliest and one of the most active of the slave trading nations, which committed Portugal to gradual suppression of the trade and authorised reciprocal (in practice, British) interception and search, though only of ships suspected of taking slaves from non-Portuguese parts of the African coast. There followed anti-slave trading agreements and formal treaties between Britain and other countries, as well as with Portugal, but in the face of organised cooperation between slave traders of all nationalities, and the continuing legality of the trade in most of the countries concerned, trying to take effective international diplomatic and naval action against it was fraught with difficulty.[5] The cost of the Preventive Squadron was controversial. It was nevertheless a relatively small force, especially to start with, for the job it had to do, comprising seven ships in 1819 (nine by 1824, and more then twenty-seven at its height in the late 1840s) with which to cover the African coast from what is now Senegal in the north, to Angola in the south. Slave trafficking in the early decades of the nineteenth century was flourishing; the captain of the *Myrmidon*, Commander Henry Leeke, estimated that in the fifteen months to October 1821 at least 190 slave ships entered the River Bonny in the Bight of Biafra.[6]

Whatever Charles Elliot had heard from his father about the injustice and horrors of slavery, his service patrolling and intervening on the slaving coasts of West Africa ensured that he confronted the inhumanity and brutality of the trade at first hand. HMS *Myrmidon* had already seen much action, as had the rest of the Squadron, by the time Elliot joined her early in March 1822. There is no reason to suppose that he was not aboard *Myrmidon* when, the following month, she attacked the Portuguese slaver *Esperanza Felix* in the waters off Lagos. Among the Africans rescued in that operation was a 13-year-old boy, Adjai, who went on to study at Fourah Bay College, Sierra Leone, was ordained, and in 1864 as Samuel Adjai Crowther, in Canterbury Cathedral, was consecrated the first Anglican bishop in Africa. It seems highly probable, too, that Charles Elliot took some part in the joint action by *Iphigenia* and *Myrmidon*, also in April 1822, when a cutting out expedition by boats of the two ships was sent to attack five slave vessels at anchor in the River Bonny.[7] The boats were under the command of George Mildmay, a senior lieutenant who later that year was promoted commander. A later account seeks to provide operational detail:

> When about four miles off, the British boats showed their colours. As soon as they came within long range they were fired at by two schooners showing no flag … Mildmay's boat was

ahead of the others, and he had to allow them to catch up, exposed meanwhile to the additional fire of two brigs and a brigantine under French colours that had joined in the fight.[8]

The two schooners turned out to be Spanish; some of the crew of the first continued to offer resistance after it had formally surrendered but the second was abandoned before boarding took place. When it did, '...a lighted match was found hanging over the hatch to the magazine, intended to blow up the ship and 325 slaves ironed in the hold'.[9] With the capture of the three French vessels it emerged that nearly 1,500 Africans had been herded onto the five slave ships. Their release was to prove one of the highest numbers of slaves to be freed in a single operation in the Preventive Squadron's endeavours over fifty years.[10]

Slave trading across the Atlantic – the notorious 'Middle Passage' – eventually ended in 1869. The West African and Cape Squadrons of the Royal Navy were then amalgamated, the Preventive Squadron having lost some 17,000 men during its existence. Some of these fatalities were in battle and some were accidental, but many were from disease, mainly malaria and yellow fever. While illness was a risk everywhere in naval service, the West African coast was well known to be especially hazardous. 'Beware, beware, the Bight of Benin! There's one comes out for forty goes in!' ran a contemporary warning. Both Commodore Mends and his son, a lieutenant, succumbed to disease and died in 1823.

Eight days following his promotion to lieutenant, Charles Elliot returned to *Iphigenia*, in which he served for a further five months. In March 1823 he was posted to HMS *Hussar*, a 46-gun fifth-rate which on 10 January 1824 sailed for Jamaica, arriving there on 21 February.[11] The Admiralty record then notes the first of Elliot's two assignments to HMS *Serapis*, from July 1825.[12] The *Serapis* had been launched as a 44-gun fifth-rate in 1782. She saw thirteen years active service before being converted for use first as a storeship in 1795, then more than twenty years later as a convalescence ship. By January 1819 she was preparing to sail for Jamaica. She is recorded as 'Flag ship, Port Royal, Jamaica', and reported at approximately monthly intervals to have been at Port Royal from July 1821 to May 1824.[13] *Serapis*'s role as a convalescence ship was a crucial one. The Caribbean was not as dangerous to health as the 'White Man's Grave' of West Africa, but the region carried major risk of disease nonetheless. In the six years before Charles Elliot took up his post in *Serapis*, Jamaica had suffered three epidemics which had taken a heavy toll of the garrison. A Parliamentary paper of 1838 noted that:

> During the above period [1817–36] the average mortality has been about 113 per thousand of the strength annually ... in 1825 about a third part of the force was cut off.... This station suffered very severely from the epidemic fevers which raged throughout the island in 1819, 1822 and 1825.[14]

A little over four months later, in mid-November, Lieutenant Elliot was appointed to the command of the four-gun schooner HMS *Renegade*, also based at Port Royal. Developed in North American waters from the early eighteenth century, the schooner's speed and manoeuvrability, and its consequent capacity frequently to evade capture, had made it one of the vessels of choice for pirates, slave-traders, and others engaged in illegal activities at sea. As the Preventive Squadron later found on the West African coast that using captured slave clippers was an effective way of pursuing slave traders, so in the Caribbean schooners were employed in policing the seas. The United States Navy and the Royal Navy cooperated in this work, but their main concerns were different, the Americans focusing on pirates and the British on slave trading. Cuba was a centre for both pirates and slavers; the United States maintained some fourteen ships in the Caribbean for action against Cuban, Spanish and other pirates, while a Royal Navy Squadron patrolled the approaches to Cuba for Spanish ships attempting to sell Africans into slavery there. Elliot's time in command of the *Renegade* was brief, little more than a month, for on 2 January 1826 he was back in *Serapis,* not this time as a lieutenant, but as an acting commander.

After her long career HMS *Serapis* was finally paid off in March 1826, to be superseded as Vice-Admiral Sir Lawrence Halsted's flagship by HMS *Magnificent*, a former third-rate 74-gun ship-of-the-line which had seen action in the wars with France, and after convoy protection work was now in service as a hospital and store ship. Charles Elliot's promotion to commander was confirmed when he transferred to *Magnificent* on 14 April 1826.

In his new rank Elliot subsequently took command, on 15 August 1826, his twenty-fifth birthday, of the 16-gun brig-sloop HMS *Harlequin*, previously in the charge of Commander James Scott. During this posting, which involved, among other things, assisting the British Consul General in Haiti with his fact-finding survey of the island, Elliot became seriously ill, though apparently not with the yellow fever by which the Consul General himself was struck down.[15] By January 1828 *Harlequin* was in Barbados, moving in July that year to Nassau in the Bahamas. Her career came to an end in 1829 when, having been deemed unserviceable, she was sold at Port Royal.

1828 and 1829 were important years for Charles Elliot. On 28 August 1828 he was promoted captain, but early in January 1829 he was discharged from the *Harlequin* and placed on half-pay, his fourteen years active service with the Royal Navy ending at this point. His naval career had been formative and demanding, and had provided him with a range of experience of people, places, tasks and situations that would stand him in good stead for the trials and challenges with which he would have to deal in middle and later life. Fourteen years from entry to captain represented a very rapid rate of progression, one which was considerably faster than that of most of his contemporaries.[16] Statistically impressive though this was, the nature of Elliot's postings suggests that he was never marked out for a long or distinguished naval career. Half his time in the navy was as a volunteer or midshipman, and of the remainder barely two and a half years had been spent in command at sea.

He was, however, still a young man. During his time in *Harlequin* helping to protect British interests in Haiti he had met and married, in 1828, the 22-year-old Clara Genevieve Windsor.[17] She had been born and brought up in Haiti by her English father, Robert Harley Windsor, and her French mother, Marie Magdeleine Jouve, along with five younger siblings.[18] There seems to be no definitive information in the available sources to suggest how Charles and Clara met, but it may be that Charles had first seen Clara in New York and subsequently recognised her in the Haitian capital Port-au-Prince.[19] Clara was related through her brother to Louis Victor Noñez, Director of Customs at Port-au-Prince, and another possibility is that Charles had professional dealings with him at some stage and social contact with friends and relations followed.[20] Whatever she thought her married future held for her, Clara had lived through unsettled times in the fledgling Haitian Republic, fitting her for the uncertainties of the several turbulent environments she would encounter over the years as Captain Elliot's wife.[21] In 1829 she gave birth to their first child, Harriet Agnes.

On leaving active service with the Royal Navy, Charles Elliot can have had little idea of what his next move would be. He had been on half pay before, for a few months between his time with the West Africa Squadron and joining the *Hussar*, and he may have entertained the possibility of resuming a naval career. That was not to be; it was a little over a year after his discharge from the *Harlequin*, having travelled to France and spent some time in Bordeaux, that he was appointed by the Secretary of State for War and the Colonies, Sir George Murray, to the post of Protector of Slaves in the newly established colony of British Guiana.

# PART TWO

# Chapter Four

# Slavery and British Guiana

As the Portuguese explorers of the of the fifteenth century ventured southwards off the west coast of Africa, gaining strategic footholds in the islands of the Atlantic as they went, they joined existing trading systems among the indigenous African communities, developing thriving commercial intercourse with them.[1] Since slave trading was already well established within Africa, Portuguese ships were able to trade slaves between coastal areas; from such commerce it was a short step to the transportation of slaves to the Portuguese islands and then to Portugal itself.

The mid-sixteenth century saw the establishment of sugar plantations in Brazil by the Portuguese, who had planted sugar cane on their Atlantic islands and then developed the industry in Brazil as a response to growing demand for sugar in Europe. Experience of slave labour had shown the economic benefits of using it for sugar cultivation and refining; other crops, including coffee and cotton, were also harvested and processed by slaves, but it was in sugar production that the majority were engaged. Other European nations were quick to learn from the Portuguese example, the Spanish, Dutch, British and French using their maritime power to acquire and exploit Caribbean and South American territories for commercial gain.

Slave labour was key to the success of their enterprises. Operating in what became known as a triangular system, specially constructed or converted ships sailed from major European ports to western Africa carrying manufactured goods.[2] These were then exchanged for native Africans who, transported to the Caribbean and to North and South America to work the plantations, constituted the slave labour force which supplied Europe with sugar and other produce on which it came to rely. The number of slaves involved was huge; it has been estimated that in the more than 350 years of the Atlantic slave trade, around 12 million people were taken from Africa, of whom some ninety-two per cent reached their destinations and about twenty-five per cent were carried in British ships.[3]

A trading system so dependent on brutality and repression inevitably engendered rebellion. By the time Brazil formally abolished slavery in 1888 there had been thirteen major slave rebellions, revolts, uprisings and wars in eight territories, as well as countless smaller disturbances. The Atlantic slave trade also caused outrage among individuals and religious and political groups in Britain, America and continental Europe, but it was some 250 years before organised pressure for abolition began, and a further twenty years before the British abolition legislation of 1807.

At the start of the nineteenth century, British possessions in the Caribbean comprised Jamaica, the Cayman Islands, Trinidad, Tobago, and territories in the Leeward and Windward Islands chains. In 1831 the former Dutch colonies of Berbice, Essequibo, and Demerara, east of Venezuela, were consolidated to become British Guiana, Britain's only colony on the South American mainland.

The three Dutch territories had taken their names from the three rivers which dominated the region, each rising hundreds of miles to the south and flowing almost due north to reach the Atlantic some 300 to 400 miles south-east of the Orinoco delta. Though the area was first visited by Europeans – a Spanish expedition – at the end of the fifteenth century, the Dutch did not start to settle it until 1580. English interest was aroused by Sir Walter Raleigh's report of his travels in the region in 1595, but decades passed during which the Dutch, French and English each sought to establish a permanent presence there. It was from the re-acquisition of an English settlement at Paramaribo, on the coast of what is now Suriname, that the Dutch developed their colonies; but the development was not continuous. Until the early nineteenth century, control of one or more of the three colonies was for short periods in the hands of the British or French, as the treaties which followed conflicts between European powers reallocated overseas possessions among them.

The Dutch colonists were keen to attract immigrants to help build a prosperous economy, but they may not have expected the scale of the influx of plantation owners who emigrated to the three colonies from the Leeward and Windward islands. Dissatisfied with the relatively poor quality of their land these mainly British expatriates came to Essequibo, Demerara and Berbice in such numbers that by the 1780s their influence had begun to eclipse the authority of the Dutch colonial government. Having de facto control of Berbice, the British took possession of the now jointly administered colonies of Essequibo and Demerara in 1796, from which time British plantation ownership, the slave population and crop production expanded even more rapidly. Despite a short-lived period again under Dutch rule following the Treaty of Amiens in 1802, when the Treaty broke down and war in Europe resumed in 1803 the colonies were retaken by the British, this time until colonial rule ended with independence as Guyana in 1966.[4] It was not until the Anglo-Dutch Treaty of 1814, however, that the territories were formally ceded to Britain.[5]

The government and administration of what became British Guiana were conducted during Dutch rule by the Dutch West India Company. The Company's main man in charge in the territory for a major part of the eighteenth century was Laurens Storm van 's Gravesande, who was Secretary then Commandeur of Essequibo from 1738 to 1750, and Directeur Generaal of Essequibo and Demerara from 1750 to 1772. Van 's Gravesande is generally credited with responsibility for the rapid development and prosperity of Essequibo and Demerara, but it was his immigration policy which eventually resulted in the takeover of the colonies by the British, whose West Indies planters he had done so much to attract. By the time he left office he had successfully guided the territory through a turbulent period of slave revolt, immigrant crime, and tribal conflict but Demerara, particularly, had now reached the point at which government would become less autocratic and more responsive to the colonists' needs. Following the report of a commission appointed by the Dutch government to look into the concerns of the planters, action was taken to implement, in 1792, what was known as the Concept Plan of Redress. The plan provided, among other things, for a single Court of Policy for the two colonies, with legislative and executive functions, while retaining separate Courts of Justice.

The last decades of the eighteenth century in the colonies were characterised by the increasing power of the planters as it speeded the weakening of Dutch authority. The appointment of the commission was a recognition that action was needed, but pressure from the planters was maintained. The size and composition of the Court of Policy – initially comprising four officials (one of whom had a casting vote) and four colonists nominated by two electoral colleges – were a continuing source of disagreement, notably so far as the 'elected' members were concerned. So also were the court's powers to approve estimates and fix budgets; 'Financial Representatives' were added but their role too was contentious. Perhaps aware of where all this might be leading, the Dutch central government was clear that the official members of the court should be more accommodating: 'the contributions for the Colonial Chest are to be regulated by the inhabitants themselves' decreed the Staten Generaal in 1788.[6] Some years later instructions were issued that the Directeur Generaal 'will take care not to leave the administration of the Colony Chest wholly to the Colony [i.e. official] Members of the Court of Policy, but will thereto admit a greater number of the Colonists...'[7]

The planters will have received with some relief the news that the first Governor of British Guiana was to be Sir Benjamin D'Urban, the current Governor of Demerara/Essequibo. Like Hugh Elliot, he had, when Governor of the Leeward Islands, been based in Antigua; as Governor there he had acquired a reputation for being sympathetic to the plantation owners. He had been appointed Governor of Demerara in 1824 and rapidly found out at first hand that its most recent history had been more turbulent than that of Antigua and would present sterner challenges. There had been a major slave revolt in Berbice in 1763-4, but in 1823, just eight years before the inauguration of British Guiana, one of the largest and most significant rebellions ever in the Caribbean and the Americas took place in Demerara.

Slave labour was used for the cultivation of coffee and cotton in Demerara, but it was in sugar production that the most money was to be made and in which the great majority of slaves were engaged. The 1823 uprising was initially planned at Plantation Success, some four miles east of the capital, Georgetown. Owned by Sir John Gladstone, who had switched his operation in Demerara from coffee to sugar, Success was one of the larger plantations in the colony. Those working there included several prominent members of the slave population who had mistakenly believed that recent instructions from the Colonial Secretary, Lord Bathurst, intended to improve conditions for slaves, meant they were to be freed. As several weeks had passed since the instructions were known to have been received in the colony, the slave leaders concluded that implementation was being deliberately stalled. Whether or not that was the case, they were justified in being suspicious of the authorities' motives. The 'Amelioration' measures had been drawn up by the Privy Council following a House of Commons resolution in March 1823 proposed by the Foreign Secretary, Canning. Pressure for such legislation had come not only from the abolition lobby but, through Members of Parliament sympathetic to their views, from the planters, whose self-interested aim was to take the heat out of both slave agitation in the colony and demands at home for abolition. The measures were essentially an attempt to steer a middle course, and as sometimes the case with compromise, in the end satisfied neither side. In March 1824 Canning gave a report back to the House on the contents of the Order in Council, in which he summarised

> the improvements government propose to effect in the island of Trinidad – First, abolition of the use of the whip with regard to females entirely – discontinuance of the use of the whip as applied to males as a stimulus to labour – restrictions on the infliction on males of punishment by the whip. Secondly, a religious establishment and religious instruction; – and in order to give time for the acquirement of that instruction, the abolition of the markets and of slave labour on the Sunday. Thirdly, encouragement of marriage among the slaves – the keeping together of families of slaves, in sales or transfers of estates; the securing to slaves the enjoyment of property, and the right to distribute it at their death. Fourthly, The admissibility of the evidence of slaves, under certain regulations; and lastly, a power to the slave to purchase his own freedom or that of his wife or children.[8]

To enquiry about other colonies he responded:

> It is the intention of the government ... after having established the system which I have explained, in Trinidad ... also to extend the experiment to Demerara and its dependants; where indeed it would have been first tried, but for the intervention of the unfortunate occurrences which have lately taken place in that colony.[9]

The 'unfortunate occurrences' involved the rebellion of several thousand slaves and the deaths of hundreds. The possibility of uprising had never been far beneath the surface and had been simmering in particular since May, 1823 when Governor John Murray resurrected instructions facilitating freedom of religious worship first sent to the Governor (Bentinck) in 1811; except that they did not, in practice, make religious observance easier for slaves because all the apparent extension of opportunity for that purpose was constrained by the need in each instance to obtain the permission of the plantation owners or managers. The reissued instructions began:

> It must in the first place be understood, that no limitation or restraint can be enforced upon the right of instruction and of preaching on particular estates; providing the meetings for this purpose take place upon the estate, and with the consent and approbation of the proprietor or overseer of such estate.[10]

They continued in the same vein – an attempt to satisfy planters, missionaries and slaves which had the effect of making matters considerably worse.

In August 1823 Governor Murray imposed martial law at the first sign of armed discontent, but despite the pleadings of the Rev. John Smith, appointed by the London Missionary Society to Demerara in 1817, and of moderate slave leaders, the uprising gathered numbers and pace. Some planters and managers were forcibly detained, but relatively little physical harm was inflicted on them. Military retribution on the other hand was swift and harsh; severed heads of alleged ringleaders were publicly displayed *pour encourager les autres*, and John Smith was imprisoned for actions which were held to indicate excessive sympathy for the slaves.[11]

Smith died in captivity of pneumonia, becoming known among the slaves as the Martyr of Demerara. News of his fate, and of the severity of the colonial authorities' response to the uprising, had a major impact in Britain. It greatly advanced the cause of the reformers, facilitating their task and setting the scene for further steps towards abolition. As has been observed, the origins of the slave trade were economic, but racist attitudes were essential in sustaining it; those attitudes were apparent in the colonists' approach to the question of religious instruction for the slave population.[12]

The London Missionary Society, established in 1796, was one of several missionary organisations in Britain set up to further, among other causes, the abolition of slavery. In Demerara it began its work at Plantation Le Resouvenir at the invitation of its owner, who believed that slaves would be less inclined to discontent if influenced by the teachings of the church. That was not how the missionaries themselves saw their objective, nor did it reflect the views of most planters, who considered that Christianity would be dangerously subversive if it became accessible to slaves. The role of the missionaries, the planters thought, should be somehow to instil contentedness in the slaves without teaching them Christianity, or indeed educating them at all. This was also the view of the local colonial authorities; a government-influenced newspaper of the day reflected their approach: 'It is dangerous to make slaves Christians, without giving them their liberty.'[13]

In the face of this hostility the missionaries had an uphill struggle. The British 1824 'Amelioration' Order in Council nevertheless obliged the planters to allow religious instruction among their slaves. In September 1825 and September 1826 the substance of the Order in Council was promulgated in Demerara and Berbice respectively in the form of Ordinances issued by the Governors. Many planters initially resisted, claiming that Britain did not have the right to legislate for the two colonies. They maintained that in accepting the capitulation of the territories in 1803 Britain had, in effect, granted them a charter, and that the relevant powers were therefore vested in the Court of Policy, not the Privy Council (Charles Elliot later set out persuasive arguments against this view).[14] Most planters, however, complied with the Ordinances, with great reluctance and not a little bad grace, making life for the slaves in respect of the legislation as difficult as they legitimately could. Providing for the local implementation of the measures previously announced to Parliament, these and similar Ordinances elsewhere required the appointment, in each of the colonies directly responsible to the British Crown, of a Protector of Slaves.[15] In Demerara the first holder of the post was Colonel Aretas William Young, a veteran of the Peninsular War who had served for significant periods as deputy to the Governor of Trinidad. He was well thought of by Governor D'Urban, but not by the home government, which viewed his reporting as inadequate and his general approach increasingly out of step with the gathering momentum towards abolition. He was suspended in 1830.[16]

# Chapter Five

# Office and Delusion

T he Amelioration legislation of 1824 was revisited with the issue of successor Orders in Council in February 1830 and November 1831, informed by the experiences of the first Protectors and taking account of the continuing debate in Parliament.

The 1830 Order was a major sweeping up exercise intended to consolidate the various proclamations, ordinances and other laws made in the Crown colonies during the previous six years. The parliamentary record notes the contents of the clauses concerned with Protectors of Slaves:

> The appointment of a protector of slaves in each of the crown colonies, saving existing offices.... The protectors not to be owners or managers of slaves on paying of a forfeiture of office. Until that forfeiture is publicly declared, all intermediate acts are to be valid. The protector may hire slaves for his domestic service if unable to hire free servants.... The protectors to be constantly resident except by the licence of the secretary of state.[1]

Importantly for Elliot, the Order also provided for Assistant Protectors to be appointed to execute all lawful instructions of Protectors. Protectors and Assistants could not act as magistrates, but were required to be kept informed of major prosecutions against slaves, and were to represent the slaves, taking action against their accusers where necessary.

The 1831 Order in Council was similarly concerned in part with what Protectors of Slaves should not do, as well as with what they should, but its main thrust was to try to tighten earlier regulation by explicitly prohibiting a number of practices used by slave owners and managers to circumvent it. The Anti-Slavery Society had some reservations but was inclined to welcome the Order as a measure which, if properly implemented, would cause Protectors to be less identified with the colonial administration and the planters and more with those whom it was their role to protect.[2] Its main additional provisions, which built on and extended the 1824 and 1830 Orders, were that Protectors were not to have any personal interest in slaves or in the land on which they worked; Protectors were to have power to enter any estate or house to make contact with a slave; slaves were authorised to bring complaints directly to the attention of the Protector, with a pass, but with impunity if a pass was refused; Protectors were to be authorised to require the attendance before them of persons complained against, and potential witnesses, and to imprison, pending further examination, any refusing to attend; and Protectors were to hold an inquest on the body of any slave dying 'in a sudden, violent or extraordinary manner'.[3,4]

Detailed though this legislation was, the appointment of Protectors of Slaves was only one of several measures introduced by the British government on the path to the abolition of slavery. Ministers were fully aware of the growing strength of public opinion on the issue, articulated persistently and at length in the House of Commons by such campaigners as Wilberforce and Thomas Fowell Buxton, but they were also conscious of the economic importance of slave-based crop production and of what the planters potentially stood to lose from emancipation. The patience of the reformers, on the other hand, was tested by what they saw as frustratingly slow progress; but they had some influential allies in government, one of whom was Viscount Howick, a personal friend of Elliot and later to become the third Earl Grey. During the period 1830–33, when his father Charles, second Earl Grey was Prime Minister, Howick was Under Secretary of State for War and the Colonies, a post which enabled him to acquire detailed knowledge of colonial practices and to lend authority in Parliament to the abolition movement.

Charles Elliot's appointment as 'Protector of Slaves to British Guiana' was notified in a letter from the Secretary of State of 2 February 1830.[5] The current Protector in Demerara, Colonel Young, was not suspended until November that year, and the newly constituted colony of British Guiana did not formally come into existence until July 1831, so it seems unlikely that Charles and Clara Elliot and their infant daughter Harriet took up residence in the colony until late 1830 at the earliest.[6]

With Elliot's responsibilities as Protector of Slaves went *ex officio* membership of the Court of Policy of British Guiana. A Royal Commission announcement of 4 March 1831 had decreed that the bodies and procedures for government and administration already in place should be continued in the new Colony.[7] Along with another new member, Elliot was admitted to the Court of Policy on 1 November 1831.[8]

Membership of the Court of Policy was not a sinecure. All members were expected to attend all meetings, which were frequent – the court met, for example, on four consecutive days after 1 November 1831, and on eight further occasions (some of which were adjourned and necessitated additional, reconvened meetings) before the end of December that year. There were now nine members: the Governor, the Chief Justice, two Fiscals (who had responsibility for law enforcement and tax collection), and the Protector of Slaves (all *ex officio*), and four members nominated from among the colonists. The court's business was varied, but much of its time was spent considering petitions, estimates, and infrastructural matters such as the state of roads, bridges and public buildings. While routine and statutory items featured frequently, other business often comprised matters raised by the colonist members. Unsurprisingly such items were usually controversial; the colonist members were planters, who used their presence on the court to protect and further their own interests.

Early in his appointment as Protector, Elliot reviewed the relevant data. Figures for the Berbice district for 1831 supplied by the Registrar of Slaves there, Mr Samuel, recorded 20,184 slaves in an overall population of 21,804.[9] At the end of May 1832 the total population of Demerara/Essequibo was 65,517 and according to its Registrar of Slaves, Mr Robertson, on 31 December 1831 the number of slaves there was 58,404.[10,11] Elliot's report as Protector of Slaves was to put the figure for the end of June 1832 at 57,358, i.e. some eighty-eight per cent of the total population.[12] His protection responsibilities thus covered around 75,000 to 80,000 slaves.[13] They worked on some 350 plantations in an area of 83,000 square miles, and Elliot could be forgiven for thinking that his task was impossible to fulfil with anything approaching full effectiveness. At the very least, he decided, he would need two properly paid Assistant Protectors, as allowed for in the 1830 Order in Council. His first recorded active participation in the Court of Policy occurred on 16 March 1832, when he read out a paper challenging the rejection of salary provision for Assistant Protectors in the Estimates.[14] Objections had been raised by the colonist members, who felt the appointment of Assistant Protectors 'unnecessary and inexpedient for a number of reasons, and that the resources of the Colony were inadequate to meet any additional expense'.[15] Elliot argued that

> it is not to be disputed that those means which it may be in the power of the Public to provide, are principally derived from the productive labor of the Slave Population, and I will beg leave to remark that this Class of His Majesty's Subjects have a most justly founded claim to a reasonable appropriation from Public sources, for the purpose of deploying the expense of an Establishment intended efficiently to protect them, and completely to ensure to them the enjoyment of their lawful rights. Looking at the objection which has been made to the appointment of Assistant Protectors on the ground that the Slaves are already sufficiently protected by the Proprietary, it is to be remarked that this was merely stated as a matter of opinion. An opinion, no doubt, however, founded upon the admission that the Slaves ought to have all reasonable protection. Here, then, the principle is distinctly recognised.[16]

Continuing to address the assertion that the interests of slaves were already adequately safeguarded by the plantation proprietors, Elliot observed that not all owners resided on their estates, and that given the size of the undertakings he would have expected more extensive reports from them. As to resources, 'the nature of the conversation [in the Court of Policy on this part of the Estimates] seemed to me to leave quite as much room for attributing the refusal to political disinclination as to difficulties of a Financial nature', and he concluded that in view of his remit for a slave population of '*circa* 70,000 souls dispersed over a vast extent of country, it does forcibly appear to me that the location of more than one Officer whose responsible duty it shall be to attend to that object alone, is indispensably necessary'.[17,18]

There had been explicit reference in a Governor's Ordinance of 21 December 1831 (a tidying up measure updating arrangements for the collection of fines and penalties) to 'the Protector of Slaves of British Guiana, and the Assistant Protector of Slaves of British Guiana for the District of Berbice', and subsequently also to 'other Assistant Protectors of Slaves of British Guiana for the District of Berbice', but this was before the discussion of the colonial Estimates.[19,20] Elliot's case had been weakened not only by the prior existence of two unpaid assistants, John MacLeod and Edward Howard Gibbon, but by their being known as Assistant Protectors of Slaves, and as Elliot admitted, 'it was observed [in the Court's consideration of the Estimates] that the duties of Assistant Protectors of Slaves were performed gratuitously, and why should not that course continue to be pursued'.[21] Elliot acknowledged what the volunteers had done, but pointed out that His Majesty's Government had no means of insisting that more time and effort be spent on slave protection, in the interests of both slaves and planters, unless there were more paid designated officials. By the interests of the planters he meant not only the economic benefits of amelioration but the serious consequences for them if more were not done:

> I am ... no friend to disorder, or disregard of authority, and I know no better way of preventing the fatal consequences of such a state of things, than by leading the Slave Population to believe that the proprietary fully adopt the views of the Government at home with regard to the amelioration of their condition, and that the observation of the whole extent of the laws in their favour is fairly ensured to them.[22]

The financial implications of Elliot's request were, however, a major factor in the planters' hostility. They were not happy with their own economic situation and were aware, as was Elliot, that the Secretary of State, Lord Goderich, had made it clear in a dispatch of 5 November 1831 that he expected 'the increased expense of a few Assistant Protectors will be abundantly provided for in the savings already made and which remain to be made in other Departments'.[23,24] So far as the planter members of the Court of Policy were concerned, there were no such savings.

Elliot's concerns did not lead to any additional resources. In the months that followed he was supplied with information and assistance by the two Registrars of Slaves, the local magistrates, and such voluntary help as he could find.

It did not take long for Charles Elliot to become disillusioned. The scale of his task meant that despite the authority with which he had been invested he could not take any practical initiatives to improve the lot of the slave population. He was dependent on others, not least for making slaves aware of his existence and of their right of direct complaint to him. That was done only patchily; but the fact was that he could not have coped with the workload at all had it been otherwise. He felt out on a limb, trying to operate between the colonial authorities, who were conscious of the potential for violence and rebellion if slaves were encouraged to air their grievances openly, and the planters, who were generally hostile to him and whose tolerance of his position rested on their belief that improving the slaves' condition might help productivity.

This economic approach was not confined to the planters. It was adopted also by Registrar Robertson in his observations on trends in the quantity and types of punishment inflicted on slaves. Analysing recent birth and death trends Robertson commented:

> The progress of the reduction of the physical strength and capacity of the Slave Population of Demerary and Essequibo is truly alarming and it is a fact which may not have been sufficiently considered , but it appears very clear that the change in this respect in the last fifteen years will have a serious and distressing influence.[25]

Since 1817 the slave population had decreased by 23,644, twenty-eight per cent, at the rate of more than 1,000 a year. Robertson was concerned about the concurrent increase in the rate of punishments administered, but also about 'the increase in the number of slaves whose age and infirmities are a drawback on its [Demerara/Essequibo's] resources'.[26] Like Colonel Young, Elliot's predecessor as Protector, Robertson appears not to have been in step with growing concerns about slave welfare, viewing the slave statistics primarily in terms of their effect on the Colony's future output. Elliot, though conscious of the economic implications, was acutely aware of the injustices being done to slaves and of the impediments being deliberately placed in the way of their education and progress. From Robertson's data, shown below, harsh treatment of slaves seemed to be on the increase.[27]

| Date | No. of slaves | Punishments in next 12 months | of which 'corporal' |
|---|---|---|---|
| 1.1.29 | 61,627 | 17,359 | c.10,000 |
| 1.1.30 | 60,599 | 18,324 | 10,077 |
| 31.12.30 | 59,547 | 21,656 | 10,889 |
| 31.12.31 | 58,404 | | |

Punishments including dark-room confinement, days in the stocks, flogging and imprisonment, were inflicted for a wide range of alleged offences. For the little over four months from mid-May to the end of September 1830 in Berbice, the Protector of Slaves reported that 4,582 punishments had been meted out. The main offences recorded were bad work and not finishing task (1,609 instances) and ranged through neglecting duty and insolence, to theft and petty larceny.[28] Other reported reasons for punishment included attempted murder, killing stock, and mutinous language.

The response of Lord Goderich to this report from Berbice is illustrative of the way in which he reacted to other reports of Protectors of Slaves. Following the structure of the report itself, he first dealt with the statistical overview and then commented on individual cases as he saw fit, with reference as appropriate to any earlier instruction or exhortation he had issued. In this instance he wrote to the Governor on 16 July, 1831 concerning

> Mr Beard's despatch dated 7 February last, enclosing the Report of the Protector of Slaves in Berbice from 14 May to 29 September 1830 ... I have observed with much regret that very little or no diminution has taken place in the punishments inflicted by the domestic authority of the owner.[29,30]

Having pointed out that 4,582 punishments on a slave population of a little over 18,000 was a rate of around one in four, Goderich drew particular attention to one estate, Plantation Utile et Paisible, 'which exhibits the extraordinary number of 420 punishments inflicted on the 145 slaves in a little more than four months', instructing the Governor to

> direct the particular attention of the Protector of Slaves to the domestic economy of this Estate, in order that his exertions may be used as the case may require, either to admonish the Slaves against the indulgence of any wantonly insubordinate feeling, or to bring the Manager to justice for abuses of his authority.[31,32]

As a supporter of the abolitionists the Secretary of State sought improvement in the welfare of slaves, but his ability to affect events on the ground in British Guiana (and elsewhere) was limited. By the time his responses to the Governor on the Protector of Slaves' reports arrived in the Colony, nearly a year had normally passed since the end of the period under review. In that time the situation on individual plantations could have changed – for better or worse – significantly, and the Protector would have taken action where he could. What the Secretary of State was able to do was to provide the Governor and Protector of Slaves with authoritative evidence of the British Government's continuing commitment to amelioration and eventual abolition.

Parliament having in 1823 expressed itself in favour of slave emancipation in principle, the debate in Britain in 1832 was about how and when. A Select Committee of the House of Commons was appointed in May 1832,

> to consider and report on the measures which it might be expedient to adopt for the purpose of effecting the extinction of slavery throughout the British Dominions at the earliest period compatible with the safety of all classes in the colonies, and in conformity with the resolutions of this House of the 15th of May, 1823.[33]

The committee's twenty-five members included Fowell Buxton, Sir George Murray, Viscount Howick, and two future Prime Ministers, Sir Robert Peel and Lord John Russell. As recorded verbatim in *The Anti-Slavery Reporter*, oral evidence was taken by the committee, both from those who sought immediate action and from those who counselled caution and delay. It also received documentary evidence, among which were 'remarks on the means of improving the system by which labour is exacted in the Slave Colonies, by Captain Elliot RN, Protector of Slaves for British Guiana, 18 January, 1832'.[34] Elliot was well aware that the humanitarian case for abolition had been accepted. His aims in providing these comments, and in his answers to specific questions posed by Lord Goderich, were not only to press for an immediate improvement in the treatment of slaves, but to make the economic argument that (slave) labour would be more productive if offered incentive rather than being subjected to punishment. After referring to the recent significant increase in the number of punishments recorded in his Protector's report for the six months ended on 30 June 1831, he continued

> The largely increasing Punishment Returns clearly prove that the actual system of coercion, extensively as it is used, is perfectly inadequate to ensure the completion of the quantum of labour, which it is loudly declared the slaves could easily finish, if they were disposed to make the effort.... It is not my purpose to contend that the slaves will work *regularly* for wages, and I am perfectly well aware that regularity of work is absolutely necessary in the cultivation of the ordinary produce of these countries; but if they know that the power to coerce them be left, surely it is rational to conclude that they would rather choose to work industriously, with a hope to acquire profit and gain time, than they would perversely determine to work ill and late, to the exclusion of all chance of advantage, and under a strong apprehension of receiving punishment.[35]

Elliot set out at some length his proposals for solving the problem of labour inefficiency. The Select Committee's attention was then drawn to what he considered a major cause of the current restlessness among the slave population, the frustration of hearing of amelioration measures agreed in Britain that never seemed to be implemented on the ground in the colony.

> It is a source of bitter complaint in this country, that the constant expectation of legislation from England is calculated to produce the most unfortunate effects on the minds of the slaves; and it is represented that the consequences of such a vague state of impatience on the one hand, and of alarm and consequent disinclination on the other, are calculated seriously to retard the progress of amelioration. If all had been done and were still doing, which might have been effected by the proprietors themselves, with real advantage to their own interests, to meet the feelings of the country, so unequivocally expressed in Mr. Canning's Resolutions of 1823, unanimously adopted by both Houses of Parliament, there would have been as little necessity, as there can have been little inclination, to legislate upon this subject at all.[36]

It was not, though, just a matter of the process of amelioration being retarded. Mindful of his job description and the formal expectations of his role, Charles Elliot felt exposed and insufficiently empowered in a situation in which he saw simmering discontent likely to escalate dangerously. Towards the end of his 'remarks' he laid the blame with the planters, but implied too that the Governor and his senior officials had been negligent in allowing matters to reach this stage. He also made it clear that given the nature of the legal requirements and the size of the country, there was very little he, personally, could do about it. He wrote

> The necessity of ameliorating legislation of a progressive tendency has, unfortunately, been forced upon the government by the disinclination to legislate effectively on this side of the Atlantic. It is superfluous to say that there is very little disposition in this country frankly to accept these laws; and the painful consequence is, that the slave has not derived all the advantage from them which it has been the object of His Majesty's Government to extend to him.... Here then is the slave population clearly convinced of the benevolent intentions of His Majesty's Government and the British public in their behalf, and perfectly sensible, on the other hand, that these intentions are frustrated to no inconsiderable extent by the feeling with which the laws are received and acted upon in this country. The probable consequence of this unfortunate state of things is seriously to be dreaded.[37]

While Elliot was clear that this situation had arisen largely because of earlier failure to legislate locally, and that the way forward was more use of the carrot and less of the stick, the Governor was less forthright; but Sir Benjamin D'Urban's cautious approach was little more than a reflection of the British Government's reluctance to proceed quickly to abolition. He was aware of the discontent among the slaves, but was careful not to antagonise the planters. Elliot's relationship with him seems to have been workmanlike but distant. He could find the Governor irritating, as he implied, with irony, in a later letter to his sister Emma: 'When I was at Demerara the governor very frequently did me the favour to send me papers and memorandums to report upon, wholly unconnected with my own duties. These trifling avocations commonly kept me out of my bed until three o'clock in the morning.'[38]

The reports and comments Elliot was required to submit to his political masters in London were not the only job-related communications he sent home. He corresponded 'off the record' with his friend Lord Howick, pulling no punches and in language stripped of diplomatic niceties. Early in 1832, around the time of his attempt to persuade the Court of Policy to provide for Assistant Protectors, he wrote a particularly blunt letter which was symptomatic of his frustration:

> As to my office it is a delusion. There is no protection for the Slave Population; and they will very shortly take matters into their own hands, and destroy the Property. The only way of saving these Countries is to give the Slaves a reasonable share in the produce of their Labour.[39]

He continued in the same vein:

> I am desperately unpopular, although I am sure I have not intended to do my duty captiously. But the fact is that this Colony is in a state of rebellion; the administration of Justice obstructed or totally defeated – no taxes paid – the most vehement clamour, not only against the Laws themselves, but against the Law-making power. What remedy for all these evils is sent out to us? Despatches full of hopes and exhortations, of advice to repent and behave better. This impunity gives strength to the growth of the Evil. The Order in Council is a dead letter and a dead letter contemned and decried in the most insulting terms. But if it were respected, would the Slave have benefited to such an Extent as he ought to be benefited, *and as he looks to be benefited?* No such thing. Setting aside the improbability of ensuring the observation of such a body of Law, I do deeply feel its inadequacy to present circumstances. You have brought forward the Slave to a certain point of civilization and intelligence, and he perceives the utter insufficiency of your

System either for his further advancement or for his controul. What should be given to the Slaves is *such a state of Freedom as they are now fit for*.[40]

While in British Guiana Charles and Clara's first son, Hugh, was born, but it was without his family that Charles returned to Britain with some urgency early in 1833. He had been called home, he later told Emma, 'because I was thought to be a person it would be well to consult in a most momentous public question'(the ending of slavery in the British Empire).[41] That he was considered to have a potentially important contribution to the debate about the method and timing of abolition was the result both of his friendship with Howick and of his assiduous reporting as Protector of Slaves. Howick will not have been surprised by the substance or tenor of Elliot's correspondence, which served to endorse his own views. He resigned his post as Under Secretary of State for War and the Colonies in May 1833 in protest at government dilatoriness over slave emancipation (though he was reinstated in the Cabinet the following year in a different capacity).[42] Elliot was grateful to Howick for supporting him, not only in his stance on slavery and for his work in British Guiana, but also in forwarding his request for compensation for financial outlay and disruption to family life – a discontent which was to manifest itself on several occasions throughout his career, as it had done with his father before him. Having obtained the endorsement of the Secretary of State, Howick passed Elliot's application on to the Treasury, commenting:

> With respect however to Captn Elliot's individual claims, Lord Goderich feels himself bound to acknowledge that His Majesty's Government are indebted to him, not only for a zealous and efficient execution of his office, but for communications of peculiar value and importance sent from the Colony during the last twelve months, and for essential services rendered at a critical period since his arrival in this country, by his exertions and personal influence with Members of the West India Board.[43]

He went on:

> His Lordship being thus sensible that Captn Elliot has contributed far beyond what the functions of his particular office required of him, to the accomplishment of objects of great public importance, is aware also that this has been done with serious inconvenience and some expense to himself, as he was sent for to return to this country with the least possible delay, and was obliged to leave his family behind him.[44]

Charles Elliot may well have reflected in later life that at this point in his career his standing with British Government Ministers was at its highest.

Despite the unrealistic expectations of his role he had worked hard and given more as Protector of Slaves than was asked (in marked contrast to his predecessor). His evidence to the Parliamentary Select Committee and his responses to particular questions put to him by the Secretary of State were important contributions to the abolition debate. He also had the satisfaction of knowing that, while observing the conventions of official communication where necessary, he had been true to his own beliefs about the inhumanity (and inefficiency) of slave labour, and had conveyed them in a forthright manner. He argued that slavery was economically unsound not only because he believed it himself, but because, as many in Parliament had recognised, the planters and their supporters were more likely to be persuaded by such an argument than by assertions about human rights. His fundamental hostility to slavery, however, doubtless influenced by his liberal education, stories of his father's time in the Leeward Islands, and first-hand experience of the Atlantic slave trade, had always been the inescapable injustice and degradation inherent in slave labour and the affront to the dignity of slaves as people. He had made it his business as Protector, notwithstanding the enormity of his task, to talk with individual slaves; a personal letter he wrote to Lord Howick in the autumn of 1832 says much about his awareness of the slaves' predicament:

> It is the merest nonsense to suppose that the Slaves are not keenly alive to the painfulness and injustice of their situation. I know a Slave – a common field negro ... who possesses that vigorous character and immense influence with the people, which would enable him to place himself, tomorrow, at the head of ten thousand of his fellows ... [He] told me once that he had learned to read; and that every night of his life he occupied himself in teaching his children to do the same. I asked him why, if he had spare time, he did not work hard so as to earn the means of buying his children's freedom, one after another. He said 'Master, I want to teach them *Knowledge*; Freedom is sure to follow'.[45]

Elliot's response revealed the importance he attached to understanding others and to forbearance:

> I did not answer as if I understood him literally, but said, it was very true that knowledge was an excellent thing – the more so as it taught us to look justly at the dependent condition of all mankind, and enabled us to bear the painfulness of our respective situations (and no situation was without pain) wisely and manfully.[46]

His role and status prevented him from more overt empathy with this man, but he knew well the frustrations and aspirations of the slave community as a whole:

What must be the feelings of the Negro population towards us? Think of their moral degradation, of the fearful wrongs they have suffered; consider their half-civilized situation, getting every hour more conscious of their own strength, and utterly void of any of those feelings which might dispose them to use it mercifully. Their confidence in every man with a white face is every day diminishing – in Government and all. Out come Laws, pretending, as these poor people may reason, to ameliorate their condition, but in point of fact rendering it not a whit less irksome.[47]

After extensive debate over many months, in August 1833 the Bill to abolish slavery in the colonies was read for its third and final time in the House of Commons and the House of Lords and passed into law, taking effect in the great majority of colonies in August 1834. Compensation to the planters was agreed in the sum of £20 million. Slavery was initially replaced by a compulsory apprenticeship system, which by the end of the decade had been discontinued.

In February 1834 Charles and Clara Elliot, and their children Harriet and Hughie, sailed in HMS *Andromache* for the Portuguese colony of Macao. Charles had been appointed to serve as Master Attendant to the Commission led by Lord Napier, Chief Superintendent of Trade in China.

# Chapter Six

# Trade and China

C hina's 4,000 years of dynastic rule had been turbulent, moving between fragmentation as external powers invaded or internal dissension divided, and consolidation as strong rulers repelled or unified. During times of relative peace Chinese explorers had travelled widely to other continents, their journeys of exploration reaching their zenith in the fifteenth century during the rule of the Ming emperors (1368 – 1644), a long period of social stability in which art, literature and commerce flourished.

The goodwill extended by China to its commercial partners incorporated a degree of condescension, an assumption that they could never expect to trade as equals. The emperors and their senior officials were aware of the power and accomplishments of some of the other states and groups of states with which they had contact, notably the Roman Empire, but it was taken for granted that none could rival their own civilization. The Chinese were not the only ones who marvelled at Chinese achievement, however. Many 'barbarians' (as the British believed China referred to foreigners) greatly admired their wealth. The mid-fourteenth century Moroccan traveller Ibn-Battuta wrote: 'Nowhere in the world are there to be found people richer than the Chinese ... porcelain in China is of about the same value as earthenware is with us, or even less'.[1] Unsurprisingly, Chinese merchant shipping was well received in Arab ports, where local conditions allowed. An historian recorded one instance:

> A report came from Mecca, the honoured, that a number of junks had come from China to the sea ports of India and two of them had anchored in the port of Aden, but their goods, chinaware, silk, musk and the like, were not disposed of there because of the disorders of the State of Yemen... The Sultan wrote to them to let them come to Jeddah and to show them honour.[2]

The Chinese traded mainly silk and porcelain for spices, gemstones and glass. Their commerce was conducted in ports as far west as the Persian Gulf and the east coast of Africa, but two of the main centres were Malacca (now Melaka) in modern day Malaysia, and Calicut (Kozhikode) on the Malabar coast in Kerala, southern India. Both these ports were frequented by Arab traders bringing merchandise from their own lands and from places further west, such as Venice. Malacca's proximity to the spice islands – the Moluccas (Indonesia's Maluku Islands) – and to the Bay of Bengal and the Indian Ocean made it an ideal place for

entrepôt trade, and it developed into a major centre which was later to
be exploited by the Portuguese, Dutch and British.

European contact with China had begun in the thirteenth century
during the rule of the Mongol Emperor Kublai Khan, through the
journeys of travellers such as the Venetian explorer brothers Niccolo and
Maffeo Polo and Niccolo's son Marco, and of Franciscan missionaries.
After the fall of the western Roman Empire in the fifth century AD,
overland trade routes between Europe and China had continued to
be operated by middle-eastern Jewish merchants, but it was travellers
from Italy – explorers, Franciscan missionaries and Papal envoys – who
laid the foundations for later, much expanded European involvement
in imperial China. The lead in religious mission to China was assumed
during the sixteenth century by the Jesuits whose founder, St Francis
Xavier, had died in 1552 on his way to China shortly before reaching
his destination. Ricci and Ruggieri, the two Italians subsequently tasked
by the Jesuits with taking their work in China forward, were to become
influential figures in the imperial court. They pursued, in addition to their
evangelism, a policy of cultural assimilation, bringing western knowledge
to China while conveying to Europe information about Chinese history
and achievement.

In 1557 Portuguese traders, who for some twenty years had conducted
their business from offshore locations, were allowed by the Chinese to
establish a base at Macao, on the western side of the Pearl River estuary.
There was no transfer of sovereignty – the Portuguese were required to
pay rent, and their activities were restricted, but the territory constituted
an important foothold from which to conduct commerce and in which
to set up education and training facilities for the promotion of Roman
Catholicism. Inevitably, other European powers showed an interest in
Macao for its trading possibilities. An attempt by the Dutch to capture
it in 1622 was repulsed, largely due to the loyalty to the Portuguese of
resident African slaves. Fifteen years later the first British approach to
Macao was made, by four ships commanded by Captain John Weddell.

Weddell was a seasoned sea captain whose buccaneering career had
involved several brushes with the law. He was now under contract to
William Courten, a wealthy London merchant and energetic entrepreneur
who was also no stranger to litigation. Weddell's visit to the south coast
of China was significant not only because it was the first by a British
expedition, but because in its contacts with the Chinese it foreshadowed
the difficulties of British-Chinese interaction for over 200 years to come.
Like his more official British successors on the China coast, Weddell's
object was trade, and like them, his dealings with the Chinese were
characterised by misunderstanding and ignorance on both sides.[3] He kept
at first to the required procedure by applying through the Portuguese for
permission to go to Canton, but after broken promises and repeated
delays lost patience, first sending a boat and then proceeding upriver,
in stages, with all his ships. Weddell received mixed messages from the

Chinese, compounded by a duplicitous intermediary, and lukewarm civility from the Portuguese at Macao. He could not have known of the agreements and informal understandings between the Chinese and Portuguese, which sanctioned Portuguese residence in Macao and monopoly of maritime trade there with China provided the Portuguese did China's bidding, not least in keeping other Europeans away from the Pearl River. The several pauses for exchange of communication allowed, almost by accident, a small amount of trade to be done, but overall, the expedition was not judged a success. Obliged to promise to leave as the price for the release of some of his compatriots being held in Canton, Weddell and his ships departed the China coast after six months. Peter Mundy, a diarist and commercial agent on the voyage, was not impressed with their treatment, '...having been for these 6 Monthes variously Crosed in our Designe, our lives, shipping, goodes etts., Molested, endaungered, Dammified, Our Principalls with Much Meanes Deteyned att Canton.'[4]

British trade in the east at this time was the monopoly of the English East India Company, but Courten was permitted to commission an expedition to China because the Company did not (yet) operate there. The Company of Merchants of London Trading into the East Indies, which had been granted its Royal Charter in 1600, had been formed from merchants and financiers to provide an organised focus for competing against other European trading powers as they sought to develop new markets in India and the Southeast Asian archipelagos. Chief among those powers were the Portuguese, who in the sixteenth century had established a sequence of trading bases between Europe and China, of which the largest concentration was on the west coast of India, and the Dutch, whose efficient and productive financial system enabled them to fund commercial expansion on an increasingly dominant scale. After three costly Anglo-Dutch wars, stemming from intense mercantile competition, the accession of William of Orange to the English throne in 1688 set the scene for Anglo-Dutch business collaboration from which the British would learn much, and finalised a rationalisation of British and Dutch trading arrangements in the east.[5] The Dutch retained Malacca (which they had wrested from the Portuguese in 1641), the Moluccas and parts of modern-day Indonesia, while the British would develop commerce in India, where the prominence of the Portuguese had faded. This apportionment was not, though, a peaceful process; it had ended with the British in 1684 being driven by the Dutch out of Bantam, the commercial base at the western end of the north coast of Java which had been the Company's first settlement in the East Indies.

During the eighteenth century the English East India Company greatly expanded its reach and influence in India. By 1805 it controlled (either directly or through local alliances) nearly all the coastal regions, especially in the east, much of the interior, and most of the fertile plains and more temperate hill areas of the northeast. It would be misleading, however, to imply that this was the result of a concerted, coordinated plan to expand; it was rather a consequence of the Company's determination to protect its own trading interests and revenue and of the personal ambitions of a number of its servants.

In 1686 the Company had been granted a new charter (one of several in its lifetime) confirming powers given in 1661 by Charles II and authorising it to use military force if necessary against, among others, native rulers.[6] A military presence, even if modest and not in evidence at the start, became essential to the maintenance of the Company's main bases in India, at Bombay (acquired from Portugal by treaty in 1661, now Mumbai), Madras (founded in 1639, now Chennai) and Calcutta (1690, now Kolkata). This support typically comprised, under overall British command, a minority of British troops and various categories of native infantry and local militias. At Bombay in the 1670s, for example, the garrison was estimated at the time by the Surgeon to the Company to number around 1,500, of whom only some twenty per cent were British.[7] In Madras in 1670 there were some 200 European troops but by 1759, according to a later account, the settlement at Fort St George was protected by five battalions of native infantry, at least 1,500 men, led by European commissioned and non-commissioned officers.[8]

The Company's military resources in the latter half of the eighteenth century were mainly deployed in the prosecution of wars in alliance with local rulers, with the twin objectives of assisting them and of furthering British interests, including territorial expansion. Such conflicts were fought against other native factions, or against other European trade competitors (who themselves formed local alliances). The Moghul Empire, which had held sway over north and central India for more than 200 years, had begun to disintegrate under attack by Maratha warriors from the western Deccan, the great plateau of south-central and southern India. The Marathas fought three wars with East India Company forces and their allies between 1777 and 1818, the last of these resulting in British control of the great majority of the Indian subcontinent.

From the early seventeenth century the Company's merchants had opened up new markets in the Bay of Bengal as British trade with the Spice Islands was gradually ceded to the Dutch. (They had also sought, with little success, to initiate trade with Japan and Siam (Thailand).) The founding of Calcutta in 1690 was attributed to Company merchant Job Charnock; it was established on an entirely new site, much as Francis Day, a senior Company man at Masulipatnam on the Coromandel coast of south-east India, had initiated the building of Fort St George close to nearby Madraspatnam sixty-one years earlier.[9] In 1756 Calcutta was attacked and captured by the forces of the Nawab of Bengal, Siraj-ud-Daula, the publicity subsequently given to the 'Black Hole' incarceration doing much to rally public opinion in Britain in support of Colonel Robert Clive and his army's vigorous retaliation. Clive's victory at the Battle of Plassey in 1757, as a result of which the process of establishing Company control over Bengal was begun, was an important turning point in the history of British India. The Treaty of Allahabad in 1765 transferred to the Company from the Moghul Emperor Shah Alam the right to collect tribute, which allowed the East India Company to exploit the agricultural resources of Bengal through land taxes and trade tariffs. The Company's taxation regime exacerbated the consequences of the disastrous famine afflicting Bengal in 1770. The famine caused the deaths of millions, and was in large part the result of the Company's policy of clearing land used for food crops, such as rice and grain, to make way for the cultivation of opium. The greater financial independence granted under the 1765 Treaty did not last long, however. Concerns about corruption and poor management by the Company's officers led the British government to legislate, first to enable it to regulate the Company's affairs, and then to bring its activities under direct British government control – the latter (in 1784)providing, among other things, that the governorships of Bombay and Madras should be government, not Company, appointments, and in effect designating Calcutta the capital of British India.

Since 1601, when the first voyage by Company ships was made under the command of Sir James Lancaster to the Spice Islands, the Company's trading priorities had greatly changed. As a joint stock company its directors' primary responsibility was to maximise revenue for its shareholders, with operational focus intended to change according to wherever the greatest profit was to be made; but in such turbulent times things were never that simple. Local power struggles and the increasingly political implications of the Company's activities in India obliged its agents to temper their ambition with large doses of pragmatism. Early in the Company's life Indian cotton and indigo began to be traded as well as spices, but attempts to pay routinely for them in kind with English woollen broadcloth failed, forcing the Company's ships to carry as payment large quantities of bullion. In the 1680s, gold and silver were much in demand by Moghul India for financing its wars with the Marathas and in Afghanistan, and cotton and silk luxury goods from India were carried to Britain in return. By the turn of the century, however, opposition in Britain to Indian manufactured products because of their effect on domestic industry resulted in legislation restricting imports to raw materials only.

The English East India Company's ships had visited the China coast since the beginning of the seventeenth century, eventually establishing a base on Formosa (Taiwan) and trading with Amoy (Xiamen), Chusan (Zhoushan) and, from a distance, with Canton (Guangzhou). Their role had frequently been that of freight carrier, transporting from China – and from Siam – goods bound for the islands of the Southeast Asian archipelagos, much as they had earlier done between Persia and India.

Portuguese Macao had long been used by European merchants as a base from which to conduct trade negotiations with the Chinese, but it was in 1689 that the first Company men were allowed to proceed to

Canton itself. They went not by ship but by boat, sedan chair, and boat again; the Company's ship *Defence* was subsequently given permission to sail upriver, but her captain, Heath, judged the river approach too risky for navigation by a large vessel.[10] The voyage to China had been undertaken on the initiative of Elihu Yale, the American born Governor of Madras,[11] who sent in overall charge of the expedition his younger brother Thomas. As with Weddell's mission more than fifty years before, Yale's attempt to establish a direct trading link with China was not a success. Captain Heath had provoked a fight in refusing to comply with the demands of Chinese bureaucracy; Chinese ransom demands were refused by Thomas Yale, the *Defence* sailed, and the prospects for promoting trade were severely set back.

Following rising discontent in England at the East India Company's apparent abuse of its monopoly and at allegations of bribery and market manipulation by Sir Josiah Child, a director and then Governor of the Company, a new 'General Society' for trade with the east was set up by Parliament in 1698 to re-establish operations on an acceptable basis. It was under the auspices of this 'New Company' that a year later the next attempt was made to secure a trading foothold in China. The *Macclesfield*, at 250 tons one of the Company's smaller ships, sailed up the Pearl River to Whampoa, the anchorage some five miles east of Canton. The Company's merchant-in-charge, or supercargo, was Robert Douglas, whose efforts to trade were frustrated by the Chinese authorities, despite being encouraged by the local customs officer (the 'Hoppo'[12]). Some trade was nevertheless done, as it was also at Zhoushan, to which Douglas sailed when after many months' detention he had finally been allowed to leave Canton. Robert Douglas's expedition has been called the most successful venture to China up to that date (1701).[13] After a disastrous attempt to found a settlement on Con Son (Pulo Condore), a small island off the south-eastern coast of Vietnam, in which Company personnel were slaughtered by the garrison, there was no appetite for trying to find another offshore base. In 1711 the Kangxi Emperor, a long-reigning, stabilising ruler who was able to take a long-term view of his country's interests, granted permission for overseas traders to establish a semi-permanent presence at Canton. Though outside the city walls and to be occupied by the foreigners for only six months each year, the establishment of the 'factories' on the waterfront at Canton marked a significant step forward for western merchants in their quest for development of the China trade. The embargo on foreign traders conducting business anywhere in China other than Canton, however, implemented in 1703, remained.

By the 1760s the balance of the Company's traded commodities had changed again. Silks and cottons were still much in demand, but proportionately they had been eclipsed by tea from China. Originally brought to Europe by the Dutch, tea was first imported by the Company to London in 1669; such had been the subsequent demand that private merchants, including some of the Company's own employees acting in that capacity, saw opportunity for enrichment and entered the market. The Company's response was to outlaw such activity as far as it could and to seek from the government monopoly rights on the import of tea to Britain, which it obtained in 1721 (at a price). When it began importing rapidly increasing quantities of the cheaper *bohea* black tea, rather than green tea only, the price fell from 16*s* lb to 7*s* lb, and by 1770 it was just 3*s* lb.[14] Tea drinking ceased to be a preserve of the fashionable rich and became widely available, hand in hand, conveniently, with plentiful supplies of sugar from the Caribbean. For the Company, the quantity of tea it was importing became a problem. Since 1768 the American colonies had preferred smuggled Dutch tea, not only because it was cheaper but because it was not subject to tax, to payment of which the American colonists took strong objection. By 1773 the Company was in a very poor financial state, largely because of huge stockpiles of tea it could not sell. The Tea Act of that year, which allowed the Company to ship tea directly to North America and undercut the Dutch smugglers, was intended to help the Company out of its difficulties, but since the tea remained taxed it inflamed the colonists' hostility still further, prompting among other things the Boston Tea Party and becoming one of the proximate causes of the American War of Independence. In 1773 the British Parliament also passed what was known as the Regulating Act, giving the government power to regulate the activities of the East India Company.[15]

British attitudes to matters Chinese during the latter half of the eighteenth century had become many and varied, but the mood in government was one of concern and frustration. Tea was now the Company's most traded commodity, and the tax on tea imports accounted for around ten per cent of British government revenue; but China's lack of interest in British and Indian manufactured goods meant that Chinese tea had to be paid for in silver bullion, to the extent that the Company's income from India was barely compensating for this drain on its resources. Added to this economic difficulty were the constraints and obstacles imposed by the Canton authorities in fees which the Company considered vastly excessive, residence restrictions, and the operation of a cartel, known as the Co-Hong, by the Chinese merchants. Further attempts to find a suitable trading base on the China coast were unsuccessful, but through the good offices of Captain Francis Light the island of Penang in the Malacca Strait was ceded to the Company in 1786.

By the start of the nineteenth century it was clear that the outflow of bullion at the required rate could not be sustained. The solution was to supply China with a commodity for which there was rapidly growing domestic demand which could not be met by China itself: opium. The opium poppy, *papaver somniferum,* had been grown as early as the fourth millennium BC, and whether or not opium was first imported earlier, there is little doubt that it was brought to China by Arab traders in the seventh or eighth centuries AD. In 1684 it was officially classed as a medicine in China, but for some fifteen years before that had come to be mixed with tobacco and smoked (rather than eaten). Joseph Rowntree later wrote that it was 'practically certain, from the absence of all mention of any opium habit by the Jesuit missionaries, by travellers, and in the Chinese records, that there was no general consumption of opium [in China] before the introduction of opium smoking'.[16] With widespread smoking came widespread addiction and abuse, and in 1729 the Yongzheng Emperor outlawed the smoking of opium and its sale in China. Then as now with banned drugs, the penalties for dealing were considerably harsher than for possession; consumers were flogged or pilloried, dealers were strangled.[17] For seventy years the Emperors nevertheless continued, despite the internal prohibition, to allow the importing of opium in order to profit from the resulting tax revenues, an ambivalence towards the drug which was to bedevil future Chinese attempts to control and eliminate it.

Until 1799 when an imperial edict banned imports of the drug, the supply of opium from India to China enabled the Company to purchase tea for export to Britain. Ever since its early days, the value of its purchases from Southeast Asia was at least three times that of the goods it sold there, the balance being met in bullion and coin. During the period 1710 to 1759 for example, exports to the east comprised goods worth £9,248,306 and bullion and coin amounting to £26,833,614.[18] During the later years of the eighteenth century the Company was able to take advantage of the involvement of the so-called 'Country' traders to substitute goods for part of the payment in bullion and coin. These India-based British and Indian private merchants – including some current and former Company men acting independently – who over the years had worked the trade routes between India, the Southeast Asian archipelagos and China, were now licensed by the Company (which formally held a monopoly of trade with China) to engage in direct commerce between India and China themselves. Their ships carried mainly opium and cotton, and the arrangement both allowed the Company to reduce the level of payment by bullion and coin and enabled the Country traders to make substantial profits.

This stratagem also meant, crucially, that the growing western – especially British – demand for tea could be satisfied. There was little awareness in Britain that opium was being used to help in the purchase of tea, but at this stage – the late eighteenth century – even had the practice been more widely known, there would have been no particular concern. In Britain the emphasis was on the medicinal use of opium; the drug was regarded as overwhelmingly beneficial and in due course became a key ingredient in a wide range of medicines such as laudanum and chlorodyne. Partly to decrease reliance on opium imports, mainly from Turkey, attempts were made to grow opium in Britain and while there was some success for a time, the venture never attained long-term commercial viability.

After the Chinese imperial ban at the turn of the century opium exports from India to China had the status of smuggled contraband. Since the Company could not itself engage in illegal trafficking, it sold off the opium crop at auction in Calcutta to the Country traders, on whom it now relied entirely to complete sales to the Chinese at Canton. Indian opium exported to China in this way continued at approximately the same annual level for some twenty years, but between 1821 and 1831 was to rise dramatically from 4,244 to 18,956 chests a year.[19]

These developments in Southeast Asia had done nothing to ease the frustration of the British government over its relations with the Middle Kingdom. In 1788 it appointed the Hon. Charles Cathcart, a Member of Parliament and a young but already distinguished soldier, to lead a mission to China with the intention of establishing diplomatic and closer trade relations there. The venture was abandoned when Cathcart died *en voyage*, and it was another four years before a further attempt was made to make official contact with the Emperor.

This time the mission was led by the vastly experienced Lord (George) Macartney, a successful diplomat and former colonial Governor. The Macartney Embassy, as it became known, was an altogether grander affair than its abortive predecessor. With the title and status of Ambassador, and an entourage of nearly a hundred men which included specialist artists and scientists and a military escort, Macartney sailed from Portsmouth in the 64-gun line-of-battle ship HMS *Lion* in September 1792.

Ten months later the expedition reached the Gulf of Zhili on the coast of north-eastern China. Contact with the Chinese authorities was made through a local mandarin who had instructions from the imperial court to make the visitors welcome. In keeping with the teaching of Confucius – 'To have friends coming to one from distant parts, is this not great pleasure?'- hospitality was generous, sometimes lavish, as the embassy made its way inland to Beijing and thence north beyond the Great Wall to the Emperor's summer palace at Jehol (Chengde).[20] The visitors were duly impressed, and held high hopes for a successful outcome to the mission. Discussion between the British and the mandarins assigned to accompany them was cordial, matters of potential difficulty being set aside lest the atmosphere become soured. The form of the ceremonial meeting to be held between the Ambassador and the Emperor was one such matter. There were other discordant notes; not all the mandarins with the party were hospitable, and after arrival at Jehol the mood of the embassy became uncertain as restrictions were applied. One of the participants later wrote: 'we had plenty within our walls, but no-one had the liberty of egress'.[21] The bewilderment of the less exalted members of the mission, if not of the Ambassador himself, is illustrated by a catering incident: 'Instead of that profusion which had hitherto crowned our board, the lower classes of the embassy found scarcely enough at dinner this day to satisfy one half of them ... We could perceive something too of a meditated disrespect, and of course felt some alarm.'[22]

After complaint to the mandarin

> in a few minutes every table was served with hot dishes, in
> the usual variety and profusion. Why this entertainment,
> which must have been nearly ready, was thus withheld, and so
> speedily produced, served as an enigma to satisfy our ingenuity,
> but which we could never solve. Indeed no other ideas could
> possibly be entertained of it, than that of an effort of Chinese
> ingenuity to try the temper of Englishmen.[23]

Despite the best efforts of both sides the question of the formalities of
meeting the Emperor could not be resolved. Macartney was willing to
follow the protocol in use when being presented to his own sovereign,
kneeling on one knee and kissing the hand, but he was adamant that
to perform the full kow-tow, kneeling on both knees three times and
touching the ground with the head three times on each occasion, would
be disloyal to the King and he would not do it. The Emperor was
predictably affronted at what he considered the arrogant disdain shown
by the British. Nevertheless, shortly afterwards he appeared to soften
his stance, sending a conciliatory message and granting the Ambassador
an audience. The spirits and expectations of the British rose once more.
There followed a series of lavish entertainments, whose conviviality led
Macartney to believe that he might at last profitably discuss with the
Emperor the objects of his mission. His attempt to do so fell on deaf
ears. Accepting that he would not now achieve all he had set out to do,
the Ambassador hoped that a final opportunity to salvage something
would be afforded by the Emperor's forthcoming return to Beijing, when
another meeting might be possible. Despite an impressive display of the
latest manufactures the British had brought as gifts, and the submission
of a written request, there was no further progress. It was made clear to
the Embassy that there was now no purpose to be served by its remaining
in China any longer. 'The manner in which the embassy was dismissed
was ungracious, and mortifying in the extreme'.[24] Lord Macartney and
his retinue set out for home on 7 October 1793.

Macartney's refusal to perform the kow-tow has sometimes been
cited as the main reason for the Embassy's failure. Its aims however
had been to establish regular trade and diplomatic relations with
China and to extend trading opportunities there, and it seems highly
improbable, given the prevailing Chinese and British views of the world
and their respective places in it, that those objectives could ever have
been achieved. The kow-tow impasse undoubtedly made things worse,
but to the imperial court the visitors from Britain, though important,
were never in the end more than emissaries from a vassal state. They
had come from further away than was usual for those bearing tribute,
but the explanatory announcement on welcoming banners en route to
Beijing had made the position clear: 'The English Ambassador carrying

tribute to the Emperor of China'.[25] Nor were the self-sufficient Chinese interested in developing trade. The clocks, porcelain, carpets, portraits and other gifts brought by the visitors were of passing interest, no more. So far as the Emperor himself was concerned, 'Strange and costly objects do not interest me. As your Ambassador can see for himself we possess all things. I set no value on strange objects and ingenious, and have no use for your country's manufactures.'[26]

Twenty-three years later, when the wars with the French were over, the British tried again. The 1816 Embassy was headed by William, first Earl Amherst. He was not a professional diplomat, but came from a well-connected family which had included a number of prominent military men. The Embassy sailed from England in early February 1816 and arrived back in mid-August the following year. There had been exploratory voyages in the eastern seas and long overland journeys in China, but only a few days had been spent in Beijing seeking to pursue the business of the mission. On this occasion the refusal to perform the kow-tow was indeed the immediate cause of the Embassy's failure. Far from making any progress, the Amherst mission had sharpened mutual antagonisms and significantly damaged the chances of improving trade and diplomatic relations.

On the south China coast the system of trading convenience between the Honourable East India Company and the Country traders (or 'private English' or 'free traders') was beginning to fray. Along with cotton, ever more opium was being shipped from India, upsetting the balance of the arrangement and, some felt, inhibiting possibilities for commercial growth. The problem could be greatly alleviated, the Country traders thought, if the Company's China trade monopoly were to cease. After sustained pressure, reflecting the longstanding disquiet of domestic manufacturers as well as the concerns of the free traders, Parliament abolished the monopoly with effect from April 1834. The consequences were not all straightforward or beneficial; one of the questions in the new situation was what should be the channel of communication between the Chinese merchants (the Co-Hong), who had been used to dealing only with the Company, and the British. To this the British response was to appoint a Chief Superintendent of Trade. The post's first incumbent was Lord Napier, whose Commission's Master Attendant was Captain Charles Elliot, RN.

## Chapter Seven

# Fizzle, Silence and Quiescence

That Charles Elliot should have been chosen to serve with Lord Napier in China was not on the face of it surprising. He had in the opinion of several members of the government (especially his friend Lord Howick) performed well in British Guiana; he came from a family distinguished for its public service; and he was personally recommended by John Francis Davis, a senior East India Company man and an accomplished sinologist (and also a friend). Davis wrote of Elliot that 'the talents, information and temper of that gentleman would render him eminently suited to the chief station in this country [China]'.[1] On the other hand, though he had served with the Royal Navy in the East India Squadron, he had had little experience of the east and none of China, and there was a sense in some quarters that the Elliot family had acquired more than its fair share of influential positions in public life.[2] (There does not however seem to be any evidence that any of his relations were instrumental in securing him this post).

Elliot's own reaction to the appointment was unsure and uneasy, perhaps reflecting a suspicion of differing views or an absence of enthusiasm on the part of those behind it. Excluding specialists such as the surgeons and interpreter, there were four levels of seniority below Napier as Chief Superintendent: the Second Superintendent; the Third Superintendent; the Secretary; and the Master Attendant, whose role was to include the oversight and management of British shipping movements in the section of the Pearl River known as the Bogue, where the river delta narrows sharply on the approach to Canton.[3] Elliot's naval experience was clearly relevant, but he would have little if any involvement in diplomacy or matters of policy, and conscious of his background and his achievements to date Elliot felt humiliated. A few days before sailing from Devonport in HMS *Andromache*, a 28-gun frigate, he wrote to Lord Howick,

> I am appointed Master Attendant at Canton with a salary of £800 a year, and certainly if I had pursued my own inclinations I should have declined the office, for when I sought employment in China I never expected it in the shape it has reached me, but it seemed to me to be my duty on public grounds to accept this appointment and I shall endeavour to discharge it faithfully'.[4,5]

Whether or not he was fully aware of the duties and the status of the job when he accepted it, he was told by Lord Glenelg, President of the Board of Control,'a few days before I left England that circumstances had prevented him from recommending me to His Majesty as one of the Superintendents'.[6,7] Whatever the 'circumstances' were it seems clear that Glenelg, at least, felt – perhaps with some embarrassment – the need to acknowledge to Elliot that a more senior position for him had been a possibility.

This general unease about his status was compounded by the awareness that he and Napier held the same service rank, that of post captain in the Royal Navy. Elliot was prepared to concede that Napier was 'a good sort of man', but was at a loss to understand why, as a sailor turned sheep farmer with no experience of diplomacy or of China, he had been chosen for his current role.[8] Napier was however a long-standing friend of the King and had been appointed a Groom of the Bedchamber, a fact to which Elliot made mocking reference. Napier's salary of £6,000, more than seven times his own, would have added to his discomfiture.

All in all, Elliot was upset, resentful and not a little bewildered by his appointment as Master Attendant, but resolved to set these feelings aside and get on with the job. He wrote frankly to his sister Emma shortly before *Andromache* sailed:

> I feel all this to be a humiliation, and a very sore one too, but I shall take very good care, that no sense of that description shall deaden the ardour of *my own efforts* in *my own behalf*. Neither am I without the conviction, that it will be very proper to wear a mask of good humor, or at least of indifference out of doors.
>
> This last stroke has not been without its advantages. It has given me the true touch of bitterness and real selfishness, without which there is no success in this world.[9]

As with others appointed to serve overseas, Charles and Clara Elliot had decisions to make about the care of their children. A letter from Charles to Emma two months before their departure shows that their inclination then had been to take with them only the 2-year-old Hughie.[10]

The correspondence between Charles and Emma, in this instance and in the coming years, reveals the extent to which Charles treated, perhaps needed, Emma as a confidante to whom he entrusted details of his feelings about his relationships and his job. His admiration for and gratitude to Clara, tempered with occasional irritation, are an indication both of his devotion to his wife and of his own tendency to impatience:

> I write Dear Emy with great difficulty, and you will excuse this illegible incoherence. Think for us. I am sure if we do resolve to leave the children, you will take every care of them, that your situation enables you to. Clara does not do herself justice. She has more sense and feeling than I have, but she seems at times to consider it *fine to talk nonsense*. She has been a great consolation to me, whenever I have really wanted affection, and self denial, and never more so than since you left us yesterday.

Poor dear, God grant that her own health may be equal to the trial which awaits her.[11]

After much agonised deliberation Charles and Clara decided that Harriet (aged four) as well as Hughie should accompany them, and that their new baby, Gilbert (Gibby), should stay behind with Emma and her husband, Lieutenant General Sir Thomas Hislop, at Charlton Villa, southeast of London.

The voyage to Macao, via Rio de Janeiro and the Cape of Good Hope, took a little over five months. Elliot's letters to his sister were much taken up with commentary on Lord and Lady Napier, who were also travelling in *Andromache*, with two teenage daughters Maria and Georgiana, the eldest of their six children. He commented on how he and Clara regarded them, and on how he thought the Napiers – Lord Napier particularly, his superior – viewed himself and Clara. The two families kept a civil distance from each other socially. There was cordiality, but no affinity:

We have as little intercourse as possible, but there seems no room for blame on either side. He does not desire to know more of me than I of him, and with this indifference there can be neither surprise to witness or fault to impute, that we are so slenderly known to each other.[12]

This observation to Emma probably reflected the sensitivity he still felt, three months into the voyage, about the level of his appointment. He could not avoid repeated mention of his dissatisfaction with the way his career was unfolding; his apparent willingness – to his sister at any rate – to make the best of it did little to conceal the hurt he continued to feel:

I am afraid I shall not be very successful, while things remain as they do now. Not that I would very willingly have you believe I think the clearness and soundness of other men's views are likely to throw my own calling into the shade but my position puts me beyond the possibility of being known or heard and I do not imagine there can be much disposition to move me forwards.

I have no complaints to make, however; there are two ways of considering such points. Upon the one hand it is irritating enough to see the people, who the state of circumstances forces over one's head but then on the other, there is something very sedative in the contemplation that thousands of abler and better men would gratefully accept what I have got.

The rottenness [of advancement through patronage and personal connection] is passing away, God's gracious name be praised, and the time is at hand when if a man does not move

higher, it will be sufficiently obvious that he ought not to move
higher.[13]

This last comment, more an expression of hope than expectation, was
perhaps an indication of a sub-conscious attempt on Elliot's part to think
positively, not least in order to counter the pain of being parted from
his infant son Gibby. He needed to feel that this sacrifice would in the
end be worthwhile, an unavoidable price to pay for what he would be
able to achieve serving his country overseas; but so far as Emma – and
presumably anyone else who cared to ask – was concerned, he gloomily
decided, at this stage in the middle of the voyage to China, that he did
not wish to return to England:

> I hope this letter will find my angel under your roof, but if he
> be not there, I am sure it will only be because you are abroad.
> God Almighty bless and preserve him. He shall not be away
> from me long. My mind is fixedly made up to sit myself down
> permanently somewhere in this Eastern part of the world – Van
> Diemen's Land [Tasmania] if I possibly can. But with England I
> have done for ever unless by a miracle I make a fortune, and
> there are no miracles nowadays.[14]

In mid-July 1834 *Andromache* approached Macao. Charles Elliot had had
a long time, too long a time, in which to dwell on his present situation,
his career prospects, and his family's future. His ponderings now came
to a swift end, as the Napier and Elliot families stepped ashore. Clara
Elliot wrote to her sister-in-law that 'There was an immediate scramble
of people to stare at the King's mandarin as Lord Napier is designated.
We were carried in chairs (most delightful conveyance) to the late Chief's
house, Mr Davis who is now our 2nd superintendent.'[15] The Elliots had
to wait several weeks in lodgings before moving into a modest house
made available to them by the East India Company rent-free until the
following May. 'I wish with all my heart', Clara wrote, 'it was for a longer
period, but many things may happen by that time.'[16]

Meanwhile, Napier wasted no time in setting the Commission's work
in train. His brief had been delivered to him in the final weeks before his
departure from England in the form of his formal Commission from the
King, a subsequent letter from the Foreign Secretary, Palmerston, private
advice from Palmerston, and a letter from the Prime Minister, Earl Grey.
Even if all parties had been conveying the same message and the Foreign
Secretary's instructions had been consistent in themselves, there would
doubtless have been differences of tone and emphasis in these several
communications which would have caused Napier some uncertainty.
As it was, Napier's task as set out by his superiors was impossible to
fulfil. He was to protect the interests of the British merchant community
at Canton; to attempt – as had Macartney and Amherst before him –

to establish regular diplomatic relations with China; to explore the possibility of increasing the number of Chinese ports at which the British could trade; to proceed directly to Canton and become resident there; and to announce his arrival at Canton by sending a letter notifying the Viceroy accordingly. These orders were at least clear; what made their execution inoperable without confusion were simultaneous instructions not to enter into new and unusual arrangements with the Chinese and to conform to the laws and usages of China. Diplomatic relations and trade expansion could not be considered other than new arrangements, and according to the laws and usages of China you could not enter Canton without a permit, let alone live there, nor did you communicate with the Viceroy except through the guild of Chinese merchants, the Co-Hong.

To these conflicting instructions were added, as if to emphasise a British view that they really could have their cake and eat it, the approach to be taken to illegal trading along the coast (the word opium, with disingenuous coyness, was not used). Palmerston wrote:

> Peculiar caution will be necessary ... with regard to such ships as may attempt to explore the coast of China for purposes of traffic. It is not desirable that you should encourage such adventures, but you must never lose sight of the fact that you have no authority to interfere with, or to prevent, them.[17]

Palmerston's equivocation on the China question was partly a consequence of his preoccupation with foreign affairs in Europe and the Middle East; China was simply nowhere near the top of his agenda, and while there might come a time at which it would need closer attention, that was for the future. His apparent indecisiveness also reflected the absence of any current crisis; that there was a question at all was the result of the British decision to change arrangements, with the ending of the Company's monopoly, for trading on the China coast. So far as Palmerston was concerned the issue would be resolved with the Chinese authorities in a manner and on a timescale of British choosing.

From the Prime Minister the message was clearer. Recognising the problems inherent in communication with so distant a country, and perhaps particularly conscious of the fraught recent history of dealing with China, Grey had written to Napier before his departure:

> You are aware of the jealous and suspicious character of the Chinese people and government. Nothing must be done to shock their prejudices and excite their fears. The utmost forbearance therefore will be required in any point of difference that may arise, and prove injurious to our commercial relations with that country. Persuasion and Con-ciliation should be the means employed, rather than anything approaching to the tone of hostile and menacing language; and I should rather recommend

where persuasion and conciliation failed, a submission for a
time or till instructions could be received from home, than a
vigorous enforcement of demands no matter how just.[18]

Napier had little choice but to accept this instruction, but the strategy
was not in line with his own thinking. During the voyage he studied
the background and context of which he thought he would need to be
aware for his task, and concluded that the policy of the Company – both
the Directors in London and its officers in Canton – had resulted in
exploitation by the Chinese, especially by local officials for personal gain:

it is evident throughout that the Select Committee [responsible
for the Company's affairs in Canton] have in many instances
acted with great indiscretion, making threats and menaces
when they had not the power of carrying them into execution,
by which they always lost their point.
  The Chinese no doubt have acted from first to last on
principles the most arbitrary and vexatious. It would lead one
to suppose that the Viceroys and Hoppos were only appointed
to make their fortunes at the expense of the Foreign Merchants,
and then retire. It is equally clear that if the British are determined
to trade on fair principles, they must *use* force, not menace it....
The trade is too valuable to them to be relinquished by China.[19]

Napier's view was based on an analysis of previous Anglo-Chinese
encounters, which he thought proved conclusively that only a robust
approach would be effective. Elaborating his thinking in a later letter to
Grey, Napier was more specific, proposing the sending of a small force
(a large one would not be needed) to China the following year with the
southwest monsoon. Its task would be to take possession of the island of
Hong Kong. This place, he thought, with its deep water natural harbour
and location near the mouth of the Pearl River, would make an excellent
base from which the British could develop the China trade.[20]

  The 'country traders', of whom William Jardine and James Matheson
were among the most prominent, were dismissive of both the former
regime – the Company – and the arrangements intended to replace
it. They wanted a firm line, but considered that they themselves were
best placed to judge what form it should take. Jardine, for one, was
personally very clear what was required, but reflected the uncertainty, if
not apprehension, of the merchant communities on both sides when he
wrote home to a colleague in June 1834 that:

The appointment of Lord Napier ... has created a sensation
here [in Canton] and in Macao.... The authorities here have
not yet made up their minds as to the reception to be given to
the Superintendent. They are waiting with much anxiety and

much will depend on his own conduct. They will probably send the Hong Merchants to him in the first instance, to whom, I trust, he will behave with great courtesy but not permit them to say a word on business. A reference will then be made to Peking by the Viceroy and others; and, should this be the case, the First Superintendent should order the Frigate he comes out in to prepare for a trip to the Yellow Sea and proceed to the Imperial Palace there to state our grievances to the Son of Heaven himself and demand redress. If this is done in good manly style I will answer for the consequences. It may do good but cannot do harm.[21]

Unrealistic though it was to entertain the idea of an approach to the Emperor, Jardine was nevertheless setting out his desire for forthright action. The Superintendent could achieve something, Jardine thought, if he focussed on demonstrating British power, especially sea power, to the Chinese; but he should not attempt to interfere with the activities of the British traders.

The Chinese view of possible developments was of course entirely different. The Co-Hong and local officials in Canton had been content with the trading arrangements hitherto, unsurprisingly since they had been established on Chinese authority and, despite their restrictions, had been adhered to by the foreigners. If the red-haired barbarians wished to seek to change them they were entitled to do so, but such a move should be a matter of communication with the Chinese according to established conventions and procedures. It was nevertheless also clear to the Chinese that they would now have to adopt a different approach with the foreigners because their new Superintendent was not a merchant, but a senior official. New instruction would be needed from Beijing as to how to deal with this new barbarian head man. A message from the Viceroy, Lu Kun, explaining this situation was accordingly conveyed to Macao by the two leading Hong merchants, Howqua and Mowqua, for Lord Napier's attention. The message informed the Superintendent by edict that he should remain at Macao until further notice, but Napier's confident eagerness to get on with things had already prompted him to leave earlier in HMS *Andromache* for Canton, arriving there on 25 July. Not having received Viceroy Lu's edict, Napier sent a letter to Lu requesting a meeting with him. The letter was peremptorily returned unread; and so began the sequence of abortive exchanges which afterwards came to be known as the Napier 'fizzle'.

Lord Napier had sailed for Canton with all members of his Commission, including the Second and Third Superintendents, the Secretary/Treasurer (John Harvey Astell), the missionary Robert Morrison, who acted as interpreter, and Charles Elliot as Master Attendant. His response to the rebuff from the Viceroy was to refuse to accept the first or any subsequent edicts, though their contents were made known to him via intermediaries.

From the New English Factory, one of thirteen premises on the Canton waterfront at which the merchants of European nations and America were permitted to carry on their business between September and February each year, the Barbarian Eye (as Napier was suspiciously called by his Chinese hosts) opined in a letter to Palmerston that there would be no progress with his mission unless the Emperor of China and his subjects were disabused of the belief that other nations, including England, were mere tributaries.[22,23] Napier was also aware that Chinese officialdom regarded trade, especially with foreigners of whose products China had no need, as relatively unimportant. He informed Palmerston of the Viceroy's explanation that 'The Celestial Empire appoints officers – civil ones to rule the people, military ones to intimidate the wicked. The petty affairs of commerce are to be directed by the merchants themselves'.[24] The merchants of the Co-Hong, who were accountable to the mandarins for the conduct of the foreigners and who were vulnerable to heavy fines or worse if the barbarians misbehaved, did their best to persuade Napier to return to Macao as Lu had ordered, but without success.

The Hong merchants issued a notice suspending trade, more to demonstrate to the mandarins that they were doing their best to pressurise the foreigners than with any serious intent to disrupt, trade being particularly slack at that time. The suspension was nevertheless a shot across the bows for Napier, who despite the lack of clarity in the instructions he had been given never lost sight of his main responsibility for the protection of British trade in China. He was also realistic about political and commercial pressures at home, writing to Grey that,

> if after a fair trial of all justifiable means I find the merchants likely to suffer, I must retire to Macao, rather than bring the cities of London, Liverpool and Glasgow upon your Lordship's shoulders; many of whose merchants care not one straw about the dignity of the Crown or the presence of a Superintendent.[25]

In what proved to be the last official gesture towards resolution of the impasse the Viceroy cancelled the suspension, casting Napier as a man doing his country a disservice: 'the tea, the rhubarb, the raw silk of the inner dominions are the sources by which the said nations' people live and maintain life. For the fault of one man, Lord Napier, must the livelihood of the whole nation be precipitately cut off?'[26] Though British dependence on rhubarb was probably overstated by Lu, and his observation no more than yet another indication of the Celestial Empire's continuing view of barbarian inadequacy, he was trying to avert open hostility. The Hong merchants, too, sought to isolate Napier by inviting the English traders to a meeting from which he was to be excluded. It never took place; Napier had rallied the British by hastily forming them into a Chamber of Commerce, one of whose first acts was to decline the Co-Hong's invitation.

Buoyed up and confident that he now held the initiative, Napier's next move was to prepare for publication to the people of Canton a broadsheet setting out his own version of events and the current situation. Its main purpose was to demonstrate to the ordinary Chinese populace, for whom Napier professed some regard, how unreasonably and ineptly their officials were behaving and how little they had at heart the interests of the population as a whole.[27] The promulgation of the broadsheet was the last straw for Viceroy Lu, who saw it for what it was, a blatant attempt to stir up popular feeling against himself and his colleagues. On 2 September it was decreed that all trade would cease until Napier left Canton. Chinese militia surrounded the factories and there was a mass exodus of servants from the foreigners' living quarters.

At the Bogue *Andromache* had been joined by HMS *Imogene*, also a 28-gun frigate, which was due to replace her in China waters. The besieged Napier now issued orders, stealthily conveyed via a merchant schooner, for the two warships to sail upriver towards Canton. They began their short voyage when weather permitted on 7 September, with the former East India Company cutter *Louisa* close astern. Fired on almost immediately first by war junks and then by the batteries of the forts on each side of the Bogue, the frigates tacked up the channel returning fire, their manoeuvrability enabling them gradually to progress relatively unharmed past the fixed-position cannon of the forts. (The story is told that Charles Elliot followed in the cutter *Louisa*, sitting under an umbrella on the open deck throughout the exchanges. If true, it was an act combining bravery and bravado which perhaps echoed some of the more flamboyant exploits of his father).

It took the frigates and the cutter four days to reach the anchorage at Whampoa. Major obstructions then placed in the river by the Chinese – sunken boats filled with rock and a floating barrier on the Canton side, and rafts loaded with combustible material to the south – served to prevent both Napier leaving the city and any communication with the frigates from the Bogue or Macao. Some of the foreign merchants, though used over many years to Chinese interference with normal commerce as a pressure tactic, now began to feel that enough was enough, and that the necessary action should be taken for trade to be resumed. With his health deteriorating, Napier reluctantly decided to withdraw to Macao. In his letter of 15 September he wrote to the merchants collectively:

> Gentlemen – My letter to Mr Boyd yesterday would prepare you for the present. I now beg leave to acquaint you that I now no longer deem it expedient to persist in a course by which you are made to suffer. I therefore addressed Mr Boyd that the authorities might provide me with the means of doing that which all parties desire, namely, to retire, and admit the opening of the trade.... I considered it my duty to use every effort to carry His Majesty's instructions into execution, and having done so hitherto without

effect, though nearly accomplished on two occasions, I cannot feel authorised any longer to call on your forbearance.

I hope, Gentlemen, soon to see trade restored to its usual course of activity; and that it may long continue to prosper in your hands.[28,29]

Any expectation that Napier's departure, since the Viceroy had insisted on it, would be straightforward and rapid, was to prove unfounded. Having regained the initiative, Lu determined not to allow Napier to leave on his own terms; not only would he only be permitted to go if *Andromache* and *Imogene* sailed away first, but the frigates' departure was also a precondition for the resumption of trade. Howqua and Mowqua, who were as anxious as the British to see the reinstatement of normal commerce, attempted to intervene but without success. In the end it fell to the surgeon, Dr Thomas Colledge, and Jardine to negotiate the final arrangements for the Superintendent to leave Canton. Viceroy Lu reported at length and with customary exaggeration to the Emperor, informing the Son of Heaven that he had dealt very firmly but mercifully with the Barbarian Eye and his intruding warships. His mercy had been such that Lord Napier had been allowed to depart in trying and humiliating conditions, instead of being executed.[30] It seems certain that the journey back to Macao had a major impact on Napier's declining health. His small boat's progress south down the Inner Passage, to the west of the river, was repeatedly interrupted for no apparent reason except to allow the local inhabitants to hurl insults and to intensify the constant disturbance of firecrackers and the banging of gongs. A journey which should have taken not more than three days took five. Fifteen days after reaching Macao Napier finally succumbed to fever. With his family around him, he died on October 11. He was buried with full honours in the Protestant Cemetery at Macao, Charles Elliot and five other naval captains, three British and two Portuguese, acting as pall-bearers.

In August in her first letter home from Macao to her sister-in-law Emma, Clara Elliot made brief but telling observations concerning Chinese enterprise and Lord Napier:

> The Chinese are the most industrious clever beings I ever read or heard of but such abominable cheats that it is painful to have anything to do with them.... I dare not say one word of official news for I conclude Charlie will tell Frederick all fully. I am such a favourite with Lord Napier and he has been so kind to *me* that I do not like to say a word of ill nature about him but I fear much he is unfit to negotiate with the Chinese they are so cunning and clever.[31]

British merchants and other old China hands resident in Macao would have concurred with her comment about Napier. Clara was nevertheless disposed to be positive about being in China; she found Macao a pleasant place and fitted in well with the expatriate community. Anxious enquiries about her infant son Gilbert featured in nearly all her letters to Emma, but she delighted in the wellbeing of Harriet and Hughie. There were tensions, nevertheless. Clara wrote later of the effect of the situation in Canton on the British families in Macao:

> We were much alarmed and inconvenienced too at one time
> for all the Chinese servants were taken from us and there was
> a report that all Europeans were to be murdered except Lady
> Napier and her two daughters who were to be taken as hostages.
> We may laugh *now* at these idle tales but I assure you at the time
> we were all much alarmed the husbands being absent at Canton
> and the poor women alone.[32]

On Napier's death the office of Chief Superintendent passed seamlessly to the Second Superintendent, John Francis Davis. Equally automatically Sir George Best Robinson became Second Superintendent and John Harvey Astell Third. In January 1835 the escalator moved again; Davis was due for home leave but retired from the Commission instead, Robinson took over as Chief and Astell as Second, and Charles Elliot came in as Third Superintendent.

The mood among the British merchants was unsettled. Jardine set about gathering support for a request to Palmerston to send a force in retaliation for the indignities suffered by the British. When received by Palmerston's successor at the Foreign Office, the Duke of Wellington, it was deliberately ignored, largely on the advice of Davis who had written to Palmerston the day after Napier died informing him that: 'In the absence of any advances on the part of the Chinese, a state of absolute silence and quiescence on our part seems the most eligible course, until further instructions shall be received from home.'[33]

Davis's decision to retire had been taken in the hope and expectation that Charles Elliot, of whom he had long been a keen supporter, would then be appointed a Superintendent. Elliot himself was aware of Davis's continuing goodwill towards him, and considered it thoroughly deserved. He confided to Emma: 'I have no doubt he will do me more than justice at headquarters, and most assuredly it would only be doing me basic justice to say, that I have worked hard, both head and hand.'[34] Elliot's relations with his new superior, Robinson, were however in stark contrast to those he had enjoyed with Davis. Perhaps partly because his reputation for incompetence and arrogance preceded him, Robinson was disliked from the start by Elliot, who accorded him scant respect. In 1828, having been reprimanded for failure to obey orders, Robinson had protested to the Select Committee in aggressive, almost insolent terms: 'Finding that my best endeavours have only exposed me to what I feel to be your very unjust censure, I must beg to decline an office the duties of which render me constantly liable to such vexatious and frivolous remarks.'[35] Charles Elliot wearily complained to his sister that 'The Su[perintendent] [Robinson] *is on my shoulders here*, dear Emy, but you need not be afraid', and then declared, making it clear that his personal strategy was to keep his head down and not make waves, 'silence and quiescence' at an individual level, ' I will commit no blunders and strive to perform no wonders.'[36]

Wonders or not, Elliot could not resist trying to remedy one of the most striking deficiencies, as he saw it, of commercial life amongst the British at Canton. Napier's instructions had indicated that civil disputes were to be settled by arbitration or persuasion, and the Superintendents were to use as much influence and authority as they could muster to that end. The Superintendents had no legal powers and while Elliot, for one, was keen to sort out difficulties himself where he could, he judged that a framework for proceeding in such matters was sorely needed.[37] He described the problem:

> Ships will repair to China for a season and perhaps never return, having on board, in many cases, Agents charged with the disposal and purchase of their cargoes, whose transactions with the resident British merchants will probably be very extensive; and in some instances it may be extremely needful to possess such means of constraining such parties to submit disputed points to investigation, <u>upon the spot</u>.
>
> …the practical problem is to shape the process … [to] secure <u>substantial justice</u> between disputants with the least possible … delay, … expense, and … interference on the part of this Commission.[38]

Elliot's proposal included examples of how the scheme would work. He advocated the use of press reports in order to have in the public domain 'a small body of useful precedents'.[39] Such transparency could be helpful in 'examples of unprincipled disinclination to adjust disputes, against … which this check of publicity may incidentally operate in a salutary manner.'[40] One of the guiding principles of Elliot's scheme, as he set it out, is instructive as an indication of the general approach to regulation which would inform his subsequent roles:

> <u>To do the least that is necessary</u> for the accomplishment of the object in view is the principle that should judge us, and perhaps in the first place the wisest course to pursue would be merely to define the <u>practice</u>, and to leave experience to indicate the points which will require more comprehensive provision. A needless burden of regulation is a great evil. I very well know (for I have had considerable experience in these matters in other parts of the world) that a copious supply of

legal remedies for anticipated difficulties is the sure precursor
of an abundant crop of subterfuge, evasion, and chicane. To
establish as sound and as few principles as we can, and carefully
to adapt our practice and proceedings, in any necessities which
arise, to those principles, is the task we have to perform.[41]

By mid-April 1835 Elliot had submitted his scheme to Robinson, who
sent it on to Palmerston asking for authorisation to introduce a system
of arbitration based on Elliot's proposals. While no authority to operate a
formal procedure was given, the Commission could handle disputes with
Elliot's principles in mind.

In the same month there was another change of offices when Astell
resigned as Second Superintendent. Elliot moved up again and the
Secretary, A.R. Johnston, became Third Superintendent. For Elliot,
ambitious but feeling undervalued, this was so far so good. After a few
months his new salary allowed him to clear his debts, much to the relief
of his wife, and enabled Charles and Clara to look forward to moving
with their children Harriet and Hughie into a new – much larger – house
on San Francisco Green, Macao. In a letter to Emma, Elliot touches on
the problem of communication and distance, and borders on self-pity in
describing his own professional position:

> The terrible drawback of this country is the immense time it
> takes for the transit of letters; making it absolutely a frightful
> thing to open one's letters when they do arrive. I sometimes
> speculate upon your whereabouts and I confess upon the whole
> I am disposed to think this letter will find you in England....
> Since poor Napier's demise, I have done the <u>whole business of
> this Commission</u>, and when I consider my former career in the
> public service I do not think I have deserved ill treatment at the
> hands of the Government. Perhaps I am needlessly disquieting
> myself but I feel I am without interest, and a man without
> interest in England must look to be trodden upon.[42,43]

Whether or not Elliot was justified in feeling so apparently sorry for
himself, his view of the world will have been affected both by a recent
illness ('a decided attack of the liver') and by an event in late January
and early February in which he suffered unexpected physical harm.[44]
A boat carrying twelve crewmen from the British merchant ship *Argyle*,
dispatched to seek help in a storm west of Macao, was intercepted
by a Chinese vessel. A ransom demand for the twelve sailors was
published, prompting the Chief, Second and Third superintendents
to seek help from the Canton authorities. Elliot, Macdonald (the
captain of the *Argyle*) and the interpreter Gutzlaff were sent with
a communication to one of the city gates. What they presented was
not in the ill-fated form of a letter that had caused so much trouble

on previous occasions, but nor was it a petition as Chinese protocol required. It was a report, for which the British considered there to be sound precedent. When Elliot and his colleagues tried to hand over the report at the gate Elliot was violently manhandled by the guards and hurled to the ground, and all three were then pushed and dragged about. Military and civil officials appeared, but refused to accept the communication because it was not a petition.[45] The sailors were later released, but the episode was for Elliot a stark reminder of the reality of dealing with the mandarins and their less sophisticated agents. His later critics would doubtless have considered that this attempt to find a middle way through the mode of communication problem, and its consequences, typified what they regarded as Elliot's misguided even-handed approach.

Robinson's attitude towards the Chinese was even more 'hands off' than Davis's. No contact was his aim, on the grounds that 'the less we have to do with the Chinese authorities and people, save when appealed to in cases of aggression and injustice, which I trust will be rare and trifling, the less apprehension may be entertained of those perplexing difficulties in which we are liable to be involved'.[46] Having penned this view to the Foreign Secretary, Robinson transferred his office from Macao to the *Louisa*, which was moored close to the island of Lintin in the Pearl River estuary. Moving his place of work to such a location was hardly expected, but it was consistent with his wish to be apart from people and situations which might disturb the tranquillity by which he set so much store. For Charles Elliot this was another example of Robinson's incompetence and insensitivity; the Chief Superintendent was signalling that not only did he not wish to communicate with the Chinese, he did not want to talk to his colleagues either.

Robinson lost no opportunity in his reports to the Foreign Secretary to defend his conduct generally and to talk up his management of affairs, but he was fighting a losing battle. In private correspondence with a personal contact at the Foreign Office Elliot was highly critical of his superior's actions, and his comments will have been brought to the attention of those who needed to know.[47] If, given his earlier acknowledgement to Emma of Davis's goodwill, Elliot really thought he was a man 'without interest', he was wrong. Davis had written before his departure from China that 'I shall probably accompany Mrs Davis home and leave Captain Elliot of the Navy as a member of the Commission. He is a very prudent and able man, well known to our Governt and should have come as Chief Superintendent instead of poor Lord Napier'.[48] He later repeated his support, writing again in June 1835: 'The Chinese have given fresh trouble by the latest account and I shall be uneasy for the state of affairs unless Elliot is immediately put in charge. Poor Robinson is quite prepared to fall back on the Company. ... Both justice and policy seem to require that such a man as Elliot should not remain below such a man as Robinson.'[49]

Since his appointment as Master Attendant, Charles Elliot's promotions had been to fill vacancies occurring above him through death, retirement and resignation. If he had blotted his copybook there may have been difficulties, but as he kept his head down and did not 'commit any blunders', his elevations were entirely predictable. His final appointment in the Superintendency, however, was anything but automatic. Robinson, unsurprisingly given his policy of inaction and the tone of his reports home, fell out of favour with Palmerston. The Foreign Secretary's communication terminating his appointment as Chief Superintendent and recalling him from China was dispatched on 7 June 1836, reaching the China coast several months later. In the same instruction Palmerston appointed Charles Elliot to the top post; but he was formally to be designated Chief of the Commission, not Chief Superintendent. The title had to be changed since, as part of the government's policy of reducing the cost of the civil service, the £3,000 salary now attached to the post was half what Robinson had been paid, and instead of two assisting superintendents Elliot had only one deputy (Johnston). The implication, for public consumption, was that the job had been downgraded, but in practice it became far more demanding – and no one in the British community in China had any difficulty in continuing informally to refer to him as Chief Superintendent. He could not of course know it, but Elliot was at the start of one of the most testing periods in the history of Anglo-Chinese relations, one which would stretch his abilities to their limits. He was however in charge, and he could no longer complain that he was being held back. He now had to demonstrate that he was indeed the right man for the job.

# Chapter Eight

# Opium Prelude

It was December 1836 when Elliot heard of his promotion. He considered, especially in the light of the non-communication policy of his predecessor, that the crucial step now was to engage in dialogue with the Chinese authorities, and quickly. Without that, he reasoned, he could not fulfil his brief, which remained as it had been for Napier two years earlier. Specifically, no progress could be made on the increasingly vexed question of opium, which stood to jeopardise the China trade as a whole. The letter which Elliot sent to the new Viceroy of Guangxi and Guangdong provinces, Deng Tingzhen, accordingly set aside British insistence otherwise and bore the superscription 'pin', signifying a communication from an inferior to a superior. Palmerston had earlier advised Elliot also that:

> It might be very suitable for the servants of the East India Company, themselves an Association of merchants, to communicate with the authorities of China through the merchants of the Hong; but the Superintendents are officers of the King, and as such can properly communicate with none but officers of the Chinese Government'.[1]

There being no time for further reference to Palmerston, Elliot chose to disregard this too, passing his letter via the Hong merchants. He knew that he would in due course have to account for these decisions, but for the present he saw, rightly, given the long time delays involved in exchanges with London, no alternative but to take matters entirely into his own hands.

Taking responsibility was not something Elliot ever found a problem, and sometimes he behaved in a rather exaggerated way as a result. He considered his current actions necessary, but nevertheless felt sub-consciously uneasy about going against government policy. As if to make the record of his position clear for future reference, he shared the burden of his unease with his sister:

> it is certain that the steps I have taken (as I learn by dispatches subsequently received) do not jump with the views of the Government. I dare say, they will be very glad eventually, that I acted as I did, but they may not choose to admit that, and for anything I can guess to the contrary they may remove me.... Their opinions upon the soundness of my proceedings,

considered merely as opinions, are of no importance to me. My
own judgment in such matters is as likely to be a reasonable
judgment, as my Lord Palmerston's. I think of what I am about,
and he neither knows nor thinks any thing about the matter.[2]

Allowing for his customary overstatement, Elliot's assessment of the
extent of Palmerston's engagement with the situation on the south China
coast was essentially correct. It could not be otherwise; quite apart from
having more pressing foreign policy issues to deal with in Europe and
the Middle East, Palmerston was in no position, at four or five months'
remove, to have anything helpful to offer the Chief of Commission on
how he should respond to events as they unfolded. Elliot's comments
about his own future were uncannily prescient.

The approach to the Viceroy, seeking permission to reside at Canton
and being appropriately addressed, was successful and Elliot arrived
there in mid-April. He had not however simply been biding his time in
the preceding few months. In the latter half of 1836 relations between
the foreign traders and the Chinese authorities had deteriorated as
resentment grew over the rising debts of the Hong merchants, both to
their foreign counterparts and to the mandarins, and over the question
of jurisdiction. The Chinese tradition of leaving foreigners to administer
their own justice over their own subjects, Elliot thought, would be
at risk if the Chief Superintendent were not given judicial authority
over British merchants including, of course, opium smugglers, who
in Elliot's view were 'men whose rash conduct cannot be left to the
operation of Chinese laws without utmost inconvenience and risk, and
whose impunity ... is dangerous to British interests.'[3] The Chinese
tradition had in any case always been subject to Chinese intervention
if the authorities thought it warranted, and in recent decades there had
been several incidents involving the deaths of Chinese subjects where
they thought it was.

1836 had also seen vigorous controversy in the Chinese government
about the opium problem. The physical effects of the drug on the
population at all levels of society, and the economic consequences of
the drain of silver to pay for it, now needed urgent action. For a time it
seemed that those calling for legalisation as a means of exercising better
control had persuaded the Daoguang Emperor to adopt such a policy, but
advocates of the elimination of opium from China altogether eventually
won the day. At Canton and in the Pearl River delta the new crackdown
was swiftly and forcefully implemented. Viceroy Deng, a supporter of
legalisation who was thought by many to be profiting directly from
the opium trade, nevertheless found it possible to carry out his duty
conscientiously. Steps were taken to prepare for confrontation with the
British and other opium traffickers, notably the construction of a new
gun battery at Cumsingmun, some twenty miles north of Macao and
opposite Lintin Island where the opium receiving vessels were moored.

In this increasingly unstable situation Charles Elliot wrote in February 1837 to Lord Auckland, Governor General of India, suggesting that a visit from the Royal Navy to the south China coast would be helpful.[4] The presence of a small flotilla of warships would send a clear message to the Chinese and (though he did not mention it specifically) strengthen his own position. That position would also be greatly assisted if he personally had more freedom of movement, and Elliot notified the Viceroy that the delay involved in his having to apply for a 'chop', or passport, each time he needed to proceed up river from Macao was impeding him in the exercise of his official duty to oversee British trade. Deng was content to waive the requirement, subject only to Elliot's notifying the Chinese authorities before each trip. With some satisfaction Elliot reported to Palmerston on 2 June 1837 that the concession meant he was now in an unprecedented position for a foreigner resident in China.[5]

The importance of this relaxation of the rules was overstated by Elliot. It was significant in that it indicated some flexibility on the part of the Viceroy, but made very little impact on the difficulties faced by the Chief Superintendent. He was having to find a way through at least five sets of competing and at times seemingly irreconcilable interests – the Chinese government (i.e. the Daoguang Emperor and his senior advisers); the local mandarins; the Hong merchants; the British and other foreign merchants; and the British government. Nor was any of these of a single mind as to the best way forward.

The Emperor had been supplied with sharply conflicting views about the opium problem. The belief that pleasure-inducing but harmful drugs are better dealt with by legalisation and control than by criminalising their use is strongly held by many in the modern world. In 1830s Qing China it was espoused by an influential band of high-ranking mandarins and academics of whom the most prominent in this context was Xu Naiqi, who as a criminal judge had had experience of the robbery, blackmail and extortion that were the widespread consequences of prohibition.[6] Viceroy Deng supported the legalisation proposals, but strong and persuasive arguments for intensified prohibition reached the Emperor before Deng's endorsement. These were from two other senior officials, who opposed legalisation for both philosophical and practical reasons and one of whom, Xu Qin, named at some length the foreign traders most involved in opium smuggling, including William Jardine, Lancelot Dent and James Innes. Though the Emperor's mind was made up before the end of 1836 and instructions were then passed to the Viceroy to investigate with a view to more stringent action, the British community – including Charles Elliot – continued to hope, well into the new year, that legalisation would become a reality.[7]

Elliot was well aware that Chinese officials on the China coast derived significant income from the illicit opium trade. In Canton successive holders of the office of Director of Customs (the Hoppo), already men of sufficient means to have purchased the post in the first place, became even more wealthy during the three years of their tenure. The system of 'squeeze' was all-pervasive; the Hoppo took a large share of the customs revenue for himself, but had to ensure that members of the Imperial Court in Beijing also had their cut. The same obligation was laid on the Hong merchants, similarly wealthy individuals whose personal income was even more directly dependent on the health of the trade with the barbarians. Unsurprisingly, they viewed with some alarm the rigorous measures against the drug now being pursued by their government. It was in the financial interests of the foreign merchants and the Co-Hong that they should maintain good relations with each other, whatever either party may have felt, but the very low opinion of Chinese officialdom held by the English frequently found a voice. Of the Hoppo the *Canton Register*, a weekly newspaper published for the foreign merchant community, had been dismissive:

> from him is neither expected nor required the political acumen, the historical knowledge, the practised habits, the civil courage, – and, above all, the honesty of intention of a real statesman. No, let him collect the Imperial duties, and strive to augment them for his own profit by any means however illegal, unjust, oppressive, and extortionate, for his system is even now tottering to its fall; but let him not … interfere with the great questions of free agency and moral right; and more particularly let him avoid meddling in those cases in which Englishmen are concerned in exercising their privileges either of unrestrained thought, or free action.[8]

The *Register's* strictures about things with which the Hoppo should not concern himself are illustrative not only of the free traders' mindset towards what they considered Chinese officials' incapability of understanding such matters, but of their estimation of their own intellectual and moral superiority. The foreign merchants were also comfortable with the trade in opium; it was seen as, and was, the one commodity which the Chinese would accept in exchange for tea, silks and other desirable merchandise, obviating the need for the English to pay in bullion and coin. With copious amounts of Chinese silver also being used as payment for opium, the foreigners made a substantial profit on the trade. If the Chinese chose to abuse the drug and themselves and become addicted, that was their problem. There was even a view that Chinese opium users themselves thought its illegal status essential for maximising supply; according to George Tradescant Lay, who worked for the British and Foreign Bible Society: 'In China every man is a smuggler in opium from the Emperor downwards.... Opium here is only contraband in the letter. It is an article that bears a duty which, to render as high as possible the traffic, comes in the shape of a prohibition.'[9]

Charles Elliot's personal position on opium was clear and known, and it did nothing to endear him to Jardine, Dent, Innes and the others.

The autobiography of his friend Henry Taylor reproduces what Elliot wrote, with his customary sniping about the perceived unimportance of his opinions, two years later:

> If my private feelings were of the least consequence upon questions of a public and important nature, surely, I might justly say, that no man entertains a deeper detestation of the disgrace and sin of this forced traffic on the coast of China ... I see little to choose between it and piracy, and in my place as a public officer, I have steadily discountenanced it by all the lawful means in my power, and at the total sacrifice of my private comfort in the society in which I have lived for some years past.[10]

Whatever his private thoughts about opium, Elliot could not afford to incur the outright hostility of the traders. They knew this, and they knew that Elliot was also concerned on economic grounds about the danger of relying solely on opium to balance the books. Jardine, protesting far too much, later placed the blame for the illegal opium trade on Chinese local officials, the Chinese government, and the East India Company – on all involved, in other words, except private British merchants like himself (and the British government, whom he did not wish to antagonise).[11] He was right in one respect, that responsibility for opium smuggling was not exclusive to one party. A Tory-leaning periodical, *Blackwood's Edinburgh Magazine*, concluded that: 'The sin of the opium trade, if sin there be, rests not with British merchants, but is divisible, in about equal proportions betwixt the Chinese and British Governments and the East India Company', and reminded its readers that:

> The East India Company first carried on the trade in opium on their own account. On the discontinuation of the direct export, the drug was still grown on their lands by their tenants on their behalf. They made public sale of it to merchants, well-knowing it was destined for export to China, where almost alone its consumption lay. The British Government and Legislature sanctioned the trade for the sake of revenue, as did the East India Company.[12,13]

In the moral argument, the East India Company was an easy target. Since losing its monopoly in 1834 the decline in its influence had gathered pace as British manufacturers had pressed further the case for free trade. In the practicalities of conducting commerce on the China coast in 1838, the British merchants found it expedient to refer, resentfully, to past years in which the Company had enjoyed a financial relationship with the Co-Hong now denied to them. Free trade they espoused in principle, but faced with little prospect of the substantial sums owed to them by the

Co-Hong ever being repaid, several sought the intervention of the British government.

Dent and his co-signatories to a letter sent for this purpose to Palmerston, via Elliot, cannot have had any serious hope of their communication being acted on. They had not involved Elliot in its composition, and some of their more prominent colleagues including Jardine, Matheson and Innes were not party to the initiative. With a hint of threat, they wrote concurrently to the Viceroy pressing the need for alternative (though unspecified) arrangements for resolving the problem of the Hong merchants' debts, complaining that:

> We bring our property from a great distance to trade with this empire, and we are compelled by its laws to place it in the hands of a few Hong merchants, nominated by the emperor. It cannot be that his majesty intends that they should retain our capital until it has nearly doubled itself by the accumulation of interest, and then pay us back only on the principal.[14]

They concluded:

> It seems to us ... that some other system is required.... As we do not feel competent to discuss this question with your excellency, we have referred it through her majesty's chief superintendent to our own gracious sovereign, who will, we humbly hope, communicate upon the subject with your emperor.
>
> In the meantime we shall gratefully receive any portion of our claims which your excellency may be pleased to order to be paid, and be prepared to listen to the suggestions which the hong merchants may propose.[15]

The fact was that as a result of the Chinese measures against opium, business had taken a significant downturn in 1837, and the foreign traders were looking for any means possible to improve their financial position. With Chinese restrictions in Canton and on the approaches to it, Jardine Matheson sought to offload as much opium as possible at locations up the coast, using force if necessary. In the absence of enough 'fast crabs' manned by Chinese crews to take opium from the store ships at Lintin up to Canton, many of the leading merchants were now using their own armed boats. Prominent among them was the aggressive and obdurate James Innes.

Charles Elliot viewed these developments with alarm. His personal antagonism towards the opium trade was well known, but purely practical considerations and the real threat, as he saw it, of a rapid escalation into conflict with the Chinese persuaded him to send Palmerston another request for British intervention. Armed smuggling was now being conducted on a provocative scale which in Elliot's assessment the Chinese authorities would not be able to ignore. Elliot's fears proved well-founded; in August and September 1837 the Emperor gave orders that the Chief Superintendent should take steps to ensure both that all receiving ships at Lintin were removed and that the illicit coastal trade ceased. Daoguang's edict was a clear indication of Chinese misunderstanding of the extent of Elliot's authority – he might be the Queen's representative but he had no powers over such unofficial activities, even though they were illegal and their perpetrators were mostly British. To a report sent by Elliot in November, Palmerston responded by repeating his original insistence that there could be no official government action either in support of, or to restrain, British opium traffickers.

In Britain, the government and Parliament had begun to take notice of the anxious communications from the Chief Superintendent and his compatriots on the China coast. They were not particularly worried about opium smuggling; their concerns centred on the reports they received of the alleged maltreatment of British subjects by a foreign power in a distant country. Perceived insult to the British flag was guaranteed to inflame the patriotic indignation of the man or woman in the street, and the press made sure that the several specific instances of unacceptable Chinese behaviour of recent decades were kept at the forefront of public consciousness.[16] In a letter in September 1837 to Lord Minto, a first cousin of Charles Elliot and at that time first Lord of the Admiralty, Palmerston was cautiously optimistic about Elliot's ability to handle the situation. He now considered that the Royal Navy could play a useful role:

> Elliot is now at Canton by the sanction of the Chinese Govt. and I hope our trade there will go on well. But it is very desirable that some good sized Ship of war should be, as much as possible, on the China Station, both to inspire the Chinese with Respect and to keep the Crews of our Merchant Men in order.[17]

Palmerston had miscalculated its potential effect, but in July 1838 the naval presence Elliot had asked for in February the previous year materialised. There were three ships: the 74-gun ship-of-the-line HMS *Wellesley*, flagship of Rear-Admiral Sir Frederick Maitland, commander-in-chief of the East India station; HMS *Larne*, an 18-gun sloop; and HMS *Algerine*, a 10-gun brig-sloop.

If the British expectation was that the squadron should simply be noted quietly by the Chinese as a reminder of who held naval superiority, it failed. The Chinese were quickly alarmed; but a note requiring an explanation from the British was returned unread because it was labelled a 'command', and Elliot's letter to the Viceroy a few days later, explaining that the purpose of the ships was entirely peaceful, was similarly returned because it was not labelled a 'petition'. The situation was then exacerbated when the Chinese fired on an unarmed British vessel they suspected of carrying opium and/or Rear Admiral Maitland up to Canton. The British ships advanced to the Bogue, and it took an eventual meeting between Chinese and British naval officers on board the *Wellesley* to clear the air. After mutual reassurance and courteous exchanges, the British squadron sailed away in early October (though HMS *Larne* remained in the region, moving to a position up the coast).

Since 2 December 1837 Charles Elliot had been with his family at Macao. The events arising from the arrival of Maitland's ships had necessitated a visit to Canton, for which he departed on 25 July. Doubtless exasperated at the continuing Chinese obsession with forms of address, he returned to Macao after a few days.

The months Elliot spent at Macao in 1838 gave him some time in which to reflect.[18] He was reasonably confident that he would be able to establish a workable relationship with the Chinese authorities, but well understood the volatility of the situation. He began to be concerned for the safety of his family – his wife Clara, their children Harriet and Hughie, and the recent addition Frederick, born in October 1837. Clara too may have felt some unease; she was aware that her husband's empathy with the Chinese caused many in the merchant community on the China coast to regard him with suspicion. She wrote to her sister-in-law early in 1838 reporting that Charles intended to send her home with the children in November. Aware (perhaps with a tinge of irritation) of the extent to which he confided in his sister, she continued: 'Charles of course tells you of his public doings and if he did not I should seem to meddle with them. He is a favourite among the Chinese but much too good. Charles declares his [own] manners and ways are really ridiculously the same as theirs.'[19] Elliot himself was worried about the children's education, telling Emma that 'My chicks here are pretty and manageable, but they need better instruction than we have the means of giving them.'[20]

Whatever domestic plans were then half-forming in his mind, in the closing weeks of the year Elliot was wholly preoccupied with yet another serious confrontation between the foreign merchants and the Chinese authorities. Since the Viceroy and his local officials could not themselves prevent opium from reaching the population of Canton, they had decided that its consumption could be discouraged by severely punishing the addicts as well as the dealers. Instances of public strangulation had had the intended effect on trade, but not just the opium trade – the harshness of the crackdown was beginning to blight all aspects of commerce. Three episodes in December quickly raised the temperature: a blatantly provocative attempt to unload opium for James Innes at the Factories, and a defiant reaction by Innes when told to leave; word of an intended execution of an opium dealer in the square in front of the Factories, in full view of all; and though that spectacle was prevented, a riot involving aggrieved merchants and large numbers of bystanding Cantonese.

Elliot was at Whampoa when he was called to Canton. After sending a formal protest to the Viceroy about the behaviour of the local citizenry, he summoned a meeting of the merchants. Focused as always on his primary duty to protect the interests of British trade, he now had no hesitation in adopting a more conciliatory policy towards the Viceroy, nor in telling the merchants why. A cooperative approach held the best hope of protecting trade; indeed without it a prolonged cessation was entirely likely. On a personal level, it would serve to make up some of the ground in Anglo-Chinese relations lost through the Maitland visit, which the Viceroy was convinced Elliot had contrived with aggression in mind. Joint action against the drug trade would also, of course, chime well with Elliot's personal hostility to the traffic in opium and the extensive British involvement in it.

He followed up the meeting, at which he made it clear that he ascribed the present turbulence to opium smuggling, with a written notice to the opium merchants informing them that they should forthwith withdraw their vessels at least as far as the Bogue; if they refused, he would not take any protective action were they to be attacked by the Chinese. By the end of December the opium boats had gone, but from Elliot's viewpoint it was equally if not more important that the Viceroy had responded positively when hearing of his initiative. Early in the new year normal commerce resumed.

Elliot could be forgiven for thinking at this stage that he was at last starting to make genuine progress in his efforts to normalise relations and build lasting foundations for the development of commerce between Britain and China. He remained realistic nevertheless. In January 1839 he set out for Palmerston – in his usual lengthy prose – his concerns about the opium trade and where it might lead:

> It had been clear to me, my Lord, from the origin of this peculiar branch of the opium traffic, that it must be more and more mischievous to every branch of the trade, and certainly to none more than to that of opium itself. As the danger and shame of its pursuit increased, it was obvious that it would fall by rapid degrees into the hands of more and more desperate men; that it would stain the foreign character with constantly aggravating disgrace, in the sight of the whole of the better portion of this people; and lastly that it would connect itself more and more intimately with our lawful commercial intercourse, to the great peril of vast public and private interests. Till the other day, my Lord, I believe there was no part of the world where the foreigner felt his life and property more secure than here in Canton; but the grave events of 12 ultimo [the intended execution and the riots at the Factories] have left behind a different impression.... In the meantime, however, there has been no relaxation of the vigour of the Government, directed

not only against the introduction of the opium, but in a far more
remarkable manner against the consumers. A corresponding
degree of desperate adventure on the part of the smugglers is
only a necessary consequence; and in this situation of things,
serious accidents and sudden and indefinite interruptions to
the regular trade, must always be probable events.[21]

Charles Elliot's reflective assessment of the position at the start of
1839 contrasted sharply with the sense of urgency prevailing in Beijing.
On 21 January it was reported in Canton that the Son of Heaven had
appointed a special commissioner to go to Canton to solve the opium
problem for good. He was given full powers and a rank which was
senior to the Viceroy. Lin Zexu's reputation for intellect, energy and
incorruptibility preceded him. Local officials from the Viceroy down
were duly worried.

## Chapter Nine

# Authority and Honour

The period from Lin's arrival in Canton in March 1839 to the commencement of full hostilities the following year has sometimes been represented as a quasi-personal struggle between Lin and Elliot, the leading figures on the two sides. They each found themselves in a position in which their main objective – for Elliot protection and development of British trade, for Lin the eradication of opium – was both obstructed by the policy of a foreign power and made hugely more difficult by the activities of their own compatriots. Each was well aware of the complexities of the situation and the number of parties involved, and neither sought to personalise their countries' differences.

Commissioner Lin's ancestors had held high office in China, though his immediate parentage was less exalted. The son of a schoolteacher, he had achieved rapid advancement in the Chinese system of public service, a meritocracy which placed the greatest emphasis on intellectual ability. On the way he had acquired wide-ranging experience as a scholar, adjudicator, statesman, administrator and all-purpose troubleshooter.[1] At 54, he was Elliot's senior by sixteen years.

Within days of taking up his post Lin set about his task with a vigour and directness which must have surprised all but the most hardened members of the mercantile community, whether Chinese, British or other nationals. After embarking on a programme for the arrest of hundreds of local opium distributors and others involved in the trade, he issued two edicts to the Co-Hong. The first instructed them to pass on to the foreign traders, for whose conduct they were formally responsible, an order requiring them to give up all the opium held in their receiving ships and never to import the drug again:

> Let them deliver up to government every particle of opium on board their store-ships.... Let it be ascertained by the Hong merchants, who are the parties so delivering it up, what number of chests is delivered up under each name, and what is the total quantity ... in order that the opium ... may be burnt and destroyed, and that thus the evil may be entirely extirpated. There must not be the smallest atom concealed or withheld.
>
> At the same time let these foreigners give a bond ... making a declaration of this effect: That their vessels, which shall hereafter resort hither, will never again dare to bring opium

with them; and that should any be brought ... the goods shall be
forfeited to government, and the parties shall suffer the extreme
penalties of the law.[2]

Lin's second command was for the Hong merchants themselves. Having
severely reprimanded them (at some length) for their longstanding and
deep involvement in the opium trade, he threatened to have one or two
of them – he did not specify which one or two – executed if they failed to
ensure the surrender of the foreigners' opium chests and the signing of a
bond. The Hong merchants

> should acquire an earnest severity of deportment, that the
> energetic character of the commands may be clearly made to
> appear. They must not continue to exhibit a contumacious
> disposition or to color over the matter, nor may they give
> utterance to any expression of solicitation.... Three days are
> prescribed, within which they must obtain the required bonds,
> and report in reply hereto. If it be found that this matter cannot
> at once be arranged by them, it will be apparent, without
> enquiry, that they are constantly acting in concert with depraved
> foreigners, and that their minds have a perverted inclination.
> And I, the high commissioner, will forthwith solicit the royal
> death-warrant, and select for execution one or two of the most
> unworthy of their number.... Say not that you did not receive
> timely notice. A special edict.[3]

When he received news of the two edicts Elliot was in Macao, expecting
the focus of the Commissioner's action to be there, at Lintin, and in the
waters of the Pearl River estuary.

Charles Elliot had had a difficult few months. After anxious soul-
searching he and Clara had eventually decided, with much sadness, that
Harriet and Hughie, now aged 9 and 7 respectively, should return to
England. As well as wishing to safeguard their education he had concluded,
correctly, that the situation would before long deteriorate to a point at
which continued residence at Macao by foreign personnel would become
unsafe, and he doubtless thought it likely in any case that his duties in
Canton and on the river in the coming months could mean long periods
of absence from his family. The two children sailed on the *Melbourne* in
mid-March; they were to join their young brother Gibby, now aged 5, at
Charlton under the care of Emma and Sir Thomas Hislop. Elliot wrote to
his sister, briefly but movingly commending Harriet and Hughie to her:

> I had resolved to write you a long letter by this sorrowful ship
> the *Melbourne*, but now the time has come I find I can do
> nothing but grieve. And in addition to this, I have upon my

shoulders a great burden of public anxiety. When you see and know these dear loves you will judge what a pang it has cost us to bid them farewell.

Harriet promises to be a glory to me, and what is better far, a dutiful and good child. Sweetly pretty and intelligent as she is, the qualities of her heart, are still higher and more lovable. My own darling Hughie, the plague and pleasure of my life, is just what Fred was at Madras in appearance, but with a bottle of quicksilver dancing through his veins instead of blood. With steady and gentle firmness, however, he is docile. The dangerous part of his character, is his extreme sensibility.[4]

Days after the Elliot children's departure the foreign traders' Chamber of Commerce met on 21 March to discuss both the threat of execution issued to the Hong merchants and the now sizeable – and highly visible – Chinese military presence in and around Canton. They persuaded themselves that they were merely agents of the East India Company and could not give up something which was not strictly theirs, but with considerable reluctance some of them agreed to surrender some opium. The quantity to be handed over amounted to a little over a thousand chests, a very small fraction of the stocks held and an even smaller one of the total traded each year.[5] It was shortly to be dismissed by Lin as a completely inadequate response to his demand.

Elliot heard about the edicts on 22 March. His reaction was that of a man provoked; gone, suddenly, was his conciliatory approach, to be replaced by firm and immediate action. After forwarding Lin's edicts to Palmerston, he ordered all British ships standing off the Pearl River estuary to make without delay for Hong Kong 'and hoisting their national colours, be prepared to resist every act of aggression on the part of the Chinese government'.[6] He then immediately went to Canton, where he indulged in some patriotic flag-raising himself, 'For I well knew, my Lord', he wrote on 30 March to Palmerston, 'that there is a sense of support in the sight of that honoured flag, fly where it will, that no one can feel but men who look upon it in some such dismal strait as ours'.[7] His next action was to summon a meeting of the foreign traders, subsequently reporting that he 'enjoined them all to be moderate, firm, and united. I had the satisfaction to dissolve the meeting in a calmer state of mind than had subsisted for several days past'.[8]

Elliot's intervention may have served, temporarily, to lower the temperature a little among the foreigners, but Commissioner Lin was bent on pressing on vigorously. The square and the area around the Factories began to fill with soldiers and militia irregulars, making much noise and seeking to intimidate the foreign community. Lin cannot realistically have expected the merchants to have agreed to his demands within the three day limit he had set; but after six days without progress, on 24 March, he tightened the screw further, closing off all access to the

Factories area except for one street, reinforcing the military presence, and ordering not only the cessation of trade but the withdrawal of all Chinese servants, compradors and other personnel working for the foreigners. His determination was unequivocal: 'If there is any attempt to evade these restrictions I, the Governor-General, and the Governor will obtain permission from Peking to close the harbour to them and put a stop to their trade for ever.'[9]

The blockade of the Factories moved the dispute between the British and the Chinese onto new ground. For Charles Elliot it was not now wholly, or even mainly, about opium, and still less about the development of trade in general, but about physical aggression by one empire against another and the infringement of personal liberty. He had been clear in his instructions to British shipping that any such behaviour by the Chinese should be resisted. He had also, in the context of the treatment of individuals, earlier declared to Palmerston that, 'till I am differently instructed, I should hold it my duty to resist to the last, the seizure and punishment of a British subject by the Chinese law, be his crime what it might'.[10] The question of how jurisdiction for the British community in China was supposed to operate had for a long time been a matter on which he had sought, without success, definitive guidance from the home government. To the Chinese, including the Co-Hong, it was simply incomprehensible that Elliot, known to all as the Chief Superintendent, could not exercise control over British subjects in China. They were at a loss to know exactly what it was he was superintending. The distinctions between the merchants' legal commercial activities and other aspects of their conduct, and between legitimate and illegitimate trade, in terms of Elliot's ability to exercise authority, were alien concepts to the Chinese. Equally alien, to the British, were the principles of group responsibility where an individual miscreant could not be identified, and arbitrarily imposed responsibility for the actions of others (which they had seen at first hand in the Chinese government's treatment of the Co-Hong).

Whatever Elliot's views of the principles at stake and of the broader picture, he had to respond pragmatically to the situation in which the British and other foreign traders now found themselves. With Lin's measures of 24 March the usual daytime noise around the Factories had abated completely as the premises were vacated by all except the foreigners, who numbered around 350. As well as the merchants they included a number of sailors and Indian servants, and the officers of the Superintendency: Charles Elliot, the Deputy Superintendent A.R. Johnston, the Secretary Edward Elmslie, and the interpreter J.R. Morrison. They were confined by more than a thousand soldiers, police and coolies, all armed with weapons of various kinds, and blockaded from the river by three rows of boats. At night the besieged community was kept awake by a constant cacophony of gongs and horns.

It was something of a shock to the foreign merchants' systems to have suddenly to turn their hands to cooking and other domestic tasks, but after a short while the atmosphere in the Factories became generally good-humoured. At the start of the blockade Elliot had written dramatically to Palmerston informing him that

> The native servants were taken from us, and the supplies cut off on the same night ... and before the gate of this hall the whole body of Hong merchants and a large guard are posted day and night, the latter with their swords constantly drawn. In short, so close an imprisonment of the foreigners is not recorded in the history of our previous intercourse with this empire.[11]

Reports to London of significant events and fast-changing situations were of course especially vulnerable to the length of time between dispatch and receipt. Elliot's communication of 30 March, along with two subsequent letters of 2 and 3 April, did not reach the Foreign Office until 29 August, nearly four months after the blockade had ended and by which time events on the China coast had moved on apace. In reality, life for the foreigners became a good deal more comfortable than might have been inferred from Elliot's initial dispatch. The Hong merchants and the interpreters played a valuable role in encouraging their coolies to ensure that a variety of food and other provisions found their way into the Factories; aided by the staff of the Hong merchants and the linguists, cooking and cleaning duties were shared among all who had been confined: sailors, Indian servants, and the foreign merchants and officers themselves. James Matheson wrote home to Jardine on 1 May, three days before the end of the six-week blockade, that 'By the kindness of Heerjeebhoy in lending us his Indian servants, with the assistance of some sailors who happened to be up, we have not only lived comfortably all along, but have entertained the remaining inmates.'[12]

So with some difficulty to start with, and with inventiveness and goodwill, the merchant community's material needs were on the whole met. They could not escape the fact, though, that their movements were being forcibly restricted by a foreign power. The humiliation and frustration were deeply felt, and by none more than Charles Elliot. His responsibility as the senior representative of Her Majesty's Government in China overrode all other considerations now, and he had to find a way out of the current difficulties. His decision, made within days of the imposition of the blockade, was startling and risky. Whatever was to happen thereafter, the priority was the ending of the blockade, and the only way to achieve this was to undertake to surrender the opium as required by Commissioner Lin. In the light of Elliot's previously robust stance this was, to all appearances, a remarkable *volte-face*. He could not have contemplated such a move without providing the merchants with a guarantee of compensation; his plan, fraught with political risk, was that appropriate compensation would be supplied in due course by the British government. Such a commitment to the merchants had to be made immediately if there was to be progress, despite there being no evidence that the government would feel obliged to honour it. The traders not only took Elliot at his word, but thought they could demand a good price. Though some of the Hong merchants considered that the promise to hand over all the opium was an overreaction, Elliot was satisfied that thus far he had made the right decisions.

Charles Elliot was able to smuggle out letters to Macao to reassure Clara of his personal safety; he also set out, with mild sarcasm and a small dose of self-congratulation, his current thinking (though in rather guarded terms) on the state of play in the stand-off with the Chinese. Ten days into the confinement he wrote to her:

> I have some promise of getting these few lines to you, and I know it will be a joy to you to hear that I am well and happy, (if I could forget your anxieties). The great point now is to get this opium delivered, so that having fulfilled my public engagement I may make my bow to his Excellency and all their other Excellencies till we come to Him in another sort of form and with another kind of business in hand.
>
> It was obviously his purpose to bully the merchants into forced and separate surrenders of their property ... But I burst in upon Him, and his measures met an officer with all the train of consequences that his treatment of me has produced....
>
> In the meantime be of good heart. Console everybody about you, and never fear for me. I shall turn up the right end uppermost.[13]

Elliot saw the surrender of the opium, as well as being necessary to secure the ending of the blockade, as a measure that would prompt British government retaliation. Such a reaction by the British would in due course cause the Chinese to be brought to terms, an essential step towards the broader objective of breaking Chinese resistance to the expansion of trade. The aim was *reculer pour mieux sauter*. His references to 'another sort of form' and 'another kind of business' indicated that he had already decided that confrontation in the form of military action was now almost inevitable, a view swiftly translated into action in a flurry of letters to Palmerston. Now nearly two weeks into the blockade, he supplied the Foreign Secretary with a preliminary account of how his intentions had been thwarted by Lin's threatening behaviour:

> It was my fixed purpose, my Lord, when I left Macao ... either to cause the merchants of my country, engaged in trade at Canton, to make solemn promises that they would abstain from connexion with the opium traffic in future, or myself, on the part of Her Majesty's Government, to undertake that no reclamation should be made if they were forthwith expelled....

> The situation ... has been entirely altered by the High Commissioner's proceedings; and his continuance of the state of restraint, insult and dark intimidation, subsequently to the surrender, has certainly classed the whole case amongst the most shameless violences which one nation has ever yet dared to perpetrate against another.[14]

In a passage which encapsulates his approach he continued with his thoughts on what should have been done, and his recommended way forward:

> It is not by measures of this kind that the Chinese Government can hope to put down a trade, which every friend to humanity must deplore; great moral changes can never be effected by the violation of all the principles of justice and moderation. The wise course would have been to make the trade shameful, and wear it out by degrees in its present form. The course taken will change the manner of its pursuit at once, cast it into desperate hands, and with this long line of unprotected coast, abounding in safe anchorages, and covered with defenceless cities, I foresee a state of things terrible to reflect upon.... I feel assured, that the single mode of saving the coasts of the empire from a shocking character of warfare, both foreign and domestic, will be the very prompt and powerful interference of Her Majesty's Government.... There can be neither safety nor honour for either Government till Her Majesty's flag flies on these coasts in a secure position.[15]

In other words, a short, sharp (and overwhelming) intervention by the Royal Navy, by preventing much more serious conflict, would be in Chinese as well as British interests. Whatever tactical advantage may have been gained by Elliot's promise to surrender the opium, compliance with Lin's other demand, that the foreign merchants sign a bond undertaking not to trade in opium again, was an impossibility for the British. Elliot was under no illusion about the meaning of 'extreme penalties of the law'; it meant summary execution for any signatory whom the Chinese subsequently considered to be trading in opium. Exercising his newly operational de facto authority, he made it clear to Lin that while accepting the need for foreigners to abide by the law of the host country, the terms of the bond were so far removed from the principles of English justice that acceptance of them was out of the question. If it were insisted on, all British traders and vessels would have to leave Canton. The death penalty as a consequence of non-compliance was explicitly spelled out in the text of a 'voluntary bond' presented via the Hong merchants at a meeting of the General Committee of the foreigners' Chamber of Commerce. Considered by the Committee on 5 April, it also required the Chief Superintendent to be in touch with the Queen:

Elliot &c., will plainly address the sovereign of his nation, that she may strictly proclaim to all the merchants that they are to pay implicit obedience to the prohibitory laws of the celestial court,- that they must not again introduce any opium into this inner land, – that they cannot be allowed any longer to manufacture opium.

From the commencement of autumn in this present year, any merchant vessel coming to Kwangtung [Guangdong] that may be found to bring opium, shall be immediately and entirely confiscated, both vessel and cargo, to the use of government, no trade shall be allowed to it, and the parties shall be left to suffer death at the hands of the celestial court, – such punishment they will readily submit to.[16]

It was not surprising that Lin wanted Queen Victoria involved. As Head of State she was regarded by the Commissioner as having the kind of authority over the British that the Emperor had over the people of China. Lin had earlier composed a long letter to the British queen requesting that she forbid the cultivation of the opium poppy and the manufacture of the drug. He made the case on moral grounds:

We are of the opinion that this poisonous article is clandestinely manufactured by artful and depraved people of various tribes under the dominion of your honorable nation.... Though not making use of it one's self, to venture nevertheless to manufacture and sell it, and with it to seduce the simple folk of this land, is to seek one's own livelihood by exposing others to death, to seek one's own advantage by other men's injury. Such acts are bitterly abhorrent to the nature of man and are utterly opposed to the ways of heaven.[17]

Copies had been freely distributed in Canton, but it never reached its destination.[18] So far as Elliot was concerned, Lin's appeal to the Queen was of no importance in the immediacy of the threat to the foreign merchant community presented by the demand to sign the bond. Since the bond could not be accepted, conditions for the foreigners could be expected to deteriorate rapidly and withdrawal from Canton, already recognised by Elliot as inevitable sooner or later, now, in late April, became urgent.

The surrender of the drug had meanwhile been proceeding as planned. Lin had set out a programme for the restoration of privileges to the besieged community, to be implemented in stages as the amount of surrendered opium increased. By 2 May the Commissioner was satisfied that his demands were being met, and he ordered the lifting of the siege. With the exception of Lancelot Dent and some fifteen other traders whom the Chinese considered the most flagrant opium traffickers, the merchants left Canton for Macao. Elliot was now concerned that if any of them should attempt to return, they would again be putting themselves at risk. Furthermore, the stand taken against what the foreign community considered to be the wholly unjust and unacceptable behaviour of Lin and his colleagues, including especially the demand that they sign a bond, would be seriously undermined.

The order that all British subjects in Canton should leave the city had been issued by Elliot on 11 May. After sailing from Canton on 24 May he arrived back in Macao. Having been away from his family for more than two months, he was relieved not only to be with them but to be able to show that he was unharmed and attending to his duties as normal. He took the earliest opportunity to write home to Emma and to Harriet, one of their sisters. He offered fond advice concerning the care of the three children, and in the same letter addressed the children themselves about how they should behave. As customary when reporting home on his own situation he was careful, while giving assurance that he was safe and bearing up, not to downplay either the severity of the difficulties he was facing or their complexity:

> I write to you both because I know you will be equally anxious about me. I am once more with my family after a pretty close imprisonment of nine weeks, somewhat shattered in health but strong in spirit...The attempt to explain what I have been doing, or why, would be hopeless indeed.'[19]

Charles Elliot was already aware that he was going to find it difficult to expound convincingly the line he had been taking with the Chinese. It would have been inappropriate, and probably alarming to her, to have reported to Emma at this stage that he had complied with the Commissioner's demand to surrender a large and valuable quantity of British-owned opium. He was, despite his assertion otherwise, dispirited and tired. He still believed that the Chinese wanted a mutually acceptable solution, and viewed his own demeanour and that of his compatriots with a degree of cynicism:

> Since I left Canton on the 24 I have received a very moderate and conciliatory note from the Governor. They are evidently desirous of accommodating matters if they can. The Chinese, dear Emy, have made me a cautious, suspicious man and I do not gabble so easily now as I was used to do 3 years since. To borrow a figure of their own, I 'investigate and enquire three times three' and then answer that it is difficult to say 'no' and harder still to say 'yes'. When they want to settle, they always find a way easily enough. When they want to confuse us, we usually spare them the trouble by doing it ourselves.[20]

Elliot's assumed authority over the British traders had held good in the withdrawal from Canton, as it had for the surrender of the opium, but influencing the merchants of other nations was a different matter. The Americans, in particular, felt under no obligation to toe Elliot's line. In the United States the prevailing view was reflected in an address to Congress by the lawyer Caleb Cushing:

> God forbid that I should cooperate with the British Government in the purpose – if purpose it have – of upholding the base cupidity and violence which have characterized the actions of the British individually and collectively in the seas of China ... I trust the idea will no longer be entertained in England, if she chooses to persevere in the attempt to coerce the Chinese by force of arms to be poisoned with opium by whole provinces, that she is to receive aid or countenance from the United States in that nefarious enterprise.[21]

Though minor players compared with the British, in terms of both the number of firms and the volume of business, the American traders in Canton had established a separate relationship with the Chinese and were now keen to distance themselves from British moves. The young and earnest Charles King of Olyphant & Co., the only American firm not to deal in opium, was a particular thorn in Elliot's side, criticising him publicly and at great length for the way he was conducting affairs. King's attack focused solely on the opium issue, greatly irritating Elliot. It led him to compose a detailed refutation, set out in a later letter to Emma, which castigated King for being critical and yet for failing to indicate how he would have done things better.[22] A raw nerve seems nevertheless to have been touched in Elliot. Given his own hostility to opium trafficking, he probably felt that the American was being not only self-indulgent but unfair and, since he had previously supported Elliot's approach, hypocritical. King's polemic was among the first of many occasions on which Charles Elliot would feel the need to justify his conduct in China.

Commissioner Lin kept his word on the return in stages to the *status quo* as the opium was handed over, though progress was stalled midway when he received an unfounded report that the British were planning to interrupt the process. From the British side the surrender of the opium was supervised on Elliot's behalf by his deputy, Johnston. For the Chinese Lin himself took direct charge, taking up residence on a boat just south of the Bogue near the island of Lankeet, where the opium was to be given up. A little short of half the promised 20,283 chests had been delivered by 19 April, after nine days. By 21 May a dispute between Lin and Johnston had been resolved, and the handover was complete. The destruction of the drug commenced early in June at Humen, then a small and otherwise insignificant town, in Dongguan, northwest of present day Shenzhen. It took some three weeks. Hundreds of workers smashed the balls of opium and poured the fragments into trenches filled with lime, salt and water, whence the dissolved drug flowed into the mouth of the Pearl River and out to sea.

At Macao Elliot could do little more than wait patiently. He hoped that either the British government would react to the injury inflicted on its citizens or, in the interests of reviving legitimate trade and of avoiding conflict, Lin would blink first and set the demand for the bond aside. As ever when he was not engaged in vigorous action or diplomatic exchange, Elliot was given to bouts of introspection. On this occasion he concluded that he was doing his best but that if that was not considered good enough, he would have to live with the consequences. He wrote in a resigned tone to Emma:

> I have had difficult things indeed to do, and my way is still among thorns and briars. As I grow older, blessed be God however, I grow more confident in his support, and less confident in the wisdom of the world's ways. I am meaning to do my duty honestly and faithfully; and if the government are not satisfied I shall leave my post with the hope that they may find as honest intentions and far more ability. My task has not been an easy one and there let that matter rest.[23]

There was never any real chance that Lin and his officials, who now held the upper hand, would give ground. So far as Lin was concerned there was no reason to; he believed that the barbarians had learned their lesson and that normal commercial relations would in due course be re-established at Canton.

The widespread tension among the foreign and local communities on the China coast  perhaps made it inevitable that this period of relative calm should have been interrupted by an event outside the control of both the Chinese and British authorities. On 12 July Commissioner Lin noted in his diary: 'Heard that at Kowloon Point sailors from a foreign ship beat up some Chinese peasants and killed one of them. Sent a deputy to make enquiries.'[24] What Lin had heard was accurate; the murdered man, Lin Weixi, had died following a liquor-fuelled brawl between local villagers and (mostly English) sailors. The exchanges between the British and the Chinese which then ensued illustrated yet again their fundamentally different notions not only of the way justice should be administered but of the nature of justice itself. Charles Elliot, aware of the danger that the affair could spark a much more serious confrontation, acted swiftly to try to identify the person or persons responsible for the death. Before the report of the incident reached Lin, Elliot was at the scene of the affray. Offering a reward, he attempted to persuade the villagers to find the culprit, who would then be dealt with according to the procedures of English law. Anxious to avoid a British sailor being subject to summary Chinese justice, Elliot's immediate aim was to convene a court and instigate a trial, as he was authorised to do under the (hitherto unused) 1833 British legislation to that effect.[25] More importantly, Commissioner Lin did not recognise any legal principle of extraterritoriality; the death of a Chinese citizen had occurred on Chinese soil and the Chinese authorities would take the necessary action. He demanded that the perpetrator be identified and handed over. Elliot arraigned six of the seamen involved and they received fines and custodial sentences but it proved impossible to establish who had caused the death. The Commissioner sought a life for a life, as Chinese justice required, and Elliot's continued refusal to surrender a murderer, coming after his refusal to allow British merchants to resume trading at Canton, was treated by Lin as another significant provocation, to which he was honour bound to respond in the strongest terms.

The Lin Weixi episode also demonstrated misunderstandings by each side of the other's psychology. The Commisioner was taken aback by Elliot's apparent intransigence – the foreigners had been forced to surrender large quantities of opium, and were therefore in an inherently weak position; how could Elliot now behave in this obstructive way? The belief that the Chinese viewed any giving of ground by their opponents as a sign of weakness was to become a major part of the argument for British retaliation, and of the subsequent criticism of Elliot's handling of affairs in China. A contemporary (British) observer of events wrote a few years later that 'Every concession on the part of Captain Elliot, or the merchants, was to him [Lin] a victory gained, and the forerunner of greater ones.'[26] Charles Elliot showed a similarly misplaced optimism about Lin's attitude; he thought he understood the Chinese and in a general way his empathy for the people was real, but he failed fully to comprehend the determined mindset of their senior officials. In his letter to Emma of 17 July he appeared sanguine, even light-hearted, about future exchanges:

> My troublesome friend the high commissioner is still here and flirts with me ever and anon. When he waxes civil I draw up and blushingly turn away. When he is a little nearer, I throw a bland word or two at him. We shall settle our little difference amicably I dare say.[27]

As with the confinement of the foreigners in the Canton factories, the measures Lin was now to take were uncompromising and effective. Except that this time the British were in Macao, it was, so far as Lin was concerned, to be very like a rerun of the Canton blockade. Once again supplies were cut off, and once again the Chinese military presence was significantly increased. This time, however, there was a way out for the British community, even if temporary and fraught with difficulty. Lin's message that if he did not surrender Lin Weixi's killer Elliot himself would be held responsible was for Elliot the last straw. He responded by putting into action a plan to evacuate all the Macao British to Hong Kong harbour, where they would be quartered on the fifty or so merchant ships until it became safe to return to Macao. By 27 August, twelve days after the Commissioner had decreed the cessation of supplies, Charles, Clara, the 2-year-old Freddy, and all British residents of Macao had decamped to Hong Kong. The decision to evacuate anticipated an edict from Lin requiring da Silveira Pinto, the Governor of Macao, to expel the British. Elliot had had little choice, but had acted in time to avoid a potentially violent and distressing encounter. The British families remained relatively safe, but had no secure source of supplies. Armed Chinese junks hovered around the Kowloon peninsula, where food and fresh water were normally to be had, obstructing access. Notices appeared on wells announcing that the water they contained was poisoned.

Though the supplies situation was not desperate, Elliot's concern that it might become so, as well as the increasing restlessness of the ships' crews at the most humid and uncomfortable time of the year, prompted him to go in person to Kowloon to try to sort something out. After hours of waiting and an agreement which was then broken, Elliot's frustration got the better of him and he permitted three junks to be fired on. The British vessels involved were the lightly armed cutter *Louisa*, a hired merchant brigantine, the *Pearl*, also lightly armed, and a boat from the recently arrived frigate, HMS *Volage*. Despite their heavier firepower the height of the junks caused their shot to pass over the British craft, whose manoeuvrability and lower line of fire enabled them to inflict significant damage. Elliot wrote later to Palmerston that he regretted allowing this action, which could have had very serious immediate consequences:

> I can assure your Lordship, that though I am responsible for causing the first shot to be fired, I did not anticipate any conflict when we left, and went accompanied [by the *Pearl* and the pinnace of the *Volage*] solely for purposes of sufficient defence against insult or attack.
>
> The violent and vexatious measures heaped upon Her Majesty's officers and subjects will, I trust, serve to excuse those feelings of irritation which have betrayed me into a measure that I am certain, under less trying circumstances, would be difficult indeed of vindication.'[28]

However unfairly treated he may have felt over recent years, and whatever he may have said in private, Elliot's communications with the Foreign Secretary had always shown the level of deference their respective positions required. This was the first time the Chief Superintendent had felt the need to express regret for his own conduct to his superior – in effect, to apologise – and was perhaps a sign that the pressures on him were beginning to erode his usual high level of self-confidence.

During these critical months of 1839 Charles Elliot was indeed under considerable strain. As well as issuing notices to the merchant community, the local Chinese population and the ships' captains, he was in frequent correspondence with Chinese officials, the Governor of Macao, individual traders and, especially, Palmerston. His letters to the Foreign Secretary set out in detail events as they unfolded and made it clear that he was in full charge. He was also careful to explain his objectives and to record his current thinking and preoccupations. Aware that his letters would not reach their destination for some five months, he knew that in due course he would be required to account for his actions. A full and reliable record would be essential for that purpose. Towards the end of August he referred to the Lin Weixi affair, reporting that American seamen had taken as much part as the British, and that if it was true that the US Consul had denied any American involvement 'he has hazarded an assertion at variance with the state of the facts.'[29] In the same communication, written from his temporary home on the *Fort William* in Hong Kong harbour, Elliot sought to draw a line under the trading arrangements with China that had prevailed hitherto:

> Your Lordship ... may be assured that I will do everything in my power to prevent the Calamity and intolerable disgrace of a surprise of this valuable Fleet of near fifty sail of British Ships by Mandarin Junks or Fire rafts; and for this purpose I have this day assumed the Military as well as the civil Superintendence of the Ships and issued the necessary directions for their defence ... English Ships or men, can never again be safe within these limits till our whole intercourse with this Empire be placed on an entirely different footing.[30]

The defensive measures taken by Elliot included approaches to the Captain General of the Philippines and the Governor of Singapore for provisions and military stores. He expected no help from the Portuguese, the Americans or any other foreign traders. He now felt, rightly, that the British community for which he was responsible was without any kind of support. He may have had some sympathy for the Portuguese, whose fragile tenant–landlord relationship with China he understood (though he talked of their 'fears and purposeless jealousy'), but the attitude of the Americans continued to annoy him.[31] He considered them especially 'capable of unworthy and vain intrigues to keep out Her Majesty's Subjects', continuing to Palmerston:

> what the Americans concede, my Lord, is scarcely conceded at all, for they trade here in point of fact not only with British capital but under the protection of Her Majesty's Government, and when things are adjusted by the powerful intervention of Her Majesty they will derive the same advantages as ourselves.'[32,33]

Elliot's irritation was hardly rational; the Americans were simply using facilities provided by another power for their own commercial advantage, as the British had been doing in Macao for more than a century. The most recent cause of his hostility was the Americans' apparent denial of any involvement in the Lin Weixi fracas, which he said (not very convincingly)

> would not have assumed its present most serious aspect if the Americans had honorably admitted the unquestionable truth of my representation, that their citizens were engaged in the affray, that it was impossible to say who the offender was, American or British, and that they never could consent to the delivering up of a man to the Chinese Government in satisfaction of a homicide brought home against no foreign individual.[34]

Two weeks passed without any communication from Lin, as a result of which Elliot informed Palmerston that 'the sober train of reflection in the mind of the Commissioner ... enables me to hold out to Her Majesty's Government the hope that we are upon the eve of some satisfactory temporary solution of actual difficulties'.[35] Despite his instinctive optimism, he must have known he was clutching at straws. Silence from Lin did not mean intention to conciliate. At the end of October came a long letter from Lin and Viceroy Deng, listing the whole catalogue of Chinese objections to British behaviour. They cited Elliot's continued failure to obey their orders to surrender the murderer of Lin Weixi; his continued failure to instruct the merchants to sign the bond; allegations that ships at Hong Kong had secretly been sending opium along the coast for sale; rumours that some families had been drifting back to Macao; and reports that foreign sailors had killed Chinese citizens at Guanghai.[36]

Lin's strictures about the bond now had, in Lin's own view, added force. In mid-October, to the despairing fury of Elliot, the British merchantman *Thomas Coutts* had entered the Bogue. Her Captain, Warner, had signed the bond, at a stroke breaching the solidarity by which Elliot set so much store. If one could do it, exulted Lin, why not all?

The Commissioner and Viceroy moved from specific alleged crimes to a more fundamental point. 'It is requisite you should know that the permission the Celestial Court gives you to trade here arises from the principle of showing tenderness towards men from afar. If you fail to obey implicitly the laws, what will be the difficulty of cutting off your commerce?'[37] They concluded:

> It seems for the most part that these foreigners cannot be aroused or influenced by good words. And We, the Commissioner and the Governor, have no course left but to send out war vessels to proceed to Hong Kong, to surround and apprehend all the

offenders, those connected with murders, and those connected with opium, as well as the traitorous Chinese concealed on board the foreign vessels.[38]

On 29 October Elliot issued a curt reply. He reiterated that he would give no protection to British traders engaged in illegal activity along the coast; he knew nothing about the reported incidents at Guanghai; and he had already dealt with all other matters contained in Lin's and Deng's communication of two days earlier. The Chief Superintendent then boarded HMS *Volage* (28 guns) and together with HMS *Hyacinth*, a recently joined 18-gun sloop, sailed for the Bogue. A mile south of the fort at Chuanbi, on the eastern side of the Bogue entrance, the two ships cast anchor. They sighted, about eight miles away, a Chinese force of fifteen war junks and fourteen fireboats.

# Chapter Ten

# War

Those who date the start of the First Opium War[1] in 1839 usually take the opening engagement to be the (first) Battle of Chuanbi, which was fought on 3 November. There was at this stage no formal declaration of war, and neither Elliot nor Lin was seeking armed conflict. In the preceding weeks there had even been a few conciliatory gestures – Elliot had proposed a search arrangement to replace the intended bond, the Chinese had suggested that the body of a drowned sailor from a British ship might serve to break the Lin Weixi *impasse* – but none had come to anything. The *Thomas Coutts* affair had caused Lin to stiffen his resolve; he ordered that unless the murderer was handed over and the bond was signed, all foreign ships should be expelled from the coast. They would have three days in which to comply. Once a last minute attempt to persuade him to rescind his order had failed, the immediate task of the *Volage* and the *Hyacinth* was to protect British merchant shipping outside the Bogue from Chinese attack. They also found themselves having to prevent the *Royal Saxon*, a second British merchantman for which the bond had been signed, from entering the river.

The exact sequence of events which triggered the Battle of Chuanbi is not entirely clear. The senior British naval officer was the captain of the *Volage*, Captain Henry Smith, a former West Indies colleague of Elliot with whom he had a good working relationship.[2] Chinese and most Western accounts agree that the *Volage* fired a warning shot across the bows of the *Royal Saxon*. At midday on 3 November, Captain Smith, with Elliot's approval, ordered the *Hyacinth* to open fire on the Chinese fleet, which had manoeuvred to facilitate safe passage for the *Royal Saxon* (and remained a threat to British merchant ships). The Chinese account makes no mention of its fleet having moved, the action by the *Hyacinth* being represented as wholly unprovoked.[3] Whatever prompted the contest it was, inevitably, one-sided. Elliot's report of the events leading up to the battle (which made no mention of the *Royal Saxon* incident) assured the Foreign Secretary that he had been 'Conscious that all had been done which was in my power, to satisfy the just demands of the Chinese officers, and [that he perceived] that the necessity had arrived for checking their hostile movements'.[4] As to the engagement itself, Elliot describes the fighting in language which reflects his own many years' experience in the Royal Navy and his familiarity with the tactics of naval warfare:

> the signal was made to engage, and all the ships, then lying hove-to on the extreme right of the Chinese force, bore away

in a line a-head and close order, having the wind on the starboard beam. In this way, and under easy sail, they ran down the Chinese line, pouring in a destructive fire.... The Chinese answered with their accustomed spirit; but the terrible effect of our own fire was soon manifest. One war junk blew up at about pistol-shot distance from this ship [HMS *Volage*], a shot probably passing through the magazine; three were sunk; and several others were obviously water-logged. It is an act of justice to a brave man to say, that the Admiral's conduct was worthy of his station. His junk was evidently better armed and manned than the other vessels; and, after he had weighed, or, more probably, cut or slipped, he bore up and engaged Her Majesty's ships in handsome style, manifesting a resolution of behaviour honourably enhanced by the hopelessness of his efforts. In less than three quarters of an hour, however, he, and the remainder of the squadron, were retiring in great distress to their former anchorage; and as it was not Captain Smith's disposition to protract destructive hostilities, or, indeed do more than repel onward movements, he offered no obstruction to their retreat; but discontinued the fire, and made sail for Macao, with the purpose to cover the embarkation of such of Her Majesty's subjects as might see fit to retire from that place, and also to provide for the safety of the merchant ships.[5]

The next few months passed relatively quietly. British trade with Canton revived, thanks to vigorous and highly profitable transhipment operations especially by the Americans, taking cotton and cloth from British ships up to Canton and bringing back tea and silk to load for the passage to Europe.

An uneasy calm pervaded Macao. Among those who had returned there were Clara Elliot and the 2-year-old Freddy. To keep themselves safe they lived largely indoors, with minimal outside contact, conscious that tensions with the Chinese in the town could quickly change to confrontation or worse. On board the *Volage* Charles had time to write to his daughter Harriet (Chachy), now 10. The letter is notable for what can be inferred about Elliot's own convictions:

> Pay good attention to your books my dear love, but pay still more to subjection and training of your nature. Say your prayers with thoughtfulness morning and evening, and never fail to read a chapter of the New Testament before you go to bed. When you begin to read the Grecian and Roman histories tell your aunt to buy Langhorne's Plutarch for you. It is a book which you cannot read too often, at least I have found it so myself.
>
> Not dear Chachy that my reading has been much or useful to me. But that book is full of ennobling sentiments and will help to elevate your character, and it is folly to think that there is

> a difference in the high thoughts which should become women
> as well as men – generosity, justice, contempt of falsehood,
> perseverance, are as needful and as good to women as to men.
> Pay good attention to your geography and arithmetic. As for
> accomplishments, my own love, cultivate these whilst you can;
> but take my advice, and strive to make yourself useful rather
> than ornamental.[6]

Much to their parents' relief, Harriet and Hughie Elliot had arrived safely at Charlton in August. By February 1840 Clara and Freddy, too, were leaving the China coast.

News of the spring blockade of Canton had reached London at the end of August 1839. When they became public the events of March and April, described by Elliot in his letters to Palmerston, had the immediate and predictable effect of causing disquiet.[7] Quite apart from the consequences for trade, the forcible confinement of Her Majesty's subjects was humiliating and should not be tolerated. In August this was also Palmerston's reaction, but other more pressing matters meant that China was still not among his top priorities. That changed in September when a more detailed account was received from Elliot, and the matter was given added urgency in December when confirmation arrived of the surrender of the twenty thousand chests. The handing over of the opium and the promised compensation were vexed issues, but by illustrating how severe must have been the coercion exercised by the Chinese, the news served chiefly to reinforce public demands for retribution in the face of insult to British honour.

If the British public felt aggrieved, Parliament had even more cause for concern, for the news from China did not enter the public domain in August as a result of parliamentary debate, but from merchant and missionary sources and the newspapers. Elliot's dispatches about the blockade were retained in the Foreign Office, their contents undisclosed to Parliament, until March 1840. The Cabinet, though, was not deprived of the intelligence from China. Since his arrival in England earlier in 1839 Jardine, along with other returned China hands and merchant houses in London, Leeds, Liverpool, Manchester and elsewhere, had been pressing for compensation to be paid. In order to oblige the Chinese to cooperate in establishing a sound basis for future trade, they sought decisive intervention on the China coast.

The Cabinet addressed the China situation on 1 October at a meeting at Windsor. It did so against a background not only of merchant lobbying, but of controversy over the morality of opium trading, and of outrage at the maltreatment of British subjects and insults to the flag. All these were now in the public domain. One of the pamphlets circulating was a version of Charles King's earlier letter to Elliot. The anti-opium moralists were supported by *The Times*, which printed a vigorous polemic by an Anglican evangelical, the Rev. Algernon Thelwall.[8] Later in October *The*

*Times* published its view that 'Our sin in growing and encouraging the trade in opium is, indeed, one of the darkest that ever invoked the wrath of the Most High God upon a people', and that 'Justice forbids that the steps taken by the Chinese to arrest a system of wrongs practised on them, under the mask of friendship, be made the pretence for still deeper injuries'.[9,10]

Before bringing the China question to Cabinet the Foreign Secretary had responded to Jardine's repeated requests for a meeting. Armed with first hand information from Jardine about topography and sailing conditions on the China coast, Palmerston presented to his colleagues a possible plan for military action. In line with opinion in the country at large, and as on other occasions during his career, he was moved primarily by the need to exact redress for the coercion of British subjects and for disregard of the honour of the Crown. Those present at the Cabinet table included the historian and staunch advocate of British education and culture T.B. Macaulay, Secretary at War, who did not need persuading, and Sir Francis Baring, Chancellor of the Exchequer, who did. Baring did not see how the Treasury could possibly fund an effective punitive expedition against China, nor compensation to the merchants, estimated at some £2 million (in 2015 terms £187 million[11]). There was debate about the compensation issue and the size – and therefore the cost – of the force to be sent, but in the end it did not take Palmerston's inclination and Macaulay's eloquence very long to result in a decision for war. The reasoning was that armed conflict, which Britain would of course win, would enable reparations to be exacted from the Chinese both for the confiscated opium and for the cost of the military campaign, and it would restore national honour. Overtly at least neither the morality and future of the opium trade, nor the desire to establish a more stable basis for Anglo-Chinese commerce in general, were major factors in the decision.

On 18 October Palmerston wrote to Charles Elliot informing him that an expeditionary force was to be dispatched and was expected to reach the China coast in March 1840. The letter arrived on 16 February on Jardine Matheson's newest and fastest clipper, the *Mor*, and lifted Charles Elliot's spirits both for its news of the British government's commitment and for the positive view it conveyed of him personally. Elliot wrote a week later to Emma that a communication from her

> had been accompanied by a private letter from Lord Palmerston announcing the determination of the government to support me, or at all events, to accept the transactions of last Spring. But his letter was most gratifying as it manifested great confidence both in my zeal and capacity. I hope he may have no reason to regret it.[12]

The situation had turned in to something of a standoff. The continuation of British trade at Canton via the trans-shipment system was in the face of a decree by Commissioner Lin that from 6 December all Chinese trade with British merchants should cease indefinitely. The decree had been endorsed by the Emperor, who had added that all British vessels should be expelled.[13] Elliot's assessment of next developments, which if there were no unforeseen events of consequence would be prompted by the arrival of the British force, was such that the safety of his family again became a major preoccupation. Governor da Silveira Pinto could not, given his constitutional position as tenant of Macao, do other than support Chinese efforts to remove the British. Isolated and under threat, Elliot decided with Clara that she and Freddy should leave – not for England, but for Singapore. As he wrote to his sister on the day of their departure in February 1840:

> My single-hearted and wise wife (for wise she is in the best sense of the word) has resolved to spare me the pain of constant anxiety while she is here, and to take the whole bitter burden to her own heart. She leaves me this morning for Singapore where she will remain till these troubles have either blown over, or till I can join her.
>
> We are again menaced with more of seriousness than usual by these perverse people, and as it is so plain to see that sharp blows must soon be struck, that I have never had one moment's comfort while dear Clara was here. Besides I owe it to my countrymen to leave no hostages here and the jubilation of the Portuguese at Macao means trick and cowardice.[14]

After conveying affectionate thanks for her care of his children, as he always did in letters to Emma, he concluded:

> Distress and anxiety dearest Emy will be my excuse for this hurried scrawl. Clara is a better correspondent than I, and she will tell you how sorely I have been beset by troubles. But be under no fear about my poor reputation … I know that I shall be able to show I have kept fast hold of right principles and ulterior objects. But for me, dear Emy, the loss and the degradation would have been equal but there would have been no *just* pretext for resenting them, and for setting all things on a firm footing.[15]

Defence of his own conduct was now to be a recurring feature of Charles Elliot's reports to his elder sister. He knew that when the expeditionary force arrived events would move on quickly, and that while his military colleagues would doubtless be ready with advice, responsibility for overall strategy would be his. Emma was to be a trusted recipient of his explanations and, on the departure of Clara and Freddy, confidante on family matters also. He was remarkably frank about his wife:

> Clara … is a good woman with many of the qualities for which I have always set you down as the wisest person I ever knew. Influenced by her sense of duty beyond the power of wrong

motives; capable of any sacrifice for honourable independence sake; clear sighted; and of a most affectionate nature. But withal, not without flaws which are much rather my reproach than hers for I might have worked them out of her nature, if I had been thoughtful and patient. As it is, she is in all things so much my superior ... that she has got to feel, poor woman (utterly without the consciousness of such a condition of mind) that she has a right to be wayward and perverse, when she pleases; and then comes the notion that waywardness and perverseness are of wholesome effect because I have been fool enough to let them work upon me.

But my own dearest Clara, I have never known her virtues and never felt how helpless I am without her till now that she has left me. She is an excellent woman in every sense of the word, and has displayed so much real tenderness, and so much wisdom during the *desperate* year I have passed, that at least it has had the one salutary effect of making me understand and love her better than I ever did.[16]

Whether Charles's main purpose here was to unburden himself of the effects of his wife's 'waywardness and perverseness', tempering his criticism with praise, or to stress the extent of his unhappiness at her departure but with the caveat that the marriage was not always plain sailing, it seems from this, and from Clara's own letters, that she was a principled and loyal spouse. She also appears to have possessed considerable emotional strength, a quality on which – often subconsciously – he relied a great deal.

Clara's fortitude would prove important to Charles for the rest of his life, for reasons now beginning to become apparent in London. In April 1840 Parliament was at last able to debate the China situation. In January the Queen's Speech opening Parliament had acknowledged that 'Events have happened in China which have occasioned an interruption of the commercial intercourse of my subjects with that country. I have given, and shall continue to give, the most serious attention to a matter so deeply affecting the interests of my subjects and the dignity of the Crown.'[17] During February questions were asked in Parliament about the government's intentions, and in March *The Times* announced that war had been declared on China.

The debate in the House of Commons, when it came, was vigorous and closely argued. It took place over three days, on a motion censuring the government for allowing the country to be brought to the brink of war. Sir James Graham, for the opposition, moved that:

It appears to this House, on consideration of the papers relating to China, presented to this House, by command of Her Majesty, that the interruption in our commercial and friendly intercourse with that country, and the hostilities which have since taken place, are mainly to be attributed to the want of foresight and precaution on the part of Her Majesty's present advisers, in respect to our relations with China, and especially to their neglect to furnish the superintendent at Canton with powers and instructions to provide against the growing evils connected with the contraband traffic in opium, and adapted to the novel and difficult situation in which the superintendent was placed.[18]

Since his communications formed a significant part of the voluminous *Correspondence Relating to China*, now made available to the House, it was perhaps inevitable that Charles Elliot's role should become a much discussed issue.[19] On the whole, government and opposition members of both Houses were at this stage supportive of him, taking the view either that he had acquitted himself well, or that if there had been omissions they were the government's fault. Graham's speech, in which he reminded the House of China's history, wealth and power and stressed the importance to Britain of not antagonising her, was followed by a robust contribution from Macaulay, who said the reason Elliot had not been invested with extra powers was that:

> down to the month of May, 1838, the Foreign Secretary had very strong reasons to believe that it was in the contemplation of the government of China immediately to legalize the opium trade, which had undoubtedly been carried on in disobedience to the existing law.... The system under which that trade had been carried on was this – it had been prohibited by law, but connived at in practice.[20]

The moral dimension was a major preoccupation of the press. *The Times* continued to fulminate about 'a lawless and accursed traffick, to be bolstered up by a flagitious and murderous war'.[21] Unaware or unbelieving of Charles Elliot's hostility to the opium trade, the Chartists, whose radical campaigning for political reform took in condemnation of imperialism in general and the opium trade in particular, referred in their publicity to 'Mr Opium Elliot ... gloating over the prospects of ... bloodshed, famine ... and multiform distress and misery.'[22]

In Parliament it was the 30-year-old future Prime Minister W.E. Gladstone who made the appeal to members' consciences, in a detailed attack on Palmerston. In the catalogue of neglect of which he accused the Foreign Secretary Gladstone also pulled no punches in criticising Elliot's actions. He made particular mention of his stance at the time of the blockade in March 1839, when Elliot had very publicly aligned himself with those who illegally traded in opium, but laid this behaviour at Palmerston's door for failing, in effect, to keep the Chief Superintendent under control and for tacitly encouraging an aggressive attitude towards the Chinese. Justice, moreover, was on the Chinese side; whatever the intricacies of authority and procedure, they had banned the importation of opium and the British had failed to comply. Gladstone confronted the calls to redress insult to the flag:

> We all know the animating effects which have been produced in the minds of British subjects on many critical occasions when that flag has been unfurled in the battlefield. But how comes it to pass that the sight of that flag always raises the spirit of Englishmen? It is because it has always been associated with the cause of justice, with opposition to oppression, with respect for national rights, with honourable commercial enterprise, but now, under the auspices of the noble Lord, that flag is hoisted to protect an infamous contraband traffic, and if it were never to be hoisted except as it is now hoisted on the coast of China, we should recoil from its sight with horror.[23]

The situation in which Britain now found itself in China, claimed Gladstone, was primarily the result of the Foreign Secretary's omission over several years properly to address the problem, and in particular his failure to give Elliot adequate authority, as the Queen's representative, to regulate the activities of British merchants. Gladstone did not propose that the country should pull back from war. It should never have been allowed to get into its present position. He did not know how long the war would last, 'but this I can say, that a war more unjust in its origin, a war more calculated in its progress to cover this country with permanent disgrace, I do not know, and I have not read of'.[24]

The Commons debate, in which eighteen members spoke, some at great length, was ended for the opposition by the Conservative leader Sir Robert Peel, and for the Government by the Foreign Secretary. Peel refuted the Government line that with preparation for war so far advanced the motion was merely party-politicking, and chided ministers for making assertions about instances of Chinese behaviour – notably the alleged poisoning of the wells at Kowloon – without adequate evidence. He accused them of using such episodes to stir up popular support. 'He knew how easy it was from the past experience of this country in similar circumstances to arouse the public indignation by the detail of individual outrages; but they ought to be perfectly satisfied of the evidence on which the allegations rested.'[25] Far from being reprehensible, there were on the contrary several other examples of conduct by the Chinese authorities reported by Elliot which showed them to be moderate and reasonable, and Peel too reminded the House that it would be against Britain's interests to antagonise China; if war were inevitable it should be undertaken with a view to normalising relations as soon as possible afterwards. The thrust of the opposition motion was not ... that the Government had not sufficient foresight to know what the Emperor of China was going to do, but that after the termination of the relation between China and the East India Company, which had continued for 200 years, and after an immense change, therefore, in the position of this country with respect to China, that Her Majesty's Government sent a gentleman to China to represent the Crown of this country, without the powers...which it was their duty to have given him, without instructions which he was competent to receive, and without the moral influence of a naval force.[26]

Palmerston's response, delivered in a tone less earnest and completely self-assured, was to hit the ball back into his opponents' court. Criticising the Government was easy, he implied, but what would the opposition have done? If the Chinese wished to buy opium and others wished to sell it to them, that free trade should not be impeded; it was not for Britain to assume the role of guardian of other countries' morals. If the government had wanted to give the Chief Superintendent wide-ranging powers to control, among other things, the opium trade and opium traders, Parliament would have to have been consulted, and the members on the benches opposite would have been the first to reject such a proposal.

The Foreign Secretary was characteristically forthright and dismissive in his demolition of the opposition's case, accusing some of their speakers, notably Gladstone, of not having properly read the papers. His defence of Elliot was fulsome:

All the Gentlemen who had spoken on the opposite side, with a few trifling exceptions, had, he was gratified to say, dwelt upon the conduct of Captain Elliot in terms more of approval than of criticism. He was happy to say this, for it was a principle which ought always to be kept in view in party contests, that whilst they struggled for power, which was an object of honourable ambition, and whilst they attacked each other with all the skill which they could command, the servants of the Crown performing important duties on foreign stations, in which duties they had no personal interest, should be unaffected by the proceedings of parties in that House. He was happy to say, that on that score he had no fault to find with the resolution, nor, save a few exceptions, with the speeches by which it was supported. He felt it due to Captain Elliot, whose zeal, courage and patience had been signally exhibited in these transactions, to clear up two points on which his conduct had been subject to criticism.[27]

The two points were that Elliot had encouraged the opium trade, and that he had tried to stop opium ships from being attacked, both of which Palmerston refuted by reference to the *Correspondence*. Graham's attempt to have the last word for the opposition foundered when he announced that he intended 'to follow the noble Lord through the various parts of his speech', at which point weary Members decided enough was enough, and forced a division.[28] The government prevailed with a majority of nine, 271 votes to 262.

With criticism of the government's handling of affairs thus narrowly set aside, the Lords had their say nearly four weeks later, on 12 May. The case against was put by Earl Stanhope, who was highly critical of Elliot as well as of the government. His emphasis was on the opium trade – Chinese motivation for wanting to suppress it, the economic as well as the ethical dimension, and (as he saw them) British connivance at its continuation and Elliot's dilatoriness in taking such action as he could to try to stop it. The debate was relatively short. Stanhope's was the only attempt of any substance to address the issue, and it was countered forcefully by the Duke of Wellington and by the Prime Minister, Lord Melbourne. The Duke expressed great sympathy for Elliot: 'he had never in his life seen on the part of the authorities in any country such language as had been written to Captain Elliot by the officers of the Chinese Government ... he had never heard of a person filling a high station in another country being treated in such a manner as Captain Elliot had been treated by the authorities of the Chinese Government at Canton.'[29]

Melbourne's contribution contained a brief description of the origin of opium trading from India, alluding to the ambivalent attitude of the Chinese authorities before and after 1796, when its importation had been decreed illegal. Of more immediate relevance were two specific points. The obligation of visitors to a foreign country to abide by the laws of their hosts was not in doubt, Melbourne said, but what was less clear was how far an official representative of those visitors should be responsible for enforcing compliance upon his compatriots. Secondly, there would have been no point at all in sending more specific instructions to the Chief Superintendent, since the situation on the ground would have changed entirely by the time they arrived.

The Prime Minister's defence of Elliot's conduct was emphatic. Stanhope, he said,

> had made a most severe, bitter, and in many respects most unjustifiable attack on the gentleman to whom were committed the interests of this country in that quarter of the globe, and who had conducted himself throughout with the greatest coolness, ability, and judgement.... Considering the situation in which Captain Elliot was placed – considering the novelty of the circumstances with which he had to deal, and the dangers by which he was surrounded – he [Melbourne] was not prepared to say, that every act was precisely the best that could have been suggested, but at the same time he was very loth, at so great a distance and in ignorance of the circumstances, to pass

any censure on him; on the contrary, so far as he could form
a judgment, that officer appeared to have conducted himself
with the greatest judgment, the greatest prudence, the greatest
firmness, and the greatest resolution.[30]

Earl Stanhope had proposed that the Queen be petitioned to take such
measures as were necessary to prevent further opium trading with China;
an amendment that no action be taken was carried without a division.
That Elliot emerged from the debates in Parliament with his reputation
largely intact was in part the result of lobbying on his behalf by his friend
Henry Taylor, at this time working closely with senior civil servants at
the Colonial Office. He had assembled a digest of Elliot's dispatches, to
which he had added comment and argument, and ensured that it was
seen by both Palmerston and the Duke of Wellington in time for the
debates. Taylor later recalled that: 'It was a successful effort ... I wrote to
my mother, 18 May 1840: "Charles Elliot has got nothing but credit on
all hands, as far as I can hear; and my digest, that is, in point of fact, his
own dispatches, have had all the effect I could have wished".'[31]

On the China coast Elliot awaited the arrival of the expeditionary
force. It would not have been lost on critics of the disproportionate
influence, as they saw it, of the Minto Elliots that including Charles the
three senior British officers now responsible for operations against China
were all first cousins. The assembling and preparation of the fleet was
within the remit of the First Lord of the Admiralty, Lord (Gilbert) Minto,
elder son of Hugh Elliot's brother Gilbert, the first Earl. The force's
formal commander-in-chief was the Governor General of India, Lord
(George) Auckland, son of Hugh Elliot's sister Eleanor. A fourth cousin,
Auckland's sister Emily (Eden), a much travelled artist and writer who
was with her brother in India, had written in January to the First Lord:

> I hope, Gilbert, you have taken care to send us out force enough
> to settle China in a short dashing manner. It must be a rapid
> business – because we *must* go home in March 1841 – and
> I suppose George will not stir till that business is done and he is
> made Marquess of Kwangfoo – then I am so afraid we sh[oul]d
> be thrilled for tea in our respectable old age.[32]

Emily did not court controversy, but she was not fazed by it; her usually
gentle, sometimes barbed, and always perceptive wit was doubtless
reinforced by her association with such contemporaries as Clerk to the
Privy Council and diarist Charles Greville, with whom she corresponded
and who was to some extent a kindred spirit in the directness with which
he expressed his views.[33] He had no time for Lord Minto:

> For a long time this government has been embarrassed by having
> such a man as Minto among them, and in such an office as First

Lord of the Admiralty, where there is enormous patronage and where the navy is the department most anxiously and jealously regarded by the country. He is in all respects incompetent … and he is besides a great and notorious jobber, and more than suspected of a want of political integrity.[34]

Highly placed members of the Elliot family were as vulnerable to criticism and personal invective as anyone else in public life, as Charles Elliot was acutely aware and as *The Times* had recently demonstrated: 'are these the people', it had demanded to know, ' – this tribe of Admiralty Elliots, from Lord Minto down – who can safely be trusted by the people of England with whatever is most dear to nations?'[35]

The early months of 1840, another period of relative quiet (though this time without the calming influence of Clara), gave Elliot space in which to marshal his thoughts and contemplate the longer term. Deciding that attack was the best form of defence, and of course in ignorance at this stage of the support he had had in Parliament, he wrote to Emma – on 12 May, the date of the Lords debate – a robust justification of his actions. His letter contained the usual solicitous enquiries about the children, and equally customary descriptions of his own feelings. Even allowing for exaggeration and his fragile mental state, it sets out concisely how he saw his own record, betraying in the process an incipient bitterness:

Be under no fear. I shall be abused, and probably removed, but *I can show* that I have saved as terrible a commercial whirlwind as ever threatened British India … I am not speaking idly when I assure you that I have resolved to answer the government *there* [in London] if they do not do me *full justice*. I know I have the heart to talk the matter of my need out. And I know that I have that to say which will cover every body concerned except myself, with condign shame.

I foresaw all; warned the government over and over again, and when the storm burst I was enabled to turn it aside by incurring personal risks and personal responsibilities, which I might easily have avoided. The Government and the Country owe me deepest thanks … It will be wise and right to give me bare justice. I want no more from them. In my condition and temper of life (if I may use such an expression) praise cannot gratify me and ill-deserved censure shall not wound or subdue me.

No man has had a harder task to perform and never was a hard task so successfully worked out…. A huge improvement, dear Emy, in affairs of commercial crisis. And where is the praise? The British Government, or at least the British Indian Government, are neither more nor less than the *Merchants* of this day. They had greatly overproduced. They had utterly disregarded any consideration of honor or prudence and it was cast upon me to relieve them of their difficulty. That has been done; but frankly the anxiety, the incessant anxiety of my situation has been almost too much for me.

You will be distressed to hear that I have *fancied* (and the fancy is terrible) that my mind is *not quite steady*. For God's sake do not mention this. I have had great difficulty at times in preserving a hold, a firm hold over my thoughts. This is a heavy wretchedness dear Emy but perhaps it is only fancy and I strive to keep myself calm.[36]

The British expeditionary force which reached the waters off Macao during the last week of June comprised vessels from Calcutta, Trincomalee and England. The majority of the ships had assembled at Singapore. They included the returning line-of-battle ship *Wellesley* (74 guns), two sixth rate frigates *Alligator* (28) and *Conway* (26), the brig-sloop *Algerine* (10), the sloop *Larne* (18), two East India Company steamships *Atalanta* and *Madagascar*, and some twenty or more transports and storeships. They carried three British and Irish infantry regiments along with marines, sepoys, artillery, engineers, and miners, a total of more than 3,500 men. What they did not have, however, was the expedition's designated commander. That responsibility fell first to the commander-in-chief of the East Indies and China station, Rear Admiral Sir Frederick Maitland, who with many others on the *Wellesley* – his flagship – had died of illness on the voyage from India. His replacement was another of Charles Elliot's first cousins, Rear Admiral George Elliot, commander-in-chief of the Cape station.[37] The appointment was not particularly welcome to Charles; he confided to Emma that:

Poor old Maitland's death was a sad stroke to me for he was very kind to me. I could have managed him more easily than I may be able to Cousin George who will probably follow him. He is a good fellow but I have no opinion of his capacity. His gravity indeed is considerable, but gravity is only the varnish of wisdom.[38]

When he was appointed to succeed Maitland, Admiral Elliot was at sea. He did not know of his assignment in time to rendezvous with the main force at Singapore, which sailed for the Gulf of Canton under the command of the most senior officer, Commodore Sir James Gordon Bremer. When Bremer arrived in HMS *Wellesley* off Macao, Charles Elliot's immediate task was to confer with him about the objectives and direction of the forthcoming campaign. The basis of their discussion was three communications from the Foreign Secretary, of which one was for the Chinese government and two were for the Elliots, now appointed, unusually, Joint Plenipotentiaries. The intention, it seemed, was that the admiral should be in overall command of the expeditionary force, but that Charles should have particular responsibility for political and diplomatic interaction with the Chinese. Such an arrangement was potentially fraught with scope for disagreement and consequent indecision, but in the event, perhaps because of kinship, there was little difficulty. In the meantime, pending Admiral Elliot's arrival, Palmerston's instructions were received by Charles Elliot and the commodore with some reservations on Elliot's part. Unlike the Foreign Secretary's earlier briefings they were operationally specific. The force was to establish a blockade of the Pearl River and then go north; it was to blockade key ports on the way, occupy the island of Zhoushan, and advance to the mouth of the Beihe River where, in addition to copies to be passed to the Chinese en route, the terms of a treaty prepared by Palmerston were to be delivered for onward transmission to the Emperor. The plan was based in large measure on advice given to Palmerston earlier by Jardine.

Despite his previous advocacy of prompt and overwhelmingly decisive action, Elliot's approach to the application of military force now reflected his overall strategy for dealings with the Chinese. Progress would best be achieved gradually and in order; there would need to be clear evidence of the seriousness of British intent, and attempting to engage Beijing without first fully controlling Canton and, preferably, part of the Yangtse basin, was in his view unlikely to succeed. Hastily imposed (and perhaps not wholly effective) blockades along the coast would not, in Elliot's view, be enough. On this occasion, however, there was unequivocally no room for discretion. The expedition set off on the 800 mile voyage to Zhoushan, which it reached on 1 July. Bremer had meanwhile ordered five ships, led by HMS *Druid* (46 guns), to enforce a blockade of the Pearl River.

Charles Elliot had not been the only one to be contemplating British offensive action in the Pearl River. Lin Zexu, now appointed substantive Governor General of Guangdong and Guangxi provinces, had authorised the reinforcement of defensive installations on the approaches to Canton, and when the British ships departed (he knew not where to) he found no difficulty in reporting that they had been deterred by the strength of the Chinese fortifications.[39] Chinese officials at Zhoushan also misinterpreted British intentions; used to equating the number of visiting foreign ships with possibilities for trade and profit they were, on seeing so great a number of vessels,

> At first ... rather puzzled. But the explanation soon occurred to them, and they guffawed with joy. Obviously the ships had assembled because of the cessation of trade at Canton. They rejoiced that "Ding-hai [Zhoushan's main town] will become a great trading centre, and we shall all make more and more money out of them day by day".[40]

With the arrival on 6 July of HMS *Melville* (74 guns), the flagship carrying the two Elliots, the British force at Zhoushan comprised fifteen armed ships and twenty-six troopships and transports. It had taken less than ten minutes' bombardment the previous day by just a few British men-of-war to end the resistance – spirited though it was – of the Chinese. There had been prior negotiation to see if conflict could be avoided, but although the local commander recognised that his guns and troops would be no match for the British force, he had felt duty-bound to fight. Before British infantry went ashore most of the population of Ding-hai had fled, leaving the town to looters and enabling many soldiers of the British force, when they arrived, to drink themselves senseless on the local liquor.[41]

With little delay the Joint Plenipotentiaries set sail for the Beihe River, but not before they had been obliged to transfer from the *Melville*, which had struck a rock and required extensive repairs, to the *Wellesley*. Elliot had sent an upbeat message to Clara, who wrote to Emma en voyage from Singapore to Calcutta:

> Thank God on 13th August, 2 days before we left Singapore, I received a joyful letter from Charlie imploring me to keep up my own spirits & to rejoice with him on the safe arrival of the Admiral and expedition in China & upon his high and new office of 'Plenipotentiary'. He tells me nothing could have been more kind & *wise too* than Lord Palmerston's support. In the event of any accident to the Admiral he is to have the entire management of the diplomatic post of the expedition and *not* the next in command.[42]

Clara was also more sanguine now about Charles's safety and her own future, and his absence made her heart grow fonder:

> Perhaps you may be surprised when I tell you the most painful part of my suspense is over. So long as Charlie remained in Macao with placards posted about offering a reward for his head there might be some danger, but now that I know he is on board a 74 surrounded by such friends, I laugh at the idea of the Chinese getting hold of him...
> ...If about February there be no chance of a return to China, I will take my passage for England and try to find consolation at least in the charge of our darlings. I cannot bring myself to hope for this. Is it not flattering & surprising too that the love of the Wife should be so much stronger than that of the mother of such 3 children.[43]

The flotilla that arrived at the mouth of the Beihe River at the end of the first week in August 1840 comprised Her Britannic Majesty's Ships *Wellesley*, *Blonde* (46 guns), *Volage*, *Modeste* (18) and *Pylades* (18), the *Madagascar* steamer and three transports – more than enough firepower to counter any Chinese attack; but the purpose of the Plenipotentiaries was negotiation and such aggression was not expected. For the British it was to be a visit of much waiting around, either requiring the necessary patience when dealing with the Chinese or involving intolerable frustration, according to temperament and point of view. The shallow waters and mud flats of the Beihe estuary obliged the ships to keep their distance from the coast for fear of running aground. When the tides allowed, Charles Elliot and Lieutenant Bingham of the *Modeste* set off with a number of ships' boats to deliver a request that the Chinese government receive Palmerston's communication. The request was granted, though the British had to wait two days for this news. It would take another twelve days for the Foreign Secretary's letter to be conveyed to Beijing, considered, and answered. The reply, inviting the British to a meeting at a hastily constructed venue near the mouth of the river, arrived as Admiral Elliot, having lost patience, was about to order an attack on the Chinese forts.

Charles Elliot's Chinese interlocutor on 30 August was Qishan, Viceroy of the local province of Zhili. Eleven years older than Elliot, Qishan had, with support in high places, risen effortlessly through the ranks of Chinese officialdom. His diplomatic skills were well developed, and his approach to negotiation with the British visitors was emollient. In the Chinese tradition of hospitality to foreigners they were guests, not intruders; if they were treated calmly and civilly the heat would go out of the situation and an amicable solution would be found. There was moreover no hurry so far as Qishan was concerned. Elliot, also (up to a point) a relatively patient man, and Qishan established a measure of *rapport*, but the Viceroy could not enter into any commitment. After six hours the meeting ended with nothing agreed except that the British would withdraw from Zhoushan once there was a settlement, and that negotiations should continue where all the difficulties had first arisen, at Canton.

Palmerston's letter, which was before Elliot and Qishan in the original and in translation, began by summarising the general objectives of the British:

> Her Majesty the Queen of Great Britain has sent a Naval and Military Force to the Coast of China, to demand from The Emperor satisfaction and redress for injuries inflicted by Chinese Authorities upon British subjects resident in China, and for insults offered by the same Authorities to the British Crown.[44]

It continued with some background – from the British point of view – before registering strong objection to Chinese hypocrisy, as the British saw it, over action against the opium trade. Why had the Chinese government moved against foreigners while doing nothing about widespread encouragement of opium importing, in defiance of Chinese law, by its own officers? At the very least, action should have been taken to seize the opium, not to subject merchants to violence. The conduct of the Chief Superintendent was supported by Her Majesty's Government; he should not have been made to do the Chinese government's work by arranging the surrender of the opium, and he had had no choice, as the Queen's representative, but to seek to protect British subjects.

The British demands made no mention of the future of the opium trade, focusing on reparation for the insult and indignity directed at British subjects and the Crown and seeking guarantees for British commerce in general:

> that the Ransom [opium] which was exacted as the price for the lives of the Superintendent, and of the imprisoned British merchants, shall be restored to the persons who paid it, and if ... they cannot be restored to their owners in the same state in which they were given up, then the British Government demands and requires that the value of those goods shall be paid back by the Government of China to the British Government, in order that it may be paid over to the parties entitled to receive it. ... The British Government demands satisfaction from the Government of China for the affront offered to the Crown of Great Britain, by the indignities to which Her Majesty's Superintendent has been subjected; and the British Government requires that in future the officer employed by Her Majesty ... shall be treated ... in a manner consistent with the usages of civilized Nations, and with the respect due to the Dignity of the British Crown. ... The British Government demands security for the future, that British Subjects ... shall not again be exposed to violence and injustice while engaged in their lawful pursuits of Commerce. For this purpose ... the British Government demands that one or more sufficiently large and properly situated Islands on the Coast of China, to be fixed upon by the British Plenipotentiaries, shall be permanently given up to the British Government as a place of residence and of commerce for British Subjects; where their persons may be safe from molestation, and where their Property may be secure.[45]

The letter also demanded that the Chinese Government recompense the British merchants for debts they had incurred from transactions with those Hong merchants who had become insolvent. Palmerston indicated that such was the importance of the matter that the naval and military force had been sent without waiting for a reply to the demands, and that its Commander had orders not just to approach within a short distance of Beijing, but before that to blockade Chinese ports, detain Chinese vessels, and occupy a convenient piece of Chinese territory.

It was hardly surprising that Qishan could not react positively to any of this. Equally, Elliot could not react entirely negatively to Qishan's stance. For practical reasons – the geography of the Beihe delta, the supply situation, the poor health of some of the troops and crew – the expedition was in no position to advance upriver, and in any case Elliot sought to avoid conflict if possible. Both Elliot and Qishan were trying to find a solution; precipitate action did not commend itself to either of them. This cautious approach, continued over the next few months, would cause both men difficulties with their respective governments.

When the British ships cast anchor at Zhoushan on the return voyage south they found that a measure of civil normality had resumed. Many who had fled at the time of the British attack had come back, and supply routines had been reinstated. The garrison, however, was in a poor state; more than a third of the occupying force were now invalids or had died and hospital care was seriously deficient. Charles Elliot had one important task, to seek the release of five Britons who had been captured and imprisoned at Ningbo. He was doubtless greatly disappointed that he was not successful; he would have been personally sympathetic to their plight as human beings, and the humiliation of British subjects abroad was something to which he, like Palmerston, reacted strongly.[46]

The Elliots reached the Gulf of Canton on 20 November. Qishan arrived nine days later, but they did not then meet. Charles conducted the British side of the negotiation from the *Wellesley*, corresponding with Qishan via messenger. The arrangement allowed considered thought to be given to each communication, but was vulnerable to delays in reply. Agreement was reached on the amount of compensation ($6 million) to be paid for the confiscated opium and for money owing from the Hong merchants, but there was a long silence from Qishan when the question of a further British trading port or ports on the China coast was raised. As the end of the year approached there had still been no more progress and Elliot's patience was wearing thin. He was now without his erstwhile adversary Lin, who had been dismissed for failing to eliminate the opium trade and expel the foreigners and had been replaced as commissioner by Qishan. He was also no longer in joint charge with his cousin the admiral, who because of continuing illness had resigned his command and left on the *Volage*. Buoyed up by his new found freedom of manoeuvre, Elliot moved the fleet upriver to a point south of the Bogue.

The second Battle of Chuanbi was to be, predictably, as one-sided as the first. The British ships now included the recently arrived *Nemesis*, a revolutionary new iron paddle steamer armed with heavy cannon, swivel guns and a rocket launcher, whose shallow draught allowed her to manoeuvre easily in rivers and creeks. A combined land and sea assault under Bremer's command was launched against the two outer forts. A force of some 1,500 marines, armed seamen and sepoys took the first (Chuanbi) with the support of bombardment from the sea by the *Nemesis* and another steamer, the *Queen*. The second fort (Taikoktow (Dajiaotou)) was swiftly put out of action by broadsides from the *Druid*, the 28-gun sixth-rate *Samarang*, and two 18-gun sloops *Modeste* and *Columbine*. The *Nemesis* wreaked havoc on a fleet of around fifteen war junks assembled in Anson's Bay, just upriver of the Chuanbi fort on the eastern side of the Bogue.

Elliot saw no need to inflict more destruction on the Chinese than was necessary. Wanting now to see whether Qishan was prepared to progress to a settlement, he sent word to Admiral Guan Tianpei from the *Wellesley* that if the Chinese were to announce a ceasefire, the British would halt their action. James Matheson thought that 'Both the Commodore and Captain Elliot appeared to have a compunctious feeling, not perhaps unnatural, at having to attack and slaughter beings so helpless and incapable of defending themselves as the Chinese'.[47] Guan obliged, enabling Elliot and Qishan to continue their exchanges. Now demonstrably able to call all the shots, Elliot steered the negotiations to a point at which a provisional agreement was reached.

The Convention of Chuanbi provided for diplomatic relations between Britain and China to be on the basis of equality; for the resumption of trade at Canton; for payment of $6million indemnity; and for the cession of the island of Hong Kong to the British. Zhoushan would be returned to China. Aware that he had come away from the Beihe without having achieved what Palmerston had required, and doubtless also that there were those of his countrymen who had become impatient with what they regarded as his vacillating behaviour, Elliot was now keen to be able to demonstrate a positive outcome. After a reconnoitre by Captain Edward Belcher and the survey ship HMS *Sulphur* the day before, possession of Hong Kong was formally taken on 26 January 1841 by Commodore Bremer, accompanied by a large contingent of naval officers and marines.

The declaration of possession was followed three days later by a proclamation by Elliot that the government of Hong Kong would be the responsibility of the Chief Superintendent of Trade and that the Chinese population would be subject to Chinese law, except that all forms of torture were prohibited. The British and other non-Chinese would be subject to English law.

The problem was that Qishan had not actually signed the Convention, and the Daoguang Emperor refused to contemplate agreement to what it set out; nor was the British government, when word of its terms reached London in April, prepared to endorse what Elliot had done. The Son of Heaven made it clear to Qishan that he regarded 'the demands of the rebellious foreigners totally excessive ... it's time to dispatch a punitive mission to suppress them.... If they try to hand over any more communications, you are not permitted to receive them.'[48] Palmerston angrily wrote to Elliot:

> You have disobeyed and neglected your Instructions; you have deliberately abstained from employing the Force placed at your disposal; and you have without sufficient necessity accepted

Terms which fall far short of those you were instructed to obtain. You were instructed to demand full compensation for the opium which you took upon you two Years ago to deliver up. To ask Parliament to pay the money was out of the question. You have accepted a sum much smaller than the amount due to the opium holders. You were told to demand payment of the expenses of the expedition, and payment of Hong debts. You do not appear to have done one or the other. You were told to retain Chusan (Ting-hai) until the whole of the pecuniary Compensation should be paid, but you have agreed to evacuate the island immediately. You have obtained the cession of Hong-Kong, a barren Island with hardly a House upon it. Now it seems obvious that Hong-Kong will not be a Mart of Trade, any more than Macao is so. However, it is possible I may be mistaken in this matter. But you still will have failed in obtaining that which was a Capital point in our view: an additional opening for our Trade to the Northward.[49]

It was as well that at the end of January 1841 on the South China coast Charles Elliot had no inkling of how the Foreign Secretary would react to the agreement he had reached with Qishan. His mood was positive; he had after all achieved significant concessions from the Chinese which would, he believed, lay the foundations for the development of British trade with China, and had maintained British honour with minimal use of force. He had still not, though, obtained Qishan's signature to the Convention, despite the commissioner's celebratory behaviour. Nevertheless, Elliot pressed on. Having with Bremer proclaimed the inhabitants of Hong Kong subjects of Her Britannic Majesty, he gave orders for the Zhoushan garrison, much depleted through disease, to withdraw and rejoin the rest of the force.

Hearing in mid-February that Qishan had been dismissed and that Chinese reinforcements were on their way, Elliot decided that immediate action was needed and brought the British ships up to launch a pre-emptive assault on the remaining Bogue forts. On 26 February bombardments led by the three 74s, *Blenheim, Melville* and *Wellesley*, overcame such Chinese resistance as there was, and by the end of the following day a smaller force including the *Nemesis*, on which Charles Elliot accompanied Captain Hall, had dispersed a flotilla of war-junks and cleared obstacles placed in the river. After little over two weeks which the *Nemesis* spent neutralising Chinese fortifications in the river passages west of the main channel, the force reached the waterfront at Canton. Many of the local inhabitants had already fled; those that had not did so now. On 20 March, with echoes of his action nearly two years earlier, Charles Elliot raised the Union Jack in the New English factory. He announced a ceasefire, and also as he had done before, a resumption of trade.

A month before, Lord Auckland, Governor General of India, had written to his cousin Lord Minto, First Lord of the Admiralty, on hearing of the Convention of Chuanbi and the acquisition of Hong Kong. Deeply unhappy at what he considered wasted opportunities for the force he had dispatched to bring matters to a head, he confided:

> I own that I have read the last reports from Charles Elliot, as I have read many upon the expedition that preceded them in extreme depression, and it is inconceivable to me how little, from the first arrival of our armament in China, those who were appointed to lead it, have grasped great prospects, and how feebly and imperfectly the instructions of the government have been executed. It is a matter for very painful reflection. We have lost one third of our soldiers.... And we have a preliminary treaty and a promise of six million dollars and possession of the island of Hong Kong subject to confirmation by the Emperor – to whom customs' duties of our new settlement are to be paid.[50]

Despite these serious misgivings, Auckland allowed the possibility that others might take a more positive view of events thus far, conceding that 'Hong Kong may become a valuable possession'.[51] He believed nevertheless that even if this proved to be the case, everything should have been done much more quickly.

With greater speed and decisiveness in mind, Auckland now sent a new commander of land forces to the China coast, the performance of the elderly Lieutenant Colonel George Burrell, the senior officer at Zhoushan, having given cause for concern. The new man was Major General Sir Hugh Gough, second-in-command at Madras and a highly distinguished and experienced soldier. Though like Burrell he was in his early sixties, he was an energetic and clear thinking commander, who soon made an impact in China. At about the same time Commodore Bremer decided to leave the coast for Calcutta, probably for health reasons. By seniority the new naval commander-in-chief became Captain Sir Humphrey Le Fleming Senhouse, of HMS *Blenheim*. Approaching sixty, he too was an officer with much experience, having served at Trafalgar and on the North American and West Indies stations.

A more robust and determined approach on the Chinese side was similarly signalled by changes in senior personnel. Qishan had submitted to the Emperor a report on the relative feebleness of Chinese military preparedness which was too honest and conciliatory for the Emperor to want to hear. Shortly afterwards, having already incurred the anger of the Emperor for his role in the Convention of Chuanbi, Qishan was recalled and replaced by a triumvirate headed by the aristocrat Yishan and including the illustrious but elderly and ailing General Yang Fang. They arrived in Canton on 5 March.

During April the legitimate trade, especially in tea, prospered. Opium smuggling also picked up along the coast, and Senhouse refused Elliot's request to prevent smaller vessels from carrying opium into the Pearl

River maintaining, correctly, that Elliot had no authority for such a move. The apparent return to something like commercial normality belied the climate of increasing tension, as the Chinese redoubled their efforts to prepare for further conflict and the British planned the next stage of their campaign. These weeks were also, for Charles Elliot, a rare opportunity for renewed focus on his family. Clara returned to Macao from India, as Charles wrote to their children on 24 April:

> Mama came back to me safe thank God – such safe a week ago in one of the clippers. It was very good of her to undertake such a voyage at an unfavourable season of the year in a small vessel. But her affection for me, and her sense of duty, made the hardship nothing. Let her always be an example to you, Harriet, for she is a devoted wife and mother, and all our best friend. She has found the house in an uncomfortable state enough, but she will soon get it to rights.[52]

Continuing with some fond advice and encouragement to Hughie and Gibby he concludes, revealingly:

> Pray to God regularly night and morning for assistance, *and remember* to ask for forgiveness for anything that your own heart tells you is wrong. I am afraid you have all inherited some of that impatience and impetuosity which are my worst faults, and if you love me, which I am sure you do, you must try to correct these defects. Give my most affectionate love to your Aunt Windsor and now my children – accept my blessing, and believe me your ever affectionate father.[53]

Elliot was probably being hard on himself in citing impatience as one of his worst faults, but he was certainly impetuous on occasion. To the military minds of General Gough and Captain Senhouse, however, he appeared differently – vacillating, indecisive, and as Gough put it 'whimsical as a shuttlecock'.[54] Gough must have been conscious also that the Plenipotentiary was in service rank two below him, far less militarily experienced, and more than twenty years his junior.

On 11 May Elliot became alarmed at the scale and pace of Chinese strengthening of defences and troop reinforcements at Canton. He cancelled a planned move against Xiamen, ordered the British force upriver to Canton, and advised those traders still in the Factories to leave. After an unsuccessful surprise attack by the Chinese on 21 May, Gough and Senhouse took the *Nemesis*, with some sixty or more boats in tow, up a channel to the west. The occupants of the boats, around three thousand soldiers, sailors and marines – almost the whole expeditionary force – disembarked two miles northwest of Canton. From there they made their way towards the northern heights above the city, which Gough had calculated would give him a position from which to launch a decisive assault. It was not to be. While Gough was assessing the likely strength and locations of Chinese resistance before making his final deployments, he received word from the Plenipotentiary telling him to not attack. '[T]he protection of the people of Canton, and the encouragement of their goodwill towards us, are perhaps our chief political duties in this country' wrote Elliot.[55] Gough and Senhouse, predictably, were extremely unhappy; they had marched their troops to the top of the hill, and as a result of a decision they considered all too typical of Elliot, now faced the prospect of marching them down again. As one of the officers with the Madras Infantry contemptuously put it: 'Here was our small army to remain for a certain number of days, barely 100 paces removed from the city walls, surrounded by many thousands of an enemy ... and in this peculiar position we were directed to remain by a post captain in the Royal Navy'.[56] The military had no choice but to comply with the instruction, however, which followed yet more negotiation between the Chief Superintendent and the Chinese. The outcome was that a ransom of $6million (the same amount as in the Convention of Chuanbi) was to be paid, the Chinese reinforcements at Canton were to withdraw, compensation was to be provided for damage and injury to property and individuals, and the British would remove their ships from the Pearl River.

They duly did, and the Chinese kept their side of the agreement, but not before Gough had dealt with what the British subsequently considered to have been a little local difficulty. The villagers of Guangdong province, as elsewhere in rural China, were both xenophobic and had little in common with city-dwellers. The inhabitants of Sanyuanli and other nearby villages in the hinterland of Canton, as customary when sensing external threat, had formed local militias. The threat represented by the foreign devils was compounded, as they saw it, by the feeble capitulation of the Canton mandarins. Some of these militias encountered detachments of Gough's troops behaving with provocative disrespect for their communities. When the desecration of graves was followed by assaults on women, they moved against the British. The skirmishes lasted a week, and involved more than a thousand villagers. Though the Chinese were primitively armed, torrential rain all but neutralised the superior weapons of the British, the encounters then mostly taking the form of hand-to-hand combat. Gough's men saw off the Chinese attacks, but the peasants regrouped; further fighting was averted when a messenger from the city persuaded the insurgents that a peace agreement had been reached, and they dispersed. From a British military perspective the Sanyuanli incident, as it became known, was a minor setback, satisfactorily dealt with, in an otherwise straightforward campaign which demonstrated overwhelming British superiority. For the Chinese, it became regarded as a major example of heroic anti-imperialist resistance, and has remained so in Chinese official consciousness ever since.

At the beginning of June British attention turned to the next phase. The plan, agreed some weeks earlier, was for the expeditionary force to sail north again to secure key ports and threaten Beijing. The force was not, though, in good shape. The operations on the river and around Canton, in heat, poor weather and often difficult terrain had taken their toll in illness and deaths. On 13 June Senhouse became a fatal casualty himself; he was buried, like Napier and Robert Morrison, in the Protestant Cemetery at Macao. Charles Elliot, too, was ill, but not until he had embarked on the first steps to settle Hong Kong.

Within days of the island's being proclaimed British some of the merchants, Jardine Matheson among the first, staked their claims by erecting temporary godowns (warehouses) on the north shore adjacent to the harbour. The development was entirely unplanned and the siting of the buildings uncoordinated, but they were subsequently connected in these early months by the construction of what became Queen's Road. Elliot made his first appointment, of William Caine as magistrate, in April, but it was not until his return from Canton in June that the first official sales of plots of land began. A further proclamation by Elliot in June, which was to have a lasting impact on the development of Hong Kong, announced that the territory was to be a free port, with no charges payable to the British government. When Elliot prepared to go north with the expeditionary force his long-standing Deputy, A.R. Johnston, was left in charge.

As Elliot and Bremer, who had returned from India as Joint Plenipotentiary, made their way by cutter to join the *Wellesley* for the voyage up the coast, the start of the main typhoon season announced itself with ferocious force. The *Louisa* lost her master overboard and was swept way off course until Charles Elliot managed to steer her to an inlet at Sanchuen. Those on board were with difficulty able to get off, but the vessel was then smashed to pieces on the rocks. Elliot and Bremer paid some local villagers to ferry them to Macao which they reached, after their boat came close to being stopped and searched by an official patrol, on 24 July. As he was about to make his way ashore, he was given the news from London that his time in China was about to end. Palmerston had written formally in early May:

> I have to state to you that Her Majesty's Government do not approve of the manner in which, in your negotiation with the Chinese Commissioner, you have departed from the instructions with which you have been furnished ... Her Majesty has determined to place the conduct of her affairs in China in the hands of another Plenipotentiary.[57]

'To this [news] Elliot made answer, that to be cast ashore at Sanchuen, and find himself adrift at Macao, was more than a man had a right to expect in one week, be he Plenipotentiary or be he not', and he quoted to the Commodore from Dryden's poem: '"Slack all thy sails, for thou art wrecked ashore".'[58,59]

At this less than convenient juncture Elliot's brother Ned, whom he had not encountered for several years, now appeared. He and his family had been blown off course and forced to seek refuge at Macao. Elliot saw to it that they were properly accommodated: 'I left my dear old Ned and his family well in my house. The day I wrecked my poor little cutter in that terrible typhoon, he was within a few miles of the place we were cast on shore.'[60]

Charles Elliot's successor as Chief Superintendent and Plenipotentiary, Sir Henry Pottinger, arrived in August. There followed several months in which instructions to cease further civil development, from the Foreign Secretary to Pottinger and from Pottinger to Johnston, were either too late in arriving or were ignored anyway. They nevertheless created uncertainty about the future, which prompted Matheson to write to Jardine in London:

> I fear that Elliot's unpopularity will in some degree descend upon his pet child.... But I know not where else we could have got as harbour equally good, more especially for large vessels. Were we able to settle this in right earnest under the acknowledged and irrevocable protection of the British Government it could hardly fail to become a considerable Emporium.[61]

The new Foreign Secretary, Lord Aberdeen, and an indecisive Parliament were equivocal about Hong Kong's becoming a permanent acquisition. In the event, Elliot's eagerness to encourage building and settlement, Johnston's enthusiastic implementation of it and Pottinger's de facto endorsement led the British government to accept the cession of the territory. Pottinger had been unsure at first; as he put it to Aberdeen:'I had no predilection for raising a colony at Hong Kong or at any other place in China' but 'this settlement has already advanced too far to admit of its ever being restored to the authority of the Emperor.'[62] Hong Kong was formally proclaimed a Colony on 26 June 1843, Pottinger becoming its first Governor.

# Chapter Eleven

# Recall, Reaction and Resolve

The news of his recall – in effect, dismissal – took Charles Elliot aback, but it was not entirely unexpected. Although he had supporters in or close to government, he had always known that his continuation in post in China was dependent on the approval of the Foreign Secretary. He had been aware, too, that by comparison with his brief he had sometimes sailed very close to the wind. It was this which prompted him to ensure, as far as he could, that there was a particularly thorough written record of the reasons for his actions. With his natural proneness to verbosity the consequence was a very lengthy collection of correspondence. In the nearly four years between assuming the duties of Chief Superintendent and the start of the war, Elliot sent more than three times as many, and usually much longer, communications to Palmerston and the Foreign Office than he received from them.[1] While most of the Foreign Secretary's letters were instructional, descriptive and broadly neutral in tone, and a few were complimentary and encouraging, some were mildly or severely critical. Palmerston's opinion, and that of the government, Parliament and the British public, of Charles Elliot might have been very different had the threatening of Canton, and the resulting concessions, occurred and been fully reported before the letter recalling him was written.[2] Instead, London heard first from General Gough, smarting from the denial of what he considered an obvious opportunity for military victory. Henry Taylor, whose expressions of support and admiration for Elliot were sometimes excessive, wrote that

> unhappily that event was first announced in a despatch from the General in command of the forces, which was unaccompanied for the moment by any despatch from Elliot (always least occupied with what most concerned himself); and the General wrote in a spirit of grievous mortification and disappointment, as if, when Elliot had prevented Canton from being taken by storm, he had substituted some tame treaty for a magnificent feat of arms. Though at the date of the General's despatch, he and Charles Elliot were living together in the same house and on cordial and friendly terms, the despatch was not shown to him, and he only knew of its tenor when the return mail brought him the results of it in a clamorous echo by the press and the people of the General's cry of distress.[3]

Coming on top of news of the Convention of Chuanbi, what was portrayed by Gough as a failure to take Canton served to reinforce negative views of

Charles Elliot's conduct. Ironically, given his previously meticulous care to explain his actions, Elliot had not written to Palmerston after the Treaty to give his side of the story – an omission he later explicitly regretted.

The Elliots – Charles, Clara and Freddy – left Macao on 20 August 1841. The official grounds for his recall, as set out in the Foreign Secretary's letter of 21 April, gave Charles a clear indication of the kind of reception he could expect from his political masters in England. He was also aware of the adverse views of his cousins in India, Lord Auckland and Emily Eden. In reports and letters to Lord Minto, First Lord of the Admiralty and to other family and friends, they had over several months been emphatic in their criticism. Auckland complained mainly because of what he saw as the waste of the force he had assembled for campaigning in China; Emily, largely from a belief that Elliot had been far too conciliatory towards the Chinese. To what extent Emily was taking the lead in this from her brother, or vice versa, can only be guessed – but Charles himself (no doubt greatly irritated by her stance towards him) was clear. He commented later to Emma about the relationship that 'Lord Minto means well but his meaning is not a very strong meaning, and poor Lord Auckland means Emily – and Emily means herself and nothing else but herself.'[4]

In his February letter to Minto conveying his misgivings about the Convention of Chuanbi Auckland admitted that he did not know how gravely the situation would be viewed at home. He was certain, though, that there would be no enthusiasm for what Elliot was reported to have done – the most that could be hoped for was a grudging acceptance:

> You may make the worst of it, and I fear that there will be strong ground for discontent and displeasure. You may make the best of it, and it is possible that Hong Kong may become a valuable possession ... I am very mad with it all. And if I seem to express myself too bitterly, tear my letter.[5]

Emily too commented vigorously about China to her correspondents at home who included, as well as Charles Greville, her brother Robert and her widowed elder sister Eleanor, Countess of Buckinghamshire. To the countess, especially, Emily passed on regularly her reactions to reports from China, and in the early months of 1841 displayed mounting frustration. She wrote in January, after castigating Admiral George Elliot for having 'made a shocking mess of China', that

> Charles is now left sole Plenipotentiary, and if he can but keep to his own mind two days running is clever enough to do very well; but he is terribly vacillating. She [Clara] wishes very much that she was with him just now, and I can fancy she might be of use in keeping him up to the mark; but she cannot go during the present monsoon, and except for the pleasure of seeing Charles again, I think she will be very sorry to leave Calcutta.[6,7]

In April Emily was berating Charles as 'totally blind to his own folly ... half the men in his position would be driven to some act of desperation'; and to her brother she complained vehemently:

> if the Opposition did not take advantage of C. Elliot's first absurd peace, they may turn the Ministry out on finding it is no peace at all, and that, moreover, he has not left himself the means of carrying on a war. There never was such a man, if he were not a positive fool. I really think he would go mad when he looks back on all he has done this year. The last act of giving up Chusan, without waiting to see if the Emperor would ratify the treaty, is the crown of all his absurdity.... Everybody wonders what will be the next news ... I don't think my national pride was ever so much hurt.[8,9]

With observations like these circulating socially among politicians and others close to government in London, Elliot's reception on his return was unlikely to be wholly welcoming. Along with Palmerston's dissatisfaction with Elliot's record in China went an urgent desire to bring matters to a head and end the conflict decisively in Britain's favour. Sir Henry Pottinger, Charles Elliot's successor, was a soldier, a veteran of Sind, Baluchistan and the Third Maratha War in the service of the East India Company. He was also a diplomat, though one with a tendency to abrasiveness.[10] Pottinger had arrived nearly two weeks before the Elliots left, on 9 August, with Rear Admiral Sir William Parker, who was replacing Bremer as the senior naval officer. With orders from the Foreign Secretary to remedy the mistakes perpetrated by Charles Elliot, Pottinger, Gough and Parker sailed north with a reinforced expeditionary force on 21 August. By early October the British had captured Xiamen and taken Dinghai on Zhoushan. Emily Eden would have been gratified; on hearing of the expedition's departure northwards, she had, with her customary tendency to simplified overstatement, written to her sister the countess, exulting that 'The General and all the Navy people seem to be in ecstasies at having somebody who will not stop all their fighting, and I should not be at all surprised if Sir H. Pottinger finished it all in six months, merely by making war in a common straightforward manner.'[11]

In the same letter Emily reports on Clara Elliot's 'anger' at the way her husband was being treated, though when she wrote thirteen days later to Lord Minto (now no longer First Lord of the Admiralty) she said she had heard that Clara

> was in a state of great exasperation, particularly against Lord A which is unjust but perhaps natural. But she is consoled by the idea that the instant Charles's story is heard he will receive the *title* and *pension* which is his due. He seems to be of the same opinion and promises written and verbal explanations which cd have broken heavily on you if you had been in the way.[12]

Charles Elliot was of course aware that he had many critics and that some, taking their cue from Palmerston, were very highly placed; but he knew also that he had had some influential supporters. They included not only the elderly and respected Tory the Duke of Wellington, but also the Whig Prime Minister Melbourne, who was prepared to concede that the January 1841 Treaty had some merit. He had written in April to Lord John Russell, then Secretary of State for War and the Colonies, setting out his view:

> Palmerston is much dissatisfied with the Chinese treaty, particularly with the amount of indemnity and the time given for payment of it, and so am I. Palmerston is, or was, for disavowing Elliot and the treaty and for renewing the demands which he was instructed to make, but which it seems he never did make. I have grave doubts of this. The treaty as it stands saves our honour and produces all the necessary moral effect. To renew the war would keep the whole thing alive, which it is of the utmost importance to close. If we break a treaty clearly concluded by our Plenipotentiary the Chinese will be convinced that we never meant to observe that or any other treaty; and if we should obtain a larger compensation, which is uncertain, it certainly will not be so much larger as to pay for the increased expense to which we shall put ourselves.[13]

The division of opinion among politicians about Elliot's conduct was to some extent echoed in the trading community in Britain and in China. Most merchants were hostile. They saw the Plenipotentiary's conduct towards the Chinese as weak and against their own interests, depriving them through the surrender of opium of an important source of revenue, and promising them compensation which the British government might not pay. An anonymous and less than accurate earlier letter to *The Times* reflected their exaggerated reaction:

> Here, Sir, is a state of things! English merchants ruined, British subjects made to fly, and perhaps all would have been destroyed but for the protection, not of Her Majesty's ships, but of a benevolent Portuguese Governor.... What, Sir, is to be the amount of ruin our Government determines to bring upon our merchants and upon our disgraced country?[14]

One notable exception to this antagonism was James Matheson, who understood and appreciated the lengths to which Elliot had gone to keep legitimate trade flowing. Though the Company was heavily involved in opium, the volume of Jardine Matheson's other business, especially in tea, meant that it had more to lose than other, smaller, firms from the cessation of trade. By establishing warehousing and other facilities there the firm had also committed itself to Hong Kong. It had no wish to see British political criticism of Elliot lead to neglect or even abandonment of the settlement with which he was so closely associated. Aware of the continuing hostility towards Elliot of other merchants, notably Lancelot Dent, James Matheson wrote to his former partner, William Jardine, in London urging his support:

> Elliot is very much hurt at the extreme animosity with which some of our neighbours are persecuting him, by petition to the House of Commons &c.... [We should] ... do all we can to defend him. For this purpose I authorise your paying liberally any lawyer or other qualified person who will defend him in the newspapers.[15]

Though by modern standards their circulations were relatively small, the newspapers were an important influence on public opinion of events on the China coast and of Charles Elliot's role in them. Two of the leading London-based titles, *The Times* and *The Morning Post*, were sharply critical of British management of affairs in China. *The Times* treated the subject in considerable detail and published correspondence from a range of interested parties. The language of *The Morning Post* could be strident; an article welcoming Elliot's recall and Pottinger's appointment was a vitriolic mixture of hyperbole and hindsight:

> Public opinion has prevailed, and 'Charles Elliot, Esq., a Captain in the Royal Navy, Chief Superintendent of the Trade of British Subjects in China, and holding full Powers under the Great Seal of Great Britain and Ireland to execute the Office of her [sic] Majesty's Commissioner, Procurator, and Plenipotentiary in China' as the late functionary delighted to write his names, styles, and titles, is now plain Captain Charles Elliot. The incompetency of the late Chinese Plenipotentiary was more than a match for the Court and parliamentary influence of the Elliots, and the Government has been forced to recall him. Sorry are we that such a step was not taken when the circumstances attendant on the delivery of the opium to Commissioner Lin were first made known in England. The history of that bungled transaction ought to have satisfied the Government that Captain Elliot was totally disqualified to discharge with dignity and advantage to the country the duties of his high office.... We are, therefore, thankful to the Government for even now recalling Captain Elliot and replacing him by an officer so creditably known in India as Sir Henry Pottinger. With all John Chinaman's craft and chicanery, he will yet find a match in plain, honest, John Bull.[16]

As well as Chartist publications, which identified Charles Elliot with the evil of the opium trade, newspapers in the major centres of population outside London were similarly disapproving of the way in which British relations with China were being handled by the Plenipotentiary.[17] Often relying on reports from Bombay, they echoed the concerns of the articles in the Indian

(English language) press, which were heavily influenced by the British Indian government. *The Times*, from the time of its report in March 1840 that war had been declared on China, had in its coverage of Parliament and the conduct of ministers also been particularly scathing about the Foreign Secretary. An editorial in the same month contrasted him with Wellington:

> But how acts Lord Palmerston? His conduct is irritating, where the Duke of Wellington counsels conciliation, and his means of defence are feeble where the Duke advises that they should be formidable! Such is the essential difference between a great man and a man who is the reverse of great.[18]

To the extent that criticism was levelled at Palmerston and other members of the government, hostility towards Charles Elliot was mitigated. For *The Times*, as for many subsequent commentators, the issue was as much about the government's handling of Elliot as Elliot's handling of China. To the questions whether Palmerston had issued clear and practicable instructions; whether Elliot had disobeyed them; and whether if he had disobeyed them it was reasonable to have done so, Charles Elliot himself had robust answers. Aware that Melbourne's Whig administration had now been replaced by the Tories under Peel, he wrote to Emma on the voyage home, from Malta, in resolute terms:

> If I had found the late Government in power and strong I should have answered their [imputation] of misconduct in my respect with an immediate appeal to the public. But I remember me that they are knowing dogs in the art of knocking down their own best friends and I will not take a leaf out of their books and help their enemies, under existing circumstances. I propose, therefore, to send Lord Palmerston in a private way a sketch of that imposture of his sorry heedlessness which might be put forward, if I had not something more of discretion and sound feeling than he has manifested towards me.
>
> My country and my family, dear Emy, have no cause to be ashamed of me. I have prevented more desperate mischief, as indeed more blunders, *saved* more millions, recovered more millions, undergone more and more danger and received worse treatment than any officer in the public employment. The government can neither give nor take from me the distinction I have made for myself and I promise you that the time is at hand *when this will be fully felt.*[19]

Then, of his relationship with Palmerston:

> The truth is that I am mainly blamed for his ignorances and waywardnesses. The little he knows of the grave matters I have

been dealing with, I taught him, and it is my just reward that I did not teach him more. He, Auckland and myself have all been learning, and it is no matter of wonderment that each should know more than the other in this ratio of our reason [closeness?] to the scene of action and more entire devotion to the matters in hand.[20]

Earlier on the voyage Elliot had met up in Bombay with one of the prominent Parsee merchants who had trading operations in China, Jamsetjee Jeejeebhoy. They did not have much time together, and after the Elliots had departed his host wrote to Charles:

Strangers may not appreciate your labors, but I can assure you that the Trading Community of India will know and feel the relief you have afforded them. You were placed alone in China, unaided by any advisers and surrounded with the most serious and overwhelming difficulties, and I know not how sufficiently to express my admiration of your untiring zeal in the Public Service. Be assured you have my hearty good wishes, and I only hope the advisers of our Sovereign will confirm and approve of all your acts.[21]

On the China coast meanwhile, Pottinger and his military commanders with their force of more than 2,500 men and thirteen warships, including the *Nemesis* and the 74s *Blenheim* and *Wellesley,* proceeded after occupying Xiamen and Zhoushan to capture Zhenhai and Ningbo. Leaving behind garrisons as it progressed, the expedition became depleted and bogged down. Further reinforcements arrived in due course and in August 1842, aboard the 74-gun flagship HMS *Cornwallis*, the British and Chinese signed the Treaty of Nanking. Among other things the Treaty opened four more ports (in addition to Canton) to the British for trade; established parity of status in official communication between the two countries; provided that the Chinese meet the expense of the war; and ceded 'in perpetuity' the island of Hong Kong to Britain.[22] What Elliot had sought to achieve gradually by patient diplomacy backed up by the threat of arms, Pottinger had forcibly accomplished in twelve months. One long-term consequence was to be the maintenance by China, at the forefront of public consciousness into the twenty-first century, of the memory of its humiliation by western imperialists.

On the voyage home from China Charles Elliot learned of his appointment as British Consul General in the Republic of Texas.

## Chapter Twelve

# Texas: Spain, Mexico and the
# United States

In 1842 Texas had existed as an independent republic for just six years. From 1821, when Mexico achieved independence from Spain, it had been under Mexican control until 1836. Before that, for some three centuries, the dominant external influence had been Spain, whose military explorers were the first Europeans to settle the Caribbean, central America, the north of South America, and what is now the southern United States. In the period from 1519 to 1521 the Spanish under Hernan Cortes had overcome the central American Aztec empire, but to the extent that their aim was the exploitation of a vast new territory, in Texas and its hinterland the early conquistadores did not achieve much success. Expeditions during the 1520s, '30s and '40s did however cover many miles over many years, some of which were spent in captivity, and allowed the accumulation of much knowledge of the indigenous Indians and their way of life.[1] They also enabled the Spanish to gain valuable information concerning the geography, climate and natural resources of the region. Progress then, and subsequently, was nevertheless slow, hampered by tenacious resistance from some of the Indian communities. Such opposition persuaded the Spanish from 1585 to adopt, successfully, a conciliatory approach, essentially gifts in return for non-aggression. Religion was a powerful influence in Spanish policymaking. The national aim, if not always locally adhered to in practice, had been articulated by King Felipe II: 'Preaching the holy gospel is the principal purpose for which we order new discoveries and settlements to be made'.[2]

Regulation by the Spanish crown of those appointed to govern and develop its overseas possessions was never wholly effective. An attempt to mitigate the harsh treatment of Indians had been included in the 'New Laws', issued by the Emperor Charles V in 1542 which had laid upon the Spanish crown courts in America the duty of ensuring that Indian interests were properly protected. They were required to investigate alleged cases of ill treatment and declared that:

> We ordain and command that for no cause of war nor any other whatsoever, though it be under the title of rebellion, nor by ransom nor in other manner can an Indian be made a slave, and we will that they be treated as our vassals of the Crown of Castile since such they are.[3]

In the late sixteenth and for most of the seventeenth century, exploration and information gathering continued apace, but a major revolt in 1680 by the Pueblo Indians of the northwest resulted in the loss of New Mexico. The main cause of the rebellion was religious oppression by the Spaniards, whose frustration at failing to convert the Pueblo to Catholicism by peaceful or violent means had led to a policy of ruthless persecution, provoking the Indians to insurrection.

Though not fully explored, let alone occupied, Texas received its first Spanish provincial Governor, Domingo Teran de los Rios, in 1691. An attempt to establish missions in East Texas proved slow and difficult, and Spain temporarily lost control of the region. To the west of Texas, however, New Mexico was reclaimed for Spain from the Pueblos by Diego de Vargas between 1692 and 1696.

During the early decades of the eighteenth century Spain's stuttering consolidation of its presence in Texas continued, and by 1722, largely as a result of the determination of the third Governor, the Marques de San Miguel de Aguayo, many new missions and garrisons had been established in East Texas. Previously strained relations between Spain and France, Spain's main competitor in North America for land and trade, had improved, in part reflecting the alliance in Europe during the War of the Spanish Succession (1701–14) between France and the Spanish supporters of Philip of Anjou, who had prevailed and succeeded to the Spanish throne.

There were failures, but the founding of new missions gained some impetus in the 1740s and 1750s. Intermarriage and Indian conversions to Roman Catholic Christianity became widespread, and by the early 1760s San Antonio's position as the chief town in southeast Texas was well established. The Spanish presence in southern North America was further extended by the provisions of the 1763 Treaty of Paris which determined the distribution of territories worldwide between the former combatants in the Seven Years War. While Britain as the victorious power (over France and Spain) was the main beneficiary, the Treaty provided that Louisiana west of the Mississippi should be transferred from France to Spain.[4]

British interest in North America, where its possessions included the whole of the eastern seaboard from Maine to Georgia and its hinterland, extended southwards with the signing of the 1763 Treaty. In giving up Havana to Spain, Britain now acquired East and West Florida, territories whose geographical position made the British a direct threat to Spanish territory in North America (New Spain). That was certainly how the Spanish saw things, taking such steps as their resources allowed to strengthen their presence along the Gulf coast of Mexico and Texas against possible British attack. Their suspicions were justified; there was no invasion, but the British lost no opportunity to try to assess Spanish military preparedness in the region.[5] Though France and Spain allied themselves with the colonists of North America during the 1775–83 American War of Independence, one consequence of its outcome was to strengthen the hand of the newly formed United States in their aspirations for further territorial acquisition to the south and west.

The last two decades of the eighteenth century in Texas saw the Spanish continuing to deal with the problem of Indian raids and seeking to establish alliances which would allow the peaceful development of their settlements. Texas Governor Domingo Cabello y Robles's inclination was to deal harshly with the Texas Indians, but he was aware of the need to establish a basis for more stable coexistence, and to that end courted the Comanches (whom he considered the lesser of the two evils) to form an alliance with Spain which would enable the Apaches better to be kept at bay.

The Viceroy of New Spain, his commandant general and his governors were much preoccupied during this period, as often before, with the international political situation, marked by the changing pattern of hostilities and alliances in Europe and its consequences for North America. The Spanish authorities at home and abroad became fearful of the republicanism and radical thought spreading throughout Europe in the wake of the French Revolution, seeing the French in North America as a subversive threat to the Indians living under Spanish jurisdiction, many of whom were recent converts to Roman Catholicism. The perceived French threat died down but was quickly superseded by equally agitated concern that the United States and Britain, which had in 1794 signed a trade and friendship agreement aimed at resolving outstanding issues (the Jay Treaty), were to mount a joint operation against Spanish Territories. Brigadier General Pedro de Nava, commandant general, wrote to Governor Muñoz of Texas in 1795:

> The King has been informed on good authority that the United States has ordered emissaries to move here and subvert the population.... For this reason you are to exercise the utmost diligence and care to avoid the entry of any foreigner or suspected person.... Especially exercise care to see that no foreigner go among the Indian nations who are our allies.[6]

The fear persisted. In 1797 the word spread that the United States and Britain intended to invade Louisiana. While no such invasion occurred, Spanish anxieties were not entirely without foundation. Following the Louisiana Purchase of 1803, when Napoleon sold Louisiana to the United States to help, among other things, defray the cost of France's escalating war with Britain, a large and vocal body of American opinion held that the Louisiana territory they had acquired included Texas. The dispute ended in 1806 with the Neutral Ground Agreement, under which territory between the Sabine River to the west and the Calcasieu River to the east would belong to neither side.

In the early years of nineteenth century New Spain, the conservative supporters of regal and viceregal rule, a system on which they depended for their status and livelihood, were opposed by American-born and much more numerous proponents of rule by junta, the interim form of government now in place in Spain. Plots and counter-plots with consequential violence characterised the years from 1808 to 1815. The most remembered insurgency was that led by Miguel Hidalgo y Costilla,[7] a priest who was at the forefront of radical thought but ill-suited to the military leadership role in which he found himself. His ill-disciplined army was defeated at the Battle of Calderon Bridge in 1811.

Mexican (and with it Texan) independence from Spain finally came in 1821. As a result of an apparently improbable alliance between leading conservatives and revolutionaries, a plan ratified by the Treaty of Cordoba provided for an independent nation in which the Roman Catholic faith would be protected and, to address a long-standing problem of discrimination, Spanish citizens born in Spain and those born in America would be treated equally. What united the two sides was a desire for change. Both the radicals and the royalists believed that their respective aims – broadly, greater fairness and social justice and the retention of traditional government – were more likely to be achieved in an independent state than in one subject to Spanish rule.

Political and social tensions were much in evidence in the new nation. A short-lived monarchy was formally replaced by a republic in 1823, and though the five years to 1828 were a period of relative stability in the Federal Mexican Republic, geographical separation and cultural differences were building antagonisms between Mexicans and Anglo-Americans that would eventually lead to war.[8]

In addition to what they considered impossible immigration constraints, frustrations for Anglo-American settlers in Texas (and those from the US who wished to join them) included perceived deficiencies in the judicial system, unwarranted military privileges, and religious intolerance. On the last two, Stephen F. Austin, a major coloniser and de facto leader of the Anglo-American community in Texas, wrote in 1832 to General Teran, commandant general, that 'These are two changes that are necessary and the man who shall carry them into effect will deserve the honored title of the Washington of Mexico'.[9]

More significant for Texas's future, however, was the question of slavery. While the colonists were clear that slave labour was crucial to the agricultural development of Texas – and to their own prosperity – government legislation, viewed over several years, was inconsistent. The Mexican authorities recognised the need to attract enterprising Anglo-American colonists for the future economic wellbeing of the country, but were also constrained by the anti-slavery principles espoused by the revolutionaries who had brought them to power.

Several years of uncertainty seemed to have ended in 1827 when the constitution of the newly formed combined state of Coahuila and

Texas contained, at Article 13, a provision that 'From and after the promulgation of the Constitution in the capital of each district, no-one shall be born a slave in the state, and after six months the introduction of slaves under any pretext shall not be permitted.'[10] This clause, which had the effect of legalising existing slaveholdings, was well received by Austin and the colonial community, who had been expecting something more draconian; but it was still not the end of the matter. A presidential decree in 1829 abolishing slavery throughout Mexico was modified to give some exemption to Texas, but the following year the Mexican government, concerned at the growing confidence and influence of Anglo-American Texans, legislated to prohibit immigration from the United States. For Austin this was a much more serious setback than any of the earlier Mexican laws against slavery, since it put the whole future development of Texas at risk. In consequence he changed his position from advocacy of slavery for practical reasons to hostility to it on moral grounds, but then came under such pressure from the settlers that he reverted to his previous stance. Austin nevertheless contemplated the permanency of slavery in Texas with practical as well as moral misgivings. He wrote to a colleague in 1831: 'I sometimes shudder at the consequences and think that a large part [of] America will be Santa Domingonised in 100 or 200 years. The wishes of my colonists have hurried me into this theory... and there is no retreat.'[11]

At the request of Austin, who had some tacit support from sympathetic local Mexican authorities, the overall ban on American immigration to Texas was lifted, but no slaves were to be brought in. The settlers had however been taking advantage of a decree of 1828 which sought to boost the size of the agricultural workforce by allowing labourers in other countries to accompany their emigrating employers to Texas. Slaves in the southern United States came to Texas formally as indentured workers under contracts which lasted more than a lifetime and they were, in practice, still slaves. Despite a law passed in 1832 limiting employment contracts to ten years, this device continued in operation throughout the remaining years of Mexican Texas.

Simmering discontent among the Anglo-American colonists escalated in the early 1830s. The imposition of customs dues, the establishment of Mexican garrisons in Texas, and what the colonists considered provocative behaviour by one of the garrison commanders, brought insurrection closer. There was some optimism when General Antonio Lopez de Santa Anna, with the expressed aim of re-establishing a liberal constitution, moved to oust the Mexican President. When Santa Anna fully assumed power in 1834 it rapidly became clear that far from adopting a more liberal form of government, Mexico was to be ruled autocratically and that much of the local authority possessed by its constituent states was to be removed.

Armed conflict began in October 1835, after another dispute about customs duties and unilateral action by militant Texans, which provoked an uncompromising crackdown by the commandant general. This time Austin saw no scope for negotiation, writing that 'War is our only resource.... There is no other remedy but to defend our rights, ourselves, and our country by force of arms.'[12] Texan resolve to resist the Mexicans was accompanied by nervousness about the slave population in the light of Santa Anna's declared view that under the law of Mexico they should be given their freedom. The capture by Santa Anna in March 1836 of the Alamo, a mission station at San Antonio, and the massacre of its defenders, did nothing to calm these fears, but they were allayed some six weeks later by the decisive defeat inflicted on the Mexican army by General Sam Houston and his Texan force at San Jacinto.

The establishment of the Republic of Texas followed a unilateral Declaration of Independence, and was formally recognised by the United States a year later in March 1837. The newly drafted constitution embedded slavery as an institution in Texas, stating that 'All persons of color who were slaves for life previous to their emigration to Texas, and are now held in bondage shall remain in the like state of servitude: *provided* the said slave shall be the bona fide property of the person so holding said slave as aforesaid.'[13] Under its first substantive president, Sam Houston, the government of Texas responded to popular will by soon seeking annexation to the United States.[14]

Ties of history and kinship and the prospect of commercial benefit were not enough to overcome the concerns of some members of the US Congress, not least over slavery, which former US President John Quincy Adams, among others, repeatedly advanced as an argument against annexation. After nearly two years without a positive response from the United States, Texas withdrew its request in 1838.

The fledgling Republic was not a stable environment. Potential settlers from the United States were wary of the disruption caused by the increasing incidence of attacks by Comanche Indians, and of the threat of military aggression from Mexico, which had never recognised Texan independence.

Houston's successor, the nationalist (and expansionist) President Mirabeau B. Lamar, saw for Texas a more promising future in commercial alliances with European powers than in any close association with the United States, and was firmly against annexation. The Europeans were cautious about links with the new Republic and were slow to recognise it. France (January 1840) was the first to complete the process, followed by Britain in November 1840 (subject to ratification) and Holland in June 1841. British recognition took the form of three treaties; answering an enquiry in the House of Commons as to whether they had been ratified, Prime Minister Sir Robert Peel said

> that there were three treaties with respect to which this country and the Government of Texas were concerned. The first was of a commercial character; the second had relation to the

abolition of slavery; and the third referred to the guarantee for the payment of a loan from Texas to the Mexican Government under the mediation of this country. These treaties were to be ratified simultaneously. The day fixed for the ratification was the first of August [1842].[15]

In Texas, Lamar was succeeded as President by Sam Houston, who had been re-elected in 1841. His second term agenda focused on establishing peace with the Indians and on improving relations with Mexico; annexation was not among his priorities. The possibility was nevertheless a worry in Britain, where anxieties were expressed in Parliament about US expansion and the reinforcement of slaveholding. MPs raised questions on these matters during 1841 and 1842, particularly, wanting to be kept up to date with developments. Information concerning the treaties was clearly crucial, but there were other issues. The Member for the Montrose District of Burghs, Joseph Hume, asked 'whether Captain Elliot was now consul-general of the Texas – where he was – whether he was now receiving pay from the Government – whether it was the intention of the Government to send him to the Texas, and when?'[16] Peel replied:

> Captain Elliot is Consul to Texas; he is at present in London; he is not in the receipt of pay, and will not be in the receipt of pay until he takes his departure; he is only detained at the instance of the Treasury, who are receiving explanations from him with respect to certain expenses incurred at Hong Kong.[17]

Hume did not follow up his enquiry, except to comment that he did not think Elliot was a fit person for the appointment. Peel's evident irritation with the manner in which Hume had spoken caused him to refer to Elliot's appointment again three weeks later, declaring that

> If the hon. Gentleman had not so put his questions, he [Peel] should not have been prevented from making some observations; and from stating, that whatever might have been the conduct of Captain Elliot in the difficult situation in which he had been placed, he must say, that although he did not know the hon. Gentleman before the intercourse he had since with him, he had every reason to place confidence in the integrity and ability with which he would perform his duties. This was a spontaneous intimation on his part, and he must declare that there was nothing in his correspondence with Captain Elliot to show that full confidence might not repose in his integrity and ability.[18]

# Chapter Thirteen

# 'This Raw Country'

From the start, Charles Elliot was not happy in Texas. He did not arrive in Galveston until 23 August 1842, after a voyage via Madeira and New Orleans. The seas had been rough for the latter stages, adding physical discomfort to the mental disquiet he continued to feel about the criticism of his actions in China. For most of the rest of the year he suffered from recurring bouts of illness. He was accompanied at this time only by his butler; Clara and the children remained in England.

In London, he had kept his spirits up, determined to show the world that he felt entirely confident about his achievements as Chief Superintendent and Plenipotentiary. Charles Greville, who met Elliot for the first time in November 1841, found him 'very amusing with his accounts of China ... animated, energetic, & vivacious, clever, eager, high-spirited & gay'.[1] He also thought Elliot would be convincing in his own defence: 'He, of course, makes his own case very good, &, whatever may be the merit or demerit of his conduct, taken as a whole, I am inclined to think he will be able to vindicate his latest exploit at Canton.'[2] Henry Taylor, too, was positive, passing one of Elliot's documents about China to Sir James Stephen, a mutual friend and Under Secretary of State for War and the Colonies.[3] Stephen was in any case disposed to be sympathetic to Elliot, making his support explicit in a letter to Taylor in March 1842:

> I have read every word of Elliot's Paper, and return it to you. Poor fellow! it is hard, indeed, to have been so misunderstood, and so abused with such a case as he has been able to make ... he was set to resolve a practical problem ... which would have baffled the seven sages of Greece when complicated by the necessity of obeying remote and ignorant Superiors, of guiding hot-headed belligerents, looking after sickly and drunken soldiers, contending with disease and tempest, negotiating with a stupid despot, and ministering to the cupidity and the pride of England.[4]

He ended on a note of realism: 'I doubt whether Elliot will ever extricate himself from the web of calumny which all these things have drawn around him. He must wrap himself up in his own virtue and be at peace, and thank God for his good spirits, and that he has done nothing to lower them.'[5]

The private letter to Palmerston which Elliot had told Emma he intended to write never materialised, but before his departure for Texas he made sure his case was fully set out for the new Foreign Secretary, Lord Aberdeen. He explained in considerable detail what he had done in China, why he had done it, and the beneficial consequences. He drew particular attention to the commercial value to the Crown of his management of trade:

> Between the 24th of March, 1839, when I was made a prisoner at Canton by the Chinese Government, and the 18th August, 1841, when I was removed by my own, we have turned a trade amounting to upwards of ten millions sterling, despatched more than fifty thousand tons of British shipping, sent to England as much produce as would pour into Her Majesty's Treasury upwards of eight millions sterling, recovered from the Chinese Treasury about 150 tons of hard silver, warded off from Her Majesty's Government pressing appeals from foreign Governments at peculiarly uneasy moments and on very delicate subjects, triumphantly manifested the prowess of the Queen's arms, and still more signally and with more enduring advantage established the character and extent of British magnanimity.[6]

Though some individuals on the Chinese side might have considered the British magnanimous, any implication that the Chinese Government did so proved to be extremely wishful thinking. In the same letter Elliot admitted to Aberdeen that he had himself been at fault in failing to send full explanatory reports to Palmerston during the eight weeks in the lull in the conflict at the beginning of 1840. On his overall approach, however, he was unrepentant. Sensitive to accusations that he empathised too much with the Chinese, his response to such criticism set out succinctly the essence of his China philosophy: 'I submit that it has been caring more for lasting British honour and substantial British interests, to protect friendly and helpful people, and to return the confidence of the great trading population of the Southern Provinces, with which it is our chief purpose to cultivate more intimate, social and commercial relations.'[7]

Compensation to the merchants for surrendered opium, about which Elliot was questioned by the Treasury before his departure for Texas, was eventually settled, with remarkable precision, at £1,267,646, 1s 3d.[8] It was a huge sum, and for Elliot to have committed the government to paying it (unavoidably without consultation and even though it was to be recouped from the Chinese) had been a major act of faith.

With China and its aftermath very much in his mind, Elliot arrived in Texas determined, as ever, to do his duty. He had no predecessor as either consul general or, as he also became, Chargé d'Affaires. Earlier in 1841 Lord Aberdeen had dispatched to Texas William Kennedy, a Scot much travelled in North America who had lived in Texas and briefly represented the new republic in London. An acknowledged expert on Texas, and with great confidence in his own abilities, Kennedy had pressed on Aberdeen the need for Britain to have an agent there to report on developments. The major concern for Kennedy was the body of Texan opinion, rapidly gaining ground, in favour of annexation by the United States. It was also a concern for the British government, but in the overall range of current foreign policy issues, not particularly urgent. When the issues of slavery in Texas and annexation had been raised in Parliament in 1836 Palmerston had told the House of Commons that 'with regard to that question [annexation] he did not think that the events which had yet occurred, afforded any ground to think that there was at present any such probability of a result of that kind as to call upon that House to agree to an address to the Crown with respect to it'.[9] In a private letter to the Chancellor of the Exchequer, Spring Rice, in October 1937 Palmerston had elaborated:

> We cannot pretend to exert much influence on the destiny of Texas; & have little to do, but to watch the course of events.
>
> Mexico will not reconquer Texas; we must see whether the Band of outlaws who occupy Texas will be able to constitute themselves into such a community as it would be decent for us to make a Treaty with...
>
> ...To us perhaps it does not very much signify what becomes of Texas, though in a Political view, it would be better that Texas should not be incorporated within the Union; commercially it would make little difference.[10]

William Kennedy's initial appointment in Texas was not to any specified post, and he accordingly had no official brief to support it. From his letters to Aberdeen requesting that he be sent, it can be inferred that his role was to observe, gather information and report back. He was volunteering his services as an unaccredited agent, he said, 'for the purpose of Watching events, and exercising whatever influence I might possess for the benefit of my country.'[11]

Charles Elliot's instructions in respect of his appointment as consul general were the standard *General Instructions for H.M. Consuls*, but Aberdeen drew his particular attention to the need for careful preservation of Consular records, and for gathering and reporting on matters concerning trade and agriculture. His salary was fixed at £1,200 per annum and he was prohibited from engaging in any commercial activity for his own benefit.[12] Elliot was unlikely to have contemplated activity of that kind – he had never demonstrated any such inclination; but perhaps conscious of his attempts to appoint paid assistants when he was in British Guiana, Aberdeen added that he was not to appoint any vice consuls without the prior permission of the Foreign Office.

The instructions for Elliot's consular duties were issued in May, 1842, before his departure for Texas. On 1 July the Foreign Secretary wrote to Elliot that now that the three treaties between Britain and Texas had been signed, 'you will take upon yourself the character and duties of HM Chargé d'Affaires to the Govt. of Texas, agreeably to the assurance that was prospectively given you to that effect by Visct: Palmerston in his dispatch dated the 4 of August last.'[13] Another letter from the Foreign Office instructed Elliot to ensure that in his communications to London he separated his consular commercial responsibilities from the diplomatic duties he was to assume as Chargé d'Affaires.[14] In his 1 July letter Aberdeen made it clear to Elliot that in his diplomatic role he

> should, at first, assume the attitude, rather of an observer than of an actor, of a passive, but not inattentive spectator rather than of an energetic agent or counseller.
>
> You will watch closely all the proceedings of the Texian Govt., not with any hostile view, but simply with the object of putting Your own Govt. in possession of such facts and circumstances as may enable them to form a just estimate of the power and character of the Texian Govt. and Nation, and to judge thereby of the value of the new relations which H.M. has formed with that Republick.

His official brief, in other words, like Kennedy's unofficial one, was to observe and report. Kennedy had arrived back in England on 20 April 1842, having spent a little over three months in Texas. After much renewed soliciting he was appointed consul at Galveston at the end of September. Aberdeen's letter explicitly confined his responsibilities to the Galveston area and stressed his subordination to Elliot as consul general. Kennedy did not arrive in Texas to take up his official post until early February 1843.

Until October 1842 the Foreign Office received little of value from Texas. Charles Elliot was unwell, and apart from some initial impressions, his communications to London during the first weeks after his arrival comprised little more than local newspapers and acknowledgement of the receipt of his formal appointment details, sent by the Foreign Office in late June and early July. He dealt with a number of local issues and reported on first meetings with the Texan Attorney General and the President, Sam Houston.

By November he felt sufficiently recovered and confident to be able to send the Foreign Secretary a fuller analysis of the situation in Texas as he saw it. His reports were informed in part by what he had gleaned from President Houston, with whom he had formed a constructive working relationship and a warm friendship. Texas, Elliot implied, had become embroiled in its current difficulties with Mexico by overreacting to the possibility of Mexican aggression. Elliot's view was that by shaping up to get its retaliation in first, Texas had inflamed the relationship between the two countries and, among other things, involved both sides in unnecessary expense on naval forces. The deterioration had been in spite of the preferences of both Houston and the Mexican President, Santa Anna, for a more conciliatory stance, but persistent localised hostilities in the border areas could not be ignored. Tensions eased, however, when a Texan blockade of Mexican east coast ports was called off in September after nearly six months. The British had been concerned for the safety of their ships operating in the Gulf of Mexico, and were anxious to ensure that Britain was seen to be entirely neutral. Following instruction from Aberdeen, Elliot had emphasised this neutrality to the Acting Secretary of State.

Though improved, Elliot's health also remained a problem. He wrote to Henry Unwin Addington, Permanent Under Secretary at the Foreign Office, early in September asking for permission to base himself on the coast at Galveston rather than inland at Austin, which had now become the Texan capital, in order to benefit from a kinder climate. In due course Aberdeen not only agreed but told him that 'in the present unsettled state of the Country' he could live wherever he judged best for the performance of his duties.[15] Elliot was of course grateful for this dispensation, but he derived at least as much satisfaction from the Foreign Secretary's remarks, in the same letter, about his 'success in China.'[16] Such was his continuing sensitivity about China, though, that he could not convey his thanks without reiterating the rightness, as he saw it, of his actions. His reply said that Aberdeen's words had

> affected me as I believe Your Lordship will have felt they would. Let me say at this conjuncture that I have always been free of self-reproach or uneasiness respecting my share in those transactions, for I knew that I had done my duty, and, under God's Providence, depended upon full success. The only ends I ever had in view ... have been accomplished; Great public and private distress was averted; a depressed and dark turn of affairs has been changed into a state of security and lasting advantage, and the principles of policy and schemes of operation which seemed to me to be sound for those purposes have not proved otherwise.[17]

The Texas brief simply to watch and report was never going to sit comfortably with Charles Elliot. Conscious of the controversy over his China activities he had assured Aberdeen that he would adhere to his instructions. Doing his duty was, as ever, vitally important; but he could not go against his instinctive need to make an impact, to contribute something extra, positive, and if possible, original. From his experience in British Guiana it had been his evidence to the Select Committee; in China it had been Hong Kong; in Texas it was a plan to safeguard British interests in North America and to secure the future of an independent Texas. Elliot set out his scheme, as he called it, in a letter to the Foreign Office of 15 November 1842, referring to it again in two more in December. Wary of engaging directly with Aberdeen with what could be construed as criticism of government policy, he took advantage of personal friendship and addressed his communications to Addington. It was however inevitable that his ideas would find their way to the Foreign Secretary, a certainty of which Elliot himself was of course aware.[18]

The maintenance of British trade and influence and a stable prosperity for Texas were the desired outcomes, but Elliot's starting point was slavery. He was to draw on his own background and upbringing, and on his experiences in the Royal Navy and British Guiana, in making the abolition of slavery in Texas a key part of his scheme. He suggested that there should be

> another Convention in this Country. Slavery to be abolished, the entire abolition of political disabilities upon people of Colour, *perfectly free trade* to be declared to be a fundamental principle; the right of voting to depend upon a knowledge of reading and writing, and pretty high money contribution to the State, with the payment charge to be made in advance, Congress to have power to *lower* the rate from time to time according to the state of the public necessities; stringent legislation against squatting, in the form of a land tax and otherwise, improvements upon the well established failure and folly of a yearly elected Legislature and other liberality of the rhodomontade school.[19]

The plan was at best unrealistic and at worst a mere flight of fancy, an example of that trait in Elliot's character which caused him to be described later as a 'political dreamer'.[20] British interests in North America, if not active policy aims, included the preservation of good relations with Mexico as an important trading partner; prevention of the spread of slavery and its eventual eradication; and containment of the territorial ambitions of the United States. Elliot was well aware that all three would be at risk if Texas became annexed to the United States. In his more pragmatic and reflective moments he must also have known that Britain, which had declared itself to be wholly neutral in the continuing hostilities between Texas and Mexico, was highly unlikely ever to attempt to impose a specific constitution on another sovereign country. Nevertheless, he was alert to the need for persistent diplomatic effort if there were to be any chance of annexation being avoided.

Elliot took much encouragement from his close relationship with President Houston, and his long 15 November letter to Addington contained much about him. He stressed that Houston was the only individual in Texas capable of consolidating the country's independence and leading it forward, though his admiration was not limitless: 'Let him speak of men, on public affairs, or the tone and temper of other Governments, and no one can see farther, or more clearly. The moment He turns to finance or fiscal arrangements, you find that he has been groping on the dark side of his mind.'[21]

The friendship with Houston was a professional positive to set against the generally dismal and difficult experience of living in Texas without his wife and family and with few material comforts. It soon bore fruit; Houston wished to achieve peace with Mexico, but wanted to do it without formality. He approached Elliot to help him, aware that permission would be needed from the British government. Houston's letter was forwarded to Aberdeen just before Elliot left Galveston for Washington-on-the-Brazos, where the President had been attending a meeting of Congress on 14 November. As he mentioned to Addington later, the journey upriver to Washington had not been without incident – he had fallen through an open hatch into the hold of the boat and dislocated a rib, an accident which ought, he conceded, to have prompted him to abide by the medical advice he had been given and to stay at Houston instead of proceeding further. He went on, however, to Washington; he informed Addington, perhaps calling to mind among other things the shipwreck of the *Louisa*, that he was 'one of the best practised men of my time to strange accidents, and hard rubs of all kinds, and I hope to come straight enough again, for all that is come and gone.'[22]

Before the year ended, Charles Elliot reiterated his thinking on future British policy towards Texas to Addington. He could not let it go, and had to be sure that the Foreign Office was in no doubt of how strongly he felt that his scheme was the right way forward:

> The people of Texas are gasping for peace, and the best bidder. I believe that the only safe solution would be a formal offer on the part of Her Majesty's Government to Texas, to secure the close of this contest upon the basis of It's consenting to place Itself in a position of *real Independence*, by an immediate and thorough organisation of It's social, political and Commercial Institutions and policy upon sound, and independent principles; an[d] further offering every reasonable facility to England to negociate such a loan as would be necessary to accomplish the proposed objects.
>
> So far as I can see there is no choice between this, and the virtual, early, and permanent lapse of Texas within the sphere of United States influence, and policy;[23]

To re-emphasise his concern about – and dislike of – United States ambition, Elliot resorted to ironic understatement in his last communication of the year to London when he commented on part of President Tyler's recent Message to the US Congress:

> It has a tang of Texas and Mexico, and is certainly worthy of attention both for coolness of purpose, and dryness of expression –
>
> 'Carefully abstaining from all interference in question[s] exclusively referring to the political interests of Europe, we may

be permitted to hope an equal exemption from the interference of European Governments in what relates to the *States of the American Continent*'

...I presume this means that United States politicians and financiers mislike disturbance on the little Island, forming the Continent of North and South America. But it is possible that this pretension of United States policy may not be equally acceptable to all 'the States of the American Continent.[24]

During the first three months of 1843 Elliot's letters to London and to the Texan Secretary of State Anson Jones were partly taken up with the questions of compensation for 'outrages' done to two British vessels by Texan ships, and land claims.[25] British subjects who had been allocated land in Texas by Mexico when Texas was a Mexican province now faced losing it through measures taken under the Republic's General Land Law of 1837. This legislation was condemned by Elliot as 'utterly unsustainable, violating universally received principles of a general nature, and carried out by Congress beyond the plain intention and limitation of fundamental authority, that is, beyond the Constitution of the Republic'.[26] The correspondence reflected the sizeable gap between Elliot's personal regard for Houston and his poor opinion of the government over which he presided. He remained intent on pressing the British government for action to end the Texas–Mexico conflict. While he accepted that France might have a role in this, he was adamant that the United States should not. He was accordingly relieved to learn that the Foreign Secretary had rejected a proposal originating from Anson Jones for tripartite intervention by Britain, France and the United States to press the Mexican government towards peace.

Elliot continued to hope that some positive progress might stem from his scheme for Texas. Peace between Texas and Mexico, and Mexican recognition of Texan independence, would remove the insecurity that encouraged Texans to look to annexation by the United States as a solution. His covering note to Aberdeen of 5 February 1843, marked 'Secret', enclosed an extract from a private letter written some days before by Houston. The President had reported that 'nine tenths of those who converse with me are in favour of the measure [annexation to the US] upon the ground that *it will give us peace*. Upon this point of our national existence I feel well satisfied that England has the power to rule!'[27] Elliot and Houston were thus at one in their wish to see Britain intervene, but Aberdeen's stance remained one of studied detachment. The Foreign Secretary's view was clear, and his response to Elliot perhaps contained a hint of irritation that the Chargé d'Affaires had been making too much of the annexation question:

With regard to the project for the annexation of Texas to the United States, which has formed the subject of some of your recent communications to this Office, Her Majesty's

3. Rt Hon. Hugh Elliot.
(The Bodleian Libraries, University of Oxford)

1. Captain Charles Elliot c. 1855 while Governor of Trinidad.
(Photograph courtesy of the Governor of Trinidad and Tobago c. 1953, from
Clagette Blake, Charles Elliot RN) (Cleaver-Hume, London 1960).

2. Minto House, Hawick, c. 1910. (Historic Environment Scotland)

4. Reading School and Playground, 1816. (Edmund Havell. By kind permission of the Old Redingensians Association)

5. Bombardment of Algiers, 1816. (Thomas Luny. Private Collection [Copyright], Royal Exchange Art Gallery at Cork Street, London/Bridgeman Images)

6. HMS *Minden* off Scilly, 1842. (Lieutenant Humphrey J. Julian. Copyright National Maritime Museum, London)

7. Slave ship captured by boats of the Royal Navy, 1824.
(Image Reference Magasin8, as shown on www.slaveryimages.org, compiled by Jerome Handler and Michael Tuite, and sponsored by the Virginia Foundation for the Humanities and the University of Virginia Library.)

8. Emma, Lady Hislop (née Elliot),
(Thomas Charles Wageman. Courtesy of
Private Collection)

9. Georgetown Harbour, British Guiana c. 1850. (Courtesy of Private Collection)

10. Henry John Temple, third Viscount Palmerston, 1844–45.
(John Partridge. Copyright National Portrait Gallery, London)

11. Howqua.
(Lamqua. Pictures from History/Bridgeman Images)

12. William Jardine. (Thomas Goff Lupton, after George Chinnery, 1830s. Copyright National Portrait Gallery, London)

13. Commissioner Lin Zexu.
(Lamqua. Courtesy of Gibson Antiques)

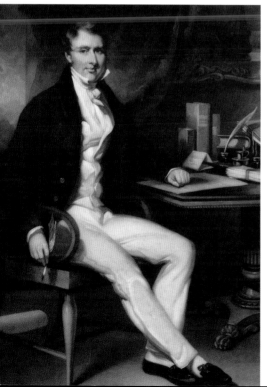

14. The Hongs of Canton, early 1830s. (Sunqua. Photo: Martyn Gregory Gallery, London)

15. (Thought to be) Clara Elliot c. 1838. (George Chinnery. Courtesy of Hong Kong and Shanghai Banking Corporation)

16. San Francisco Green: Houses of Mr Whiteman ('the forty-pillared house') and Captain Elliot, and Monte Fort, Macao. (George Chinnery, 1836. Copyright Victoria and Albert Museum, London)

17. The Bocca Tigris from the South. (Chinese Artist c. 1840. Photo: Martyn Gregory Gallery, London)

18. Commissioner Lin Zexu overseeing the destruction of Opium at Humen, June 1839. (Chinese Artist. Pictures from History/ Bridgeman Images)

19. James Matheson. (Henry Cousins, after James Lonsdale, 1837. Copyright National Portrait Gallery, London)

20. Emily Eden, 1835. (Simon Jacques Rochard. Copyright National Portrait Gallery, London)

21. *Nemesis* destroying junks in Anson's Bay, 1841. (Edward Duncan. Copyright National Maritime Museum, London)

22. Major General Sir
Hugh Gough.
(after Sir Francis Grant, 1854.
Copyright National Portrait Gallery,
London)

23. Hong Kong Island and Harbour, c. 1860. (Nam Ting. Photo: Martyn Gregory Gallery, London)

24. Sir Henry Pottinger.
(Sir Francis Grant, 1845. Copyright UK Government Art Collection)

25. George Hamilton Gordon, fourth Earl of Aberdeen, c. 1847.
(John Partridge. Copyright National Portrait Gallery, London)

**26. President Sam Houston.**
(Daguerreotype, studio of Mathew Brady. Courtesy of the Library of Congress LC-USZ62-110029)

**27. President John Tyler.**
(Charles Fenderich. Courtesy of the Library of Congress LC-USZ62-7266)

**28. Port of Galveston.** (*Illustrated London News*, January 1845. Courtesy of the Library of Congress LC-USZ61-293)

**29. Government House, Mount Langton, Bermuda, mid-1850s.** (from *Bermuda: a Colony, a Fortress, and a Prison* by Anonymous, Ferdinand Whittingham) (London, Longman, Brown, Green, Longmans and Roberts, 1857).

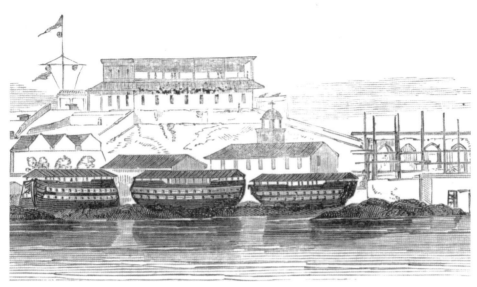

30. Convict hulks at Ireland Island Bermuda. (from sketch in *Illustrated London News*, July 1848. Private Collection [Copyright] Look and Learn/Illustrated Papers Collection/Bridgeman Images)

31. Governor's Cottage Residence, Trinidad, 1857.
(Michel J. Cazabon. Courtesy of the Yale Center for British Art, Paul Mellon Collection)

32. Harriet (née Elliot), Hon. Mrs Russell. (Camille Silvy, 1860. Copyright National Portrait Gallery, London)

33. Henry George Grey, third Earl Grey, 1861.
(Camille Silvy. Copyright National Portrait Gallery, London)

34. Sir Henry Taylor.
(Julia Margaret Cameron,
1864. Copyright National
Portrait Gallery, London)

35. Plantation House, St Helena, 1857.
(from St Helena: a Physical, Historical and Topographical Description of the Island by J. C. Melliss (London, Reeve and Co., 1875).

36. St Helena, Jamestown from the Sea. (Nineteenth century. Photo: Martyn Gregory Gallery, London)

Government do not think it necessary to give you any instructions at the present moment on that subject, further than to desire that you will assure the President of the continued interest which the British Government takes in the prosperity and independence of the state of Texas.[28]

Aberdeen's hands-off approach was reinforced shortly afterwards by the reports and views of Richard Pakenham, Elliot's former opposite number in Mexico, who had recently returned home. Pakenham, a career diplomat, was relatively unconcerned about the possibility of annexation. He thought Texas would be annexed, either to Mexico or to the United States, but did not see any cause for British alarm. Houston's private communication in May to Elliot, on the other hand, reflected considerable urgency. His language in describing the United States' motives was uncompromising, even extreme, and he was unhappy that the US was unwilling to respond positively to an armistice proposed by Santa Anna:

The genius as well as the excitability of that people, united to a bold and generous daring, impel them to war. Their love of Dominion, and the extension of their territorial limits, also, is equal to that of Rome in the last ages of the commonwealth and the first of the Caesars.

The Continent of North America is regarded by the people of the United States as their birth-right – to be secured by policy, if they can, by force, if they must. Heretofore Texas has been looked upon as an appendage to the U.States...

...I regret that our friends in the U.States should have any uneasiness on the Subject of Santa Anna's propositions. If we were to judge from the Newspapers, as well as from private correspondence which I receive, we might conclude there was danger of my being favourable to retrocession to Mexico; and as for the subject of Texas becoming a British Colony and abolition in Texas ... I can neither sympathise with the distress of our friends, nor can I entertain commiseration for their ridiculous credulity.[29]

Elliot then forwarded to Aberdeen, marked 'Secret', a copy of Houston's letter. Either the level of unspoken understanding between Elliot and Houston was very high indeed, or Elliot was being more than a little disingenuous when he assured the Foreign Secretary that while he was aware that contents of the letter were intended to be confidential to himself, 'I am also persuaded that General Houston must have felt they would be made known to your Lordship'.[30] For Elliot a particular sensitivity was slavery; Houston had referred to abolition in conversation as well as in his letter, indicating that some Texan as well as US newspapers had suggested that the British government had insisted on abolition as a condition of its mediating in the conflict with Mexico. Elliot reported that he had assured the President that the slavery question had not been mentioned to him in any communication from London.

By the spring of 1843 Charles Elliot was grudgingly familiar with his new posting, and his preoccupations became again as much personal as professional. He was waiting to be joined by Clara, who sailed from England on 15 April, the day on which he arrived back in Galveston from Washington-on-the-Brazos. He wrote hurriedly to Emma conveying concern and affection for his family and bemoaning his own fortunes, as he had done so often before:

> I have only this moment landed from the Houston Steam Boat, after a wearisome journey to and from Washington and have just time to write these lines for the New Orleans Boat to say that I am well. Poor brave Clara; according to her last letter this was the very day of her departure from England and a bitter, bitter hour it must have been to her. She is coming to a wretched country in a wretched condition, but I know she will be glad to share my exile and I can only hope that it will not be for long. Thank my own dearest boys for me, for their nice letters. I have been a disappointed and a troubled man in life, but say to them, dearest Emy, that I should think myself repaid indeed, if the hope of contributing to my happiness should keep them *steadily good*.[31]

In early May Elliot departed for Havana to rendezvous with Clara, leaving his diplomatic duties in the willing hands of William Kennedy, for whom dealing with diplomatic correspondence was a welcome diversion from his consular responsibilities for trade and production returns. En route, at New Orleans, Elliot wrote to Aberdeen. Elation at the prospect of seeing Clara again no doubt influenced his mood to make what must have seemed to the Foreign Secretary rather a presumptuous request:

> I use the freedom of this communication to mention to Your Lordship that I am troubled with an Ague contracted in a long and painful Service in hot Countries, and I should consider it a favor if Your Lordship would sanction my passing the months of July, August and September in the Mountains of Kentucky where I have been advised as there are Springs of great virtue for complaints of that kind. I have the less reluctance in proffering this request, as I can always be at my post within two weeks from that Situation, and be in the constant receipt of tidings from Texas of ten days or a fortnight's date. It may also be added that Congress in Texas does not meet till December, and the Officers of the Texian Government usually disperse during the hot season.[32]

In the event, and in the absence of any reply from Aberdeen, Elliot did not go. Pressure of work kept him busy throughout the summer as Mexico's fraught relationship with Texas continued to be the subject of frequent correspondence between himself, Percy Doyle (the new British Charge d'Affaires in Mexico), and Aberdeen. Despite any initial misgivings on the grounds that nothing less than immediate recognition of Texan independence would do, Houston decided to accept Santa Anna's offer of an armistice and published a proclamation to that effect on 13 June. Later analyses of diplomatic exchanges during these months raised questions about real as opposed to apparent motives, tacit understandings behind formal communications, and leakage of information. Elliot was in the thick of it, interpreting Aberdeen's instructions rather than following them to the letter, and losing no opportunity to express his support for Houston and his moderate policy towards Mexico. He also found himself having to explain to Aberdeen that he had not been the source of newspaper reports in Boston and New Orleans that Britain was seeking to impose abolition on Texas.

China was never far from his mind. On 6 June he wrote at length to Lord Minto.[33] With the best of intentions, Clara had mentioned that she had commented to Minto on the absence of any reference to Charles in a recent parliamentary debate about China. Elliot was concerned lest there should be any suspicion of lobbying on his behalf; he did not wish to alienate any of his relatives, and with the possible exceptions of Emily Eden and Auckland, did not believe any of them bore him any ill will. Equally, he was not going to miss an opportunity to underline yet again the rightness of his actions in China, while maintaining – rather unconvincingly – that he was unmoved by criticism: 'The truth is that whilst I am always glad of assent to the general character of my measures in China, come whence it may, the contrary does not disturb me for ... I have done nothing and left nothing behind in China that the country has cause to regret.' Pottinger, he asserted, had arrived in China to find systems already in place and impediments already removed, and with a sideswipe at the Foreign Office commented that 'Chinese Mandarins were not the hardest to manage in China, and Pottinger seems to have managed those without tails to their heads with more skill and good fortune than myself.'[34] Elliot could not resist making explicit mention of his alleged disobedience of Palmerston's instructions, sardonically asking the rhetorical question

> whether the nation would choose to give up Hong Kong at this time, for some more opened ports, and some more millions of dollars than have hitherto been safely opened, or punctually paid up ... I do not find that orders were sent out (or at least acted upon) to undo what I had done.[35]

Consistent with the apparently ambivalent approach he was now taking to communications from London – passing on to the Texan government Aberdeen's advice on the merits of nominal Mexican sovereignty over Texas while stressing to Doyle that only immediate acceptance of Texan independence would do. Using China as an example, he was emphatic that instructions had to be sensibly applied:

> I believe I should have no difficulty in satisfying the reasonable part of the public that there was no obeying the letter of the instructions in our hands without totally breaking up the China trade, to the great advantage of the Court of China, and our own serious injury, and without rendering it impossible for the force to have subsisted on the Coast of China for six months. It was my part to remember *what* the instructions *meant*, as well as *what* they said.[36]

Clara's arrival in Texas was a great comfort to him, but her full endorsement of the dissatisfaction Elliot felt with life there encouraged him to redouble his efforts to be sent somewhere else. Clara complained to Emma that 'If Charles had committed murder, theft, or any other grave crime & been sent to Botany Bay, it is more than possible we should have found there a more desirable place of residence than Galveston.'[37] In the same vein, Charles bemoaned their situation some weeks later, also in a letter to his sister: 'No language can convey to you any adequate idea of the wretchedness of life in this raw country..'[38] A specific request by Elliot to the Foreign Office on 4 August to be given a different posting because of ill health met with a negative response; Addington informed him that Aberdeen would however be willing to grant leave of absence for convalescence if he wanted it.[39]

Diplomatic activity on the future of Texas during the summer of 1843 took place in London and Washington DC as much as in Texas and Mexico. In July a meeting was held in London of prominent individuals from Texas and the United States to discuss abolition in Texas. Those present included Stephen P. Andrews, a Houston lawyer and fervent abolitionist. A report sent back to the US Secretary of State, Abel P. Upshur, set in train a series of alarmed repercussions which was to provoke the United States to action. The report was written from London by General Duff Green, a newspaper owner, industrialist, and close associate of President Tyler. Green was a strong supporter of the institution of slavery and was deeply suspicious of British motives. Andrews, he told Secretary Upshur, had been sent by the abolitionists in Texas to negotiate with the British government. Green said that he had learnt

> from a source entitled to the fullest confidence ... That he [Andrews] has seen Lord Aberdeen, and submitted his *projet* for the abolition of slavery in Texas; which is, that there shall be organised a company in England, who shall advance a sum sufficient to pay for the slaves now in Texas, and receive in payment Texas lands; that the sum thus advanced shall be paid over as an indemnity for the abolition of slavery; and I am authorised by the Texan minister [in London, Ashbel Smith]

to say to you, that Lord Aberdeen has agreed that the British Government will guaranty the payment of interest on this loan, upon condition that the Texan Government will abolish slavery.[40]

Green's attempt to reinforce antagonism towards Britain found a receptive audience. If they had had any doubts, Secretary Upshur, former Vice President John C. Calhoun and President Tyler were now convinced that Britain's overriding aims were the abolition of slavery in Texas and the prevention of further territorial expansion by the United States. The distinction in the official British Government line, that Britain wanted to see an end to slavery everywhere but had no wish actively to intervene to that end in any slave-holding country, was not one in which the Americans placed any trust. Green went further, believing that there was no altruism or philanthropy about Britain's abolition policy, but that she sought the eradication of slavery to halt the growth in the United States' economy. US commercial expansion, Green held, was adversely affecting British trade in the region, which had been weakened by the abolition of slavery in the British West Indies. In Britain, fuel was added to the fire when Aberdeen evaded a question in the House of Lords about abolition in Texas, maintaining that the ongoing negotiations between Mexico and Texas made it inappropriate for him to comment.[41] At the same time as the parliamentary exchange, Upshur and Calhoun were corresponding over next moves, working up a plan – and each other – towards annexation by the United States. Responding to a letter from Upshur, Calhoun cast Britain firmly in the role of villain:

> You do not, in my opinion, attach too much importance to the designs of Great Britain in Texas. That she is using all her diplomatick arts and influence to abolish slavery there, with the intention of abolishing it in the United States, there can no longer be a doubt...
>
> That her object is power and monopoly, and abolition but the pretext, I hold to be not less clear. Her conduct affords the most conclusive proof. No nation, in ancient, or modern time, ever pursued dominion & commercial monopoly more perseveringly & vehemently than she has. She unites herself in the ambition of Rome and the avarice of Carthage.[42]

Unaware of these machinations, Charles Elliot was much encouraged to receive from Doyle a copy of the instructions sent to him by the Foreign Secretary following the July meeting of US and Texan abolitionists in London. Doyle was informed that Aberdeen had told a leading member of the meeting that

> if the State of Texas should confer entire emancipation on all persons within its territory, and make that decision

permanent and irrevocable, H.M. Govt. would not fail to press that circumstance upon the consideration of the Mexican Government as a strong additional reason for the acknowledgement by Mexico of the independence of Texas.[43]

Elliot felt that at last abolition was moving nearer centre stage, writing enthusiastically to both to Aberdeen and to Doyle. His euphoria was short lived. Despite the known view of the US Chargé d'Affaires in Texas, William S. Murphy, and of the US minister in London, Edward Everett, that the British position on abolition in Texas was no cause for concern, in the rumour-ridden climate of alleged plots and conspiracies Secretary Upshur, to his great satisfaction, was instructed by President Tyler to offer an annexation treaty to Texas.[44]

The offer was communicated by Upshur on 18 September to Isaac Van Zandt, the Texan Charge D'Affaires in Washington DC, and thence to President Houston. At this wholly unexpected development Van Zandt was taken aback, and Houston deeply troubled. Elliot too was surprised, and would have been greatly disappointed. Upshur had conveyed a sense of urgency, asking that Van Zandt seek a response from Texas in time for it to be considered at the next meeting of the US Congress. In a long letter reporting all this to Aberdeen, Elliot described how he had asked the President what he intended to do.

> General Houston answered that Mr Van Zandt would be instructed to communicate verbally that it did not seem to the government of Texas to be convenient or necessary to entertain such proposals at all, till the Senate of the United States had manifested its readiness by resolution to treat with Texas, upon the subject of Annexation.[45]

Such a pause would give Houston one more chance to see if Britain would exert influence on Mexico finally to recognise Texan independence, and Elliot relayed the President's insistence that

> Her Majesty's Government might rest assured that with the Independence of Texas recognised by Mexico, He would never consent to any treaty or any other project of annexation to the United States, and he had a conviction that the people would sustain him in that determination. He had formerly been favorable to such a Combination. But the United States had rejected the proposals of the Country in its time of difficulty; neither was the subsequent conduct of that Government calculated to induce the Government and people of Texas in this mended state of things, to sacrifice their true and lasting advantage to the policy of party in that Country.[46]

For the remaining two months of 1843 there was little diplomatic activity on the annexation question as Texas awaited the United States' reaction to Houston's message. During November a relatively minor incident involving alleged disrespect to a British ensign caused the temporary suspension of diplomatic relations between Mexico and Britain. Half offering this difficulty as an excuse – he would probably have proceeded anyway – Elliot used the lull in annexation negotiations to write at length to Aberdeen about the navigability of the Rio Grande both for commercial purposes and in case, he implied, the stand-off with Mexico deteriorated into open conflict. Elliot was in his comfort zone dealing with this kind of issue, but he was aware that supplying unsolicited information and opinion in such detail to the Foreign Secretary at this juncture was a surprising and potentially irritating thing to do. He was therefore anxious to ensure that Aberdeen understood that he knew this, 'Hoping Your Lordship will ascribe this intrusion to it's true motive, that is, a desire to further the public Service'.[47]

Since the Foreign Office knew that Elliot was unhappy in Texas, it will not have been greatly surprised to hear from him in mid-December, not from Galveston but from New Orleans. He had gone there, he said, for health reasons, 'chiefly for better advice and convenience than I can find in Texas for an instant [having] fallen into a very weak state of health', but he was hugely relieved to be away from Galveston, as was Clara.[48] He had written to Emma in the summer with condolences on the death of her husband, Sir Thomas Hislop, adding that 'Clara is satisfying herself as well as is possible in this desperate hole, but I will not consent to keep her in such a place beyond the expiration of the summer months'.[49] The Elliots did not leave for a new posting, as Charles had hoped and requested, but an extended temporary relocation was a welcome change.

In New Orleans Elliot met Henry Clay, the influential former US Secretary of State. He was glad to receive Clay's reassuring opinion, expressed several times, that 'no scheme of that kind [the annexation of Texas] either by treaty, or in any other form, could be carried through the Senate of the United States'.[50]

# Chapter Fourteen

# 'Knavish Tricks'

One diplomatic benefit of being in New Orleans was that Charles Elliot could gauge for himself the popular mood in the United States towards possible Texan annexation. It was not Washington DC, but it nevertheless allowed him a realistic perspective on the exaggerated reports and rumours circulating in Texas. He explained to Aberdeen that, though recovering, his health had hitherto prevented a return to Galveston. In mid-February 1844 he wrote again:

> It has been so generally reported in Texas that a scheme of Annexation to the United States by treaty, is in an advanced state, that I consider it right to notice these reports to Your Lordship; remarking that nothing of the kind has transpired here, and that the statement is not believed by persons of great knowledge and weight in this Country.[1]

Aberdeen had reacted strongly to Tyler's Message to Congress of December 1843 in which, in a passage about the need to end the war with Mexico, the President had implied British interference in Texan affairs. In a letter of 26 December to Pakenham, now British Minister to the United States, the Foreign Secretary instructed him to 'take the opportunity of observing to the Secretary of State [Upshur], that the language of the President, when speaking of the measures which the U.States may hereafter have occasion to adopt, ill accords with this condemnation of the supposed designs of other powers...'[2] Probably sensing the damage it might do to diplomatic relations between Britain and the United States, Pakenham ensured that at this stage the contents of the letter went no further than himself.

Whatever advantage Elliot may have had by being closer to American opinion in New Orleans, political scheming in Texas in his absence ensured that the annexation issue remained active. How much of this Elliot would have been able to influence, or even known about, had he been there is an open question. Without at this stage any firm guarantees from the United States about the terms of annexation, Houston and his government remained unsure what would be the best deal for Texas. Though attitudes in the US towards annexation were keenly divided between the abolitionist north and the expansionist south, the ardently annexationist President and Secretary of State were moving things forward. In mid-January 1844 Secretary Upshur told William S. Murphy, the US Chargé d'Affaires in Texas, that the point had now been reached at which the US Senate would approve an annexation treaty, a view also held by Van Zandt. Houston continued to keep his options open, conducting armistice negotiations with the Mexicans while seeking a guarantee of US protection in the event of a commitment to annexation. The Americans increased the pressure, warning Texas unequivocally about alleged British intentions. Murphy gave Anson Jones an assurance, without authorisation, that 'neither Mexico nor any other power, will be permitted to invade Texas, on account of any negotiation which may take place, in relation to any subject upon which Texas, is, or may be invited by the United States to negociate'.[3]

Murphy was subsequently reprimanded for making this commitment but, crucially, it gave Houston added encouragement to pursue discussions with the United States. As Texas was allowing Mexico and the United States to form differing impressions of her intentions, Mexico was behaving with similar guile towards the United States and Texas. Upshur sought to persuade the Mexicans both of the reasons for the US wishing to annex Texas (chiefly to stem British influence and interference) and of future US support for Mexico as a neutral state. Like Texas, Mexico hedged its bets, aware of the weakness of the American position inherent in the divide between the northern and southern states, especially on slavery. Away from Texas, Elliot was unaware of these intrigues. In the wake of Tyler's Message Aberdeen had not only written to Pakenham, but had drawn into the Texas affair the French government, whose support for Britain in its concerns over American designs on Texas was readily forthcoming.

The gap in Charles Elliot's preoccupations occasioned by his distance from current diplomacy was filled, predictably, by China and by his health. In January he sent a long letter to Emma discoursing again on his role in China and giving his current perspective on its aftermath, saying that there was nothing pleasant in his present situation to write home about. By mid-March his health showed some improvement, but he was not inclined to be too positive. He wrote to his sister: 'I have just time for one line to tell you that I am better, but still desperately weak. I am off to Texas today, for only a very few days, however, for my doctor tells me that I must go away immediately to the northward'.[4] In the same letter he mentioned also the illness, of great concern to Clara and to himself, of their baby daughter Emma Clara, who remained in a 'very, very precarious condition'. A little earlier he had asked the Foreign Secretary for permission to go north for the sake of his health, as advised by his doctor, from whom a medical certificate was enclosed. Dr Rushton's note emphasised that it was essential, if Elliot was to become fully well again, that he should move to a more temperate climate to the north as soon as possible. He continued:

> I conceive that your attack of severe Dysentery has proceeded from a debilitated state of the Digestive Organs, brought on by long residence in tropical Climates, and am satisfied that your

continued residence either here, or in a latitude as low as Texas, would be attended by a great risk of a return to your present Complaint, and from the consequences of such a return you have everything to dread.

Under these circumstances, I conceive it your duty, at whatever sacrifice, to leave our hot and humid Climate, for one more dry and bracing.[5]

In his covering letter to Aberdeen, Elliot took advantage of the opportunity by expressing a wish to return to Europe, but dented his credibility by saying that Rushton's certificate advised this, which it clearly did not. He probably thought, in any case, that such a move would not be sanctioned, and implied as much by indicating that

if Your Lordship shall be of the opinion that it would be more convenient for the public interest that I should not go so far from my post at present I would endeavour to find suitable change on the Northern parts of this Continent, and return to my duties as soon as my health enabled me.[6]

The following week he wrote to Aberdeen informing him that he would indeed be going north. His first task however was to return to Texas, to find out closer to hand what was going on, and in particular what had prompted the government to dispatch a special emissary to Washington DC.

Texas had sent General J. Pinckney Henderson, a firm supporter of annexation, to join Van Zandt in negotiations with the Americans. It was probably the clearest indication yet that annexation was being taken seriously and that its implementation was a real possibility. In an exchange of correspondence between Elliot and Anson Jones, the Secretary of State informed Elliot that it was in the Texas Congress that policy had changed. The mood there had turned more strongly against Mexico; it had become

very apparent the Government of Mexico were indisposed to any settlement upon reasonable and admissible terms ... intelligence from our Commissioners beyond the Rio Grande engaged in conducting the terms of the Armistice was of a very unfavorable character, and the people of this country tired of uncertainty and delay naturally turned their attention to annexation, the door to which had just been unexpectedly opened, as the most certain remedy for existing evils.[7]

Nevertheless, Elliot told Aberdeen, Houston himself remained committed to Texan independence. Unless and until provided with hard evidence to the contrary, Elliot wanted to see the best in people; he certainly did not want to think now that Houston might be being less than straight with him. The President had only authorised the Henderson mission to Washington, Elliot said, to pre-empt a resolution of Congress which would have removed his control of the annexation issue.

Upshur, with whom Van Zandt had been formulating the detail of a treaty of annexation, met with a fatal accident at the end of February. Van Zandt was immediately concerned that the constructive progress of the negotiations would stall, but he need not have worried. The new Secretary of State was John C. Calhoun; not only did the process continue apace, but the unauthorised assurance given earlier by Murphy was in large measure legitimised. Calhoun wrote to the Texan negotiators: 'I am directed by the President to say that the Secretary of the Navy has been instructed to order a strong naval force to concentrate in the Gulf of Mexico, to meet any emergency; and that similar orders have been issued by the Secretary of War, to move the disposable military forces on our southwestern frontier for the same purpose.'[8] The treaty between the United States and Texas was finalised, signed, and laid before the US Senate on 22 April. It had with it related correspondence, including the letter from Aberdeen to Pakenham of 26 December 1843, which had found its way to the US Government in February. Aberdeen's intention had been to rebut any suggestion that Britain's main purpose was abolition, but his mentioning Britain's stance towards slavery in general had prompted Calhoun to represent Britain as intent on imposing abolition everywhere, including Texas. In the light of this, said Calhoun, the United States could 'no longer refuse, consistently with their own peace and security' to respond positively to Texas's request for annexation; but Calhoun had misjudged the American people's reaction to his enthusiasm for annexation.[9]

Charles Elliot wrote to Aberdeen in May from New Orleans reporting on these developments. In line with public opinion the Senate had not ratified the treaty, and Elliot clung to his belief that if only Mexico could be persuaded to recognise Texan independence then there would be no appetite in Texas for annexation. He wrote:

> It may, I think, be depended upon… that if Mexico can be induced to acknowledge the Independence of Texas, the Government and people would reject any renewed overtures for annexation to the North American Union. Their recent consent has been less the result of a desire to form part of that Union, than of a belief that the agitation of such a project would dispose the Government of Mexico to acknowledge their Independence.[10]

Elliot may or may not have been right in his assessment of how Texas would react to Mexican acceptance of independence, but he had no evidence for his assertion about the reason for Texas's acceptance of annexation. It was another example of the wishful thinking to which he was prone. He also had other things on his mind, not least plans for the improvement of his health. With a reference to the presidential aspirations of Henry Clay, and no doubt agreeably surprised by the response to his leave request, he wrote to his sister:

> My dearest Emy,
> The last mail has brought me leave of absence to return either to Europe or to proceed to any northern part of the United States. I was very much tempted to go at once to Europe, but upon the whole I have thought it better to remain in the neighborhood of my post, at all events till the annexation affair is fairly set to sleep. So far as I can judge there is no chance of carrying it during the present administration's time, and if Mr Clay should succeed, still less. We are going to the Springs in the Mountains of Virginia, which are said to be of great virtue for complaints of the kind that I have been afflicted with.[11]

The Elliots left for Virginia leaving Consul Kennedy as the senior British representative in Texas. Before he departed, Charles Elliot suggested to Aberdeen that the most efficient route for contact between the Foreign Office and himself would be via the British Consul in Boston, and said he had made it clear to Kennedy that he was not to get involved in diplomacy; he was to 'confine himself strictly to an unobtrusive and prudent discharge of his Consular duties.'[12] Elliot's relationship with Kennedy was not close. There had been little contact since their first meeting. That had been cordial enough, but Kennedy clearly found it irksome, with his greater knowledge and experience of Texas and its people, to be excluded from the diplomacy now shaping the country's constitutional future. His dissatisfaction was compounded by the absences of the superior officer entrusted with this role, who was now about to be away again, for an unspecified but almost certainly longer period than hitherto.

Elliot had also asked Kennedy to forward to London any 'informations ... during my absence, which he may judge to be of interest.'[13] Kennedy lost no opportunity to do so, writing to Aberdeen frequently while Elliot was in the United States. His first letters were mostly on matters of disagreement between himself and the Chargé d'Affaires in which he was implicitly critical of Elliot. Subsequently he supplied information in his consular brief on such things as port charges, and people and ship movements. He also reported on what he had been able to glean of diplomatic and political developments.

Charles Elliot did not return to Galveston until December. During his absence the annexation issue had continued to command the attention of politicians and diplomats in Texas, Britain, Mexico, the United States and now, again, France. Aberdeen had instructed

Lord Cowley, the British Ambassador in Paris, to propose to the French Government a plan for the British and French to act jointly to persuade Mexico to acknowledge Texan independence. The Foreign Secretary had first held explanatory meetings with Mexico's man in London, Tomas Murphy, and with the Texan Minister in Britain, Ashbel Smith. He informed Charles Bankhead, Doyle's successor as British Chargé d'Affaires in Mexico, of what he had said to Cowley: if Mexico recognised independence, Britain and France would guarantee protection of both independence and the Mexico–Texas border from interference by any other country. Aberdeen had made it clear to Murphy that if Mexico did not accept Texan independence, Britain would not oppose the annexation of Texas by the United States, nor would it act on border issues. Should France assent to this proposal, Aberdeen advised Bankhead on 3 June,

> we propose to send out forthwith a fit person to Texas, in the unavoidable absence of Captain Elliot, who will be instructed to ascertain as accurately as he may be able the state of publick opinion and feeling with respect to the projected annexation of Texas to the United States, under the security of the joint guarantee above described.[14]

Importantly, Aberdeen was explicit that abolition in Texas should not be a condition of the recognition of independence by Mexico. Since she had herself accepted Texan independence without such a stipulation, Britain was in no position to suggest that it be required by Mexico.

A proposed annexation treaty was again considered by the United States Senate on 8 June. The northern states, motivated by opposition to the acquisition of a state committed to slaveholding and by the risk of war with Mexico, as well as personal antipathy to Tyler and Calhoun, ensured its defeat by thirty-five votes to sixteen. As Pakenham wrote to Aberdeen some three weeks later, this did not mean that the annexation question had gone away, and he warned the Foreign Secretary in blunt terms of his view that if Britain and France tried to implement the proposal for joint action, the United States would annex Texas forthwith.[15] In Texas, Houston's exasperation with the annexation issue reached new levels. His disillusionment caused concern in the United States, now taken up with a forthcoming presidential election in which a committed annexationist, James K. Polk, had emerged as the Democrat candidate against the Whig Henry Clay.

By the end of June, Charles Elliot had taken up residence in the mountains of what became West Virginia. He wrote to Aberdeen from Blue Sulphur Springs, a spa resort built ten years earlier which had attracted some notable visitors, including Henry Clay and Presidents Andrew Jackson and Martin Van Buren. He was aware that he was falling far short of what would normally be expected of a Chargé d'Affaires in such a rapidly changing political situation. His tone in places was tentative and pleading:

> I have the honor to report that I am ready to proceed to my post whenever my presence there may seem to Your Lordship to be desirable; and I would add that I have written privately to Mr Pakenham some days since, to say that I shall be prepared to return to Texas at any moment that He may see reason to recommend that course.
>
> Through the press of this Country I learnt that the treaty of annexation had been rejected by the Senate of the United States.... But I suppose it may be taken for granted that the subject of annexation will be renewed again in some form, at the next regular Meeting of Congress in the United States, if not at a called Session, and perhaps with more probability of success than has attended the treaty.[16]

He concluded 'I take the liberty to repeat to Your Lordship that communications to me, addressed to the care of Her Majesty's Consul at Boston, will always reach me within a few days arrival at that point'.[17]

With Elliot to all intents and purposes *hors de combat*, Bankhead in Mexico new to his post and caught up in the country's political turbulence, and Kennedy causing irritation through unauthorised attempts to involve himself in diplomacy, it was Pakenham who was Aberdeen's main source of information and advice from the New World. His warning letter of 27 June quickly persuaded Aberdeen to stall his plans for an Anglo-French initiative; Cowley was instructed to inform the French of the British change of policy; and the French Foreign Minister, Guizot, agreed to the deferment of the project. While Britain and France waited during the summer and autumn of 1844 for the outcome of the US presidential election, changes of leadership were afoot in Mexico and Texas. Santa Anna's bellicose threat to invade Texas to prevent US annexation faded as his own position became increasingly fragile and he was eventually ousted. In Texas Anson Jones was elected to succeed Houston as President and began to exert influence well before formally taking up office in December.

By mid-July Elliot had moved to White Sulphur Springs, a short distance to the southeast, and in August was in Washington DC. After letting the Foreign Secretary know that he had been in correspondence with Henry Clay, and was therefore retaining some involvement with the political situation, Elliot referred to the opportunity he had been given to leave North America:

> Your Lordship will have observed from my despatches that I did not consider it suitable to avail myself of the permission to return to Europe in the condition of affairs which had come about, by the time that it reached me, neither have I liked to do

so till replies to the intelligence of the failure of the treaty shall have reached me, either directly, or through Mr. Pakenham. In the mean time I am glad to find that Mr Pakenham agrees with me in thinking there is no need for my return to Texas till we shall be further instructed from England.[18]

and he ended with his now familiar expression of dutiful availability 'Your Lordship is aware that I am ready for any service that may be charged to me'.[19] He was reassured to have Pakenham's endorsement of his continuing absence from Texas, though it was probably given at least partly because Pakenham thought Elliot had been away for so long that he would be unable easily to pick up the reins again and might do more harm than good if he were to return. The Elliots moved on again during August. Charles's health may have been gradually improving, but Clara was in poor shape; Emma was informed from 'near New York'[20] that she was again 'very alarmingly ill'.[21]

Clara duly recovered enough to travel. On his way up to New York, Elliot had visited Pakenham in Washington DC and at the same time had written to Aberdeen seeking authorisation to delay his return to Texas until the beginning of November. He was torn between the call of duty, which told him he should be back in Galveston as soon as possible, and a personal desire to stay away as long as he could, not only for the sake of his own and Clara's health, but because of a strong dislike of Galveston itself with its primitive amenities, lack of agreeable distractions, and inhospitable climate.

At the end of October he wrote to the Foreign Secretary from Philadelphia, indicating his intention to leave for Texas between the 7 and 10 November, having first called in to see Pakenham again. As if to underline his seriousness about returning, he concluded 'May I request that any despatches to my address may once more be addressed to the care of Her Majesty's Consul at New Orleans.'[22]

Charles Elliot arrived back in Galveston on 7 December, but without Clara and their 2-year-old daughter Emma. He later said in a letter to Aberdeen 'owing to the severe sickness of my child I have been compelled to leave my family amongst strangers in a hotel at Philadelphia'.[23] Clara and Emma were to remain in the north, Elliot hoped, for as long as their health and recuperation required. He would have wished to stay there with them, but duty dictated that he re-immerse himself in diplomacy in Texas without further delay.

Elliot's first reports to London on his return to Texas were taken up with his initial impressions of the annexation situation, and with the substance of a meeting in Washington-on-the-Brazos with Anson Jones, now installed as President, who like his predecessor was not wholly committed either to independence or to annexation. Elliot was in less doubt than perhaps he should have been that the Texan government was opposed to annexation, but made clear to the President his view that if the popular will was in favour then that would prevail. For Elliot, there was even now a chance that if Mexico would recognise Texan independence, the popular preference for annexation would fade. He reported that Jones too

> did anxiously hope that Her Majesty's Government would use it's immediate and decisive influence with Mexico, to propose the recognition of Texas.... He does not doubt if it were in the power of this Government to declare to the people of Texas that such a proposal was before them, He and his friends would have strength enough to turn them aside from any further thought of annexation.[24]

Aberdeen was also supplied by Elliot with a pen portrait of the President, so that he would be able to assess Jones's trustworthiness and his likely approach to the annexation question and reaction to any British proposals. Elliot thought the President

> remarkably cautious and reserved, and with a moderate degree of the skill and firmness of his predecessor he will probably be able to controul affairs very materially with much less appearances of direct interposition than General Houston, and with less stormy opposition.[25]

This favourable assessment of Anson Jones was in stark contrast to the letter (marked Secret) composed the following day about the disruptive activities of General Duff Green. Green had been in Texas as US Consul since the end of November, living up to his reputation for mischief making and irresponsible business activity. It was not strictly necessary to trouble the Foreign Secretary at this juncture, but in part to show that he was now fully functional again, and in part consistent with his innate tendency to dramatize, Elliot wrote:

> circumstances satisfy me that his true position here is that of secret agent to the unshrinking advocates of annexation in the United States, or should I rather say of extended mischief against Mexico, for it is manifest that their objects are not limited to the annexation of Texas only.... The foundation of all his Schemes is the incorporation of a land Company ... with the management of their affairs in the hands of a Director appointed by themselves, powers to levy and maintain troops for defence *against Indians*.[26]

Elliot's conclusion was that Green was not planning against Indian attacks, but for aggressive action against Mexico, and that to this end Green was seeking 'to transfer almost all the powers of the Constituted Authorities of this Country ... to a Confederacy of political Speculators and Capitalists in the United States.'[27] Whether or not Elliot was right about Green's intentions, Green had overstepped the mark as far the Texan President and Attorney General, Ebenezer C. Allen, were concerned. Green had publicly maintained that it was Elliot, not the government, who was shaping Texas's policies, a claim also reflected in his correspondence with Major Andrew Jackson Donelson, the US Charge d'Affaires in Texas: 'Capt. Elliot arrived here [at Washington-on-the-Brazos] last night. He promises that in case Texas will pledge herself against annexation England will obtain the consent of Mexico for her Independence.'[28] President Jones accordingly cancelled Green's authority to function as Consul, a development subsequently reported by Elliot to Aberdeen.[29]

The early months of 1845 brought differing perceptions of where the annexation issue stood. The election of James K. Polk as United States President, due to assume office in March, reinforced the determination of the pro-annexationists in the United States, even though their opponents still thought Congress would never agree. In Mexico the Foreign Minister in the post-Santa Anna government, Cuevas, showed some inclination to entertain recognition of Texan independence but before going further sought rather more robust evidence of support from Britain than had so far been forthcoming. Aberdeen held to his position of moral support for Mexico but nothing more tangible. He urged Mexican recognition of Texas but wished at all costs to avoid any confrontation with the United States. In Texas itself Jones, like Houston before him, professed himself against annexation, but was now more aware that the wishes of his fellow Texans might leave him no choice.

Charles Elliot continued to hope and believe that Mexico could be persuaded to recognise Texas and that annexation could be avoided. He was low in spirits; he was without his family; he not heard from London for some months, and he had not yet fully re-engaged with developments after his absence in the United States. His frustration found expression in a communication to the Foreign Secretary which, with its enclosure of over 7,000 words, was one of the longest he ever sent. The enclosure consisted of notes he had written for possible future use, angrily criticising Calhoun's pronouncements that abolition in British colonies had been a failure, and that the decreased production of sugar in those territories 'he considers to be entirely attributable to the change from forced to free labour'.[30] There was much invective against Calhoun personally for his 'incredible ignorance' and other alleged shortcomings, but Elliot's main thrust was that abolition was not primarily, or even at all, about economics.[31] It was a matter of common humanity, and history would 'record this measure of emancipation ... as the worthiest deed ... the mightiest victory that any people ever achieved over their selfishness and cupidity, for the sake of justice, and the cause of the helpless and oppressed, to the end of time'.[32] It was not surprising that he put pen to paper about Calhoun's views; he felt passionately about slavery and his work in British Guiana thirteen years earlier had supplied him with first-hand knowledge and experience. That he chose to send these notes to Aberdeen at this particular time was perhaps an indication of how his mood was affecting his judgement, and he knew that it was quite possible that they would be of no interest, in which case 'I will take the liberty (with my excuses for the trouble to which I have exposed Your Lordship) to ask that they may be forwarded to my Sister Lady Hislop.'[33]

On the same day, no doubt with Calhoun in mind, he wrote gloomily to Emma: 'You will imagine that I am leading a wretched life enough in this vile hole ... this Texas question has come to be the grand centre of all the lies and [?injury] and knavish tricks of the American Politicians...'[34] In February, however, Elliot received an instruction from Aberdeen dated 31 December requiring him to act with extreme caution over the annexation question – a policy which, he was gratified to note, he had already been following.

In the last week of March the policy of caution gave way to bolder tactics. In a despatch of 23 January the Foreign Secretary set out the views of Her Majesty's Government on the Texas independence issue as they then stood, but the substance of his communication was a November report from Bankhead in Mexico of a meeting he had had with Santa Anna. The President had indicated that Mexico might at last be prepared to entertain the idea of Texan independence. There were, needless to say, conditions, some of which were unacceptable, but it was a start, and Aberdeen was now moved to seek French support for a new joint initiative. The following week, on 3 February, he forwarded to Elliot a copy of a parallel communication from Guizot to the French Chargé d'Affaires in Texas, Alphonse Dubois de Saligny. 'Upon receipt of this Despatch [his 23 January letter]', Aberdeen instructed Elliot, 'you will immediately confer with the French Charge d'Affaires ... and you will lose no time in bringing the subject jointly before the Texian Government'; and he concluded, 'you will do well to avoid all unnecessary mention of the Government of the United States, and all comment upon their Policy'.[35]

March 1845 was a critical month in the annexation saga. Just as a more positive stance was being adopted by Mexico, in the United States the outgoing President Tyler had obtained the formal support of the Senate and issued instructions to Donelson to make an offer of annexation to the Texan government. Concurrently, Elliot was meeting with Ashbel Smith, now returned from Europe and appointed Texan Secretary of State. Smith was sure that the mood of the Texan population was inclining more towards independence, provided of course that Mexico would recognise it on acceptable terms. He asked that Elliot convey to Aberdeen – which he did – the basis on which Texas would wish to proceed and to which he believed Mexico would consent: that Mexico would immediately recognise Texas as independent; that Texas would undertake never to annex to, or be annexed by, any other country; and that the matter of territorial boundaries and indemnities be subject to negotiation, with external arbitration if necessary.

At the end of the month Charles Elliot found himself centre stage. Following Aberdeen's instructions, Elliot and de Saligny met in Washington-on-the-Brazos with Ashbel Smith and Anson Jones. The outcome, as reported by Elliot, was threefold: an agreed memorandum pledging Texas for ninety days not to annex to any other country, and including the basis for proceeding which Smith had previously discussed with Elliot; agreement that as evidence of goodwill and serious intent Smith should return to London, where he was much respected; and that Elliot should go 'with the utmost despatch and secrecy to Mexico in order to make a fresh explanation to the Ministers of our Courts there of the extreme difficulty of the President's situation, and the urgency of immediate promptitude, and exact conformity to the preliminary arrangement here submitted.'[36] Here, more than three and a half years after leaving China, was an opportunity for some action, a prospect Elliot welcomed. He did express reservations to Aberdeen about the plan: 'Personally considered, if I may venture to include a personal consideration, it is distressing to me on several grounds; but the President attached so much importance to it, and my Colleague [de Saligny] advocated it so strongly that I have thought it my duty to go'.[37] Since he had himself proposed the mission in the first place, this was a little disingenuous. He was quick to move into cloak-and-dagger mode:

> I shall of course take every practicable precaution to keep my visit there strictly secret and shall not remain one day longer than may be necessary for the purpose of full explanation. With the intention of concealment I shall cause it to be understood that the *Electra* has gone to Bermuda with dispatches to meet the homeward Mail, and that She will drop me at Charlestown, to which place I have for some time been expecting that Mrs Elliot would pay a visit.
>
> I shall also ask the Commander not to anchor at Vera Cruz, but to send me into any English or French Man of War lying there, as an officer charged with despatches for Her Majesty's Minister at Mexico, and the ship will go away, and be reported by another name. It is also my purpose not to return to this place [Galveston] or New Orleans from Mexico, but if possible to land somewhere in the United States where I am not known, and to return to New Orleans in some unobserved manner. I hope to be there by the 1 May in time to receive my despatches by the April Mail.[38,39]

The following day, 3 April, HMS *Eurydice* arrived at Galveston with communications from Bankhead in Mexico, and it was to that ship that

Elliot transferred after leaving Galveston for the voyage to Vera Cruz, from where he travelled up to Mexico City.[40]

Elliot's mission to Mexico had to be conducted so as not to arouse United States' suspicions of British interference, and it had to be carried out quickly to avoid undue delay before the US annexation offer was submitted to the Texas Congress. It went well to the extent that the objective with Mexico was realised. The Mexicans agreed to cease hostilities with Texas on the assumption, subject to negotiation on the details and confirmation by the Mexican Congress, that Texas would continue independent.

When news of Elliot's intended visit to Mexico reached Aberdeen he was at once concerned, not about its aims but the manner of its execution. He conveyed his worries to the Prime Minister, Peel:

> The only part of the transaction which I do not much like, is the journey of Capt. Elliot to Mexico at the request of President Jones, and his attempt at concealment. This cannot succeed, and it will make English agency appear too active, and too hostile to the United States. The Texian Government has taken a great responsibility on themselves by acting in opposition to the wishes of the people, and after all it is very doubtful if their decision will be confirmed by the Congress [of Texas]. Much will depend on Mexico and here unfortunately there is very little reason to expect anything like discretion or common sense. It is their last chance, and if they do not now secure the independence of Texas, annexation is certain.[41]

Peel agreed; but in Mexico, Elliot, Bankhead and the French and Spanish ministers (with whom Bankhead had been working on the Texas question) were elated at the positive response from the Mexicans, which was formally confirmed on 19 May. On his way back to Galveston on the French brig *La Perouse* Elliot even allowed himself some upbeat comments to his sister, writing (after describing 'all the suffering of the last two months'):

> But praise be to God, my first item of business has come to a right conclusion and I am now going back to Galveston with the preliminaries of peace signed upon the basis of acknowledgement of Texas by Mexico. It is hard to think that the Texians will prefer annexation upon disadvantageous terms, with the certainty of a war, to peace and independence.[42]

On his arrival in Texas Elliot began to realise that his optimism had been misplaced. President Jones announced the agreement of Mexico in a proclamation, in which it was clear that the British had played a key part in the negotiations. He recommended a Convention for wider discussion and to try to head off the annexationists. The proclamation had the effects of alarming American agents and officials, re-igniting suspicions of British plots and intrigue against the United States, and laying Jones open to charges from the people that his government was being manipulated by Britain. Well before the proclamation rumours had begun to circulate in the United States that Britain had been involved. At some point during his mission Elliot had been identified, as Aberdeen and Peel had feared, and reports of 'The Man in the White Hat' appeared in the US Press. Once the outcome of the mission had been made public, no attempt was made to conceal Elliot's role in it. Sensing that his continued presence in Texas was likely to be inflammatory and counter-productive, he decided to leave for the United States. He wrote a private letter to Bankhead explaining that

> I am on the point of leaving this Country for I really do not think it proper to remain here whilst this Convention is sitting. The Measure is purely revolutionary, and I see no suitable excuse for remaining in Texas whilst the people are unlawfully, or at all events beyond the Law, debating on the extinction of their Nationality, and the violation of their compacts with the Powers who have treated with them.[43]

He continued: 'My health too is shaken heavily, and I have private distresses with which I will not trouble you, but they are sad to bear'.[44] Bankhead was not happy, urging Elliot to reconsider his decision to go:

> it is absolutely necessary that this Legation should be *accurately* informed from time to time of what is going on in Texas – and, moreover, Lord Aberdeen particularly enjoins you to do so [stay] in his Instruction of 3 May.
> I take the liberty of adding that my opinion is fully supported by my French Colleagues and by the Mexican Government.
> I send this by HMS *Persian*, and I fervently hope that She may arrive in time to prevent your putting your plan into execution.[45,46]

She did not. Elliot had left for New Orleans, from where he intended to go on to New York, nearly two weeks earlier. The Texas Convention voted on US Independence Day, 4 July, to reject independence and commit itself to annexation to the United States, to take formal effect in February 1846.

It was in New York that Charles Elliot received a letter from Aberdeen concerning his role in the formulation of the proposal for the recognition of Texan independence and in its conditional acceptance by the Mexico. 'Her Majesty's Government', said the Foreign Secretary, approved of 'the energy and ability with which, in conjunction with M. de Saligny, you prosecuted this matter with the Government of Texas'; but that was not the main point of the communication.[47] He continued:

> It might have been preferable, however, that you had not proceeded in person to Mexico; and at all events it would have been better if you had not proceeded thither secretly, or under a feigned name or character, inasmuch as the mystery which necessarily attended such secret expedition was liable to give rise to erroneous notions and false interpretations of our motives and intentions, especially on the part of the United States.

Another rebuke from another Foreign Secretary; but Elliot was not as discomfited as he had been over China. His personal circumstances – poor health, dislike of his environment, family worries – gave him a different perspective on his professional activities. He knew that his duty in Texas was to work against the odds. Like Aberdeen, he had been fully aware that Texas's independence was very unlikely to be able to survive the growing force of public opinion in favour of annexation. He also understood the importance for Britain of keeping the peace with the United States. Whether he thought through the consequences were his mission to be discovered is doubtful; if he did, he may well have concluded nevertheless that the attempt was worth the risk. It seems more likely that he had full confidence in his ability to maintain the necessary secrecy and did not think beyond that. His response to Aberdeen's criticism, written shortly after receiving it and in the belief that he had made an important contribution to the cause of Texan independence, maintained that speed and secrecy had been essential to his mission if intervention by the United States was to be avoided. Elliot said he had believed, and still did, that there would have been some positive outcome since

> even if it failed the completion and subsequent publicity of the conditions recommended to Mexico by the Governments of Her Majesty and the King of the French could in no way prejudice the public interest but would on the contrary subserve them. The want of conclusive proof in the sight of the people of Texas and of this Country, of the dispositions and ulterior motives of Her Majesty's Government had already furnished the advocates of Annexation with their most powerful means of sustaining it. I believed therefore that moderation on the part of Mexico, even at that late hour, and unequivocal evidence of the character and extent of the arrangement supported by Her Majesty's and the French Governments would deprive Annexation of the chief pretext which had given it so much strength here.[48]

If Elliot had indeed believed it, this rather contorted argument was at best wishful thinking, and the likelihood is that it was regarded as such by Aberdeen. Before concluding Elliot could not resist commenting on the coverage his mission had received in the American newspapers:

> I may at least observe that the mystery adverted to was no more than was necessary to conceal my destination. What has been said on this subject in the press of the United States is merely that kind of unscrupulous attack and misrepresentation to which persons are liable in the discharge of their public obligations, and in this particular case is no more than the natural consequence of a faithful attempt to perform my duty to my own Country, and I must give myself permission to add, no bad evidence of the extent to which the success of these proceedings has been felt to interfere with the easy accomplishment of bad and dangerous schemes.

This, too, was unconvincing. His dismissive contention that a hostile press was a 'par for the course' inevitable consequence for a public servant seeking to do his duty was something which, in his more reflective moments, he probably did not believe himself; but its tone was an indication that he was prepared to meet Aberdeen's rebuke forcefully.

The Foreign Secretary did not wish to prolong the correspondence concerning Elliot's Mexico mission and did not refer to the matter again. Elliot, though, had also found himself in the firing line shortly before, this time in connection with his relationship with the consul, William Kennedy. In March the previous year, 1844, Elliot had written to Aberdeen, privately and unofficially, alleging that Kennedy's health

> not merely bodily, but I fear mental, has given way to the effects of strong drink ... I ought to have mentioned to Your Lordship before this that I had no confidence in Mr Kennedy's temperance or discretion.[49]

Proposing that the Consul should be given leave of absence in England, Elliot was clear that he could not 'consider Mr Kennedy to be in a sufficiently secure state of mind to fulfil his trust with uniform steadiness.'[50]

Elliot wrote again to Aberdeen in May 1845, this time officially, complaining in strong terms about Kennedy's conduct towards him. It had, Elliot said, been so improper as would have justified Elliot's suspending him. Aberdeen was clearly annoyed. He was blunt in his criticism:

> I regret that you should have thought it your duty to make Charges so serious against Mr Kennedy without adducing

any evidence in justification of them. I regret also the tone in which those Charges are made. You have, moreover, entirely misapprehended your own position and authority, in supposing that you have the power to suspend a person who has been appointed by The Queen to reside and act as Her Majesty's Consul at Galveston.[51]

He asked Elliot to provide evidence and detail for each of the allegations he had made. Elliot will have sent a response but, like the allegations themselves, it is not in the Foreign Office papers. It seems likely that the long-standing acrimony between Elliot and Kennedy, which found expression in Elliot's complaints about Kennedy's drink-related behaviour, was also fuelled by Kennedy's encroaching on diplomatic business which was properly in the domain of the Chargé d'Affaires. Where the blame for that lay is an unanswered question; Kennedy had ideas above his station, but Elliot's repeated absences from Texas left the consul as the senior British official there.

Elliot's absences and the Kennedy matters were finally put to rest by Aberdeen in letters to Elliot on consecutive days in September. Aberdeen expressed his regret that Elliot had let his irritation get the better of him in making the accusations against Kennedy, but he was willing to take in to account the poor state of Elliot's health, and admitted that while the government would have preferred that he had stayed in Texas, it did not attribute any blame to him for not doing so.

During the late summer of 1845 the Texas Convention and its committees were engaged in formulating proposals for the Constitution of the new US State of Texas. There were issues which prolonged the exercise, notably the question of what territory the State would actually cover. Elliot was in correspondence with Bankhead about his decision to leave Texas, explaining at greater length than before that while his health was a factor, he felt that he had done all he could towards the prevention of annexation or the mitigation of its consequences. Though Bankhead was of the same status, it is clear that he was greatly respected by Elliot, who was anxious to be well regarded by him. To Aberdeen, Elliot maintained his flow of reports on the current situation as he saw it. He described the American naval and military build-up in Texas, preparatory, as he had presciently observed to Bankhead, to what he was sure would become a war between the United States and Mexico. He was in no doubt who was responsible for the impending hostilities, informing the Foreign Secretary that he had been strengthened in the belief

> that the movement of the United States troops beyond the Sabine was made mainly to commit the Legislatures and people of the two Countries beyond all possibility of retraction. But beyond that motive, I cannot but think, that the advance of the American

force, within the territory which the Government of Texas in the preliminary conditions sent on to Mexico palpably admitted to be subject to Negotiation and compromise, affords conclusive proof that the Government of the United States desired to provoke hostilities by Mexico; probably with the view to the sudden seizure of certain positions on the Coast of California.[52,53]

His correspondence was not, of course, all official. From the Elliots' temporary home at Rockaway, a summer holiday area on Long Island, New York, Charles had written to Emma in July with condolences on the death of their sister Harriet.[54] There seems no evidence that they were close, but like Clara, Harriet had married a naval officer, Captain (later Admiral Sir) James Plumridge. In August there was happier news; Charles was able to send congratulations on the confinement of Emma's daughter Nina, who the previous year had married her second cousin William, the third Earl Minto.[55] She gave birth to a son, later to become the fourth Earl and Governor General of Canada.

In October Elliot still clung to the hope that appropriate action by Mexico could prevent annexation, but by the end of 1845 none of the main players in the drama, on whatever side, was in any real doubt that annexation would take place. That certainty did not mean, so far as Britain at least was concerned, that diplomatic activity could be relaxed. When he wrote his two letters to Elliot in mid-September, Aberdeen had told the Chargé d'Affaires to await further instructions. Elliot replied somewhat defensively on 6 October saying that he had always intended to return to New Orleans if events so required. Aberdeen's response this time allowed no further discussion:

> Until the final Annexation of Texas to the United States shall have taken place, Her Majesty's Government consider it indispensable that you should be at your post at the Seat of Government in Texas, in order to maintain the Communications between the two Governments, and to keep Her Majesty's Government regularly and authentically informed of all that takes place in Texas.
>
> I have therefore to desire that you will forthwith repair to your post, and that you will remain there until you receive orders from Her Majesty's Government to leave it.[56]

On his way back to Texas Elliot learned from Pakenham that the resolutions for annexation had been passed by both Houses of Congress and had been approved by the President. He arrived in New Orleans on 4 January. A few days later the matter of the mission to Mexico raised its head again, this time in the *New York Herald*. The newspaper had published on 22 December some outspoken criticism of Elliot, especially his venture's attempted secrecy, in a letter by Polk's Secretary of State James

Buchanan to Donelson. Elliot's conduct, Secretary Buchanan said, had excited feelings of indignation throughout the country. He continued:

> These are not confined to any party, but pervade the whole community. One of its good effects has been to render us, to a very great extent, a united people on the question of annexation. It is scarcely possible that his conduct can be approved by his government ... Captain Elliott, in his efforts, has transcended all reasonable bounds. To assume the character of a secret negotiator of the government of Texas with Mexico, in a hostile spirit towards the United States, to conceal his agency in this matter, by pretending that he had left Galveston for Charleston, when his destination was Vera Cruz, and then to prevail upon Mexico to consent to the independence of Texas on condition that Texas should never annex herself to the United States – these acts, taken together, are at war with all the recent usages of diplomacy, and with the character of the British government, which is generally bold and frank, if not always just, in its policy towards foreign nations.[57]

Elliot's scheming would be thought ridiculous, Buchanan concluded,

> But what is far worse on his part, by obtaining the consent of Mexico to the independence of Texas, he has deprived that power of the only miserable pretext which it had for a war against the United States, whilst he has fomented among the Mexican people a spirit of hostility against us which may plunge that ill-fated country into such a war.[58]

Precisely as Aberdeen had feared, this was a propaganda gift to the pro-annexationists. Despite Buchanan's strictures, the annexation die was already cast, and the assertion that Elliot might be responsible for precipitating a war was without credibility. Elliot knew nevertheless that the letter could do his own reputation substantial damage, and was quick to explain himself to Aberdeen, writing at considerable length on 8 January. Buchanan's censure, he implied, was essentially a case of sour grapes that he had succeeded with the Mexicans. His concealment had been necessary, and he had initially indeed been intending to travel to Charleston; but most of Elliot's letter was taken up with the case, yet again, against annexation and – which is unlikely to have gained him much sympathy – with some highly critical and sweeping criticism of the American people and their institutions. He was careful to say that this was not his intention, but his reassurance was unconvincing:

> I know that there are as many reasonable and honest persons in the United States as in any other part of the world,

proportionately to the population. But it is unhappily equally true that if there were many times more; the course of public events would not be materially altered, or there is a great preponderance of ignorance, prejudice, and rashness, not only in the body of the people, but in the councils of the Nation, sinking more and more palpably to a very low level, by the rapidly deteriorating operation of universal suffrage.[59]

Elliot argued that this was all a consequence of a move from representative to pure democracy, which he alleged had been shown to be unstable and incompatible with true freedom. The fact was, however, that he had been stung into an intemperate overreaction. Anyone reading his letter who was not aware that it was not typical of his communications would have been seriously concerned. As it was, Aberdeen did not respond.

The Government of the Republic of Texas was formally dissolved on 16 February 1846. In the early months of that year Charles Elliot was busy keeping the Foreign Secretary informed of military and political developments; correcting what he saw as inaccuracies and possible false impressions from earlier reports; and putting in place arrangements – mostly to do with British ships previously contracted to trade with the Republic – for dealing with the new authorities in Texas. His health was still poor, and shortly after dissolution he moved again from Galveston to New Orleans. On 3 April Aberdeen wrote to Elliot formally terminating his appointments as Chargé d'Affaires and Consul General with effect from the ending of the Republic, and instructing him to return to England as soon as convenient. Then, in another letter the same day, as if he had thought his first note rather peremptory, 'With reference to my dispatch of this day's date ... I have much pleasure in acquainting you that Her Majesty's Government have highly approved the zeal and intelligence with which, ever since your appointment, you have executed the duties committed to your charge.'[60]

The stress and discomfort of the Texas years were now at an end. The Elliots arrived back in London on 16 June. From next door to his sister Emma's house in Wilton Crescent, Charles wrote to the Foreign Secretary about his future. He was, as always, short of money: 'Deprived of my post by circumstances in Your Lordship's knowledge, I beg to express my readiness, and I hope I may add my earnest desire for early re-employment, for I have no fortune, and a large family entirely dependent on me.'[61]

Though hampered by ill health, Elliot's motivation and intentions in Texas had been largely creditable. He had made mistakes, of which the execution of the Mexico mission was the most public, and his relationship with Kennedy had been problematic. He had nevertheless established a close working rapport with Presidents Jones and, especially, Houston and communicated constructively with the British Chargés d'Affaires in Mexico and the United States, and with his French counterpart.

Whether or not the prevention of annexation was ever a realistic prospect, Elliot worked conscientiously to give the British aim of Texan independence the best chance of success that circumstances would allow. While he was aware of the need not to provoke the United States, that was a higher priority for Aberdeen and the British government than it was for him. For Elliot the containment of slavery – a first step towards its abolition in North America – was of equal or greater importance.

From later in 1846 until 1848 the United States fought and won a controversial war with Mexico, one result of which was that Mexico relinquished its claim to Texas. In 1861, following the election of the abolitionist Abraham Lincoln as President of the United States, Texas and initially six other southern slaveholding states, followed by a further four, broke away from the Union and formed the Confederate States of America. The Union victory in the ensuing Civil War saw the passing in 1865 of the Thirteenth Amendment to the US Constitution, by which slavery in the United States was abolished.

Charles Elliot's request for early re-employment was successful. He was able to write in August to his friend the former Lord Howick, now third Earl Grey and Secretary of State for War and the Colonies: 'I accept the Government of Bermuda very thankfully...an appointment which from many circumstances is peculiarly acceptable and agreeable to me.'[62]

# PART THREE

## Chapter Fifteen

# 'A Delightful Residence'

Patronage still played a major part in colonial appointments in the first half of the nineteenth century, but such appointments were regarded by the political and civil service establishment as of lesser standing and less desirable than, for example, those made by the Foreign Office to diplomatic posts. Colonial governorships were often difficult to fill and the arrangements for selection haphazard. Sir William Molesworth, briefly Secretary of State for the Colonies before his death in October 1855, was of the view that 'Men of superior ability will not go there.'[1] Sir James Stephen was later to write that 'Not to be a Governor of a Colony is one of those blessings, the diffusion and general enjoyment of which renders us insensible to their value.'[2] Nevertheless, postings to the colonies offered independence and adventure for younger men and opportunities for more experienced individuals, often ex-soldiers, to exercise real responsibility in unfamiliar environments.

In the 1840s there was no recognised career pattern for colonial government officers, including the Governors themselves. The first official reference to a Colonial Service had been as recent as 1837, when the Secretary of State for War and the Colonies, Lord Glenelg, had issued a set of Colonial Rules and Regulations. The intention was to consolidate the various regulatory requirements to make them better understood and observed. Glenelg acknowledged that this would to start with be an imperfect exercise, but he was confident that the collected standing regulations would 'at least, form a basis for future improvements; and will, probably, tend to the immediate introduction of a better method, and of greater certainty in the despatch of the duties of the Governors, and other Public Officers in the Colonial possessions of the Crown'.[3]

Elliot was now 45. If the Governorship of Bermuda was seen by some as a sideways or even a downward career move, to him it was a welcome relief from the trials of being based in Texas. Aberdeen, who had resigned as Foreign Secretary two months earlier, was in no doubt that the appointment would be welcomed by Elliot and took the trouble to write to him shortly after it was announced:

> After your exertions and long sufferings in unhealthy climates, you must look with satisfaction to the prospect of passing some years in a delightful residence ... I really feel obliged to Lord Grey for having made this appointment, as your services had given you strong claims upon me to which I was no longer able to attend.[4]

Some four months after returning from Texas, during which their preparations were punctuated by the inevitable social engagements including a banquet given by the Lord Mayor of London, Charles and Clara Elliot sailed for Bermuda. According to the Bermuda press, they were due to leave England on 20 October in an Indiaman, the *Mariner*.[5]

Bermuda is the longest established of the United Kingdom's remaining overseas territories. Named after Juan de Bermudez, the Spanish sea captain who discovered them in 1505, the islands which comprise the Bermuda archipelago did not receive their first settlers until 1609. They came from the ship *Sea Venture*, one of a fleet chartered by the Virginia Company to replenish the struggling colony of Virginia with people and supplies. The *Sea Venture* was blown off course during its voyage to America by a severe storm and was wrecked off Bermuda. Though most of the shipwrecked passengers did eventually make their way to Jamestown, Virginia, those who remained in Bermuda formed the core of a permanent settlement from 1612, when Richard Moore assumed office as its first Governor, appointed by the Virginia Company in whose control the islands then lay. For a time the territory was known as the Somers Isles after Admiral Sir George Somers, a key figure in the foundation of the colony. From the Somers Isles Company, the Virginia Company's successor, responsibility for gubernatorial appointments passed to the Crown in 1684. It was subject to the ultimate authority of the British monarch as head of state, but Bermuda had been, from 1620, a self-governing colony with its own parliament. After an initial and unsuccessful concentration on agriculture, the colony turned to the sea for its main sources of income. Shipbuilding, whaling and especially privateering became established enterprises, but by the nineteenth century the islands were not remotely self-sufficient. When Elliot assumed the Governorship imports for the previous year (1845) at £140,015, almost entirely from the United States, had been nearly seven times the value of exports, £20,884, which went to Britain and the West Indies.[6,7]

For Britain, Bermuda's value was primarily strategic. Work on developing the dockyard into a major facility for the Royal Navy had been started in 1813 during the American War of 1812–15. In 1818 the main base for the North American and West Indies squadron was transferred to Bermuda from Halifax, Nova Scotia, giving British warships better access to the coast of the United States, should hostilities break out again, and to the Caribbean to counter piracy and slave trading.

During the middle years of the nineteenth century Bermuda had another, more controversial, role. From 1823 it was used for penal purposes, with most of the convicts accommodated in prison hulks off Ireland Island near the dockyard. They typically numbered between 1,300 and 1,700, distributed between up to five hulks and prison on land, under the authority of a Superintendent of Convicts supported by (among others) Surgeon and Chaplain Superintendents.[8] Shortly before Elliot was appointed it had been decided that the Superintendent of Convicts should be discontinued as a separate post and the duties subsumed within the responsibilities of the Governor. Sensing that here was a significant addition to his role, and conscious as ever of his own shortage of money, Elliot raised the matter with Grey before his departure. Elliot said he fully recognised the importance of this work, and would give it as much attention as he could,

> But looking to the probability of an increase in the number of convicts at Bermuda, to the actual conditions of the Establishment there ... and to the growing solicitude of Her Majesty's Government and Parliament upon the whole subject of Convict management, I certainly do feel that the regulation and adequate supervision of this branch of my duty will form an anxious and large claim upon my thoughts, time, and personal attention.[9]

He thought that the use of convict labour for naval works, on which he considered he had some expertise of his own to offer, would make it appropriate for him to receive an extra allowance. The main thrust of his request, though, was for funds to cover his expected extra workload: 'I trust Your Lordship will see reason to recommend to the Treasury that I should receive an allowance for the maintenance of a Private Secretary, in consideration of the increased duties cast upon me by the direct Superintendence of the Convict Establishment at Bermuda.'[10] Grey gave instructions that Elliot should be told his application was premature, and that he should wait until he was in Bermuda and had been able to assess at first hand what would be needed before considering re-submission.

Bermuda's strategic importance was recognised in a level of salary for the Governor that was slightly more generous than its relatively small size – some twenty-one square miles and a population of 9,930 – would have justified.[11] Governor Elliot's income comprised an annual salary of £2,199 from parliamentary grant throughout his eight-year tenure, plus £500 from the Colonial Treasury, together with small amounts from fees and rents which varied from year to year and an allowance for a housekeeper and boat crew, all amounting to some £300 per annum.[12,13] His predecessor was an army lieutenant colonel on full service pay, but the regular salary of the Governor before that, Sir Stephen Chapman, in 1834 was £2,835, one below the median figure (£3,000) for thirty-one colonial governors, lieutenant governors or equivalent at that time.[14] Elliot was not being especially hard done by, but he was always conscious of his lack of significant private means and of the prospect of acquiring any. No opportunity should be lost, as he saw things, to press for additional income.

The Elliots, Charles, Clara and their children Gibby, Freddy and Emma, disembarked at Bermuda on Christmas Day, 1846. Before long Charles and Clara were into the social round, attending a lavish ball which had the dual purpose of welcoming them and of honouring the commander-in-chief of the North America and West Indies station, Vice Admiral Sir Francis Austen and his family.[15] Two weeks after arriving Elliot wrote to Grey on the question of additional staff. Anxious to get his governorship off to a good start and to redeem himself in the eyes of his friend Grey, he withdrew his request. 'I am persuaded', he said, 'I shall receive from the legal and other Public Officers of the Colony all needful Counsel and assistance in the Superintendence of the Convict Establishment which has devolved upon me by virtue of my Office'.[16]

Lieutenant Colonel William (later Major General Sir William) Reid, who was Governor from 1839 to 1846, is much lauded in historical accounts of Bermuda as probably the most successful and well-regarded Governor the colony ever had, making his tenure the hardest of acts for Elliot to follow. Reid was a military engineer who had served in the Peninsular War and in the war with the United States of 1812 to 1815. As it was for Elliot, Bermuda was Reid's first appointment as a colonial governor. His reputation derived from a wide-ranging, energetic desire to improve the prospects of Bermuda and its people, which he translated into vigorous action. Notwithstanding the introduction of standing regulations by the Colonial Office, colonial governors generally had, and continued to have, considerable latitude to act on their own initiative as individuals.[17] In Bermuda's case this freedom was tempered by the territory's governance arrangements as a self-governing colony, but Reid's persuasiveness and popularity were such that his schemes and projects usually attracted wide support. It was in 1844 during his Governorship that the Gibbs Hill lighthouse, the tallest in Bermuda and believed to be the oldest cast-iron lighthouse in the world, was built by the Royal Engineers. As an engineer himself, Reid was well placed to take a close and informed interest. Perhaps his most important contribution, however, was his largely successful effort to revive agricultural activity in the islands, long since virtually abandoned as inefficient and ineffective. He also sought to improve educational opportunity for the populace, a venture that was prompted in part by the need to ensure prospects for newly emancipated slaves.

Charles Elliot too was keen to make his mark as a pro-active governor. He nevertheless realised that he could do worse than continue to build on the work done by Reid. The Elliot years were for Bermuda largely ones of consolidation, but at the same time eventful. Much of a colonial governor's time was necessarily taken up with routine, formal and minor matters. He was required for example to report quarterly to the Colonial Office that he had been present and functioning for the preceding three months; to seek permission for certain appointments and promotions; and to sign off the annual statistical and financial report (the Blue Book) of the colony for submission to the Colonial Office.

On the domestic front, the Elliots settled early in 1847 into the Governor's residence at Mount Langton on Main Island overlooking the capital, Hamilton, and its harbour. The house – more modest than the present 1892 built Government House – was set in some forty acres of grounds, an extensive area which caused Elliot to worry about its maintenance. It was not long before he again sought extra staff, this time not with funding from the British government but with help from his family. He would provide the money himself. He wrote whimsically to Viscount Melgund:

> I write a few lines to ask a favour of you. We have got a sort of domain round my palace consisting of 40 or 50 acres of sand and marsh and the little improveable soil, but which nevertheless produce, *tant bien que mal*, wherewithal to furnish our table with vegetables, and some amount of what the imaginative of my Kingdom have the face to call hay to keep out the starvation of the horses. What I want you to do is to ask Selby to induce some painstaking industrious cross between the gardener and the farmer to come out here and be my Bailiff or Chief Commissioner of the Woods and Forests. I would give him £50 per annum and find him a lodging and he should sell for his own profit whatever there was of surplus from the kitchen garden after supplying our Royal table.[18,19,20,21]

Governor Elliot was later to become much concerned with the convict population of the colony, but in his first year there were other preoccupations. In July 1847 Grey asked him with some urgency for his comments on some earlier correspondence about Bermuda's defences. The British government was keenly aware of the need properly to maintain Bermuda, 'the Gibraltar of the Atlantic' as it was sometimes called, as a strategic base. 'The subject [the colony's defences] is one of the very highest importance', Grey wrote, 'the possession of these islands in time of War with the greatest value to us as a naval station and the injury to which we might be exposed by their falling into the hands of any other power is equally obvious'.[22] By 'any other power', Grey meant primarily the United States, with which - as Elliot well knew - a climate of mutual suspicion continued to exist and whose expansionism was perceived to threaten British interests in the Caribbean.

All requests for major grants to colonies, for defence as for any other purpose, were scrutinised by Parliament, acting as the Committee of Supply. Some such proposals were vigorously contested, colonial expenditure being recognised as potentially a substantial drain on the country's resources and in need of tight control. Five years earlier the government had nevertheless voted Bermuda a special allocation of £18,126 for the purchase of land on which to build new barracks nearer the shore for more effective defence.[23] With his naval service background Elliot took a keen interest in maritime projects, including non-military as well as defensive works (he had, for example, in March taken a hands-on part in an operation to improve harbour access by using explosives to widen the approach channel.)[24] He found no difficulty in replying to Grey's request for comments, which he did at some length on 8 October.[25]

It was also in July that Elliot took up the cause espoused by Reid of reinvigorating agriculture. In a bid to encourage each of the nine parishes to take systematic responsibility for developing agriculture in the interests of the whole community, especially the poorer parts of it, he wrote an open letter to parish leaders, which was published in the *Bermuda Herald*:

> The high price of Provisions in the Markets to which the Inhabitants of these Islands chiefly resort for supplies, must be a subject of anxious reflection to every thoughtful person in the Country.
>
> Moved by this impression, I recommend the Magistracy and influential Inhabitants of the several Parishes meet together ... to consider what means there may be of stimulating the industrious cultivation of Ground Provisions ... and particularly of inducing the extensive planting of Irish Potatoes...
>
> I should also suggest that a Committee of benevolent and experienced Persons should be named in each parish, charged with the task of drawing up and distributing directions concerning the preparation and cultivation of the Soil. And I think it would excite more general attention to this subject if each parish would raise small funds by subscription ... for defraying the charge of a monthly examination and published statement of the said soil in cultivation...
>
> I would also recommend that every effort should be made to encourage the rearing and stalling of cattle...
>
> There is reason to apprehend that privation and suffering can only be averted from the poorer classes of people in these islands by the rigorous and concerted exertions of the whole Community; and I have confidence that the Magistracy and the leading Inhabitants of the respective Parishes will devote themselves to the objects of this letter with zeal, intelligence and liberality.[26]

It is not clear how far this appeal for collective action and money was effective. Though Bermuda was formally a Crown Colony, with overall authority vested in the Governor appointed by the Crown, its self-governing status meant that on internal matters such as education, welfare, and agriculture the Governor could only recommend, rather than determine, policy. The two instruments of government in addition to the Governor were the House of Assembly and the Council, which had been in place for many decades and were overdue for reform, largely on grounds of cost. The ten-man Council sat both as the Executive Council, chaired by the

Governor, and as the Legislative Council, but the main concerns related to the House of Assembly, which comprised thirty-six members, four elected from each of the nine parishes, and whose chairman could change from meeting to meeting. To the problems of expense – members were paid $2 for each day on which they sat, however short the meeting – were added criticism of the unfairness of the wealth qualifications for electing and standing for election; of time wasting with unnecessarily repetitive resolutions; and of persistent slowness of action. Reid had wanted to see reform but had not achieved it. According to a contemporary observer, Governor Elliot was similarly frustrated, being moved to address the Assembly in 1849 in forthright terms: 'This slow and costly transaction of the simple affairs of a very small community, is no doubt attributable to the cumbrous inaptitude of the legislative machinery'.[27]

Elliot's initiatives in the field of education, however, brought tangible results. William Reid had founded Bermuda's first library and was himself a meteorologist of some repute, but it fell to Elliot to promote more systematic educational provision for the population as a whole. An Act 'for aiding in the Establishment of Schools', passed in August 1847, established a Board of Education for Bermuda. Eleven months later Elliot submitted to the House of Assembly the Board's First Report. During the year Board members had visited all schools from which requests for aid had been received, noting inadequate provision generally of books and stationery and a high degree of absenteeism. Progress had nevertheless been substantial; between 1846 and 1847–8 the number of 'free' schools (those mainly funded by Christian charities and colonial grant) had increased from seventeen to twenty-four, the number of pupils in them from 700 to 1,064, and support expenditure from £595 to £1,153 per annum.[28]

Elliot could derive considerable satisfaction from this development, which was a significant step forward for the education of young people in Bermuda. The establishment of an eponymous primary school in 1848 in Devonshire parish, which continues to thrive today, is a permanent reminder of his commitment to improving education in the islands.

1848 also marked a change of commander-in-chief of the North America and West Indies Station. After four years in the post Sir Francis Austen retired at the age of 74 and was succeeded by Vice Admiral Sir Thomas Cochrane, tenth Earl of Dundonald. As Lord Cochrane he had distinguished himself in the Napoleonic Wars, becoming much admired (and feared) by the French. Like Elliot, Dundonald was no stranger to controversy. He had been expelled from Parliament, dismissed from the Navy and stripped of his knighthood after he was found guilty of fraudulent stock exchange dealings in 1814. His conviction was vigorously disputed, Cochrane himself protesting his innocence for the rest of his life. Though he was reinstated in the Royal Navy in 1832, he declined active service until his knighthood was restored in May 1847. Like Austen, he assumed the North America and West Indies command in his seventies and retired from active service after relinquishing the post.

Dundonald's years as commander-in-chief, which ended in 1851, did not feature any of the heroics of his earlier career. The role of the squadron continued as it had been under Austen, the routine protection of British trade interests in the region, especially during the American–Mexican war of 1846–8, and the disruption of slave trading, notably by Brazil. Of the 159 ships of the Royal Navy on overseas duties in 1845, deployed on eight stations around the world and in 'particular service' task forces, the North America and West Indies Station accounted for twenty-five.[29] Only eleven, however, were fighting units; the others comprised support vessels of various kinds including receiving, hospital and supply ships and, importantly, convict hulks.

The lack of any major military operations should have allowed the fortification of the Bermuda naval base to proceed unhindered. Initially the Royal Navy had established a base at St George's in the east of the islands, but towards the end of the eighteenth century moved its centre of activity to Ireland Island in the west, where land had been acquired for a much larger development. The project was beset in its early years by labour supply problems. Local manpower was scarce, and was more productively employed in traditional Bermudan work such as small ship construction. The solution, which was to remain in place for nearly forty years, was convict labour. In 1823 the most recent in a series of amending and consolidating Transportation Acts had permitted the employment of convicts on public works in the colonies. The fortification of the dockyard in Bermuda and the building of associated defences were deemed an entirely appropriate use of this new dispensation. In 1824 the *Antelope*, a former troopship, arrived in Bermuda from Britain with 300 convicts and 200 Marines on board. Progress on the development of the dockyard was painfully slow, however. It was a challenging project, involving major land reclamation and the construction of long breakwaters. To early labour shortages were added inadequate provision of the necessary machinery and frequent storm damage. After more than a decade in which very little had been achieved, the recently arrived Earl of Dundonald was typically forthright in his comments on the subject, reporting to his naval masters in London that

> there was nothing in the Yard to defend – the space enclosed by ramparts is an entire void, except the half finished Victualling Store, and 2 small wooden buildings to be pulled down. The space is incapable of holding the Dockyard and the Victualling Yard. There is not a Shed in which the Sails of the Flag Ship can be fitted, not even space for setting up a Spunyarn reel out of the rays of the Sun. Water cannot be got for the Ships; the glacis should be plastered and tanks built.[30]

Dundonald was moreover highly critical of what he saw as the vast amounts of money wasted on building ever more fortifications, when what was needed were gunboats to provide a mobile defence capability. The mistaken policy so far followed had resulted from a lack of appropriate naval involvement in the planning. If there had been any, he said, savings would have amounted to 'many hundreds of thousands of pounds, perhaps a million ... I assert that gunboats not only would suffice, but are by far the most available, and easily the cheapest defensive force amongst [these] rocks.'[31] The need for Bermuda, especially the naval base, to be properly defended was not in doubt, but the question of how that should best be achieved led to protracted debate between London and the colony over several years. Governor Elliot, of whom Dundonald was generally supportive, was to submit in 1851 a twenty-seven page memorandum to Earl Grey requesting various defensive improvements. Perhaps with the operations of the *Nemesis* in the Pearl River delta ten years earlier in mind, and in line with Dundonald's view, he placed considerable emphasis on the provision of

> 2 small iron steam boats ... such rapid means of concentration and movement of troops in a country abounding with defensive positions from one end of it to the other and with the sea penetrating into all parts of it ... would be a more effective as well as a much more economical reinforcement than an additional battalion of infantry without those facilities'.[32]

Though Grey was sympathetic, the official response was negative, on grounds of cost and because, it was said, the navy could itself manage any critical situation that might arise.

The frequent correspondence between Governor Elliot and the Secretary of State in the summer of 1848, other than routine business, was almost entirely taken up with convict matters. The two men had very different concerns, however. Elliot was anxious to see an improvement in prisoners' living conditions generally, while Grey reflected the British government's major preoccupation with Ireland and the Irish, Irishmen now comprising a sizeable proportion of the convict population of Bermuda. His focus was John Mitchel, a lawyer and journalist whose alleged revolutionary nationalist activities had resulted in a conviction for treason and a sentence of fourteen years transportation. Grey informed Elliot that Mitchel was being sent to Bermuda, and anxious to avoid any action that would risk his subsequently acquiring martyrdom status amongst his compatriots, suggested that he be housed in hospital accommodation

> since he is supposed to be of a consumptive tendency, if not already labouring under decided consumption, & that it is highly important he should be so treated as to find no ground for its being alleged hereafter, that his life has been lost owing to the manner in which his sentence has been carried into effect.[33]

It was Elliot's view, however, that if Mitchel were to be accorded this kind of special treatment – there were no prisoner patients in the hospital – there would be an even greater risk that the resentment of other prisoners could boil over into severe disorder. As he had done before, Elliot decided that as the man on the ground his own judgement should prevail; he had Mitchel accommodated not in the hospital (the newly converted convict hulk *Tenedos*) but in the *Dromedary*, one of the regular prison hulks. He was nevertheless keen to show that he understood Grey's concern, informing the Secretary of State that Mitchel would be in the custody of 'a firm but discreet and humane man', and adding that he would be kept apart from the other prisoners.[34] To the disquiet of Irish Protestants in Parliament Mitchel had already, in transit to Bermuda, been given what they considered unjustifiable privileges, but the fact was that he was no ordinary convict. Being careful not to go too far, Governor Elliot, along with others in authority in Bermuda, recognised his status as a highly erudite educated political prisoner and ensured, as Grey would have wished and as Mitchel himself acknowledged, that his living conditions were tolerably comfortable. Having been provided with books and various other items Mitchel wondered in his diary whether

> With all these appliances, both for bodily health and mental dissipation, with liberty to write for, and receive any books I please from home (except political periodicals), with sufficient space to exercise in the fresh sea-air, with abundance of good food, and a constant supply of fresh water, and paper, and pens ... it would be possible to live here for some indefinite number of years, or even for the whole fourteen, should nothing happen to cut them short.[35]

Unease continued to be expressed in Parliament about the undue leniency allegedly being shown to Mitchel. In July, Elliot was able give assurances to Grey's satisfaction that his treatment was appropriate – and went further, indulging in some of the exaggeration to which he was prone: 'With his health shattered and his spirit broken I venture to suggest whether it may not be humane and wise to send him to Australia on conditional freedom or the ticket of leave.'[36] In due course Grey undertook to respond to this suggestion, but in the meantime had more pressing concerns, about security. He had alerted Elliot some weeks earlier to the possibility that an attempt might be made from the United States to kidnap Mitchel, and urged the Governor to take every precaution to prevent his escape to America. Elliot duly promised to take firm action, including if necessary the imposition of martial law, should there be any unrest amongst the Irish in Bermuda in the approach to the forthcoming US presidential election. The Democratic candidate General Lewis Cass displayed, Elliot said, 'exaggerated hatred to England, inordinate vanity, and perfectly unscrupulous ambition'.[37] The supposed threat of attempted abduction never materialised. Mitchel eventually sailed for Cape Town in April 1849 and on to Van Diemen's Land (Tasmania), from where he escaped to the United States in 1853. Elliot's proposal that Mitchel should leave Bermuda on health grounds was not primarily because he was a highly controversial figure, though that was a factor. Mitchel's spirit was not broken, but his health was indeed in a very poor state and despite his less harsh treatment his future looked bleak.

The conditions under which convicts were housed in the hulks were oppressive and insanitary. Elliot was concerned that the inmates' environment should be drastically improved. Most Bermuda convicts served out their sentences, generally seven or fourteen years, in the colony with no prospect of betterment; but Elliot's communications with London on the urgent need to ameliorate their conditions in Bermuda went further. He sought also to persuade the British government that there should be increased opportunity for onward transportation to Australia, where some hope of a better life could be offered. He was particularly concerned about the predicaments of the Irish and juvenile convicts. Of the Irish he reported, with reference to the Great Famine, that

> many of them were convicted of stealing food, and agrarian offences; the first, no doubt, chiefly attributable to the dreadful calamity which befell the poorer classes of people during the last two years, and the last in a high degree to the inflammatory practices of others, in the time of desperate need.[38]

He wondered whether

> Her Majesty's Government may be pleased (taking all these circumstances into consideration, on the return of a state of comparative tranquillity in Ireland), to permit me to appoint a Commission in this colony, for selecting individuals from the Irish prisoners, whom it may be permissible to recommend for removal to Australia, on the ticket of leave or conditional pardon. These prisoners are for the most part friendless men in humble stations of life, and your Lordship will feel that they are entitled to any extenuating considerations which I can advance on their behalf, whilst they are conducting themselves steadily and submissively at this depot.[39]

Elliot made it clear, without any hope of immediate change of judicial practice, what he thought of the sentences meted out to many of the boy convicts who had recently arrived in Bermuda:

Poor and scanty food and the hard things of their infancy have for the most part left these lads with a lower stature and more childish appearance than their age alone would suggest, though it will shock H.M. Government to learn that twelve of them are under sixteen years of age, and that of the thirteen-year-olds one has been sentenced to fifteen years transportation for sheep-stealing![40]

In November 1848, five months after submitting his request, Elliot had in place criteria for choosing 250 Irish prisoners to sail to Australia, and by 1851 was able to house some 600 convicts in a newly constructed stone jail on Boaz Island instead of on board the hulks.[41] He could subsequently feel some satisfaction that he had played a key role in beginning the process of abandoning the hulks and, eventually, of discontinuing convict transportation to Bermuda.

Family and health matters were never far from Charles Elliot's mind. He and Clara decided to send Gibby, now aged 14, home in April 1848 to the East India Company's college at Haileybury. He was thought by his father to be bright and well able to cope with the demands that would be made of him. A year later Clara also returned to England, with a view to going abroad for the summer. It seems probable that her plan was to travel in Europe, possibly for her health. Elliot hoped that if she did go, she would be able to take Gibby with her. In any event, Hughie (aged 18) was to accompany his mother. At this stage Elliot appears to have had great confidence in Gibby, and found no difficulty in making highly critical remarks to him about his elder brother, whose academic motivation and progress had been sadly lacking:

It is high time that he [Hughie] should be doing something for himself. He is a good natured creature, as ever lived, but very volatile and idle. If I have any luck he will get a Cavalry Cadetship, and as I often tell him unless his horse has more brains than the animal on his outside they will come to no good ... Hughie has thrown away if not a fortune at least the life of a gentleman.... Do not you play the same foolish trick for Heaven's sake.[42]

Charles Elliot was not particularly well at this time. The nature of his illness is not clear, but it seems likely that it was a recurrence of the dysentery that had dogged him in recent years, especially while he was in Texas. Whatever it was, it persisted. In May 1852 he successfully applied for leave of absence to go to England to seek medical advice. In a briefing note a colleague reminded Herman Merivale, who had succeeded Sir James Stephen as Permanent Under Secretary, that 'Governor Elliot obtained leave of absence last year [1851] to come home on the ground of ill-health, but did not avail himself of it', and thought that the present

Secretary of State Sir John Pakington would probably 'not refuse the same indulgence to a Governor, who has managed the affairs of his Colony so well, and who unfortunately still stands in need of medical assistance in England'.[43,44] Elliot had not indicated a period for his leave, but Pakington granted it on the assumption, made clear to Elliot, that he would return to Bermuda as soon as his health allowed.

Return he did, leaving London at the end of October 1853, after more than a year in England. Having learned with great concern of the outbreak of yellow fever in Bermuda, he was anxious to ensure that the necessary measures were taken to help end it and to relieve the suffering of the bereaved. The colony had experienced yellow fever epidemics before, but this was the most widespread to date. It claimed the lives of more than 800 in total, with the greatest concentrations amongst the convict establishment and military personnel.[45]

In the weeks before he embarked for Halifax, Nova Scotia en route to Bermuda, Elliot had lobbied vigorously for authority to release convicts back to England according to the length of sentence served and subject to satisfactory behaviour. Completion of approximately one third of a man's sentence would suffice to secure his release. Those incapable of further labour should also be returned home. Elliot conveyed his request with great urgency to the Duke of Newcastle, Pakington's successor as Secretary of State, who lost no time in instructing his officials to proceed. Merivale wrote to Henry Waddington, his opposite number at the Home Office:

> I am directed by the Duke of Newcastle to request that you will state to Viscount Palmerston [now Home Secretary] that His Grace considers it an object of pressing importance to take some immediate and decisive steps with respect to the release of a proportion of the convicts who are now employed on public works at Bermuda. This measure, His Grace would point out ... is at this moment the more essential from the fearful mortality which has been occasioned by the epidemic which now prevails in that island. The Duke of Newcastle is of opinion that the Governor of Bermuda should be authorised to make immediate arrangements.[46]

As well as seeking powers to repatriate convicts, Elliot requested funds with which to help those survivors most affected by the epidemic. Sir Charles Trevelyan, Assistant Secretary to the Treasury was asked to lay the request before the Treasury Commissioners. When Elliot reached Halifax the news from Bermuda was as bad as he had expected, prompting him to make another plea for the Treasury to grant his request for funds as soon as possible. By mid-January 1854 he was able to report to Newcastle that the sum available for the relief of yellow fever sufferers and their dependants, £1,055, had been distributed, as agreed by a small committee including the Colonial Secretary and the Mayor of Hamilton, to 183 widows and children.[47]

Governor Elliot had been satisfied in December that the epidemic was at an end, declaring 4 January a 'Day of Prayer and Thanksgiving' for deliverance. The passing of the disease marked a decisive point for him. 'In this state of circumstances', he wrote to Newcastle, 'I venture to hope that Your Grace will be pleased to consider my respectful request to be relieved from the administration of this Government as soon as the convenience of the Service may admit of such an arrangement'.[48]

January was a busy month for Elliot. He already knew that his next appointment was to the Governorship of Trinidad, but there was still work to be done in Bermuda. Follow-up action after the epidemic included thanking (at great length) the commander-in-chief North America and West Indies, now Vice-Admiral Sir George Seymour, for his assistance in sending crucial medical and other aid from Halifax. He also forwarded to the Secretary of State a list of twenty-one prisoners who had worked with particular dedication as nurses during the outbreak; the remainder of their sentences was to be cancelled, and with five others specially commended, they were to return home. All was not thanks and reward, however. Convicts were aware of the less harsh approach now being taken towards them. Lest any should assume more leniency than was justified, Elliot saw fit to issue a warning. He transmitted to Newcastle

> a copy of a memorandum I have caused to be read to the prisoners with the purpose of discouraging malingering ... a column will be inserted on all lists of recommendation for Her Majesty's clemency showing the actual number of days in each year that each candidate for release before the expiration of sentence has been in the actual performance of the work allotted to them.'[49]

The tidying up completed, Elliot wrote to the Secretary of State saying that he had done all he had to do in Bermuda and that on his departure the administration of the government of Bermuda would devolve (temporarily) to Colonel Montgomery Williams, Royal Engineers. The Governor's last formal communication was the standard certificate of attendance and diligence, suitably extended: 'I certify that I have been in the execution of my duties from the 1st of January last to this 13th day of February, when I have embarked on the Brigantine *Daphne* to proceed to assume the Government of Trinidad.'[50]

By most reckonings, Charles Elliot's Governorship of Bermuda had been generally successful. He had not accomplished all he would have wished, particularly in so far as the colony's machinery of governance was concerned, and his attempts to revive agriculture seem not to have had any enduring effect. The fortification of the naval base and the defensive development of the territory remained a work in progress for many years to come. A leading historian of Bermuda referred to the years 1839 to 1854 as 'the great period of Reid and Elliot'.[51] Whether or not that description is justified, Elliot's work in widening educational opportunity in the colony is properly remembered as a significant achievement. Of at least equal importance were the initiatives he took to improve the conditions and prospects of the convict establishment, which were consonant with the eventual abolition of transportation to Bermuda, and with the evacuation of all convict prisoners by 1863. Elliot's concern to alleviate the suffering caused by the yellow fever epidemic was much lauded in the Bermuda press, perhaps in the knowledge that his health had been problematic and could have resulted in his remaining in England for longer, proceeding then direct to Trinidad instead of returning to Bermuda.

## Chapter Sixteen

# Back to the Caribbean

In the twenty-five years since Charles Elliot completed his active service in the Royal Navy much had changed in the West Indies. The apprentice system which had replaced slavery in several British colonies after its formal end in 1834 had been followed in Trinidad and elsewhere by an influx of thousands of labourers from Asia, largely India and China. The hope was that this process of replacing the enslaved workforce would lead to the restoration of the sugar and cocoa-based economy of the island to its previous level of prosperity. Though less affected by the economic consequences of emancipation than several other West Indian colonies, it took Trinidad's sugar industry some twenty years to recover. The immigration from many different European, African, Arab and Asian cultures which was in full flow during the 1850s continued into the twentieth century.

Since 1797 when the British took the island from the Spanish, an acquisition ratified by the Treaty of Amiens in 1802, there had been nine substantive (as opposed to interim acting) Governors of Trinidad. They had ranged from the controversial and harsh (Colonel Thomas Picton) to the benevolent and enlightened (Lord Harris).[1] Harris was Elliot's immediate predecessor, in office from 1846 to 1854. A man of considerable private means, some of which he used for the benefit of the colony, he is remembered in Trinidad as a progressive innovator who was responsible for improving the infrastructure and educational provision of the island. As in Bermuda, it was Elliot's lot to follow a highly successful governor. Unlike Bermuda, however, Trinidad was despite Harris's reforms not a happy environment in which to live. The island's abundant natural resources suffered from inefficient management and the islanders felt neglected by the British government. Harris had himself written to Grey in 1848 of the downturn in Trinidad's economic fortunes, that it was

> pitiable indeed to witness a fine colony daily deteriorating; a land enjoying almost every blessing under heaven, suffering from a shock from which it does not rally; but the deepest pang of all to an Englishman, is to see the hearts and affections of a whole population becoming alienated from the country which he loves.[2]

It was no surprise to Elliot when he arrived in 1854 to find that the colony had not yet fully recovered from the yellow fever epidemic which had swept the Caribbean and spread to Bermuda and elsewhere. In one of its regular news reports, 'From the West Indies', the *Bermuda Royal Gazette* had drawn particular attention in September 1853 to the prevalence of the disease in Trinidad.[3] Of even greater concern was an outbreak of cholera later in 1854, which spread alarmingly quickly throughout the island. In the capital, Port of Spain, the population was literally decimated. Not until news came from Britain that cholera had been shown to be a water-borne disease could effective action, including the filling in of wells near cesspits and the installation of water pipes, be taken to stem the epidemic.

The recently arrived Elliot family, now comprising Charles, Clara, 17-year-old Freddy and 14-year-old Emma, attempted to settle into their new surroundings. The task was made difficult by the Governor's residence, which had – like many other dwellings on the island – fallen into a state of serious disrepair. Yet the lushness and tropical beauty of the environment made a deep impression. The sense of wonder overcome by intense frustration is vividly and entertainingly described by Freddy, writing to his aunt Emma:

> My mother tells me that you want a long and true account of Trinidad. Accordingly I begin by telling you it is a paradise, but, as some person said, the paradise of toads and lizards, of which I think there are more in this island than in any place I have visited. The country is precisely beautiful, more than partly, and not sublime, at least in its present state, for I have not yet seen it in what is called the 'dry season'. The town, Port of Spain, is the best built in the West Indies, and boasts a church which would be beautiful anywhere ... we found the house [the Governor's residence] in the most complete state of dilapidation ... the Honourable the Council has, I am told, been spending 500 a year on it, which does not say much for the brightness of their wit.... My mother was, as she generally is after a sea voyage, very unwell, for nearly a month, however, (as I foretold) she recovered, and is now getting things a little in order. They have nearly (this hole being at last condemned) finished a little cottage for us, in the grounds. It will be very pretty, and I am afraid very hot, an inadequate residence for the Governor of an Island like this, who has to give dinners of more than 20, and balls of 500 people; our servants alone are twelve in number without gardeners...
>
> The various views are exquisite ... the colouring is gorgeous, which seems to be effected through the atmosphere, for a ribbon, faded in England, becomes vivid here. Scarcely a tree but has its blossom, some yellow, some red, &c. You may picture the effect

produced by such trees, mingling their colours with the masses of different shades of green, high up on the mountains, and the whole contrasted with the very blue sky.... But Trinidad, though so beautiful, is somehow a country in which few people can live, without being by turns, horribly irritable, and desperately indolent. The Island, as well as most individuals, is deeply in debt, so my father has the pleasant task of reducing, modifying, regulating, and all that style of thing. In fact, he comes rather unfortunately after Lord H — who having his private income, could well afford to spend all his salary in the country.... Here ends my history of Trinidad.... My opinion is, taking all things into consideration, that the sooner we get out of this place the better for there is a kind of continual oppression which affects people more or less, being to some a kind of punishment very like the dripping of water on the head, very pleasant at first, but becoming unbearable.[4]

Despite the developments initiated by Governor Harris, Trinidad remained in urgent need of further infrastructural improvement. Obtaining Colonial Office sanction for the money needed to achieve them was a continuing matter of argument with London. Harris, perhaps in the knowledge that if absolutely necessary he could find more cash from his own resources, had frequently spent first and sought permission later. A polite but firm note to Harris from the Parliamentary Under Secretary, Frederick Peel, is illustrative:

> I am to state to you ... that the Duke of Newcastle has no authority to sanction the very wide variations stated to exist between the estimated and actual expenditure of the years 1852 and 1853 – but His Grace will be happy to transmit to the Lords Commissioners of the Treasury any explanations of the several items which Your Lordship may wish to offer in addition to the notes which you have affixed to some of them in the return.[5]

Elliot too had plans for the public good requiring more funds than were immediately available, but he also needed adequately to house himself and his family. The cottage to which Freddy referred in his letter, though newly built and in good condition, was not fit for purpose. More accommodation was needed; the urgency was such that Governor Elliot committed the additional expenditure without delay. Having received a statement of justification from Elliot, Newcastle was sympathetic. Merivale passed on to the Treasury Elliot's explanation that 'the enlargement of this cottage was a work of urgent necessity inasmuch as the Government House was in such a state of dilapidation as to be dangerous.' and with a bureaucratic flourish informed the Lords

Commissioners that 'Under these circumstances the Duke of Newcastle is of the opinion that Governor Elliot was justified by the 11 Art. Chap.X Sec. 1 of the Rules and Regulations in taking this Vote of £700 without previous Authority from the Secretary of State.'[6,7]

For financing public works on the island, Elliot adhered to the procedural book. What was now required, a need made all the more urgent by the yellow fever epidemic, was more hospitals. He sought from Britain financial authorisation for new hospitals at Port of Spain (£7,000) and the second town San Fernando (£2,000), along with a 'lunatic asylum' (£3,000) at the former and a jail (£2,000) at the latter. Merivale informed Sir Charles Trevelyan at the Treasury that

> To meet this expenditure Governor Elliot recommends that authority should be given to the Legislative Council [of Trinidad] to raise a loan of £15,000 of debentures on the credit of the Colony & he encloses a Resolution of the Council pledging themselves to make good the payment of such loan and interest upon it.[8,9]

Merivale added that the Secretary of State (now Sir George Grey) was not prepared to propose a Treasury guarantee for the loan, but would recommend that the Trinidad authority should go ahead as suggested by Elliot subject to a moderate rate of interest of the order of six per cent.[10] There were also other construction initiatives, not all of which came to fruition. One which did was the canal known as Hart's Cut at Chaguaramas in the north-west of Trinidad, a shortcut which benefited fishermen and other local sailors. A scheme to export timber for shipbuilding for the Royal Navy was envisaged, but samples sent to Portsmouth and Woolwich were found not hardy enough for the English climate. Unsurprisingly, given his naval background and the prominence of the navy during his years in China and Bermuda, its role and requirements were for Elliot an abiding interest. He was keen to persuade his masters in London of the strategic potential of Trinidad, in particular for the development of Chaguaramas Bay as a naval base.[11] His was a lone voice on this subject in the colony; one of the leading merchants described his attention to strategic possibilities as a 'peculiar hobby'.[12]

The government of Trinidad at colony level was now, thanks again partly to changes implemented by Lord Harris, organised on what became a common pattern for Crown colonies – Governor, and Executive Council and Legislative Council with overlapping *ex officio* membership. Local government, however, was in Elliot's view in need of further reform. Each of the main organisational units, the wards, had its own warden but there were thirty-nine of them. Even though the island had, for purposes of government, been divided in two by Harris, nineteen or twenty wards in each part were too many for effective communication with the colonial authorities. An Ordinance was passed in August 1854, 'making certain amendments and alterations to the warden's ordinance, and making it lawful for the governor to form such and so many wards as he shall see fit into ward unions, and to appoint one warden for the several wards comprised in such union'.[13] The resulting scheme consisted of nine ward unions of two to six wards each, with a warden appointed for each Union.

During the first year of his term of office, from March 1854 into the early months of 1855, Elliot was at his most proactive as Governor. That this period of activity was relatively short can be attributed to several factors, personal as well as professional, which subsequently required him to react and manage rather than promote and innovate. He was left with little or no room for advancing the progress of the island.

Compared with Bermuda, Trinidad was strategically unimportant to Britain, and presented different challenges for a governor. With ten times the land area, its population was seven times the size, growing rapidly through immigration, and racially complex; the full economic benefits of its mostly fertile soil and tropical climate had yet to materialise; and as noted above its infrastructure, despite improvements, was still inadequate.[14] The colony required committed leadership and governance, and resources to match. Elliot was now in his mid-fifties. He had made a good start to his Governorship, but continued to be prone to bouts of illness. He was also increasingly worried about his family, in particular his wife's health and his children's education and prospects, and about money. Promotion to rear admiral on the Reserve List did little to lift his spirits.[15] As always in times of stress or despondency, his letters to his elder sister became more frequent and more anxious for response. When he became especially agitated he was not beyond a little sarcasm:

> My dearest Emy, I know you have resolutely determined every day for the last five weeks to congratulate me on this step towards one's last [?] that I have just taken – But the moment slipped by, and I let you off with the fellow feeling that the spirit was strong, but the – pen – weak.[16]

In this gloomy mood, Elliot's time in China, never far from his thoughts, became again a matter for explicit comment. He wrote

> I have always, in my [?account] of events, congratulated myself that the overland post was not in existence as far as China (at least) when I was there. If the Chinese, Gough, Senhouse, *et hoc genus omne*, had been reinforced by leading articles from the 'Times' a month old then the land force would have [?walked] away or been burnt up in the flames.[17]

Freddy, who never felt settled in Trinidad and was now 18, went home to England to his aunt Emma in August 1855. The many letters from Charles to his sister between July and November contained repeated concerns about Freddy and his future, but the anxieties were in reality as much to do with the possible financial impact on Elliot himself as with what was best for his son. He was emphatic at this point that Freddy should not go to Haileybury. He pleaded with Emma that

> <u>all applications</u> for a Haileybury appointment would be quite useless in the first place, and are quite contrary to my wishes for Freddy if that were not the case. If Freddy can <u>win</u> an Indian appointment by his own efforts I shall be greatly pleased, both for his own sake and for mine.[18]

Nevertheless, by the end of November he seems, very reluctantly, to have been persuaded that Haileybury was the right way forward. After a taxing time dealing with the cholera outbreak and continuing to be dogged by family worries, a confused depression had taken hold. He wrote to Emma:

> I am meditating retirement from public life, for I do not see what I have to struggle for. The government could not issue me with a pension … the difficulty I shall find in meeting the cost of Freddy's education at Haileybury and his outfit. Clara and the child [Emma] ought to go for home this spring, and I do not I think have the heart to remain without them…. If I do go to Europe in 1856, I should proceed via the W.I. to France; and then Hatty would come and see us.[19]

He was not contemplating going to England, he said, because, 'I should certainly not risk refusal by asking the government for any further employment, and having nothing to collect from them, I may spare myself the [?hurt] and [?calumny] of an English journey'.[20]

Following the organisational and public building initiatives of his first few months and the cholera epidemic, Governor Elliot found himself under sustained pressure from radical activists. From the start of British administration in Trinidad there had been repeated requests for some form of representative government, all of which had been refused. Elliot was sent a memorandum early in 1855 from residents seeking constitutional change for the island, which he forwarded to the Colonial Office. The reform being pursued included involvement in government by the educated minority, essentially, the planters, a development to which Elliot was firmly opposed. The way forward, he believed, was not the immediate representation of a privileged group, but the eventual enfranchisement of the population as a whole. As he put it: 'The disciplined and griping spirit of a narrow Corporation is always more hurtful to a community than the temporary and capricious excitements of enlarged constituencies, ignorant and impressionable as they may be'.[21] His message to the Colonial Office was that Trinidad was simply not yet ready for full representative government. The population was 'rapidly strengthening not in increasing proportions of intelligence and capital, but by a Heathen Immigration, and as regards the Immigration from the neighbouring regions for the most part by indigent and ignorant people'.[22]

The radicals' ambitions derived added impetus from the parlous economic state of the colony. The twin threats of reduced public expenditure and higher taxes reinforced their desire for representation. Low prices in Europe during the first six months of 1854 had depressed the island's income, added to which the government in London was exerting renewed pressure to balance Trinidad's books, a strategy fully supported by the new Governor. The Treasury had minuted the Colonial Office at the start of the year with a shot across the bows, trusting that the individual measures proposed by Lord Harris would 'have the effect of raising a Revenue at least equal to the estimated Expenditure'.[23] Should that not be the case, it would

> become necessary to instruct the Governor to consider carefully before the Estimates for another year are prepared what reductions may be necessary in the expenditure, as it is manifestly impossible to continue the system which appears to have existed and to vote year after year Estimates [of expenditure] exceeding the Revenue of the Colony.[24]

Senior officials at the Colonial Office during 1855 included not only Lord John Russell (Secretary of State), but Elliot's brother (Thomas) Frederick, and his lifelong friend Henry Taylor. Taylor agreed with Elliot's view that for the present Crown Colony status was appropriate for Trinidad, but sensing the danger of growing confrontation, Russell wanted from Elliot some proposals for bolstering confidence in the Legislative Council.[25] The Governor did not come up with anything new; in an upbeat report in early June, covering the (rather late) submission of the Blue Book for Trinidad for 1854, he merely expressed the hope that recent changes – by which he meant mainly the introduction of ward unions – would 'gradually furnish safe and convenient means of introducing a new admixture of the representative principle into the constitution of the Council of Government'.[26]

In Trinidad the momentum for reform was maintained. In October a public meeting in Port of Spain chaired by the mayor passed what amounted to a vote of no confidence in the legislature. It decided to set up a standing committee with a watching brief, to be known as the (Trinidad) Reform Association. From then on positions on both sides – colonial government and would-be reformers – hardened. The Reform Association began direct communication with the Secretary of State for the Colonies, now Henry Labouchere, articulating its opposition to higher taxation and maintaining that if unavoidable it should be levied on the whole population according to their ability to pay. The Association's Chairman, Anthony Cumming, sent Labouchere a note of four resolutions passed at a public meeting, which had been followed by a meeting of the Association's Committee on 20 November.[27] Concurrently, Elliot was writing to Sir George Grey, now Home Secretary, complaining at length about troublesome minorities. 'As an old servant of the Crown in these regions and rather stagnant communities, in which criticism is out of all proportion more plentiful than performance' he contemptuously alluded to

> those phases of perverse mischief (more or less chronic in these contracted communities) springing from that combination of idleness, extravagant self-importance, disregard of public time, and scramble for notoriety, on the part of a handful of persons, which forms the basis of what passes current under the sounding description of public opinion, in these little societies.... Their real purpose is to get the public finances under their management. Truly influential members of the Community who are steadily occupied, have neither time nor disposition to take an active share in clamorous agitation and in indiscriminate abuse.[28,29]

More in the same vein followed early in the new year. In a place in which most adults had been born into slavery, he said, it was inevitable that there were many 'uninstructed, dependent and … very idle people … too easily impressionable by any handful of unscrupulous persons who may seek for their own Ends to practise upon their ignorancies and their Conflicting religious and Caste prejudices'; all of which meant that in Elliot's view there was not yet anything in the colony that could properly be called public opinion.[30]

While the Secretary of State endorsed Elliot's plans to consolidate various offices in Trinidad to reduce expenditure, not everyone in the Colonial Office was unequivocally in support of the Governor. Perhaps because he knew Elliot so well and sensed an uncharacteristic level of animosity on his part, it was Henry Taylor who took issue over the role of the Reform Association, which Elliot had described 'an unauthorised association permanently organised for the purpose of watching the Government and Legislation of the Colony'.[31] Taylor held that 'in the absence of a representative polity or of the means of forming one, the educated portion of the Colonists shd. not be discouraged fm. watching the course of public affairs & expressing their opinions', then adding 'though they would doubtless do so with more credit to themselves and more public usefulness if their opinions were carefully and dispassionately formed and expressed with temper and propriety'.[32]

During this tetchy correspondence Charles Elliot, on 26 February 1856, tendered his resignation, as he had confided to his sister two months earlier that he might. The strain of his personal and professional responsibilities had been taking its toll for many months and his health was a continual problem. In April he told Emma that he was 'perfectly free of fever, but convalescing, I think, more slowly than I have done after any of my terrible attacks'.[33]

Elliot's judgement seems to have been affected by these pressures such that problematic professional issues were allowed to engender personal antagonisms. One involved the Reform Association member and first elected Mayor of Port of Spain, James Kavanagh, 'a wicked Irish Rebel' Clara called him, 'who has [?] acted as though he [was] the Governor'.[34] Like Henry Taylor, Elliot could not abide incivility. Of Kavanagh he wrote that 'Persons who have known him long acquaint me that his vehement malignancy of language ... almost amounts to madness, and it is charitable to hope that his rancour does spring from a disturbed judgement, and not from deliberate wickedness.'[35]

A continuing clash with the Italian Vincent Spaccapietra over his appointment as Archbishop of the Roman Catholic Archdiocese of Port of Spain was more serious. Spaccapietra had taken up his post in April 1855, the first non-British or Irish prelate to head the Roman Catholic Church in Trinidad, but whereas for previous appointments Rome had first informed the Colonial Office, no such notification had occurred this time.[36] Relations between the British and the Vatican became less than cordial. The deterioration did not last, however, except in Trinidad itself, where Governor Elliot refused to countenance the support of a non-UK national from colonial funds. Despite a Colonial Office assurance that there was no objection to such an arrangement, Elliot was adamant and the archbishop gave no ground either.[37] There was agitation and public protest from the Catholic community, which considered Elliot's policy to be contrary to the spirit of the 1797 Articles of Capitulation in which freedom of religious practice was guaranteed. The 'Catholic Committee' played a prominent role in the dispute under the leadership of its president, James Kavanagh, whose anti-English feeling was well known. The hostile reaction to the stance of the Governor and the Legislative Council was full of foreboding for Elliot, who feared that if Spaccapietra were recognised 'Trinidad would probably become the transient residence of a succession of the most intriguing and dangerous Italian and other foreign ecclesiastics'.[38] Elliot was convinced that such foreign influences would inevitably generate hostility to British interests, especially so far as language was concerned. He firmly believed that people should use the language in which the laws they live under are written, maintaining that 'Nothing could be better calculated to obstruct such a result than habitual intercourse with a foreign priesthood, ignorant of the English language and quite naturally less friendlily disposed to the Government and constitution of England than of their own countries.'[39] Whether or not this confrontation triggered Elliot's resignation, it did nothing for Elliot's reputation in the Colony, since Spaccapietra had become a well-respected and popular figure, not least as a result of his work in caring for those affected by the cholera epidemic.[40]

Though he had resigned, Elliot did not leave Trinidad until October. In April Labouchere wrote to him acknowledging that his many years of service in the tropics entitled him to relief from any further employment in the West Indies.[41] He was perhaps aware of Elliot's unheeded earlier preference, set out in a minute from Taylor 'that he would go as a point of duty and in obedience to orders wherever he might be sent, but he wished it to be known that he did not wish to be sent to British Guiana or Trinidad'.[42] Labouchere did not now rule out service elsewhere, but probably treated Elliot's resignation as an intention to retire. The award of a KCB at this time, announced officially in *The London Gazette* on 22 July, was consistent with such a view on the part of the Secretary of State. In one of his periodic resentful reflections on China Elliot later implied, cynically, that if he had been less conscientious he could have achieved higher honours, but for now he was delighted, and was clear whom he had primarily to thank: 'Nothing can have been more handsome than the manner in which this [?business] has been communicated to me.... The person to whom I am really indebted for this and for almost all that of good has befallen me in life is my dear old friend Taylor.'[43]

Towards the end of June Elliot told his sister he expected to sail for Europe the following month, an expectation which proved unduly optimistic.[44] In the remaining months of his Governorship the stand-off with members of the Reform Association continued. In a confidential letter written, unusually at this stage in his career, in his own rapidly deteriorating handwriting, Elliot dismissed them as having 'cast themselves into complete discredit amongst the respectable portion of this community by their unscrupulousness of assertion, and violence of abuse'.[45] Whatever the 'respectable' members of society thought, and whether or not they were justified in so doing, the Reform Association took advantage of Elliot's impending departure. Its Chairman, Anthony Cumming, visited London in September to convey the Association's concerns direct to the Secretary of State. Among other things, misuse of funds and general financial mismanagement, it was claimed, made it essential that the system should be changed to allow popular representation in decision-making on taxation and expenditure, and in the framing of legislation. These demands were not met, but Labouchere required Elliot to change the Colony's budget plans for 1857 to eliminate the possible use of reserves, and to sort out with the Council the contentious question of the level and funding of immigration.[46]

Elliot's planned exit in July having proved impractical, his departure was further postponed by a renewed outbreak of cholera in September. It was thankfully short-lived, and the Elliot family left the island in the last week of October. The usual farewell addresses from sections of the community, delivered with due formality, were as noteworthy for the responses they elicited from the Governor as for their own content. With the Council, Elliot took the opportunity to draw attention to a marked improvement in the colony's financial position. He attributed this to an upturn in trade, reduced public expenditure, and the re-imposition of export duty. Better crop yields had been responsible for the first, but Elliot himself took credit for the last two – the export levy against vigorous opposition from the planters and landowners.[47] To the clergy, the Governor stressed the value of education. In reply to an address from a group of former slaves, who considered themselves to have benefited from Elliot's Governorship, he was happy to extol the virtues of local self-government. As a result of recent changes in legislation, he said, public affairs and finances were being successfully managed locally, with those in Port of Spain and San Fernando now wholly under local control and without central government supervision. Gratified by the ex-slaves' address, Elliot followed it by telling his masters in London that the emancipated class had been decorous in trying times; there had been much 'inflammatory public declamation'.[48]

For Charles Elliot Trinidad had been an uncomfortable experience. Lord Harris' term immediately before him had been less financially constrained. Harris had been popular with the white Creole community, in part because he had succeeded in implying that much of the responsibility for the colony's ills lay with the British government.[49] Elliot recognised the difficulties the planters had in remaining competitive against slave-owning economies such as Brazil and Cuba. He sought with some success to alleviate this problem through mass immigration from Asia, consolidating the relevant legislation in the Immigration Ordinance of 1854; but his background and experience of empathy with slave populations and of the intransigence of planters predisposed him to significant hostility from the Trinidad elite, drawing sustained criticism from its leading members.[50] One of these, Dr L.A.A. de Verteuil, a reformer and author who was prominent in the Roman Catholic and French communities, was especially forthright. He wrote of the Spaccapietra affair that Elliot's 'partial and vexatious policy has been condemned here, not by the catholics only, but, it may be said, by the whole community.... The measures adopted by the governor are viewed with extreme jealousy and suspicion by the catholics, and may prove an unhappy source of ill-feeling'.[51] De Verteuil's treatise on

Trinidad conveyed his own strongly reformist and partisan messages, but there seems no doubt that a sense of unfair treatment and relative neglect by Britain extended beyond narrow sectional interests. Elliot had not managed the discontent well. He was by instinct a conciliator, but as Governor of Trinidad his approach became confrontational. After little more than two years the various stresses affecting his performance – illness, family anxieties, fatigue, and the strain of governing a colony under financial pressure from London and with vigorous opposition from its most influential inhabitants – had become too much.

# Chapter Seventeen

# Intermission

Rear Admiral Sir Charles and Lady Elliot and their daughter Emma Clara reached the south coast of England on 14 November 1856. Despite his earlier intention to sail to France rather than direct to England, and perhaps because of the delays in leaving Trinidad, going to continental Europe was postponed. They met up with Charles's sister Emma, and remained in London over Christmas and New Year. In the midst of family reunions and social engagements, Charles was in correspondence with Labouchere about the financial situation in Trinidad.[1] By April the Elliots had travelled to Switzerland, to the Hotel des Bergues, Geneva.

Pleased and relieved though they had been to return home, Charles and Clara Elliot's priority now was rest and recuperation. Charles, at least, felt he had made a good start. With guilty apologies, probably for not communicating sooner, Clara wrote to her sister-in-law:

> By this time you will have [?abused] me to your heart's content – with good cause – but you will have [?] how little I am to be depended upon in my [?] and dilapidated condition...
>
> Charles is in raptures, declaring that he would be well satisfied to pass the remainder of his days here, but he is an old Fox and wishes to persuade us to be satisfied. We remain at this Hotel until the 1st.[2]

As Charles will have been well aware, their luxury existence in the Hotel des Bergues could not continue.[3] The family transferred in May to the comfortable but more modest Hotel du Faucon in Lausanne, on the north shore of Lake Geneva. It was, as Charles put it to Emma, 'a pleasant and quiet hotel, and though the place appears to be very dull, I think we are all better & satisfied.'[4] During the rest of the summer in Lausanne Charles's correspondence with Emma was taken up not only with domestic matters, but also with China, specifically the Canton campaign and Charles's role in it. China had often impinged during the years since 1841, but with time now to reflect at greater length, it became a major preoccupation. As Charles and Clara began to feel some benefit from their new-found lifestyle, they received worrying news from their son Hughie, of which Emma was immediately informed.

> You will hear with great sorrow that we have just received a letter from dearest Hughie ... giving a disquieting account

about his health. He has been examined by a committee of medical men, and they have [?with concern said] that one of his lungs does not act well, as he phrases it. He says that he had for some months past been troubled with a nasty cough.[5]

There was a better outlook some five weeks later, though Charles warned that Hughie would need constant care. Concern about Hughie was to some extent balanced by a visit from Freddy, who had completed his time at Haileybury and was to take up a position in the Indian Civil Service the following year. He left Switzerland for England on 8 September, his father a little presumptuously alerting his Aunt Emma: 'thinking it very doubtful whether you will be in town I have directed Freddy in that case to invade the 'Elliot Circus' in Chester Square.'[6] Clara was subsequently annoyed to find that whatever he had been told, Freddy had not gone directly home. He had broken his journey in Paris and was still there at the end of December, so failing to convey in time and in person his mother's Christmas good wishes to his aunt.[7]

As summer gave way to autumn Charles, and presumably Clara, decided they would feel better if they moved on. He wrote from an hotel in Montpellier near the south coast:

this weather has taken a churlish turn, and an [?] sky and wet atmosphere ... have persuaded me to break up my commitments and get me gone to either [?] or ... to Bordeaux, where I have some old friends who I should be pleased to shake by the hand again before we all go to sleep.'[8]

Bordeaux it was. For Charles and Clara this was a nostalgic return to a city they had last visited before the assignment in British Guiana. For Clara Bordeaux was of particular significance as the birthplace of her mother, Marie Magdeleine Jouve. The Elliots stayed initially at the Hotel de France, from where Charles duly reported to his sister:

I have assembled my force here, and after 27 years of absence, and many strange accidents by fire and flood, we shall on Monday next (D.V.) occupy an hour in my old friend [?...'s] property, distant about a mile from the Palace that we inhabited in days of yore, where my dearest Hatty eat grapes and bread nobbed with garlick to make her fat.'[9,10]

By the spring of 1858 the family had found themselves other accommodation in Bordeaux and had settled in, though Charles visited England at this time. For how long and for what purpose is not clear, but his schedule included an interview with Lord Stanley, Secretary of State for the Colonies, on 19 March.[11] Emma seems to have been especially organised and content with life, writing in March to her aunt in very positive terms and sending good wishes on what appears to have been their shared birthday:

> How I envy Papa his trip to England. It would be so pleasant to see you, Hatty and her dear children again but if I must tell the truth I confess I should be very sorry to leave my books & my Governess.[12] She is a very clever person and I hope we may remain some time in Bordeaux if it is only to profit by her instructions. I have found an excellent Music Master and if practising and perseverance will do the work I am determined to become a tolerable pianiste...
>
> You would like the situation of our apartments here. They are facing the principal Promenade of the town and we have a fine view of the Theatre which is a beautiful building perhaps one of the finest in Europe.... We are also quite close to a large Promenade called the Quinconces; there is a fair being held there now and being on the banks of this beautiful river it could not be better situated. Poor Mamma has suffered a great deal from a very bad cold but she is better now in fact the whole state of her health has been much better during these last few months.... By the by this is our birthday and I wish you many happy returns of it dear Aunt Emma.[13]

Emma Clara's optimistic report about her mother's health was to prove misplaced. Clara again became ill, now more persistently. In July Charles was reporting to his sister that Clara was still too unwell to write; she remained so until shortly before the end of August, when the Elliots moved again.[14] This time, with health considerations very much in mind, it was to a small spa town in the foothills of the Pyrenees, Bagneres de Bigorre. At first it looked as if the change had worked. Charles wrote that Clara 'is I think I may safely say getting through her heavy need as steadily as we have any right to expect ... considering what her state was when we left Bordeaux fifteen days since ... we have deep reason for thankfulness.'[15] By February however there had been a substantial deterioration; on 23 February Clara had been without food or drink for nearly three days, and over the following four weeks she became very weak. Charles's growing anxiety is apparent from his increasingly frequent letters to Emma during this period, though it had occurred to him that causing his sister great concern too might not be the best thing to do. On 1 March he wrote:

> It is only after a very strong effort that I have been able to make up mind to tell you of our deplorable condition. Today is Tuesday, and my beloved has not taken <u>one single crust of bread</u> or <u>one sip of water</u> since last Wednesday at 5 o'clock, that is a space of <u>144 consecutive hours</u>...'[16]

Further bulletins followed. After a few days there were again some signs of improvement. Elliot planned at this point to take Clara to England a week later if she was well enough to travel, but again the recovery proved illusory. In the middle of March the news was that Clara had had another relapse lasting nearly three days, and was even weaker.

Clara's health did in the end recover sufficiently for the journey to England. It is not clear exactly when the family travelled, but by mid-1860 they were back in London staying at one of the many temporary addresses they were able to use. Charles Elliot never owned any property. The nature of his work, always on the move and subject to being sent to far-flung places at short notice, meant there was no need for a permanent residence in Britain; nor, because neither he nor his father were first or eldest surviving sons did he inherit any fortune by way of property or in any other form. Correspondence suggests that between 1860 and 1863 the Elliots lodged, as well as with Emma Hislop at 56 Chester Square, at two other London addresses, 20 Clarendon Villas and 53 Inverness Terrace. Additionally, in April 1861 the census records Charles, Clara and Emma Elliot, now aged 19, as residing at 31 Kensington Park Gardens with two servants, Sarah [?Peare] and Mary Vane.[17]

As befitted a person of his seniority and experience Charles became again, as he had been on his return from China, a well-known figure on the London social and political scene.[18] Though there was no repetition of the more serious illness from which she had suffered in France, it seems that Clara was far from generally well, and did not always accompany Charles at social engagements. An undated letter from Clara, probably written sometime in 1861, indicates some difficulty in her relationship with Harriet (and some impatience on the part of her husband):

> Just a line to tell you how grateful am to my dearest sister [?Clarisse], who seeing my miserable position at Dr. Mee's with her own eyes has taken the responsibility of having me under her care. Hatty, she has been a good angel to me.... Yr. father tells me that you are under much uneasiness about me. Why my dearest Child did you not believe the evidence of your own eyes.... Kiss my darlings for me ... my blessings to you my dear child. Your father hurries me.[19]

Had Harriet failed to appreciate her mother's frailty, or declined a request to look after her?

Charles too had family matters to deal with. He became embroiled in a curious correspondence involving the Rev. C.E. Birch of Wiston Rectory, Colchester, and his own son Gibby, who was now 27. Gibby had attended Haileybury and was duly pursuing a career in India, but his personal life was turbulent. He was beset by debt problems, and had at this time a 4-year-old son, Charles. Gibby had married Sarah Rebecca Rowell in Bombay in October 1855 and Charles had been born the following July. It is not clear what happened to Sarah, but in July 1860 Gibby had written to Birch asking to place his son with him. 'I am unable to tell you where he is', he admitted, 'but he was to be with his Grand Aunt Lady Hislop.'[20] Charles Elliot first heard about all this when he received a letter from Birch in September informing him of the request and then saying that at present the boy was in the charge of his daughter, a Mrs Bushell. Elliot told the Rev. Birch in effect that it was up to Gibby what arrangements he made for his son, but he was clearly irritated, objecting in a letter to Gibby to Birch's 'attempting to require me to interfere in a matter in which I have never had any word from you.'[21] The correspondence appears to have ended, inconclusively, shortly afterwards.

Elliot's wish to continue to be involved in current affairs was much in evidence. His experience and thoughts were sought and generally welcomed, though perhaps predictably, given the sensitivities, China does not seem to have featured in them. In April 1861 he was a witness at the Parliamentary Select Committee on Colonial Military Expenditure, giving his views on troop levels in colonial garrisons, with special reference to the West Indies. He was also in touch with Lord Grey (the third Earl, his friend of longstanding), now out of office but still active. An eleven-page letter to him from Elliot in June consisted of a series of rather rambling observations on current US, Spanish and French activities and policies in the West Indies. He expressed particular concerns about Haiti and Santo Domingo, but the letter is unfortunately most notable for the sharp deterioration in his handwriting; never the easiest to read, it is tolerably legible at the start but by the end hardly any words can be deciphered.[22] Without the services of the copywriters on whom he could call as a colonial governor, the problem of written communication remained with him for the rest of his life.

Involving himself in matters of national policy helped Charles Elliot to feel engaged, but it was not enough to mitigate his personal anxieties. Chief among these was Clara. Though the Elliots' time in Switzerland and France had helped initially, by the time they left for England Clara's health had shown no overall improvement. Earlier, when he departed from Trinidad, Charles was focused on the need for a stress-free change of scene and climate. He seems then to have had no intention of seeking another appointment, but neither had he expressed a firm commitment to retire altogether from public life. What concentrated his mind now, towards the end of 1861, was his wife's fragile condition and, specifically, how he was going to able to continue to fund the special care she needed. He was promoted vice admiral in January 1862, but he was a retired officer on half pay and on the reserve list. The ever-changing complex regulations governing naval pay currently provided that half pay retired personnel on the reserve list who were flag officers (i.e. who had attained the rank of commodore or above) were all to be paid at the same rate, set in 1860 at £456 per annum.[23] Greater income, guaranteed accommodation, and a peaceful environment were now needed. Around the turn of the year he submitted a successful application for the Governorship of St Helena. He explained the background a year or so later to his civil servant brother, T.F. Elliot of the Colonial Office:

My dear Fred,

Yours of the 27 reached me Saturday but too late for the post. I applied for St Helena about 15 months since when I was almost without hope that my dear one would ever be restored to me. The formidable inroad on my very small income of her separate care in anything like adequate comfort and otherwise reliable circumstances, made it necessary that I should attempt all that depended upon me to increase my means of meeting my expenses. That, in short, was a state of things in which sacrifice of personal feelings or risks of other kinds were not to be weighed for a moment and I asked for St Helena at that time because I supposed that it either was or would very shortly become vacant, and I imagined it could hardly be refused to me. It is a doubtful point whether I should not keep my half pay if I accepted this offer. The Order in Council is not before me and it would depend entirely on the exact wording of the regulation whether I should not do so. I am now a Vice-Admiral and am [?] the highest rate of half pay in that rank exceeds 2000 a year. But, on the other hand, I am only on the reserve list and therefore still on the half pay of a <u>Rear-Admiral</u> .[24]

He ended wearily: 'What are we doing, dear Fred, or proposing to do for the rest of our pilgrimage? and how is dear old Taylor? "Our sills of life are careering down"'[25]

Charles, Clara and Emma Clara returned once more to the Hotel du Faucon in Switzerland for a short time. By June 1863 they were at Madeira, en route to the South Atlantic island colony of St Helena.

# Chapter Eighteen

# Last Posting

It is tempting to think of St Helena first as a place of exile because of its association with Napoleon, who was banished to the island in 1815 until his death there in 1821. Its remoteness, some 1,200 miles from the coast of southern Africa, fitted it for such a purpose, but in the eighteenth and early to mid-nineteenth centuries St Helena was also of strategic importance as a port of call for ships sailing between Europe and south and east Asia. The island is said to have been discovered for Portugal by the navigator Joao da Nova Castella, in May 1502 on the saint's day of St Helena of Constantinople. The Portuguese, Dutch, and English used St Helena at various times during the sixteenth and early seventeenth centuries for re-provisioning their ships, often fighting each other in the process. Though the Portuguese had constructed the first buildings there, no attempt was made to settle the island until 1659 when the English East India Company, having been given a charter to govern by Oliver Cromwell, sought to do so. It was not an easy task. St Helena is small, around forty square miles, and at that time suffered from the ravages of wild goats and rats. It could never be self-sufficient, but despite the difficulties of attracting colonists, was retained for strategic reasons. Apart from a six-month occupation by the Dutch in 1672–3, St Helena remained a Company possession until 1834, when it became the responsibility of the British Crown.

As in Bermuda and to an extent in Trinidad, it fell to Charles Elliot to take over from a successful and popular Governor. In his seven years in office Sir Edward Hay Drummond Hay had been responsible for the construction of several important buildings and public works, notably the main drainage system for the capital, Jamestown. To reassure its readers that Elliot might not necessarily prove less able and well regarded than his predecessor, the local press cited his Bermuda Governorship:

> Sir Charles brings with him a goodly experience of the duties and troubles of governing a Colony. The government of Bermuda was entrusted to him for a period of nearly eight years, and we well remember with what anxiety his friends watched his opening career. Sir Charles, then Captain R.N., assumed that government on the removal of a truly learned, amiable and efficient Governor, whose like the Bermudians feared they might never see again.[1]

Describing the ways in which Elliot was 'perfectly successful' as Governor of Bermuda, the newspaper added that he was 'ably assisted by his amiable and very accomplished Lady in carrying out those pleasurably social duties which more particularly become ladies'.[2] The comment reflected one widely held contemporary view of the role of women, but it also indicated the important part Clara Elliot played in Charles's official as well as his personal life.[3]

Charles, Clara and Emma Elliot disembarked on St Helena from the mail steamer *Briton* at the beginning of July 1863, relieved that the voyage had not had to be extended to the Cape – presumably because of adverse weather – as had been feared. The new Governor was sworn in at a meeting of the Colonial Council on 3 July.[4] By August the family was installed in the Governor's residence, Plantation House. Built in 1791–2 for the East India Company, it has had a chequered history. In 1832 the Governor moved out because of damp. Though it was re-occupied four years later, the house continued to have problems. As in Trinidad, the Elliots were confronted on their arrival with accommodation in need of serious attention. Clara conveyed mixed feelings to her sister-in-law: 'We are at last in our exquisite and beautifully situated home ... though the house is imperfectly cleaned from such a condition of filth and squalor as I could not have believed it possible.'[5] The house was made habitable, but as well as thorough cleaning it needed structural and external maintenance for which funds were not forthcoming. In 1873, a few years after the Elliots' departure, the Governor was instructed either to lease the property or to sell it, and reside at another, smaller, house. Despite the external elegance of its construction and its imposing position, on higher ground some three miles inland from Jamestown and fronted by a long sweep of sloping lawn, Plantation House was not a place for gracious living during the 1860s.

St Helena was not unknown to Elliot, who had visited the island briefly late in 1819 during the return voyage of HMS *Minden* from the East Indies Station. For the new Governor there were several pressing concerns. Chief among these were the scourge of termites ('white ants') which were causing severe and widespread damage to buildings and their contents, and juvenile crime and vagrancy.

Elliot formulated a programme for the reconstruction of several termite affected public buildings in Jamestown, using iron, stone and teak hardwood.[6] His application to the Colonial Office for a loan for this work was successful, approval being accompanied by authorisation to raise the taxes necessary to fund the interest and provide a sinking fund. An official view was that hitherto there were 'strong grounds for considering the inhabitants of this little island very lightly taxed.'[7]

The cornerstone of Elliot's plan to counter vagrancy and youth violence was the establishment of 'Reformatories' in which offenders would be placed in custody and required to undertake useful employment to fund their keep. Once deemed 'cured' of their delinquency, they would be trained in craft skills that would enable them to make positive contributions to the communal good. 'It is', Elliot wrote, 'better to spend largely for deterring men and particularly youths from criminal tendencies by instruction and an effective plan of reformatory training, than to spend largely for recruiting the prison strength by old offenders and undisciplined youthful offenders'.[8]

The Ordinance which was intended to give effect to Elliot's reform of the penal system was passed in 1865, towards the end of an initial period of intense activity aimed at achieving significant progress on several fronts, much as had happened in Elliot's previous governorships. During these early years the Government Savings Bank of St Helena was established and a public market was introduced, as well as the waterworks being enlarged to provide for better fire control and more plentiful supplies for shipping. The payment to be made to shipping lines for mail ships to call additionally at St Helena en route to the Cape became a matter of contention, resolved after more than a year when the contract was awarded to the Union Steamship Company. In addition to measures to deal with white ants and delinquency, Elliot also proposed to the home government initiatives on such diverse subjects as the establishment of a new naval depot on the island (unsuccessful), the importation of cochineal insects from Tenerife (successful) and measures for improving the efficiency of the garrison (partially successful).

Postal traffic initiated between St Helena and the Colonial Office was not all one way. A notorious American slave ship captain, Francis Bowen, had been captured by the British and sent to St Helena to be handed over, under the US-British 1862 Treaty for the Suppression of the Slave Trade, to the US authorities for punishment. Austen Layard, Parliamentary Under Secretary at the Foreign Office, had asked the Colonial Office find out from the Governor of St Helena 'in what manner Bowen was disposed of'.[9] Elliot replied that Bowen had been permitted to leave St Helena on a US whaling vessel, prompting Layard to tell Sir Frederic Rogers, Colonial Office Permanent Secretary, to instruct Elliot that he should in future ensure that such people were placed directly in the hands of US officials. The incident sparked a spirited exchange of memoranda between the Foreign Office and the Colonial Office about the interpretation of the Treaty; there appears to be no evidence of any clear outcome.

A more constructive correspondence took place between the Foreign and Colonial Offices on the problem of termite infestation. Rogers was informed in September 1863 that the Foreign Secretary, Earl Russell, had instructed HM Consuls at a number of locations in Brazil, including Pernambuco and Rio de Janeiro, to report on measures used there 'for counteracting the mischief caused by the ravages of the white ants'.[10] The replies suggested various remedies according to the sites or items to be treated, such as tar and a mix of sugar and arsenic, along with more general advice about vigilance, cleanliness and the avoidance of damp. Whatever measures were tried, none was entirely successful, and though the use of different building materials prevented further structural damage, termites remained on St Helena.

Compared with Trinidad, the day-to-day business of the Governor was small scale. The population of the island had been dramatically increased from time to time for particular reasons, such as the substantial number of extra troops deemed necessary to guard Napoleon, and in its capacity as a destination for liberated African slaves, but the settled population in the nineteenth century typically numbered between 4,000 and 7,000. The 1861 St Helena census recorded a total population of 6,444, of whom the garrison accounted for 948.[11] The apparatus of government was appropriately also small. In Elliot's time the colony's Executive (and Legislative) Council comprised, according to its minutes, only the Governor, the Chief Justice, and the Garrison Commander, with the Colonial Secretary. Legislation approved by the Council was required to be posted for public scrutiny for one month, before being placed again before the Council for final endorsement. There were otherwise no consultative arrangements, enabling the Governor and Council to take and implement decisions quickly (subject to subsequent report to London). Publication of draft legislation did nevertheless have some effect; the procedure was tested in August 1863 when an Ordinance proposing various measures to improve public health was successfully challenged. Alterations were made when the Council next met and the Ordinance was duly passed into law.[12]

The relatively small size of the Government of St Helena and of the population it served meant that the Governor could quickly get to know many of the key individuals in the island's life. Elliot's normal briskness was therefore soon in evidence in changes of personnel where he thought there was good cause.

The Headmastership of the Government High School had become an issue before Elliot's arrival. In such a small community as St Helena some doubling up of roles was inevitable if all necessary functions were to be covered, but Governor Drummond Hay had determined that the incumbent, the Rev. George Bennett, could not properly fulfil the roles of both Rector of Jamestown and headmaster. Bennett was informed while he was on leave of absence of the termination of his appointment as headmaster, and he then resigned from the rectorship. The testimonial to him in the local press in March 1863 was full of praise for him as rector, but his decision had been made.[13] Bennett's successor as Headmaster was the Rev. Robert W. Gray. Perhaps partly because of a plurality of roles, as in the Bennett case – Gray was also the Bishop's Private Secretary and Canon of the Cathedral– Elliot gave Gray notice that his services would not be required beyond the end of 1866.[14] Gray's response was immediate and forthright. He told the Governor that he intended to write direct to the Secretary of State, Edward Cardwell, about Elliot's notification, which he considered unjust and illegal. In forwarding to Cardwell Gray's letter of intent, Elliot said his decision had been

> influenced solely by what I consider to be the advantages to the community in the important respect of the steady instruction

and guidance of the better classes at the Government High School.... I should wish to observe that the number of pupils at the Government High School when the late Head Master the Reverend Mr Bennett left in 1862 was forty-five, the number at present has declined to sixteen, neither am I able to attribute this considerable fall off in the number of pupils to any remarkable diminution in the number of the youth who would normally seek instruction at such an institution.[15]

The establishment by Elliot of a special Board of Investigation did not prevent the matter from escalating into a bitter and protracted dispute in which Gray also made allegations against others, including the Colonial Secretary, whom he accused of auditing false accounts. Things came to a head in November 1866 when Gray resigned. He wrote that

the injury done to me by His Excellency's illegal suspension of me from my appointment as Head Master of the Head School in this island ... has made it necessary for me to take such steps in an action at Law against His Excellency as will render it impossible for me to continue in any service of which His Excellency is the head...

I beg therefore to tender to His Excellency my resignation of my appointment as Head Master.[16]

Efforts to find a successor as headmaster failed because, it was said, the salary was too low and the cost of living too high. The role of acting headmaster had been assumed by W.M. Griffith, Assistant Master, who also thought he had grounds for complaint; firstly that he had not been appointed headmaster, and secondly that he had received what he considered a paltry addition ($£10$) to his salary for his acting role over five months. In June 1867 Elliot proposed that the salary of the headmaster's post be increased, but that future appointments be made for two years in the first instance. An appointment was eventually made. Having failed in his first attempt at redress Gray tried again in September 1869 by seeking a new investigation of his case, a request which the Secretary of State, Earl Granville, refused.

Elliot also had concerns about the reliability of J.H. Hartley, Medical Officer of the Liberated Africans Department at Rupert's Bay. He recommended, apparently successfully, to the Duke of Newcastle that Hartley be replaced, and that his duties

should in future be confined to an officer directly connected with Her Majesty's service. It is a post of considerable trust, demanding habits of unfailing steadiness, and I see much reason for earnestly submitting this change to Your Grace's support – at the close, therefore, of Mr Hartley's leave of absence.[17]

The replacement would be on the establishment of the garrison, 'with directions that his services should be placed at the disposal of the Colonial Government for employment in the Liberated Africans Department at Rupert's [Bay].'[18] Nor was the judiciary exempt from scrutiny. Elliot proposed that the work of the Summary Judge, who dealt with cases of petty debt, should be taken over by the Stipendiary Magistrate and the office of Summary Judge abolished. In this instance, however, Newcastle demurred.

Not all personnel matters were problematic. In January 1867 the Custodian of Napoleon's tomb and former residence at Longwood, M. de Rougemont, came to the end of his appointment. As Elliot observed, the tomb and the house were visited each year by large numbers of people, and during de Rougemont's tenure there had never been any disturbance or need for police intervention. That was perhaps just as well; the island's police force was economically staffed – one officer in charge and nine other policemen. It was the subject of an allegation of inefficiency which obliged Elliot to write to the Secretary of State, the Duke of Buckingham and Chandos (to whom the complaint had been made) in an attempt to rebut the charge. In a population of around 6,500 (including the garrison), he said, there had over the five years since his arrival been forty convictions at General Quarter Sessions, of which the majority were for larceny.

1864 and 1865 were difficult and ultimately traumatic years for Charles and Clara Elliot in their personal lives. A few months after the family's arrival in St Helena the 22-year-old Emma Clara became engaged to the Rev. George Pennell, Vicar of St Paul's, who was 26 and whom she had met en voyage. The development was a cause of great concern to her father, who had made his disapproval clear before the engagement was announced. The situation was fully and feelingly described by Emma Clara in a letter to her aunt in April:

> I have known Mr Pennell intimately for the past 6 months and I am as certain as one can well be of anything that he is well calculated to make me happy and I hope that by God's help I shall be able to do my duty to him and to make him happy. We came out together from England and he proposed to me at the end of August 63. Papa did not wish to acknowledge any engagement then because Mr. Pennell's means were small.[19]

Charles was against the engagement, but he had not forbidden it. George Pennell was seeking a Chaplain's appointment at Rio de Janeiro; if successful, Charles had said, he would not oppose the couple's plans. Pennell's Rio application did not succeed. Charles was insistent that the engagement be broken off, but Emma Clara was adamant and in the end persuaded her father, with great reluctance, to give his approval. She told her aunt, 'I consider myself a very lucky girl', adding 'Maman is quite well and always busy around the house. Papa I am afraid finds this place dull.'[20]

At about the same time Clara Elliot confided her own reservations to her sister-in-law, giving also an approving indication of her daughter's good works and some reasonably contented observations about Charles' present life:

> Emma is very useful in visiting the poor (if poor there be in a worldly sense) persuading them to send their children to the Sunday School, and so on. Of her own private affairs, I leave you to judge from Charles and her own account. It will be a pang to me if she leaves us, but I shall feel sure that all is arranged for us better than we could do ourselves. There is not much society here for Charles, but this want leaves him more time for duty ... about once a month we have a Man of War and have been very fortunate, for the greater number of the Captains and Officers we have been able to receive have been gentlemanlike and fit companions for Charles. I feel a great ease that it is in his power to entertain his brother naval officers. They will now know him as he deserves to be known.[21]

While Elliot's concerns about his daughter's wedding intentions were mainly financial, especially in the light of his own perennial money worries, there were other factors. Emma Clara was, of all Charles's and Clara's children, the one they knew best. Her siblings had all spent long periods away from their parents, staying with their Aunt Emma, at school, or travelling. Emma Clara had been with Charles and Clara all her life, sharing their unsettled existence with all its excitements, discoveries, frustrations and disappointments. They were desperately keen to see her make a happy, stable and enduring marriage. A brief shipboard romance with an impecunious clergyman did not seem likely to deliver that. A further dimension was that George's father, Richard Croker Pennell, was a close, probably the closest, colleague of Charles Elliot. He had been appointed Colonial Secretary and Registrar in 1844, and had served under four previous Governors. There is no indication that Elliot's working relationship with him was other than generally cordial, though there will inevitably have been occasions on which Pennell's long experience and Elliot's desire for reform came into conflict. It is not clear what view Richard Pennell took of his son's engagement, but he was probably more kindly disposed to it than was Elliot.

At the wedding the bride's father and the groom's sister Jacquelina were witnesses. A few weeks later Charles wrote sadly and anxiously to his sister:

> My child was married on 3rd June, God's will be done. All that remains to be hoped is that she may have acted best for her own happiness. So far as I can judge the young man is a *really delight*[ful] clergyman and in *every* respect *well-conducted*.

But, looking *at the thing* from *my point of view* I think *he* has acted selfishly & that *she* has been *out of all measure irrational*. However what is past is past, & I can only grieve that I cannot do more for her. They will of course be miserably poor, and as children come, I foresee nothing but a life of care, & pinching & unavailing regrets…

I am very sorrowful dearest Emma and do not affect to conceal from you that this marriage has been a terribly staggering blow to me. So far as I can see, it is an extremely rash thing indeed.

[ps] Clara is well & has been much wise throughout this distressful business of poor Emma's. I pity that child from the bottom of my heart. My thoughts are with her more and more.[22]

Emma Clara became pregnant in July. There is a hint in a letter to her aunt shortly before her expected confinement that she had not always been in the best of health during the pregnancy. She was apprehensive, but as was her nature sought to be positive. From St Paul's Vicarage she wrote in April 1865,

I expect a certainly most interesting event to us to take place before the end of this month praise God or quite early in May. I am thankful to say that I am perfectly strong and well now and have had so <u>little</u> to suffer and so <u>much</u> to be grateful for up to this present moment that I feel it would be worse than folly to look forward with anything but hope and trust.[23]

George and Emma Pennell's son, Clement Hope, was born before the end of April. On 21 May, two days before his christening, Emma Clara died of septicaemia.[24] The devastation caused to her parents was inevitably overwhelming. Her new husband, who lived for a further forty-seven years, never remarried. Charles's grief was compounded by extreme anxiety about Clara, who though maintaining some kind of mental equilibrium, lost an alarming amount of physical capability. As always in such circumstances, he wrote repeatedly to his elder sister. This a month after Emma's death:

Knowing how deeply anxious you will be for the latest tidings of us, I send this line to say that my dearest Clara, continues in the same *perfectly satisfactory condition* mentally considered but still distressingly low in other respects. May God grant to her some measure of bodily energy & the continuance of her present mental calmness & usualness of manner & appearance…

My own darling Child's voice is still in both our ears, & her form is never long out of our poor memories. God's will be done.[25]

A further letter followed in July and another in August:

> You will see that I have but slight hope that my dearest will ever recover her strength of mind or body....You will remember how active she was, & till my ...[?] left us she could walk as far as I could (& much more reliably). Now she does *not walk at all*, & the only exercise she takes is a drive with me in the afternoon if the weather permits. She sleeps pretty well, but does not get up for breakfast. In short, her forces are *diminishing*, both *bodily* and *mental*.[26]

The tablet placed in the nave of St Paul's by Charles and Clara speaks of Emma Clara's spirit, diligence, friendship to the poor and her sweetness as a companion. It is a memorial both to her and to Hughie – a grim reminder that Charles and Clara had lost not only their younger daughter but also their eldest son, who had become a captain in the Bombay cavalry, married in 1860 and died at sea on June 8 1861, aged 29.

Although still grieving and very anxious about Clara's health, Elliot seems to have applied himself to his work again with minimum delay. He proposed the reform of the jury system, urged on the Colonial Office action to improve the defensive capability of the island, and resumed his initiatives on the environment, seeking to build in particular on his longstanding interest in trees. He had imported to St Helena Bermuda cedars and Mexican and Norfolk Island pine, and sent some Norfolk Island pine seeds to his cousin, the third Earl Minto, whimsically hoping that 'they will ... serve to remind the generations to come that [?we] thought of them in the days of Queen Victoria who will be President of the Confederation of British States when these trees are 180 feet high.'[27,28] Elliot's most lasting botanical contribution to St Helena, however, was the cultivation of cinchona plants, from whose bark anti-malarial quinine was extracted. The Director of the Royal Botanic Gardens at Kew, Dr Joseph Dalton Hooker, who had visited St Helena many years earlier, had commented that cinchona might profitably be grown on the island's mountains. With Elliot's agreement he dispatched Joseph Chalmers, an experienced gardener, to take charge of a project to that end. Work began July 1868. In April 1869 Elliot wrote to Hooker at length, discussing progress, and by the time planting was completed in December 1869 there were estimated to be 10,000 cinchona plants at various stages of growth.[29] The full potential of the scheme was never realised. Elliot's successor took no interest in the project, which was neglected and then abandoned. Uncultivated, invasive cinchona now grows on St Helena, but with harmful effects on other species of plant.

While the island was on his mind, Dr Hooker also wrote to the Colonial Office about a familiar, long-standing and intractable problem, 'hazarding conjecture that the introduction of insectivorous birds might check the propagation of the white ants in St Helena.'[30] The suggestion was passed to J.C. Melliss, Colonial Surveyor, who had a keen interest in flora and fauna. Several species of birds from England, mostly sparrows, were subsequently imported, though with what effect on the ants is not clear.[31]

Elliot moved in September 1865 to full admiral on the retired list. In the midst of bereavement and anxiety about Clara the promotion will have done little to lift his spirits, and had no effect on his remuneration. So far as his debts were concerned, however, he expected his Governor's salary of £2,000 per annum to serve the purpose he had intended when he applied to be posted to St Helena.[32] He could now envisage a life free of such burdens, though this had been only a small grain of comfort in his extreme despondency after the marriage of Emma Clara. He wrote near the end of June 1864: 'As soon as I have paid off the remaining encumbrances on my insurances, I shall get the ship [?] to Timbactu [?] and spend the last of my days there or thereabouts. Another year and a half (if I live so long) will see me out of this island. But that is a long time to look forward to at my age.'[33]

There was a gradual improvement in Clara's health and demeanour during the three years following Emma Clara's death. It was aided by her religious faith, her interests in gardening and music, and the regular company of her grandson, who was always known by his second name, Hope.[34] George Pennell and Hope stayed at Plantation House for three weeks in November 1867; 'they were very happy weeks to us' Clara wrote, continuing, 'I love all children, particularly my grandson. Hope's visit was music in this house though sometimes he used to shout very loudly not in anger but to be heard [as] the house is very large'.[35] Charles continued to apply himself conscientiously to his work, in a position now to reminisce occasionally, and not just about China. Receipt of his niece Nina's *A Memoir of Hugh Elliot* prompted a generally favourable reaction from Charles, and some appreciative comments about his father:

> I must leave it to you, dearest Nina, to imagine the feeling with which I have read your book, judiciously and tenderly compacted in all aspects, according to my firm judgement ... what my dearest father lacked will doubtlessly be diligently noted and solemnly and sternly rebuked by those whose nack or pleasure is to find the fault that is in men and things. What my father possessed in larger perspective than 99 men out of every hundred in the public service (military or civil) was a generous sense of duty, a head brim full of resource, courage to match, and an eye sure and swift to see the right moment for action, in all circumstances of crisis; and never more so than when those circumstances were perilous.[36]

Several of the traits Charles most admired in his father were also part of his own character, and it was unsurprising that Henry Taylor agreed with Nina that Charles was the sibling who most resembled Hugh.[37]

One of Charles Elliot's characteristics was a persistent restlessness. At a relatively early point in most of his postings he had expressed a frustrated desire to be somewhere else. Such wishes were entirely unrealistic; but to his own and others' benefit, his restlessness was more usually channelled into productive energy. That, along with kindness, courtesy and gentle manners, was said by a leading historian of St Helena to have won for him the respect and affection of the islanders.[38] Another account says that he 'continually endeavoured to advance the welfare of the island', and that 'He had to contend with many difficulties, especially with the diminishing revenue.'[39]

That the revenue to the colonial government was diminishing was apparent most dramatically at the end of Elliot's tenure. In January 1869 Elliot sent a note to Buckingham about revenue and expenditure for the previous year. He explained that

> The Revenue of this Island depends mainly on receipts at the Custom House – In other respects the receipts one year with another are liable to little fluctuation – It will be noted in the Abstract of the Customs Revenue for the years 1867 and 1868 that it has fallen off in the whole year 1868 compared with the previous year to the heavy extent of £3,576.14.4 that is to say between a fourth and a fifth of the Ordinary Customs Revenue on an average of some years past.[40]

The failure of the Customs Revenue, Elliot said, was 'owing probably to that general stagnation of business which seems to have prevailed in all parts of the world in the same period.'[41] From the opening of the Suez Canal in November 1869, the position deteriorated still further with an acceleration of the reduction in the number of ships using the island begun with advent of steam some years earlier. In due course St Helena's wider economy, of which servicing and supplying ships had been a major part, suffered a serious decline.

The minutes of the meeting of the St Helena Council (also called the Board by Elliot) held on 24 January 1870 record a statement from the Governor:

> I have the honor to announce to the Board that the Queen has been graciously pleased to appoint Rear Admiral Charles G.E. Patey to succeed me as Governor of St Helena.
>
> He may be expected to arrive here on the 2nd or 3rd Proximo and desiring that his residence may be ready for him I propose to leave the Island by the Mail from the Cape of Good Hope due on the 27th or 28th Instant.
>
> In conformity with the Commission under the Great Seal providing for the Government of this Island, the administration thereof, after my departure and until Her Majesty's further

pleasure thereon shall be known, will devolve on the Honorable the Colonial Secretary.[42]

The Grateful duty remains to me Honorable Gentlemen of the Council to tender to you collectively and individually my hearty thanks for the public spirited and judicious assistance I have always received from you at this Board and elsewhere in the discharge of the Queen's service.

May God continue to keep you and all the dwellers on this Island under His Merciful protection.[43]

Despite the very short formal notice of their departure, Charles and Clara Elliot left their third island colony on the mail steamer *Cambrian* on 29 January. This time it really would be for retirement.

Chapter Nineteen

# The Final Chapter

Afew weeks after their departure from St Helena the press reported
that Charles and Clara Elliot had sailed 'for Madeira, en route to
spend the rest of the winter there and in Switzerland'.[1] It is not
clear when precisely they returned to England, but by January 1871 they
had taken up residence in Withycombe Raleigh, a south Devon village
next to the coastal town of Exmouth.[2] The house and grounds rented by
the Elliots were large. When the property was put up for sale by its owner
some years later, it was described by the auctioneer as

> situate about one mile and a half from the town of Exmouth ...
> built a few years since by the present owner, standing high in its
> own grounds, and commanding extensive land and sea views,
> approached by a carriage drive and lodge entrance, containing:-
> Entrance Hall, 4 large and lofty reception rooms, 12 bedrooms,
> 2 dressing and 1 bath ditto ... wine, beer and coal cellars, and
> all necessary domestic offices.[3]

Outside there were '[a] large walled kitchen garden stocked with choice
fruit trees, conservatory and greenhouse, large yard with good coach
house, stable, harness room, cowsheds, piggeries &c &c, together with
about 24 acres of orchard, arable and meadow land'.[4]

By comparison with Plantation House, St Helena, this may have
been technically downsizing, but it is clear that Charles Elliot had no
intention of living out his remaining years in modest circumstances. The
Elliots had no difficulty making full use of the accommodation, receiving
frequent family visits and entertaining their grandchildren. The house
became a periodic destination for Hope Pennell and his father George,
who had left St Helena in 1871 and until 1876 was one of the clergy at
the newly built St Jude's Church, South Kensington. Their visits were
a source of much happiness for Charles and especially Clara, who had
now recovered from the depression and trauma of the St Helena years
and was enjoying the opportunity to pursue her enthusiasms for music
and gardening. On the date of the 1871 census, 2 April, the residents
comprised Charles and Clara, seven servants including a footman and
two cooks, and daughter Harriet Russell with her four children, Maud,
Edward, Charles (all teenagers) and Katherine, aged 9.[5] Correspondence
between Clara and the Elliot's son Freddy and daughter-in-law Marcia
during the year following June 1871 shows that the house was visited by
their four young children, who had remained behind in England when

Freddy returned to India with his wife to resume his career in the Indian Civil Service.[6]

For Charles the retirement years were few. He died on 9 September 1875, shortly after his seventy-fourth birthday and after an illness which, as implied by his brother Fred – now Sir Frederick – caused him much distress. Fred wrote to their niece Nina ten days later:

> I did not communicate with you at the time of poor Charles' death, for I knew you must hear direct from Hatty. At the end it was a relief from a condition which no-one could desire to be prolonged. His characteristics were above all his gallant, generous spirit and the kindest of hearts. There is something remarkable in hearing, wherever one goes, the <u>affection</u> with which he is spoken of by persons of every degree.[7]

Forty-eight hours later he felt the need to write again:

> Poor dear Charles' death has, as you divine, depressed me much – not only for the loss of him, tho' I do lament it most sincerely – but on account of the general reflections it cannot but awaken...
>
> Two things above all it has always seemed to me that a man should wish to find in a retrospect of his life, if he has time for a retrospect – first that in some way or other (and the ways are infinitely various) he should have earned the fruits of the earth he has consumed – this for his self-respect – next as to his enjoyment of the term granted to him, that he has felt (too happy if it has been requited) some true and thorough affection.
>
> I think that poor Charles might be conscious of both these things. He fulfilled the tasks that fell to him with all his strength and with a noble disregard of self-interest; what devotion he felt and showed to the companion of his life we all know, and I do believe that although her mind was clouded for so many years and thus gave him a saddened close, she truly loved him, and that he found in her much happiness.[8]

There is a hint here that though her final years with Charles were happy, Clara was not as mentally fit as she had once been. In her widowhood she went in due course to live with her nephew (Hugh) Maximilian, known as Maxey, the son of Charles's brother Hugh Maximilian who had died in 1826 aged 24. Maxey, who was a retired post captain in the Royal Navy, his wife Mary, Clara and three servants were living in 1881 at 160 Castle Street, Reading.[9]

The freehold of the Elliot's home was advertised for sale by auction in February 1876, along with many of its contents, including 'the Handsome and Modern Household Furniture, china, glass, brilliant plate chimney glasses, Brussels carpets and rugs, plants, mowing machine, and various other effects, appertaining to a gentleman's mansion'.[10] The executors of Charles Elliot's will, written in St Helena in 1866, were Sir Frederick Elliot, John Stilwell and William Ford. Summary details, as was normal practice for distinguished figures, were widely reported in the national and local press. The personal estate amounted to less than £8,000, according to the announcement.[11] Charles bequeathed all his income to Clara. On her death £100 was to go to their daughter Harriet (Chachy/ Hatty) 'to purchase some token of the tender regard of himself and his wife'.[12] Of the majority of the estate, one third was left to grandson Hope and two thirds to sons Gibby and Freddy. In his letter to Nina Fred comments that 'He [Charles] will not have left much more than £5,000 in money, but there is a pension of £120 to Clara as Admiral's widow, or perhaps £130 in all on account of a pittance of a Naval annuity for which he subscribed'.[13]

The bequest to Hope proved significant; it appears to have enabled him to live all his adult life – as a bachelor with his father until the latter's death – without any other source of income.[14] George Pennell died as vicar of Stadhampton, Oxfordshire, in 1912; Hope lived on in Oxfordshire and died, apparently intestate, in 1951. His was a long and perhaps at times lonely life. Charles and Clara's three surviving children were similarly (for the time) long-lived. Harriet, whose husband had succeeded to the de Clifford barony and predeceased her in 1877, died in 1896 aged 67. Gibby had a long career in the Bombay Civil Service, spending some time in Australia. By 1891 he was back in England with his third wife Ann and his son by her Launceston Elliot, who was to become a champion weightlifter and Britain's first Olympic gold medal winner.[15] Gibby died in October 1910 at Mottingham, Kent, aged 77.[16] Freddy served for thirty-six years in the Indian Civil Service, rising from Assistant Magistrate and becoming a District Judge in 1881.[17] He retired in 1894, eventually settling with his wife Marcia in Exmouth, and died in 1916 at the age of 78.[18]

Of Charles's siblings, Emma, his elder sister and lifelong correspondent and confidante, died while Charles was in St Helena, in 1866. She was 72. His brother Gilbert, with whom he was at school in Reading and who had become ordained, served for more than forty years as Dean of Bristol. Ned (Edward Francis), who visited his brothers at school and appeared unexpectedly at Macao, entered the Indian Civil Service and became Chief Magistrate at Madras, returning to England and living in retirement in Harrow.[19] Fred, Charles's only other surviving brother, was 72 when he died in 1880.

Charles's body was buried in the churchyard of St John in the Wilderness at Withycombe on 15 September 1875.[20] Clara moved with Maxey – now a rear admiral – and his wife to The Bury, Hemel Hempstead, where she died on 17 October 1885.[21] Despite her frequent bouts of ill health and frailty towards the end, she had lived into her eightieth year.

# Epilogue

Most of the judgements passed on Elliot have inevitably been based on the China years, since it was in that period that he was most in the public eye. The chorus of political, military and press disapproval which characterised the contemporary view of him, despite the influential support he also had, has served to shape the views of several commentators since. Many of the assessments by historians have focused on the question of Elliot's instructions from Palmerston, whether he can be said to have followed them – in spirit if not to the letter – and if not, whether he was justified in that disregard. If it is the case that Secretaries of State for the Colonies 'regularly claimed that the disadvantages of distance and imperfect local knowledge were more than offset by the Department's command of superior wisdom, accumulated experience, and impartial, panoramic views', the same was surely at least equally true of the Foreign Office.[1] Despite Hong Kong's subsequent conspicuous success, according to the commercial criterion of mid-Victorian Britain, Elliot's pivotal role in its beginnings was never widely acknowledged. Napier suggested, Elliot acted, and Pottinger ratified – but it was Pottinger's speedy and decisive use of force that most commended itself to the popular mood.

Elliot's personality was such that he was able to live with the injustice, as he saw it, of the criticism of him over China. It never left him, but it did not prevent his fulfilling, on the whole effectively, his subsequent assignments in Texas and as a colonial governor. Most views of him as a person have been benign, though there have been exceptions which have been very wide of the mark – Hanes and Sanello's description of him as 'the typical myopic, uninformed foreigner' is surely an example.[2] As his niece Nina later implied, many of his character traits were inherited from his father – a streak of flamboyance, physical courage, wit – but Elliot was also a man of contrasts.[3] He could be impetuous, yet appear vacillating; anxious yet sometimes insouciant; generally realistic but also capable of being swept along by idealism and grand strategy. His ambitious plan for Texas and Mexico, as the historian Ephraim Douglass Adams concluded, was 'entirely in character; a dreaming intriguer, political theorist, and philanthropist ... and he lacked the statesman's poise'.[4] On the other hand, Adams's assertion that after being discredited by failure in China, Elliot 'was sent to Texas merely to find a place for him – an excellent proof that Texas was not then considered an important post in diplomatic policy' is questionable.[5] Elliot's letter of appointment as Charge d'Affaires clearly held out the possibility that his observing and reporting role might have to develop into something more active and, by implication, more important. Furthermore slavery and trade, both matters of major concern in Britain's relations with the new Republic, were areas in which Elliot had had first hand operational experience.

While the role of patronage in Elliot's professional life should not be exaggerated, it should not be underestimated either. Joining the Royal Navy would have been a relatively straightforward matter for someone of his class, without the need for any special pleading, but it seems inescapable that background and connections (though not individual members of his family) played a major part in launching him on his post-naval career. Elliot demonstrated ability in British Guiana, but there was nevertheless caution about his suitability for higher things. Writing after the Elliots arrived in China, Sir James Stephen felt the need to explain to the Foreign Office that Elliot was 'without a very systematic education', but that 'he had acquired a mass of knowledge respecting all the practical business of life'.[6] There is no evidence that his leaving school aged 14 and not going to university affected Charles Elliot's future – either his career itself or how he felt about it. Fourteen years in the Royal Navy encompassing a wide variety of deployments on five different stations was more than enough to give him confidence in his experience.

That underlying self-assurance was to prove essential for Elliot's subsequent assignments, and for the difficulties that many overseas civil servants faced. The discomfort of long sea voyages, recurring illness, and the heartache and worry of separation from close family were all hardships which Charles and Clara Elliot bore over many years, but for Charles, as for other senior officers of the Crown, the sense of duty to his country was paramount. As Hoe and Roebuck have shown, Charles and Clara sustained each other, she understanding his responsibilities and supporting him in their discharge.[7] It is clear from the correspondence that Emma Hislop also played an important role. Charles' elder sister was the sibling to whom he related most closely. According to Henry Taylor, whose admiration extended to Emma and who was for a period a frequent visitor to the Hislops at Charlton, she had some of her brother's attributes. 'She is ingenuous, impetuous, and vivacious in her talk and manner, and essentially discreet in her conduct', he wrote. She had 'the charm of a bright intelligence, not uninformed by books as well as by commerce with society, and especially, I think, foreign and diplomatic society, Lady Hislop had a faculty, rarely to be met with in lively women, of giving rest to the weary.'[8]

Taylor's autobiography was published in 1885, ten years after Charles Elliot's death. The praises which were showered on Elliot as Earl Athulf in Taylor's play *Edwin the Fair* (quoted in the autobiography with commentary), and in the poem *Heroism in the Shade*, are the most fulsome expressions of support for him to have appeared in writing. When the play first appeared in 1842 it was influential in presenting Elliot's China

activities in a more positive light. The character Wulfstan the Wise, whom
Taylor based on his friend the poet Coleridge, describes Athulf:

> Earl Athulf's disposition shall I then
> Duly develop; him shall I disclose
> As one whose courage high and humour gay
> Cover a vein of caution, his true heart,
> Intrepid though it be, not blind to danger,
> But through imagination's optic glass
> Discerning, yea, and magnifying it may be,
> What he still dares: him in these colours dressed
> I shall set forth as prompt for enterprise,
> By reason of his boldness, and yet apt
> For composition, owing to that vein
> Of fancy that enhances, prudence which wards
> Contingencies of peril.[9]

Courageous, cautious, intrepid, discerning, daring, prudent – the picture
is again one of contrast, even contradiction. What seems certain is that
Charles Elliot was a complex character. That complexity gave rise to
unpredictable, sometimes bizarre, behaviour on occasion, but it never
affected his essential professionalism. One testament to that came from
an unlikely source; in an observation mainly intended to be critical of the
British government, the Irish dissident John Mitchel commented that 'it
is one of the privileges of a superior officer in the British service to invent
and publish any story he pleases to screen himself and government at the
expense of a subordinate – and one of the duties of inferior officers to
support him in his story, though to their own ruin'.[10] Giving as an example
the captain of the ship on which he had travelled to Bermuda, he continued

> Captain Wingrove can tell something of that practice – and so
> could Captain Elliot, from his experience in China. Perhaps
> you do not know that he acted in China according to his
> plain instructions, and when the transaction was supposed to
> have turned out unfortunate, and Parliament and the press
> were raving, he durst never plead those orders, but had to let
> ministers make up what story they liked.[11]

It was Elliot's experience in China that most thoroughly illustrated his
liberal background and beliefs. His well-known abhorrence of the opium
trade made him unpopular from the start with the merchants whose
commerce he was charged with overseeing. Taylor was clear that while
Elliot deplored the violent methods used by the Chinese against opium
dealers and users 'he still felt that on our side the quarrel was tainted in
its origin.'[12] Elliot's empathy with the Chinese people (as opposed to their
government), and indications that they respected him, were regarded

with suspicion by his colleagues and superiors. Edward Belcher, captain of the survey ship HMS *Sulphur*, recounts how, when the British force was poised to take Canton, on the Chinese side 'the ominous white flag was again displayed, and for some hours there had been repeated cries of "Elliot, Elliot!" as if he had been their protecting joss'.[13] Above all, his determination to rely on force of arms as a deterrent to strengthen his negotiating position, and to use it only as a last resort, was contrary to the prevailing military and popular ethos. Austin Coates, the historian and former Hong Kong Assistant Colonial Secretary, wrote perceptively of Elliot that

> at every critical juncture he deliberately took care to demonstrate to the Chinese that he resorted to arms only under provocation, and he never missed an opportunity to enter into peaceful negotiations. In doing so he steered a miraculous course between the conflicting orders of his conscience, his superiors and his exceptional insight into Chinese realities.[14]

As Julia Lovell has put it, setting the consequences of Elliot's approach in operational context, 'It was perhaps the dismissal of Charles Elliot that marked the true turning point in this war: from here on, the campaign would be more about gunboats than diplomacy'.[15]

Elliot was never, in anyone's estimation – except possibly Henry Taylor's – a national hero or role model. He made mistakes, and it would be wrong to suggest that what he achieved was at all times the result of a clear strategy or tactical plan; but it can be argued that the sum of his contributions in a variety of arenas to different causes, viewed over his whole career and in the light of what was expected of him, has been underrated. The conclusions he drew from his experience as Protector of Slaves helped towards the framing of abolition legislation; the combination of negotiation and military force in China led to the ceding of Hong Kong and opening of more ports to trade; and determined diplomacy in Texas, despite health-related absences, almost succeeded against the odds in delaying, if not preventing, annexation by the United States. His naval career had been steady and competent rather than spectacular, and except for Trinidad his colonial governorships were successful assignments in which important progressive initiatives were undertaken. He could be paternalistic, vacillating, rash, and sometimes self-absorbed but his views, including those on racial and gender equality, were ahead of his time. He was essentially a patriotic man of principle who, while making his personal opinions clear, never in the end allowed such opinions to interfere with the discharge of his official responsibilities as he saw them.

It has been his role in China on which Elliot's reputation has been largely based. The last word is perhaps best left to the American merchant W. C. Hunter. He had been visited in 1853 by the French traveller the Abbe Huc, who recounted a meeting with the exiled former Commissioner Qishan. Drawing on what the Abbe had told him, Hunter subsequently wrote of Elliot that

> Throughout the difficult position in which he was placed after the death of Lord Napier, as HM's Chief Superintendent at Canton, and however grave the events to which the opium surrender gave rise, it was remarkable the personal esteem in which he was held by the Chinese authorities, by the Co-Hong and particularly its chief, How-Qua, who would say 'Elut No.1 honest man'.[16]

# Genealogies

## Charles and Clara Elliot's children and grandchildren

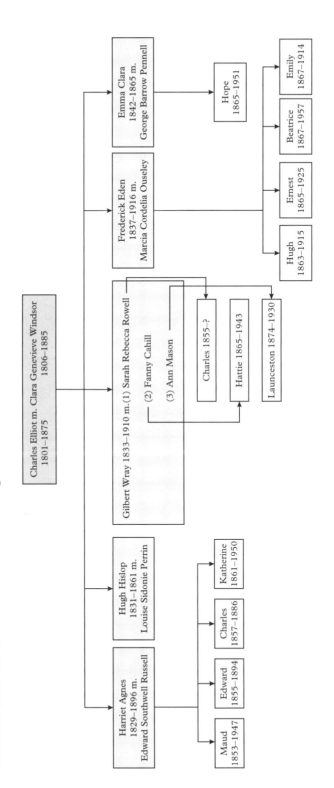

**Charles Elliot's Siblings, Nephews and Nieces**

Hugh Elliot m. Margaret Lewis ? Jones

Henry c.1793-1842 m. Margaret Masterton

Emma 1794-1866 m. Sir Thomas Hislop

Edward 1796-1866 m. Isabella Hardie

Harriet c.1799-1845 m. James Plumridge

Gilbert 1800-1891 m. (1) Williamina Brydone (2) Frances Dickinson

Charles 1801-1875 m. Clara Windsor

Maximilian 1802-1826 m. Mary Lys

Frederick 1808-1880 m. (1) Jane Perry (2) Elizabeth Bromley

Caroline c.1812-? m. William Forster

Charlotte 1838-1893

Hugh (Maxey) 1826-1900

Harriet Hugh Gilbert Frederick Emma

Emma (Nina) 1824-1882

Georgina 1839-1883

Frederick 1847-1910

Emma 1842-1921

Margaret 1838-1907

Harriet 1841-1897

Augustus 1826-?

Margaret 1828-1901

Gilbert 1829-?

Emma 1831-1887

Mary 1834-?

# Charles Elliot's Aunts, Uncles and Cousins[i]

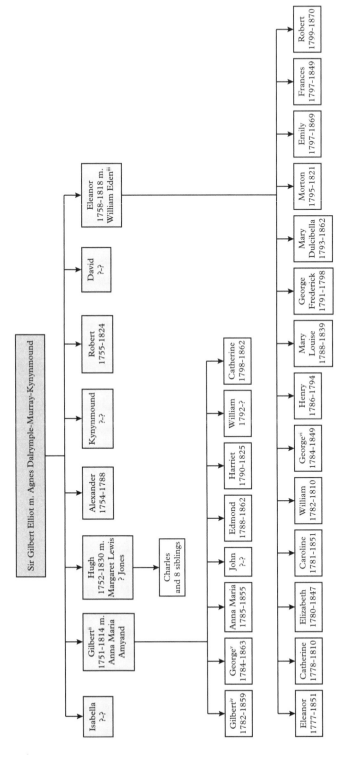

[i] Names of children of Sir Gilbert Elliot and of the 1st Earl of Minto as listed in *Collins's Peerage of England* (Collins, London, 1812), Vol. VIII, 560–561.
[ii] 1st Earl of Minto
[iii] 1st Baron Auckland
[iv] 2nd Earl of Minto
[v] Admiral
[vi] 1st Earl of Auckland

# Appendix 2

# Timeline

## Monarchs, Ministers and Mandarins
in office during Elliot's post-naval career[1]

| | Sovereigns | Prime Ministers | Secretaries of State | Permanent Secretaries[2] |
|---|---|---|---|---|
| | | | **Colonial Office**[3] | |
| British Guiana 1831-1833 | William IV | 2nd Earl Grey | Visct. Goderich | Sir Robert Hay |
| | | | **Foreign Office** | |
| China 1834-1841 | William IV | Visct. Melbourne | Visct. Palmerston | John Backhouse |
| | Victoria | Duke of Wellington | Duke of Wellington | |
| | | Sir Robert Peel | Visct. Palmerston | |
| | | Visct. Melbourne | | |
| Texas 1842-1846 | Victoria | Sir Robert Peel | Earl of Aberdeen | Henry Addington |
| | | Lord John Russell | | |
| | | | **Colonial Office** | |
| Bermuda 1846-1854 | Victoria | Lord John Russell | 3rd Earl Grey | Sir James Stephen |
| | | Earl of Derby | Sir John Pakington | Herman Merivale |
| | | Earl of Aberdeen | Duke of Newcastle | |
| | | | Sir George Grey | |
| Trinidad 1854-1856 | Victoria | Earl of Aberdeen | Sir George Grey | Herman Merivale |
| | | Visct. Palmerston | Sidney Herbert | |
| | | | Lord John Russell | |
| | | | Sir Wm. Molesworth | |
| | | | Henry Labouchere | |
| St Helena 1863-1870 | Victoria | Visct. Palmerston | Duke of Newcastle | Sir Frederic Rogers |
| | | Earl Russell[4] | Edward Cardwell | |
| | | Earl of Derby | Earl of Carnarvon | |
| | | Benjamin Disraeli | Duke of Buckingham & Chandos | |
| | | William Gladstone | Earl Granville | |

---

1 To show who held office and the sequence of their appointments; lengths of tenure of ministers varied from a few months to several years
2 Formally Permanent Under-Secretaries of State
3 Secretaries of State were Secretaries of State for War and the Colonies until 1854 when a separate Colonial Office was established.
4 Formerly Lord John Russell

# Appendix 3

# Ships

## In which he served
### HM Ships of Elliot's career in the Royal Navy, 1815–1829
### (Admiralty record ADM/196/4/161)

| Name | Vessel | Rate | Guns | Station/ Squadron | Elliot's Rank and Years of Service | |
|---|---|---|---|---|---|---|
| *Leviathan* | Line-of-battle ship | 3rd | 74 | Mediterranean | Volunteer (1st Cl.) | 1815-16 |
| *Minden* | " | " | " | " | Midshipman | 1816 |
| " | " | " | " | East Indies | " | 1816-20 |
| *Starling* | Cutter | - | 10 | Home | " | 1820 |
| *Queen Charlotte* | Line-of-battle ship[1] | 1st | 100 | " | " | 1820-1 |
| *Iphigenia* | Frigate | 5th | 42 | West African | " | 1821-2 |
| *Myrmidon* | Small Frigate | 6th | 20 | " | " | 1822 |
| *Iphigenia* | Frigate | 5th | 42 | " | Lieutenant | 1822-3 |
| *Hussar* | Frigate | 5th | 46 | West Indies | " | 1824-5 |
| *Serapis* | Frigate[2] | 5th | 44 | " | " | 1825 |
| *Renegade* | Schooner | - | 4 | " | "[3] | 1825 |
| *Serapis* | Frigate[4] | 5th | 44 | " | Actg. Commander | 1826 |
| *Magnificent* | Line-of-battle ship[5] | 3rd | 74 | " | Commander | 1826 |
| *Harlequin* | Brig-sloop | - | 16 | " | "[6] | 1826-8 |
| " | " | " | " | " | Captain[7] | 1828-9 |

1 Flagship
2 Flagship, in use as a convalescence ship
3 In command
4 Convalescence ship
5 Flagship, in use as a hospital and store ship
6 In command
7 In command

# Notes and References

## Prologue
1  Andrew Yanne and Gillis Heller *Signs of a Colonial Era* (Hong Kong, Hong Kong University Press, 2009), 42

## Chapter One: Forbears, Father and Family
1  G. F. S. Elliot *The Border Elliots* (Edinburgh, David Douglas, 1897), 21
2  Ibid., 287–8
3  Dennis Rodwell *The Minto House Debacle,* Context (Magazine of the Institute of Historic Building Conservation) Vol.36, Dec. 1992, at ihbc.org.uk/context_archive/36/minto.htm (accessed 1.7.2012). Minto House was demolished, amid much controversy, in 1992.
4  MP for Selkirkshire 1753–65 and Roxburghshire 1765–77
5  See H.M. Scott *Elliot, Hugh 1752–1830 diplomat and adventurer* in *Oxford Dictionary of National Biography* (Oxford University Press, 2004)
6  Countess of Minto *A Memoir of the Right Honourable Hugh Elliot* (Edinburgh, Edmonston and Douglas, 1868)
7  Henry Taylor, 1800–86, writer and civil servant
8  Taylor to Elliot, 27 March 1869 in Edward Dowden *Correspondence of Henry Taylor* (London, Longmans, Green and Co., 1888), 289, at https://archive.org/details/correspondenceof00tayl (accessed 26.2.2016)
9  See Carl G Slater *The Problem of Purchase Abolition in the British Army 1856-1862*, Journal of the South African Military History Society Vol 4 No 6, Dec.1979, at http://samilitaryhistory.org/vol046cs.html (accessed 16.7.2012). Slater notes that the purchasing of commissions for children was 'originally conceived as a means of providing for the male orphans of deserving officers, but it quickly degenerated into a major abuse that was not abolished until the Duke of York's administration as Commander-in-Chief at the end of the [eighteenth] century.' The refusal to confirm Hugh Elliot's commission in 1771 may in part have been because the practice was already falling into disrepute.
10  Scott *Oxford DNB* and Clagette Blake *Charles Elliot RN 1801-1875 A Servant of Britain Overseas* (London, Cleaver-Hume Press Limited, 1960), 2
11  See Jeremy Black *British Diplomats and Diplomacy 1688–1800* (University of Exeter Press, 2001), 44
12  Quoted in Scott *Oxford DNB*
13  Jacques Rambaud (ed.) *Memoirs of the Comte Roger de Damas (1787-1806)* at http://archive.org/stream/memoirsofcomtero00damauoft#page/306/mode/2up (accessed 18.7.2012).
14  Sources vary on the surname, some suggesting, since both words appear in her name, that it must be either Lewis or Jones; but Lewis Jones also seems possible.

15 Countess of Minto *A Memoir*, 338

16 Ibid. The Raphael painting was the Virgin, Child and Saints Sixtus and Barbara (1512), better known as *The Sistine Madonna*, which had been in the *Gemaldegalerie Alte Meister* at Dresden since 1754

17 Quoted in Black *British Diplomats...*, 161

18 Ibid., 97

19 Ibid., 101

20 Ibid., 5

21 The year of birth of [Theodore] Henry Elliot is not known, but he is referred to as the 'eldest son' in the *Morning Post's* announcement of his marriage, at http://www.themastertons.org/james_masterton_gogar_braco.html (accessed 2.8.2012)

22 Minto papers, ms 11084 f264, 7 September 1802, Hugh Elliot to Lord Minto. The reference to nine children suggests that Harriet and Carrie were elder sisters to Charles, or that there were other, unidentified, siblings.

23 Scott *Oxford DNB*

24 Blake *Charles Elliot RN*, 4. Blake ascribes the absence of further diplomatic appointments to a government decision, but also suggests that Elliot himself opted for a career change.

25 Minto papers, ms 11084 f268, 9 March 1808, Hugh Elliot to Lady Minto

26 Ibid., f270, 12 May 1808, Hugh Elliot to Lady Minto

27 Ibid., f278, 6 June 1810, Hugh Elliot to Lord Minto

28 Quoted in Hoe and Roebuck *The Taking of Hong Kong*, 9

29 John Buchan *Lord Minto: A Memoir* (London and Edinburgh, Thomas Nelson and Sons Ltd., 1924), 5 'I was not aware that Providence was one of your allies' ... 'The only one, Sir, whom we do not pay.'

30 Quoted in Buchan *Lord Minto*, 118

## Chapter Two: Minor to Midshipman

1 Countess of Minto *A Memoir*, 338

2 Ibid.

3 FO70/21/8-11, 4 July 1803, Hugh Elliot to Lord Hawkesbury

4 Blake *Charles Elliot RN*, 4

5 FO70/27/194-195, 25 August 1806, Hugh Elliot to Charles James Fox

6 Minto papers, ms 11084 f282, 8 June 1810, Hugh Elliot to Lord Minto

7 See TAB Corley *Valpy, Richard (1754–1836) schoolmaster*, *Oxford DNB*

8 Oliver Oldfellow (Benjamin Bradney Bockett) *Our School: Or Scraps and Scrapes in Schoolboy Life* (London, John Wesley & Co., 1857, reprinted Kessinger Publishing, 2009)

9 Minto papers, ms 13138 ff157-159, Ned to Emma, 22 May 1814

10 The extent of reductions in naval expenditure after the wars with France was controversial; opponents claimed that it left the Royal Navy ill able to discharge its growing non-war commitments such as suppression of slave-trading, piracy and smuggling. See C.J.Bartlett *Great Britain and Sea Power 1815-1853* (Oxford, Clarendon Press, 1963) passim

11 Anna Maria, Lady Minto (1752-1829), Hugh Elliot's sister-in-law and Charles's aunt, whose husband Gilbert had died in 1814; her role in supplying careers guidance to the 14-year-old boy was clearly significant.

12  Minto papers, ms 11789 f33, 12 February 1816, Hugh Elliot to Lord Minto

13  On the closure of the Academy (in 1806 renamed the Royal Naval College) in 1837 institutional provision for officer education and training ceased until 1863 when it resumed on HMS *Britannia*, moored in the River Dart; the Royal Naval College at Dartmouth opened in 1905 and was renamed Britannia Royal Naval College in 1953.

14  William R. O'Byrne *A Naval Biographical Dictionary: comprising the Life and Services of Every Living Officer in Her Majesty's Navy, from the Rank of Admiral of the Fleet to that of Lieutenant, inclusive* (London, John Murray, 1849) 332

15  J. J. Colledge and Ben Warlow *Ships of the Royal Navy* (Newbury, Casemate-UK, 2010), 227

16  Samantha Cavell *Playing at Command: Midshipmen and Quarterdeck Boys in the Royal Navy 1793–1815* MA thesis Louisiana State University 2006, 24 at http://etd.lsu.edu/docs/available/etd-03312006-200152/unrestricted/Cavell_thesis.pdf (accessed 13.9.2012)

17  Data in Robert Mackenzie *The Trafalgar Roll: The Ships and Officers* (London, Chatham Publishing, 2004), quoted in Cavell *Playing at Command,* 106, indicates that each of the sixteen 74s at Trafalgar had between fifteen and twenty-five midshipmen and volunteers (first class).

18  Cavell *Playing at Command,* 21

19  The scale of the activity is discussed persuasively and in detail in Robert C. Davis *Counting European Slaves on the Barbary Coast,* in *Past and Present* No.172 (Oxford University Press, August 2001) 87-124

20  See Andrew Lambert *The Last Sailing Battle Fleet: Maintaining Naval Mastery 1815-1850* (London, Conway Maritime Press, 1991), 184

21  William Laird Clowes *The Royal Navy – A History from the Earliest Times to the Present* (London, Sampson, Low, Marston and Co., 1901), quoted Blake *Charles Elliot RN,* 8

22  Brian Lavery *Empire of the Seas* (London, Conway, 2009), 235

23  Quoted ibid.

24  George Grover to his father, 29 August 1816, *Official Catalogue and Guide, Chelsea Royal Naval Exhibition, 2 May 1891,* 32 at http://www.ebooksread.com/authors-eng/1891-may-2-chelsea-royal-naval-exhibition (accessed 29.9.2012)

25  Data in William James *The Naval History of Great Britain 1793-1827* (London, R. Bentley, 1837), Vol. VI, 408 at http://pbenyon.plus.com/Naval_History/Vol_VI/Contents.html (accessed 1.10.2012)

26  Ibid.

27  *Minden* in *Index of 19th Century Naval Vessels,* data from William James *The Naval History of Great Britain* at http://www.pbenyon.plus.com/18-1900/M/03033.html (accessed 5.10.2012)

28  See Sugata Bose *A Hundred Horizons. The Indian Ocean in the Age of Global Empire* (London and Cambridge Massachusetts, Harvard University Press, 2006), 45

29  Antigua, Bermuda, Bombay, the Cape, Gibraltar, Jamaica, Malta, Nova Scotia, Quebec and Trincomalee

30  Noted in HA Colgate *Trincomalee and the East Indies Squadron 1746 to 1844* unpublished MA thesis University of London 1959, 293

31 From ADM1/190, correspondence of commander-in-chief East Indies with Admiralty, 1817-1820, and ADM7/561, Royal Navy ships and movements, 1814-1824

32 ADM1/190, Sir Richard King's letters written from '*Minden*, Trincomalee'

33 *Minden* in *Index of Nineteenth Century Naval Vessels*

34 It may also explain a reference in a letter by Charles Elliot of 21 March 1839 in which he describes his son Hughie as being 'just like Fred [Charles's brother] was at Madras in appearance'; see Hoe and Roebuck *The Taking of Hong Kong*, 228

35 ADM7/561/347 *Minden*

36 *The Gentleman's Magazine*, Vol.89, 1819, part 2, 185

37 The Second Earl, Hugh Elliot's brother the First Earl having died in 1814

38 Minto papers, ms 11789 f39, 9 October 1819, Hugh Elliot to Lord Minto

39 Ibid. f44, December 1820, Hugh Elliot to Lord Minto

40 ADM7/561/284 *Iphigenia*

## Chapter Three: Commission to Captain

1 See Harry W. Dickinson *Educating the Royal Navy: Eighteenth– and Nineteenth–Century Education for Officers* (Abingdon, Routledge, 2007), 31. There had been provision for schoolmasters to be appointed to Royal Navy ships since 1702, but numbers had been relatively small.

2 Quoted ibid., 32

3 Based on the careers of fifty officers joining the Navy between 1788 and 1820; data in *William Loney RN – Background* at http://www.pdavis.nl/Background.htm (accessed 28.10.2012)

4 For an illustrative and informative account of the twelve years from 1807 to 1819, and of the role of the Royal Navy in suppressing the slave trade thereafter, see Sian Rees *Sweet Water and Bitter: The Ships that Stopped the Slave Trade* (London, Chatto & Windus, 2009), 26-49 and following.

5 The other countries included Spain (1817) and The Netherlands (1818)

6 Noted in Philip Aubrey *Preventive Squadron – The Royal Navy and the West African Slave Trade 1811-1868* (Julian Corbett Prize Essay, University of London, 1948), 27

7 'Cutting out' was the term for a surprise attack by small boats on larger stationary vessels, with the object of capturing or cutting the target out of future service.

8 Aubrey *Preventive Squadron*, 29. This seems a plausible description of the encounter; the author does not cite his source.

9 Ibid., 30

10 It is estimated that between 1808 and 1860 some 150,000 Africans were freed by the Squadron from around 1,600 slave ships (Royal Naval Museum, Portsmouth at http://www.royalnavalmuseum.org/visit_see_victory_cfexhibition_infosheet.htm (accessed 3.11.2012))

11 ADM7/561/361 *Hussar*

12 ADM196/4/161. For the key dates in Elliot's naval career Blake *Charles Elliot RN* relies on O'Byrne's *Naval Biographical Dictionary*, to which reference is also made in Hoe and Roebuck *The Taking of Hong Kong*. O'Byrne cites brief periods on ships not mentioned in the Admiralty record, the schooner

*Union* (June to August 1825) and the brig-sloop *Bustard* (immediately before joining the *Harlequin*). A further variation from the Admiralty record is that O'Byrne cites only one period of service in *Serapis* (January to April 1826), not two.

13  ADM7/561/516 *Serapis*

14  From *Statistical Report of the Sickness, Mortality and Invaliding Amongst the Troops in the West indies* quoted in Frank Cundall *Historic Jamaica* (London, The West India Committee, 1915), 77 at http://archive.org/stream/cu31924020417527#page/n9/2up (accessed 15.11.2012)

15  See Charles Mackenzie *Notes on Haiti, made during a Residence in that Republic, Vol.1* (London, Henry Colburn and Richard Bentley, 1830), 334: 'During my illness my brother, two of the Vice-Consuls, and my excellent friend, Captain Elliot of the Harlequin were also laid up with dangerous sickness' at http://archive.org/details/notesonhaitimade01mack (accessed 20.11.2012)

16  Based on the careers of thirty-eight captains who had joined the Royal Navy between 1788 and 1820; data in *William Loney RN* – accessed as in Note 3 above. Twenty had served twenty-five years or more before promotion to captain.

17  Clara's role in Charles Elliot's life, as a wife and mother, and in his subsequent career, is sensitively and thoroughly described in Hoe and Roebuck *The Taking of Hong Kong*, which has been the source of much of the material on Clara Elliot in this account.

18  See Hoe and Roebuck *The Taking of Hong Kong*, 258

19  Ibid., 239-240, Note 25 to Chapter 9

20  See *Descendants of Archibald Kane in Haiti* at http://genforum.genealogy.com/haiti/messages/1296.html (accessed 22.11.2012). Clara's brother Robert Alexandre Windsor was married to Marie Louise Isabella Kane, whose mother, Jeanne Julienne Bonnet, had married Noñez after the death of her first husband, Isabella's father, Archibald Kane.

21  The Republic of Haiti had been founded in 1804 following a slave revolt against the French.

## Chapter Four: Slavery and British Guiana

1  The islands included Madeira, the Azores, and Cape Verde, and Sao Tome and Principe in the Gulf of Guinea.

2  Notably from Amsterdam, Bordeaux, Bristol, Cadiz, Liverpool, Lisbon, London, Nantes and Seville. Many minor ports were also involved.

3  For a summary of the worldwide implications of slave trading, see James Walvin, *The Slave Trade* (London, Thames and Hudson, 2011), 7–19

4  Under Article III of the Treaty of Amiens 'His Britannic Majesty restores to the French Republic and its allies, viz. His Catholic majesty [Spain] and the Batavian republic [the Netherlands] all possessions and colonies which respectively belonged to them…'

5  The Treaty restored to Holland the colonial territories it held in 1803 with the exceptions of Berbice, Demerara/Essequibo and the Cape of Good Hope.

6 Quoted in G.W.Bennett *A History of British Guiana, compiled from various authorities* (Georgetown, Demerara, L. M'Dermott, 1875), 112 (published (no date given) in digitised form, British Library Historical Collection)

7 Ibid.

8 Hansard, House of Commons debate *Amelioration of the Condition of the Slave Population of the West Indies*, 16th March 1824, at http://hansard. millbanksystems.com (accessed 18.12.2012). Lord Bathurst gave a similar summary in the House of Lords on the same day.

9 Ibid.

10 *Demerara: Further Papers ... Copy of Documentary Evidence Produced Before a General Court Martial* (House of Commons, 1824), 6,7, quoted in Viotti da Costa *Crowns of Glory, Tears of Blood* (New York, Oxford University Press, 1994), 175

11 Governor Murray was subsequently presented by the colonists with a valuable (1,200 guineas) piece of plate, in recognition of his leading role in the suppression of the revolt (see Henry G. Dalton *The History of British Guiana* Vol.1 (London, Longman, Brown, Green, and Longmans, 1855), 361).

12 See Walvin, *The Slave Trade*, 128

13 The Royal Gazette, 1808, quoted in Odeen Ishmael *The Guyana Story (from Earliest Times to Independence), 41: The Anti-Slavery Movement in British Guiana*, 2005, at http://www.guyana.org/features/guyanastory/guyana_story. html (accessed 20.12.2012)

14 Minto papers, ms 21219, ff1–12

15 Of the fifteen British Caribbean colonies at this time only four were in this category, Demerara/Essequibo, Berbice, St Lucia and Trinidad; the remaining eleven all possessed some form of representative government. The other 'Crown' colonies were the Cape of Good Hope and Mauritius.

16 See Phillip Buckner *Young, Sir Aretas William* in *Dictionary of Canadian Biography Online*, Vol. VI 1821-1835 at http://www.biographi.ca/009004-119.01.php?&id_nbr=3204 (accessed 21.12.2012)

## Chapter Five: Office and Delusion

1 Hansard, House of Lords debate *Condition of Slaves in the West Indies*, 8 February 1830, Order of the King in Council at http://hansard. millbanksystems.com (accessed 4.1.2013)

2 Full title 'The Society for the Mitigation and Gradual Abolition of Slavery Throughout the British Dominions', founded by – amongst others – the veteran abolitionists Thomas Clarkson and William Wilberforce

3 For a summary and the Anti-Slavery Society's reaction see *The Anti-Slavery Reporter* No 92, January 1832, Vol. 5 No. 1, 1-5, *New Slave Code: Protectors and Assistant Protectors* (London, London Society for the Abolition of Slavery Throughout the British Dominions, 1833) at http://archive.org/stream/antislaveryrepor005soci# (accessed 2.1.2013)

4 Ibid.,3

5 *Public Record Office Lists and Indexes, XXXVI List of Colonial Office Records* (London, HMSO) 1911, noted in Blake *Charles Elliot RN,* 13

6   Buckner *Young, Sir Aretas William*, DCBO

7   See CO 114/12, *Minutes of the Proceedings of the Court of Policy, British Guiana*, 195–6

8   Ibid., 58-9

9   CO 116/178, *Blue Book of Statistics, Berbice 1831*, 114

10  Noted in Richard B. Sheridan *The Condition of Slaves on the sugar plantations of Sir John Gladstone in the colony of Demerara, 1812–49* in New West Indian Guide/ Nieuwe West-Indische Gids 76 (2002), no.3/4, Leiden, 264 at http://www.kitlvjournals.nl/index.php/nwig/viewFile/3455/4216 (accessed 14.1.2013)

11  Minto papers, ms 21219 ff 95-102. Robertson's figures also give numbers of slaves according to crop cultivated: sugar (47,456); cotton (2,859); and coffee (2,555). In smaller numbers, slaves were also engaged in other tasks, such as working with cattle (385).

12  CO 116/159 *Report of the Protector of Slaves, Demerara and Essequibo, January – June 1832*

13  i.e. including Berbice, which as a separate colony had had until June 1831 its own Acting Protector of Slaves, the Registrar Mr Samuel, who had held the post in the absence of the Protector, Mr Power, since January of that year.

14  CO 114/12, *Minutes of the Court of Policy*, 188-94

15  Ibid., 189

16  Ibid., 189–90

17  Ibid., 190

18  Ibid.

19  *An Ordinance for Assimilating the Manner of Proceeding for the Recovery of the Fines and Penalties Provided in the Slave Ordinances in the United Colony of Demerary and Essequebo, and of Berbice Respectively* in *The Essequebo and Demerary Royal Gazette*, December 1831 at http://www.vc.id.au/edg/18311231rg.html (accessed 15.1.2013).

20  Ibid.

21  CO 114/12, *Minutes of the Court of Policy*, 191

22  Ibid., 193

23  Ibid., 203 – the planters had commented, for example, that 'it is notorious that the duties paid on sugar exceed the residue of gross sales'.

24  Ibid., 202

25  Minto papers, ms 21219 f97, quoting Robertson, who had been Registrar of Slaves in Demerara/Essequibo since 1817

26  Ibid.

27  Ibid.

28  CO 116/146, *Report of the Protector of Slaves, Berbice, May–September 1830* Table A, 108-110 (standard form numbering in Protectors' reports)

29  Henry Beard, Governor of Berbice 1821–31

30  CO 116/146, 1

31  Ibid.

32  Ibid., 5

33  *The Anti-Slavery Reporter* No. 104 December 31, 1832, Vol. V No.13, 313, *Analysis of the Report of a Committee of the House of Commons on the Extinction of Slavery* at http://archive.org/stream/antislaveryrepor005soci#(accessed 22.1.2013)

34  Ibid., 463

35  Ibid., 464

36  Ibid., 465

37  Ibid., 466

38  Minto papers, ms 13135 ff5-7, 25 January 1834, Charles Elliot to Emma Hislop.

39  Bell, K.N. and Morrell, W.P. (eds.), *Select Documents on British Colonial Policy, 1830–1860* (Oxford: The Clarendon Press, 1928), quoted in Blake *Charles Elliot RN*, 18

40  Ibid., 18-19

41  Minto papers, ms 13135 ff5-7, 25 January 1834, Charles to Emma.

42  Under-Secretary of State for Home Affairs, until July 1834. He was subsequently Secretary at War (1835-1839) and Secretary of State for War and the Colonies (1846–52)

43  Minto papers, ms 21217 f2, 2 March 1833, Howick to the Treasury.

44  Ibid.

45  Grey papers, ms GRE/B148/8, 9 October 1832, Charles Elliot to Lord Howick.

46  Ibid.

47  Ibid.

## Chapter Six: Trade and China

1  Ibn-Battuta *Rihla*, quoted in Joe Studwell *The China Dream* (London, Profile Books, 2002), 6

2  Ibn Taghri-Birdi *A History of Egypt, 1382–1469 AD*, quoted in Gavin Menzies *1421 The Year China discovered the World* (London, Bantam Press, 2002), 71

3  A detailed account of Weddell's activities in China is provided in Austin Coates *Macao and the British 1637-1842, Prelude to Hong Kong* (Hong Kong, Oxford University Press, 1988), 1-27

4  Peter Mundy *The Travels of Peter Mundy in Europe and Asia 1608–1667* quoted in Frank Welsh *A History of Hong Kong* (London, Harper Collins, 1993), 550

5  See Niall Ferguson *Empire: How Britain made the Modern World* (London, Penguin Books, 2003), 22-23

6  See John Keay *The Honourable Company: A History of the East India Company* (London, Harper Collins, 1993), 177

7  J. Fryer *A New Account of the East Indies and Persia … 1672–1681*, cited ibid., 137

8  F. E. Penny *Fort St George, Madras: A Short History of Our First Possession in India* (London, Swan Sonnenschein & Co. Ltd., 1900), 36, at http://archive. org/details/fortstgeorgemad00penngoog (accessed 6.3.2013)

9  Day's and Charnock's successors, who with those at Bombay were the men in overall charge of the East India Company's Indian settlements, were formally designated Presidents, though they were more usually known as Governors or Governors-General. Until the Presidency of Madras came into being, the Company's activities on the Coromandel coast were the administrative responsibility of the Bantam Presidency. Its trading in the Bay of Bengal was under the aegis of Madras initially, but was accorded Agency status in 1681 and by 1700, after a period in which it was again subject to Madras, had become independent as the Presidency of Bengal, centred on Calcutta.

10  Keay *The Honourable Company*, 206–07

11  After whom Yale College (now Yale University) Connecticut was named.

12  From the Cantonese 'hoi poi', an abbreviation of the Mandarin title held by the superintendent of South Sea Customs (see Frank Welsh *A History of Hong Kong*, 27)

13  Keay *The Honourable Company*, 209

14  Ibid., 349

15  The Act's provisions included the granting of additional powers to the Governor General of Bengal (at that time Warren Hastings), in effect establishing Bengal as the senior of the three Presidencies and the Governor General as the British government's officer in overall charge of its Indian territories.

16  Joseph Rowntree (1905), quoted ibid.

17  Martin Booth *Opium: A History* (New York, St Martin's Griffin, 1998), 109

18  Hosea Ballou Morse *Chronicles of the East India Company* quoted in Michael Greenberg *British Trade and the Opening of China 1800-1842* (Cambridge University Press, 2008), 6

19  Greenberg *British Trade and the Opening of China*, 221 (Greenberg notes that the figures, taken from Morse *International Relations Vol.1*, are from a number of different original sources and may not be entirely accurate; but the overall trend is clear).

20  Quoted in Christopher Hibbert, *The Dragon Wakes: China and the West 1793– 1911* (Harmondsworth, Penguin Books, 1984), 4.

21  Aeneas Anderson *An Accurate Account of Lord Macartney's Embassy to China; carefully abridged from the original work* (London, Vernor and Hood, 1798), 78 at http://archive.org/details/accurateaccount00ande (accessed 11.4.2013).

22  Ibid., 78–9

23  Ibid.

24  Ibid., 98

25  J.L.Cranmer-Byng *An Embassy to China: Being the Journal Kept by Lord Macartney during his Embassy to the Emperor Ch'ien-lung, 1793-94* (Longmans, 1962) quoted in Hibbert *The Dragon Wakes*, 13.

26  Quoted in Greenberg *British Trade and the Opening of China*, 4.

## Chapter Seven: Fizzle, Silence, and Quiescence

1  W. C. Costin *Great Britain and China, 1833–1860* (Oxford, The Clarendon Press, 1937), 31

2  See Chapter One

3  More properly Bocca Tigris (the Mouth of the Tigris, the name by which the Pearl River was known to the East India Company)

4  Salary in 2015 terms, £93,793 (illustrative – Bank of England inflation calculator at http://www.bankofengland.co.uk/education/Pages/resources/inflationtools/calculator/flash/default.aspx (accessed 10.4.2016)

5  Grey papers, ms GRE/B84/10/12, 23 January 1834, Charles Elliot to Lord Howick

6  Hoe and Roebuck assert (*The Taking of Hong Kong*, 6) that Elliot did not realise what he was being offered; it is possible that he had been actively encouraged to believe that a more senior post was intended.

7  FO17/6/34-7, 13 August 1834, Elliot to Lord Palmerston.

8 Minto papers, ms 13135 ff8-9, 21 February 1834, Charles Elliot to his sister Emma (Hislop)

9 Ibid., ff5-7, 25 January 1834.

10 See Minto papers, ms 13135 ff1-2, 3 November 1833, Charles to Emma (quoted in full in Hoe and Roebuck *The Taking of Hong Kong*, 12).

11 Minto papers, ms 13135 ff1–2, 3 November 1833, Charles to Emma.

12 Ibid., ff10–12, 10 May 1834.

13 Ibid.

14 Ibid.

15 Ibid., ms 13137 ff4–6, 24 August 1834, Clara Elliot to Emma Hislop, quoted in Hoe and Roebuck *The Taking of Hong Kong*, 20. Davis had been the senior East India Company official in China before its monopoly and predominant formal role there ended in April 1834.

16 Ibid.

17 *Correspondence Relating to China*, 1840, 36 (223), 5, Parliamentary Papers, quoted in Peter Ward Fay *The Opium War 1840-1842* (New York and London, W.W. Norton & Company, 1976), 69.

18 Quoted in Glenn Melancon *Britain's China Policy and the Opium Crisis: Balancing Drugs, Violence and National Honour, 1833–1840* (Aldershot, Ashgate Publishing Ltd., 2003), 36.

19 From the letters and journals of William John, ninth Lord Napier, quoted in Priscilla Napier *Barbarian Eye: Lord Napier in China, 1834, The Prelude to Hong Kong* (London, Brassey's, 1995), 88.

20 See Napier *Barbarian Eye*, 159.

21 William Jardine Private Letter Books, Ch.3, 127, June 1834, Jardine Matheson papers, quoted in Robert Blake *Jardine Matheson Traders of the Far East* (London, Weidenfeld & Nicholson, 1999), 69.

22 Napier was also referred to by the Chinese in writing, more insultingly, by characters which translated as 'Laboriously Vile', though this was probably not as offensive in Chinese usage as Napier and the British took it to be (see Brian Inglis, *The Opium War* (London, Hodder and Stoughton, 1976), 97).

23 See Napier *Barbarian Eye*, 124-125

24 *Correspondence of Foreign Secretaries with Superintendents,* 1834–1839, Napier to Palmerston, 14–17 August 1834, Parliamentary Papers 1840, xxxvi, no.7, quoted in Costin *Great Britain and China, 1833–1860*.

25 Ibid. no. 11, Napier to Grey, 21 August 1934, quoted in Costin *Great Britain and China*, 24.

26 *Correspondence Relating to China*, 1840, 36 (223), 24, quoted in Fay *The Opium War*, 73.

27 See Napier *Barbarian Eye*, 132.

28 William Boyd, the merchants' secretary.

29 From the letters and journals of Lord Napier, quoted in Napier *Barbarian Eye*, 184–85.

30 See Napier *Barbarian Eye*, 191

31 Minto papers, ms 13137 ff4–6, 24 August 1834, Clara Elliot to Emma Hislop, quoted in Hoe and Roebuck *The Taking of Hong Kong*, 27.

32  Minto papers, ms 13137 ff7–11, 9 November 1834, Clara to Emma, quoted in Hoe and Roebuck *The Taking of Hong Kong*, 33.

33  Parliamentary Papers (Blue Book) (selected Foreign Office papers), 44, quoted ibid., 40.

34  Minto papers, ms 13135 ff13-15, 19 January 1835, Charles Elliot to Emma

35  Quoted in Hsin-pao Chang *Commissioner Lin and the Opium War* (New York, W.W.Norton & Company Inc., 1970), 64.

36  Minto papers, ms 13135 ff13–15, 19 January 1835, Charles Elliot to Emma.

37  See Derek Roebuck *Captain Charles Elliot RN, Arbitrator: Dispute Resolution in China Waters, 1834–6* in Arbitration International (1998) 14:2, 185-212 at http://arbitration.oxfordjournals.org/content/14/2/185 (accessed 12.1.2016).

38  Quoted ibid.

39  Ibid.

40  Ibid.

41  Ibid.

42  'without interest' i.e. in whom no-one is interested

43  Minto papers, ms 13135 ff16–17, 28 April 1835, Charles Elliot to Emma.

44  Ibid.

45  See Chang *Commissioner Lin*, 66–67.

46  FO/17/14, 16 October 1835, Robinson to Palmerston.

47  The contact, Lennox Conyngham, is said by Blake (*Charles Elliot RN*, 28) to have been a friend of Elliot's; Hoe and Roebuck (*The Taking of Hong Kong*, 45) suggest he may have been a private channel of communication with Palmerston set up by Davis. 'Private correspondence' was both used as a means of frank communication, often usefully in advance of official messages, and not infrequently cited in Parliament by ministers as a reason for non-disclosure of information.

48  FO 17/12/174–6, 8 November 1834, Davis to John Barrow (Second – later Permanent – Secretary to the Admiralty, 1804–6, 1807–44), quoted in Hoe and Roebuck *The Taking of Hong Kong*, 49–50

49  FO 17/12/341, 26 June 1835, Davis to John Backhouse (Permanent Under-Secretary at the Foreign Office, 1827–42), quoted in Hoe and Roebuck *The Taking of Hong Kong*, 50.

## Chapter Eight: Opium Prelude

1  *China: Opium War and Opium Trade* Parliamentary Papers No. 65, 123, quoted in Hoe and Roebuck *The Taking of Hong Kong*, 57–8.

2  Minto papers, ms 13135 ff18–19, 17 February 1837, Charles to Emma.

3  Hansard, speech by Sir James Graham, House of Commons 7 April 1840, quoted in Harry G. Gelber *Opium, Soldiers and Evangelicals, England's 1840–42 War with China, and its Aftermath* (Basingstoke, Palgrave Macmillan, 2004), 54.

4  See Jack Beeching *The Chinese Opium Wars* (New York, Harcourt Brace Jovanovich, 1975), 67–8. George Eden, First Earl of Auckland, was a first cousin of Charles Elliot.

5  See Chang *Commissioner Lin and the Opium War*, 74–5

6 Ibid., 85–8

7 Ibid., 91

8 *Canton Register* editorial 7 January 1834, quoted in Chang *Commissioner Lin and the Opium War*, 82

9 Lay papers, 17 April 1838, quoted in Peter Ward Fay *The Opening of China*, in Maggie Keswick (ed.) *The Thistle and the Jade, A Celebration of 150 Years of Jardine Matheson* (London, Frances Lincoln Limited, 2008), 81.

10 Henry Taylor *Autobiography* (London, 1885), from a communication by Elliot of 16 November 1839, quoted in Hoe and Roebuck *The Taking of Hong Kong*, 52.

11 See Chang *Commissioner Lin and the Opium War*, 49.

12 *War with China and the Opium Question* in *Blackwood's Edinburgh Magazine*, Vol. 47 (London and Edinburgh, 1840), 380 at http://google.co.uk/books?output=html&id=xbPQVntE8mEC&jtp=380 (accessed 9.9.2013).

13 Ibid.

14 Quoted in *The Chinese Repository* Vol. VI, May 1837 to April 1838 (Canton, 1838), 544 (unabridged facsimile, Elibron Classics Replica Edition, 2005).

15 Ibid.

16 These episodes included the strangling in 1784 of the gunner of the *Lady Hughes*, who in firing a salute had accidentally killed one of the crew of a small chop-boat lying nearby.

17 Minto papers, ms 11810 ff31–32, 13 September 1837, Palmerston to Minto.

18 Also, according to Blake (*Charles Elliot RN*, 30) to draw and paint; Hoe and Roebuck (*The Taking of Hong Kong*, 60) find no evidence to support this view and suggest a possible confusion with an earlier Elliot on the China coast, Captain Robert Elliot (no relation), who was an artist.

19 Minto papers, ms 13137 ff15–17, 25 February 1838, Clara to Emma, quoted in Hoe and Roebuck *The Taking of Hong Kong*, 63.

20 Minto papers, ms 13135 ff20–21, 13 October 1837, Charles to Emma.

21 Hansard, quoted in speech by Lord Ashley (later the Earl of Shaftesbury), Suppression of the Opium Trade, House of Commons, 4 April 1843 at http://hansard.millbanksystems.com (accessed 2.10.2013).

## Chapter Nine: Authority and Honour

1 For an informed and thorough account of Lin's career see Chang *Commissioner Lin and the Opium War* 121–4.

2 J. R. Morrison's translation, quoted in *The Chinese Repository* Vol. VII, May 1838 – April 1839, 612–3

3 Ibid., 619

4 Minto papers, ms 13135 ff24-5, 21 March 1839, Charles to Emma

5 See Greenberg *British Trade and the Opening of China 1800–42*, 112–3: opium imports at Canton rose from an average of around 4,500 chests a year between 1800 and 1821, through around 10,000 a year from 1821 to 1830–1, to 40,000 in 1838–9.

6 Circular from Charles Elliot to Her Majesty's Subjects, 22 March 1839, Parliamentary Papers *Correspondence Relating to China*, 1840, 363, at https://archive.org/stream/CorrespondenceRelatingToChina1840 (accessed 12.11.2013)

7 Letter Elliot to Palmerston, 30 March 1839, ibid., 357.

8 Ibid.

9 Arthur Waley's translation from *Ya-p'ien Chan-cheng Tzu-liao Ts'ung-k'an* [*Corpus of material about the Opium War*] (Shanghai 1955) Vol.II, 245, quoted in Arthur Waley *The Opium War through Chinese Eyes* (Stanford, Stanford University Press, 1968), 36.

10 Letter Elliot to Palmerston, 2 January 1839, Parliamentary Papers *Correspondence Relating to China*, 1840, 340 (accessed 12.11.2013). Elliot's statement followed a report in the same letter of a discussion with Howqua. In that exchange Elliot had explained the earlier attempt made in the House of Commons to regularise the position in the abortive China Courts Bill of 1838, in which Palmerston had sought to extend provision for admiralty and criminal courts (passed into law in 1833 but not acted on) also to allow civil cases. Howqua had listened sympathetically but 'he desired to know what more was wanted, and how was it possible to preserve the peace, if all the English people who came to this country were to be left without control?'

11 Letter Elliot to Palmerston 30 March 1839, Parliamentary Papers *Correspondence Relating to China*, 1840, 357 (accessed 21.11.2013).

12 Jardine Matheson papers, Canton 553, quoted in Chang *Commissioner Lin and the Opium War*, 156.

13 Minto papers, ms 13140 ff101–2, 4 April 1839, Charles to Clara.

14 Letter Elliot to Palmerston 6 April 1839, Parliamentary Papers *Correspondence Relating to China*, 1840, 386–7 (accessed 15.12.2013).

15 Ibid.

16 *The Chinese Repository* Vol.VII, May 1838 to April 1839, 650–1 (unattributed 'close translation').

17 Ibid., Vol.VIII, May 1839 to April 1840, 10-11, quoted in Chang *Commissioner Lin and the Opium War*, 135

18 It is not clear why, or who was entrusted with its delivery.

19 Minto papers, ms 13135 ff26–7, 29 May 1839, Charles to Emma and Harriet, quoted in Hoe and Roebuck *The Taking of Hong Kong*, 81–2

20 Ibid.

21 Quoted in Edgar Holt *The Opium Wars in China* (London, Putnam & Company Ltd., 1964), 101.

22 See Minto papers, ms 13135 ff32–5, 23 February 1840, Charles to Emma

23 Minto papers, ms 13135 ff28–9, 17 July 1839, Charles to Emma.

24 Quoted in his translation in Waley *The Opium War through Chinese Eyes*, 55.

25 See note 10.

26 W.D.Bernard *Narrative of the Voyages and the Services of the Nemesis from 1840 to 1843* (London, Henry Coulburn, 1844), 196.

27 Note 23 above.

28 Letter Elliot to Palmerston 5 September 1839, Parliamentary Papers *Correspondence Relating to China*, 1840, 446 (accessed 6.1.2014).

29 FO 17/32/153–7, 27 August 1839, Elliot to Palmerston.

30 Ibid.

31 FO 17/32/194-196, 3 September 1839, Elliot to Palmerston.

32 Ibid.

33 Ibid.

34  FO 17/32/236–239, 8 September 1839, Elliot to Palmerston.
35  FO 17/32/250–254, 23 September 1839, Elliot to Palmerston.
36  Some sixty miles southwest of Macao.
37  J. R. Morrison's translation, in FO 17/33/182-194, 27 October 1839, Lin and Deng to Elliot.
38  Ibid.

## Chapter Ten: War

1   Otherwise known as the First Anglo-Chinese War or simply the Opium War.
2   Also Elliot's nearly exact contemporary (born 1804, promoted post captain 1829); knighted and appointed admiral before retiring.
3   See translated extracts of Lin's subsequent report to the Emperor, quoted in Julia Lovell *The Opium War* (London, Picador, 2011), 94.
4   Letter Elliot to Palmerston from HMS *Volage*, Hong Kong, 5 November 1839, Parliamentary Papers *Additional Correspondence Relating to China*, 10 -11 (accessed 24.1.2014).
5   Ibid.
6   Minto papers, ms 13135 f202, 8 November 1839, Charles Elliot to (daughter) Harriet.
7   See for example those of 30 March and 6 April (notes 11,14 and 15, Chapter Nine).
8   Algernon Thelwall *The Iniquities of the Opium Trade with China: Being a Development of the Main Causes which Exclude the Merchants of Great Britain from the Advantages of an Unrestricted Commercial Intercourse with that Vast Empire. With Extracts from Authentic Documents* (London, W. H. Allen and Company, 1839).
9   'Proceeding with our View of the Opium Question' *Times* (London, England) 23 October 1839 The Times Digital Archive, Web, 5 July 2014
10  'The Opium Question' *Times* 25 October 1839, ibid.
11  Illustrative, Bank of England Inflation Calculator (accessed 14.2.2017).
12  Minto papers, ms 13135 ff32–35, 23 February 1840, Charles to Emma.
13  See Chang *Commissioner Lin and the Opium War*, 206.
14  Minto papers, ms 13135 ff36–37, (undated) February 1840, Charles to Emma
15  Ibid.
16  Minto papers, ms 13135 ff32–35, 23 February 1840, Charles to Emma.
17  Hansard, Queen's Speech, House of Lords, 16 January 1840, at http://hansard.millbanksystems.com (accessed 24.2.2014).
18  Ibid., War with China, House of Commons, 7 April 1840 (accessed 27.2.2014)
19  The form in which the *Correspondence* was presented, unordered, not indexed and long, generated much criticism. W.E.Gladstone said in the debate that it had been given to the House 'in one vast, rude, and undigested chaos which the wit of man is incapable of comprehending'.
20  Hansard, War with China, House of Commons, 7 April 1840 at http://hansard.millbanksystems.com (accessed 27.2.2014)
21  'Editorial' *Times* (London, England) 7 April 1840 The Times Digital Archive, Web, 5 July 2014.
22  *The Charter*, quoted in Lovell *The Opium War*, 107.
23  Hansard, War with China – Adjourned Debate, House of Commons, 8 April 1840, at http://hansard.millbanksystems.com (accessed 6.3.2014).

24 Ibid.

25 Hansard, War with China – Adjourned Debate, House of Commons, 9 April 1840, at http://hansard.millbanksystems.com (accessed 10.3.2014).

26 Ibid.

27 Ibid.

28 Ibid.

29 Hansard, War with China, House of Lords, 12 May 1840 at http://hansard. millbanksystems.com (accessed 10.3.2014).

30 Ibid.

31 Henry Taylor *Autobiography* (London, Longmans, Green and Co., 1885), 295.

32 Minto papers, ms 11795 ff59-61, quoted in Hoe and Roebuck *The Taking of Hong Kong*, 107–8.

33 See *Miss Eden's Letters* ed. Violet Dickinson (London, Macmillan, 1919, reprinted General Books LLC, Memphis, 2012) Chapters XI and XII, 81-105. Greville achieved posthumous notoriety with the publication of his *Diaries*, parts of which caused serious offence amongst the political establishment.

34 Philip Wilson *The Greville Diary* (1927), 21 February 1840, Vol.2, 506, quoted in Hoe and Roebuck *The Taking of Hong Kong*, 108.

35 Leading article *Times* (London), 2 March 1840: 4 The Times Digital Archive, Web, 5 July 2014

36 Minto papers, ms 13135 ff40–42, 12 May 1840, Charles to Emma.

37 Son of Hugh Elliot's brother Gilbert, Ist Earl of Minto, and brother of the First Lord of the Admiralty.

38 Minto papers, ms 13135 ff38-39, 23 March 1840, Charles to Emma.

39 See Waley *The Opium War through Chinese Eyes*, 103.

40 *Ya-p'ien Chan-cheng*, Vol.IV, 630, quoted ibid., 108–9

41 For a detailed contemporary account of the occupation of Zhoushan see Lieutenant John Ouchterlony *The Chinese War: an Account of all the Operations of the British Forces from the Commencement to the Treaty of Nanking* (London, Saunders and Otley, 1844)

42 Minto papers, ms 13137 ff34-37, 31 August 1840, Clara to Emma.

43 Ibid.

44 Palmerston to 'The Minister of the Emperor of China' 20 February 1840, quoted in H B Morse *International Relations of the Chinese Empire*, Vol. 1, Appendix A (London, New York: Longmans, Green and Co., 1910).

45 Ibid.

46 The prisoners, who had escaped from the wreck of a survey vessel and been transported in cages to Ningbo, did eventually return south with the main force.

47 Jardine Matheson Archive, James Matheson Private Letter Books, vol. 6, 13 January 1841, 50-51, Matheson to Jamsetjee Jeejeebhoy.

48 Mao, *Tianchao de bengkui (The Collapse of a Dynasty)* (Beijing: Shenghuo, 1995) 212-213, quoted in Lovell *The Opium War*, 136.

49 Palmerston to Elliot, 21 April 1841, extracts quoted in Maurice Collis *Foreign Mud* (London, Faber and Faber Limited, 1946) 300–1. The young Queen Victoria joined in, conveying indignant exasperation about the Convention – and Elliot – to her uncle Leopold, King of the Belgians.

50  Minto papers, ms 11793 ff82-84, 19 February 1841, Auckland to Minto

51  Ibid.

52  Minto papers, ms 13140 ff129-130, 24 April 1841, Charles to the children (Harriet (Chachy), Hughie and Gibby).

53  Ibid.

54  Sir Robert S. Rait *The Life and Campaigns of Hugh, First Viscount Gough, Field Marshal* (London, A. Constable, 1903), vol.1, 168, quoted in Gelber *Opium, Soldiers and Evangelicals*, 121.

55  FO 17/52, 24 May 1841, Elliot to Gough and Senhouse, quoted in Fay *The Opium War 1840 – 1842*, 294.

56  Duncan McPherson MD *Two years in China, Narrative of the Chinese Expedition from its formation in April 1840* (London, Saunders and Otley, 1843), 143–4.

57  Minto papers, ms 21216A, 3 May 1841, Palmerston to Elliot (printed in *Papers Relating to China 1839–40 and 1841*).

58  Henry Taylor *Autobiography*, Appendix, *Charles Elliot's Operations in China*, 367–8.

59  Ibid.; though either Elliot was misquoting Dryden, or Taylor Elliot (or possibly both). The lines appear in Dryden's *Ode to the Pious Memory of the Accomplished Young Lady, Mrs Anne Killigrew, Excellent in the Sister-arts of Poesy and Painting:* Slack all thy sails, and fear to come,/Alas, thou know'st not, thou art wrecked at home! (*Oxford Book of English Verse* (Oxford, Clarendon Press, 1961), 478).

60  Minto papers, ms 13135 ff 45–46, 26 October 1841, Charles to Emma.

61  Blake *Jardine Matheson Traders of the Far East*, 110.

62  G.B. Endacott *A History of Hong Kong* (Hong Kong, Oxford University Press, 1964) 34.

## Chapter Eleven: Recall, Reaction and Resolve

1  Parliamentary Papers *Correspondence Relating to China* 1840, passim (accessed 28.6.2014).

2  On 21 April 1841 (see Chapter Ten, note 49). The letter ended 'You will no doubt, by the time you have read thus far, have anticipated that I could not conclude this letter without saying that under these circumstances it is impossible that you should continue to hold your appointment in China.'

3  Henry Taylor *Autobiography*, 299–300.

4  Minto papers, ms 13135 ff51–54, 26 June 1843, Charles to Emma.

5  See Chapter Ten, 116 and note 50

6  *Miss Eden's Letters* Chapter XII, 15 January 1841, Emily to Eleanor, Countess of Buckinghamshire

7  Ibid.

8  Ibid., 6 April 1841, Emily to Eleanor.

9  Ibid., 12 April 1841, Emily to Robert Eden.

10  See George Pottinger *Sir Henry Pottinger, First Governor of Hong Kong* (Stroud, Sutton Publishing, 1997) 160.

11  *Miss Eden's Letters* Chapter XII, 8 October 1841, Emily to Eleanor.

12  Minto papers, ms 11796 ff58-59, 21 October 1841, Emily to Lord Minto.

13  Lloyd Sanders *Lord Melbourne's Papers* (1889), 493–4, 30 April 1841, Melbourne to Russell, quoted in Hoe and Roebuck *The Taking of Hong Kong*, 158.

14  MERCATOR 'Calamitous Events in China' *The Times* 15 January 1840: 5. The Times Digital Archive, Web, 16 July 2014.

15  Jardine Matheson Archive, James Matheson Private Letter Books, vol.6, 23 January 1841, 63–4, Matheson to Jardine.

16  *The Morning Post*, 8 May 1841, at http://www.britishnewspaperarchive. co.uk (accessed 7.8.2014). The reference to Pottinger's reputation in India for forthright action was intended by the newspaper to show that his appointment was, as it put it in the same article, a 'warning to such nations on our Indian frontier as may have heard of the exploits of the late Plenipotentiary'.

17  See for example *The Birmingham Journal*, *The Leeds Times*, and *The Liverpool Mercury*, 1840–42

18  'The memorandum by the Duke of Wellington' *The Times* 19 March 1840:4. The Times Digital Archive, Web, 16 July 2014.

19  Minto papers, ms 13135 ff45-46, 26 October 1841, Charles to Emma.

20  Ibid.

21  Minto papers, ms 21217 ff20-23, 20 October 1841, Jamsetjee Jeejeebhoy to Charles.

22  The four additional ports were Xiamen, Fuzhou, Ningbo and Shanghai.

## Chapter Twelve: Texas: Spain, Mexico and the United States

1  See Donald E. Chipman and Harriett Denise Joseph *Spanish Texas 1519-1821* (Austin, University of Texas Press, 2010), 28–47.

2  *Comprehensive Orders for New Discoveries*, 1573, quoted in *The Oxford History of the American West* (New York and Oxford, Oxford University Press, 1994), 52–3.

3  From *The New Laws of the Indies*, quoted in Hugh Thomas *The Golden Age: The Spanish Empire of Charles V* (London, Penguin Books, 2011), 480

4  There had been an unpublished agreement the previous year (The Treaty of Fontainebleau) that the whole of Louisiana should go to Spain; under the 1763 Treaty the eastern half was allocated to Britain.

5  See for example Carl A. Brasseaux and Richard E. Chandler *The* Britain *Incident 1769–1770: Anglo-Hispanic Tensions in the Western Gulf* in Southwestern Historical Quarterly Vol. 87, April 1984, 368 at http://texashistory.unt.edu/ ark:/67531/metapth117150/m1/425/ (accessed 19.10.2014). While the leaders of a British delegation to Veracruz sought reparations for the loss of the ship *Britain*, some of their colleagues covertly gathered detailed information about the state of Mexican defences.

6  de Nava to Muñoz, Chihuahua 30.7.1795, Bexar Archives, Austin, University of Texas, quoted in Odie B.Faulk *The Last Years of Spanish Texas 1778–1821* (The Hague, Mouton & Co., 1964), 114–5.

7  Subsequently known as The Father of Mexican Independence.

8  For a description of the contrast between the respective characteristics and outlooks of the Mexicans and their neighbours to the north, see Eugene Campbell Barker *Mexico and Texas 1821–1835: University of Texas research*

*lectures on the causes of the Texas revolution* (New York, Russell & Russell Inc., 1965), 1–6

9  Quoted in *Mexico and Texas 1821–1825*, 70.

10  H.P.N.Gammel (comp.) *The Laws of Texas 1822–1897* (10 vols.; Austin, 1898–1902), 1, 424, quoted in Randolph B. Campbell *An Empire for Slavery: The Peculiar Institution in Texas, 1821–1865* (Baton Rouge, Louisiana State University Press, 1991), 21.

11  Austin to Samuel May Williams, 16 April 1831, in Eugene Campbell Barker (ed.) *The Papers of Stephen F. Austin* (Washington and Austin, 1924–8), II, 645, quoted in *An Empire for Slavery*, 28–29. Santo Domingo, present day capital of the Dominican Republic, had been overrun by Haitian forces in 1821 and subsequently forced to abolish slavery.

12  He wrote as chairman of the Central Committee of Safety of San Felipe. Quoted in Eugene Campbell Barker *The Life of Stephen F. Austin: Founder of Texas, 1793–1836* (Nashville, 1925), 481, and in *An Empire for Slavery*, 40.

13  From the Constitution of Texas, General Provisions, Section 9, quoted in *An Empire for Slavery*, 46.

14  David G. Burnet had been interim President during the first, transitional, six months of the Republic.

15  Hansard, Texas, House of Commons, 26 April 1842 at http://hansard. millbanksystems.com (accessed 18.11.2014).

16  Ibid., Consul-General of Texas, 3 May 1842.

17  Ibid.

18  Ibid., Captain Elliot – Texas, 24 May 1842.

## Chapter Thirteen: 'This Raw Country'

1  Lytton Strachey and Roger Fulford eds., *The Greville Memoirs 1814–1860* (London, Macmillan, 1938), vol. IV, 422, 19 November 1841, quoted in Hoe and Roebuck *The Taking of Hong Kong*, 199.

2  Ibid.

3  Stephen had trained as a lawyer and later became Regius Professor of Modern History at Cambridge.

4  Minto papers ms 11789, f203, Stephen to Taylor, 11 March 1842.

5  Ibid.

6  Minto papers ms 21218, ff1-54, Elliot to Aberdeen, 25 January 1842.

7  Ibid.

8  In 2015 terms, £129,299,892 (illustrative – Bank of England inflation calculator at http://www.bankofengland.co.uk/education/Pages/resources/ inflationtools/calculator/flash/default.aspx (accessed 11.4.2016). See Minto papers ms 21217, ff47–50, memorandum from Sir Charles Trevelyan, Assistant Secretary, Treasury to H.U.Addington, Permanent Under Secretary, Foreign Office, 3 September 1846.

9  Hansard, Slavery in Texas, House of Commons, 5 August 1836 at http:// hansard.millbanksystems.com (accessed 10.12.2014).

10  Broadlands mss., GC/MO no.29, quoted in Kenneth Bourne *The Foreign Policy of Victorian England 1830-1902* (Oxford, Clarendon Press, 1970), 228–9.

11 Ephraim Douglass Adams (ed.) *British Diplomatic Correspondence concerning the Republic of Texas, 1838-1846* (Austin, The Texas State Historical Association, 1918), 46–7, Kennedy to Aberdeen, 6 November 1841 at http://archive.org/stream/britishdiplomati00grea# (accessed 11.12.2014).

12 In 2015 terms, £126,185 (illustrative – Bank of England inflation calculator (accessed 11.4.2016)).

13 FO 75/4, ff5–6, Aberdeen to Elliot, 1 July 1842.

14 FO 75/3, f26, Addington to Elliot, 28 June 1842.

15 FO 75/4, f53, Aberdeen to Elliot (unsigned), 3 December 1842.

16 Ibid.

17 Aberdeen papers ms 43126, ff42–43, Elliot to Aberdeen, 15 January 1843.

18 See Blake *Charles Elliot RN*, 74.

19 *British Diplomatic Correspondence*, 125–30, Elliot to Addington, 15 November 1842 (accessed 5.1.2015).

20 See Ephraim Douglass Adams *British Interests and Activities in Texas 1838–1846* (Baltimore, The Johns Hopkins Press, 1910), 115.

21 FO 75/4, f145, Elliot to Addington, 11 December 1842.

22 Ibid., f142.

23 Ibid., f158, Elliot to Addington, 16 December 1842.

24 Ibid., f161, Elliot to Addington, 28 December 1842.

25 The ships were the *Eliza Russell* and the *Little Penn.*

26 FO 75/6, ff44–47, Elliot to Aberdeen, 23 January 1843.

27 FO 75/6, ff75–78, Elliot to Aberdeen, 5 February 1843.

28 Ibid., ff 9–11, Aberdeen to Elliot, 18 May 1843.

29 *British Diplomatic Correspondence*, 208-213, Houston to Elliot, 13 May 1843 (accessed 26.1.2015).

30 Ibid., 205, Elliot to Aberdeen, 8 June 1843.

31 Minto papers ms 13135, ff49–50, Charles to Emma and Clara, 15 April 1843.

32 *British Diplomatic Correspondence*, 186, Elliot to Aberdeen, 12 May 1843 (accessed 29.1.2015).

33 Minto papers, Elliot to Minto, 6 June 1843, quoted in Hoe and Roebuck *The Taking of Hong Kong*, 207–9.

34 Ibid.

35 Ibid.

36 Ibid.

37 Minto papers ms 13137, ff44–47, Clara to Emma, 16 July 1843.

38 Ibid., ms 13135, ff55–58, Charles to Emma, 6 September 1843.

39 See *British Diplomatic Correspondence*, 267, Addington to Elliot, 3 October 1843 (accessed 5.2.2015)

40 Green to Upshur (undated fragment), quoted in Frederick Merk, *Slavery and the Annexation of Texas* (New York, Alfred A. Knopf, 1972), 12.

41 Hansard, Texas, House of Lords, 18 August 1843 at http://hansard.millbanksystems.com (accessed 9.2.2015).

42 Calhoun to Upshur, 27 August 1843 quoted in Merk, *Slavery and the Annexation of Texas*, 21.

43 Aberdeen to Doyle, 31 July 1843, quoted in Adams *British Interests and Activities in Texas*, 138

44 Murphy and Everett nevertheless had their own theories about British intentions: Murphy thought that Britain sought Texas' re-annexation to Mexico, Everett that Britain wanted to see Texas commercially strong enough to rival the United States.

45 *British Diplomatic Correspondence*, 271–8, Elliot to Aberdeen, 31 October 1843 (accessed 10.2.2015)

46 Ibid.

47 See *British Diplomatic Correspondence*, 283-286, Elliot to Aberdeen, 2 December 1843 (accessed 11.2.2015).

48 Ibid., 289, Elliot to Aberdeen, 29 December 1843 (accessed 13.2.2015).

49 Minto papers ms 13135, ff51–53, Charles to Emma, 26 June 1843.

50 *British Diplomatic Correspondence*, 289–91, Elliot to Aberdeen, 31 December 1843 (accessed 13.2.2015).

## Chapter Fourteen: 'Knavish Tricks'

1 *British Diplomatic Correspondence*, 299, Elliot to Aberdeen, 17 February 1844 (accessed 24.2.2015).

2 Quoted in Adams *British Interests and Activities in Texas*, 157.

3 William R. Manning, ed., *Diplomatic Correspondence of the United States: Inter-American Affairs, 1831–1860* (Washington, 1932-1939), Vol.XII, 328, Murphy to Jones, 14 February 1844, quoted in David M. Pletcher *The Diplomacy of Annexation: Texas, Oregon, and the Mexican War* (Columbia, University of Missouri Press, 1975), 132.

4 Minto papers ms 13135, ff66–67, Charles to Emma, 18 March 1844.

5 *British Diplomatic Correspondence*, 301, Rushton to Elliot, 7 March 1844 (accessed 7.3.2015).

6 Ibid., 300, Elliot to Aberdeen, 7 March 1844 (accessed 7.3.2015).

7 Ibid., 311–2, Jones to Elliot, 25 March 1844 (accessed 8.3.2015).

8 Senate Documents, 28 Cong., 1 sess. (ser.435), no. 349, 11, Calhoun to Van Zandt and Henderson. 11 April 1844, quoted in Pletcher *The Diplomacy of Annexation*, 55.

9 Quoted in Adams *British Interests and Activities in Texas*, 164.

10 *British Diplomatic Correspondence*, 324-325, Elliot to Aberdeen, 10 May 1844 (accessed 16.3.2015).

11 Minto papers ms 13135, f68, Charles to Emma, 20 May 1844.

12 *British Diplomatic Correspondence*, 325, Elliot to Aberdeen, 20 May 1844 (accessed 19.3.2015).

13 Ibid.

14 Quoted in Adams *British Interests and Activities in Texas*, 171.

15 See Pletcher *The Diplomacy of Annexation*, 160.

16 *British Diplomatic Correspondence*, 342–33, Elliot to Aberdeen, 22 June 1844 (accessed 2.4.2015).

17 Ibid.

18 Ibid., 349–50, Elliot to Aberdeen, 10 July 1844 (accessed 4.4.2015).

19 Ibid.

20 Minto papers ms 13135, f73, Charles to Emma, 29 August 1844.

21 Ibid.

22 *British Diplomatic Correspondence*, 372, Elliot to Aberdeen, 28 October 1844 (accessed 4.4.2015)

23 Ibid., 444, Elliot to Aberdeen, 8 February 1845 (accessed 30.4.2015).

24 Ibid., 399, Elliot to Aberdeen, 28 December 1844 (accessed 15.4.2015).

25 Ibid., 397.

26 Ibid., 401–2, Elliot to Aberdeen, 29 December 1844 (accessed 17.4.2015).

27 Ibid.

28 Andrew J. Donelson papers, Manuscripts Division, Library of Congress, Vol.10 (1844-1845), Duff Green to Donelson, 20 December 1844, quoted in Blake *Charles Elliot RN*, 99.

29 *British Diplomatic Correspondence*, 407, Elliot to Aberdeen, 2 January 1845 (accessed 17.4.2015).

30 Ibid., 412, Elliot to Aberdeen, 15 January 1845 (accessed 28.4.2015).

31 Ibid., 414.

32 Ibid., 415.

33 Ibid., 410.

34 Minto papers ms 13135, f78, Charles to Emma, 15 January 1845.

35 *British Diplomatic Correspondence*, 432–3, Aberdeen to Elliot, 23 January 1845 (accessed 28.4.2015).

36 Ibid., 464–5, Elliot to Aberdeen, 2 April 1845 (accessed 2.5.2015).

37 Ibid., 468.

38 HMS *Electra*, 18-gun sloop.

39 *British Diplomatic Correspondence*, 468, Elliot to Aberdeen, 2 April 1845 (accessed 3.5.2015).

40 HMS *Eurydice* was a two-year old, fast, 24-gun frigate commanded by Captain George Elliot, son of Charles' cousin Rear Admiral (later Admiral Sir) George Elliot with whom Charles had served in China.

41 Peel papers, British Museum, Aberdeen to Peel, 11 May 1845, quoted in Merk *Slavery and the Annexation of Texas*, 170–1.

42 Minto papers ms 13135, f80, Charles to Emma, 23 May 1845.

43 *British Diplomatic Correspondence*, 503, Elliot to Bankhead, 11 June 1845 (accessed 7.5.2015).

44 It is not clear what were the 'private distresses', but they may have been anxieties about his family, not only Clara's and their daughter's health, but the behaviour of their youngest son Gibby, whose persistent habit of lying had been the subject some months earlier of a pleading letter to him from his father to desist – see Hoe and Roebuck *The Taking of Hong Kong*, 212–3. Four days later, on 15 June, Elliot wrote to Aberdeen citing an attack of ague and fever and saying that he was going to New Orleans for the sake of his health. He indicated that he would then go on to New York (while always being ready, if the situation required it, to return to Texas).

45 In Aberdeen's instruction the importance of a coordinated approach between Bankhead, Elliot and de Saligny was a key element – see *British Diplomatic Correspondence*, 481–5.

46 *British Diplomatic Correspondence*, 507–88, Bankhead to Elliot, 29 June 1845 (accessed 7.5.2015).

47 Ibid., 508–9, Aberdeen to Elliot, 3 July 1845 (accessed 10.5.2015).

48 Ibid.

49  Aberdeen papers ms 43126, ff50–51, Elliot to Aberdeen, (no date) March 1844.

50  Ibid., ff52–57, Elliot to Aberdeen, 26 March 1844.

51  Ibid., 493–4, Aberdeen to Elliot, 3 June 1845 (accessed 19.5.2015). Adams notes that the withdrawal of Elliot's complaint letter and related correspondence (see next paragraph) was the only instance of exclusion in the whole of the *British Diplomatic Correspondence concerning the Republic of Texas*.

52  The Sabine River had formed Texas's eastern boundary with the United States since Texan independence in 1836.

53  *British Diplomatic Correspondence*, 550, Elliot to Aberdeen, 13 September 1845 (accessed 22.5.2015).

54  See Minto papers, ms 13135, f84, Charles to Emma, 31 July 1845. Harriet's date of birth is not clear from the records, but at death she was probably not older than 50.

55  Ibid., f89, Charles to Emma, 15 August 1845.

56  *British Diplomatic Correspondence*, 562, Aberdeen to Elliot, 3 December 1845 (accessed 26.5.2015).

57  *New York Herald* archives 2336, 22 December 1845, at fultonhistory.com/my%20photo%20albums/All%20Newspapers/New%20York%20NY%20Herald/index.html (accessed 26.5.2015).

58  Ibid.

59  *British Diplomatic Correspondence*, 576–81, Elliot to Aberdeen, 8 January 1846 (accessed 27.5.2015).

60  Minto papers, ms 21217, ff45–46, Aberdeen to Elliot, 3 April 1846.

61  *British Diplomatic Correspondence*, 619–20, Elliot to Aberdeen, 18 June 1846 (accessed 27.5.2015).

62  Grey papers ms GRE/B84/10/14, Elliot to Grey, 28 August 1846.

## Chapter Fifteen: 'A Delightful Residence'

1  Quoted in Hugh Tinker *Victorian Colonial Governors* in *History Today* Vol.40, Issue 12, 3, 12 December 1990 at http://www.historytoday.com (accessed 27.4.2016).

2  Caroline Stephen *The Right Honourable Sir James Stephen: Letters* (1906), 207–8, quoted in Hoe and Roebuck *The Taking of Hong Kong*, 222.

3  *Rules and Regulations for the Information and Guidance of the Principal Officers and Others in His Majesty's Colonial Possessions, 1837* quoted in Anthony Kirk-Greene *On Crown Service* (London, I.B.Tauris & Co Ltd., 1999), 9.

4  Minto papers, ms 21217, f52, Aberdeen to Elliot, 13 September 1846.

5  CO 41/2, *Bermuda Royal Gazette*, 27 October 1846.

6  Imports in 2015 terms, £14.7 million (illustrative – Bank of England inflation calculator at http://www.bankofengland.co.uk/education/Pages/inflation/calculator/index1.aspx, accessed 3.7.2015).

7  CO 41/41, Bermuda Blue Book 1846.

8  At the start of 1848 the hulks were *Coromandel, Dromedary, Medway, Tenedos* and *Thames*; all had initially been in service as warships and subsequently converted for prison use.

9   CO 37/114, ff359–362, Elliot to Grey, 17 October 1846.

10  Ibid.

11  CO 41/41, Blue Book 1846 (1843 census).

12  Salary in 2015 terms, £231,235 (illustrative – Bank of England inflation calculator, accessed 11.4.2016).

13  CO 41/41 Blue Book 1846 and CO 41/49 Blue Book 1854.

14  CO 325/20 Colonial Governors' Salaries at December 1834.

15  Austen was an elder brother of the novelist Jane Austen.

16  CO 37/116, ff7–8, Elliot to Grey, 6 January 1847.

17  For elaboration of this theme see Kwasi Kwarteng *Ghosts of Empire: Britain's Legacies in the Modern World* (New York, PublicAffairs, 2011), passim.

18  Melgund was later to become the third Earl of Minto; he was the husband of Elliot's niece Emma (Nina) and son of his cousin Gilbert, the second Earl.

19  Ephraim Selby, factor (manager) on the Minto estate; see John Evans *The Victorian Elliots in Peace and War* (Stroud, Amberley Publishing, 2012), 12.

20  £50 in 2015 terms £5257 (illustrative – Bank of England inflation calculator, accessed 11.4.2016).

21  Minto papers, ms 12256, ff302–303, Elliot to Melgund, 14 April 1847.

22  Grey papers, ms GRE/B84/10/15, Grey to Elliot,1 July 1847.

23  In 2015 terms, £1,906,032 (illustrative – Bank of England inflation calculator, accessed 11.4.2016).

24  Reported in the *Bermuda Royal Gazette* – see Blake *Charles Elliot RN*, 113.

25  CO 37/118/24.

26  CO 41/4, *Bermuda Herald*, 1 July 1847.

27  Quoted in Anonymous, Ferdinand Whittingham *Bermuda, a colony, a fortress and a prison: or, Eighteen months in the Somers' Islands* (London: Longman, Brown, Green, Longmans, & Roberts, 1857), 90 (Reprinted USA, Scholar's Choice, 2015).

28  CO 41/2, *Bermuda Royal Gazette*, 18 July 1848. Support expenditure figures in 2015 terms: £72,250 and £140,007 respectively (illustrative – Bank of England inflation calculator, accessed 11.4.2016).

29  Admiralty *The Navy List* (London, John Murray, 1821-1881), quoted in John Francis Beeler *British Naval Policy in the Gladstone-Disraeli Era, 1866–1880* (Stanford, Stanford University Press, 1997), 28.

30  Quoted in Ian Stranack *The Andrew and the Onions: The Story of the Royal Navy in Bermuda 1795-1975* (Bermuda, Bermuda Maritime Press, 1990), 14.

31  Quoted in Henry Campbell Wilkinson *Bermuda from Sail to Steam: The History of the Island from 1784 to 1901,* Vol.2 (London, Oxford University Press, 1973), 600.

32  Grey papers, ms GRE/B84/10/40, Elliot to Grey, December 1851.

33  Ibid., ms GRE/B84/10/18, Grey to Elliot, 29 May 1848.

34  Ibid., ms GRE/B84/10/22, Elliot to Grey, 26 June 1848.

35  John Mitchel *Jail Journal; or, Five Years in British Prisons* (New York, *The Citizen*, 1854), 68, at https://archive.org/details/jailjournalorfi00mitcgoog (accessed 21.8.2015).

36 Grey papers, ms GRE/B84/10/24, Elliot to Grey, 10 July 1848. The Ticket of Leave system for convicts was essentially one of parole after probation.

37 Ibid.

38 CO 37/122, ff 51–52, Elliot to Grey, 22 June 1848.

39 Ibid.

40 CO 37/122, f93, Elliot to Grey, 3 July 1848.

41 See CO 37/123/11.

42 Minto papers, ms 13140, ff145–147, Elliot to Gibby, 5 April 1849.

43 CO 37/141, f38, internal Colonial Office memorandum, 26 May 1852.

44 Ibid.

45 See Wilkinson *Bermuda from Sail to Steam*, 607, and Averil Kear *Bermuda Dick* (Lydney, Lightmoor Press, 2002), 108–9.

46 CO 37/144, ff172–175, Merivale to Waddington, 22 October 1853.

47 In 2015 terms, £128,107 (illustrative – Bank of England inflation calculator, accessed 11.4.2016).

48 CO 37/144, f404, Elliot to Newcastle, 24 December 1853.

49 CO 37/146, ff95–97, Elliot to Newcastle, 24 January 1854 .

50 CO 37/146, f146, Elliot to Colonial Office, 13 February 1854.

51 Wilkinson *Bermuda from Sail to Steam*, 600.

## Chapter Sixteen: Back to the Caribbean

1 Picton was killed in action at Waterloo and posthumously feted as a military hero, but he had previously been tried for his involvement in the torture of a slave girl while Governor of Trinidad.

2 Harris to Grey, quoted in L.A.A. de Verteuil *Trinidad: Its Geography, Natural Resources, Administration, Present Condition and Prospects* (London, Ward and Lock, 1858), 343 (Reprinted London, Forgotten Books, 2015).

3 CO 41/3 *Bermuda Royal Gazette* 27 September 1853.

4 Minto papers, ms 13138, ff209-224, Freddy to (aunt) Emma, 26 August 1854.

5 CO 296/22 f22, Peel to Harris, 4 March 1854.

6 Ibid., ff25–26, Merivale to Treasury, 12 June 1854.

7 Ibid.

8 In 2015 terms, £1,457,142. Preceding sums mentioned for the individual projects would translate to £680,000; £194,285; £291,428 and £194,285 respectively (Illustrative – Bank of England inflation calculator at http://www.bankofengland.co.uk/education/Pages/resources/inflationtools/calculator/flash/default.aspx (accessed 11.4.2016).

9 CO 296/22 ff28–29, Merivale to Trevelyan, 24 June 1854.

10 The Secretary of State was a nephew of Charles second Earl Grey and former Prime Minister.

11 CO 295/191, ff124–133, Elliot to Labouchere, 24 January 1856.

12 CO 295/193, Hume to de Verteuil, 1 May 1856, quoted in Donald Wood *Trinidad in Transition: the Years after Slavery* (Oxford, Oxford University Press, 1968), 16.

13 Quoted in de Verteuil *Trinidad*, 212.

14 The population at the 1851 census was 69,600; immigration in 1852 and 1853 totalled 4,775; 1851 population by place of birth: Trinidad 58%, British (presumably West Indian) Colonies 15%, Africa 12%, 'Foreign' 7%, India 6%, UK 1%, quoted in Daniel Hart *Trinidad and the Other West India Islands and Colonies* (Trinidad, The 'Chronicle' Publishing Office, 1866), 66–70 (Reprinted USA, Scholar's Choice, 2015).

15 Announced in *The London Gazette*, 8 May 1855.

16 Minto papers, ms 13136, f4, Charles to Emma, 27 June 1855.

17 Ibid.

18 Ibid., f28, Charles to Emma, 10 October 1855.

19 Ibid., ff50-52, Charles to Emma, 25 November 1855.

20 Ibid.

21 See Mary Cumpston *Radicalism in Trinidad and Colonial Office Reactions 1855–6* in *Historical Research* Vol. 36 Issue 94, 12 October 2007, 153-167 at onlinelibrary.wiley.com/ (accessed 23.10.2015).

22 Ibid.

23 CO 295/186, ff192-193, Trevelyan to Merivale, 20 January 1854.

24 Ibid.

25 See *Radicalism in Trinidad*, 157.

26 CO 295/188, ff199–201, Elliot to Russell, 1 June 1855.

27 CO 295/190, ff298–303, Cumming to Labouchere, 24 November 1855. See also *Radicalism in Trinidad*, 159.

28 CO 295/189, ff316–324, Elliot to Grey, 6 December 1855.

29 Ibid., ff345–349, 8 December 1855.

30 CO295/191, f76, Elliot to Labouchere, 22 January 1856.

31 See *Radicalism in Trinidad*, 162.

32 CO 295/191, ff172–173, Colonial Office minute, 27 March 1856.

33 Minto papers, ms 13136, f57, Charles to Emma, 9 April 1856.

34 Ibid., ms 13137, f243, Clara to Emma, 24 December 1855.

35 CO 295/189, ff345–349, Elliot to Grey, 8 December 1855.

36 Spaccapietra's three predecessors since the British took control had been appointed Vicars Apostolic; Port of Spain became an archdiocese in 1850, Rome taking the view that its new status obviated the need for reference to the British government concerning archiepiscopal appointments.

37 See Gertrude Carmichael *The History of the West Indian Islands of Trinidad and Tobago, 1498–1900* (London, Alvin Redman, 1961), 245, quoted in Hoe and Roebuck *The Taking of Hong Kong*, 220.

38 CO 295/189, Elliot to Grey, 6 December 1855

39 Ibid.

40 For a detailed explanatory account of the Spaccapietra affair see Wood *Trinidad in Transition...*,199–205

41 CO 295/191, ff458–460, Labouchere to Elliot, 15 April 1856.

42 Quoted in *Radicalism in Trinidad*, 164.

43 Minto papers, ms 13136, ff59–61, Charles to Emma, 10 May 1856.

44 Ibid., ff17–72, Charles to Emma, 27 June 1856.

45 CO 295/192, ff20–21, Elliot to Labouchere, 12 June 1856.

46 See *Radicalism in Trinidad*, 164.

47 See Hart *Trinidad and the Other West India Islands and Colonies*, 153. Revenue in 1856 increased by 29% on 1855; expenditure fell slightly by 0.4%. Imports increased by 20%, exports by 48%.

48 CO295/192, ff261–263, Elliot to Labouchere, 7 October 1856.

49 White Creole i.e. those of European descent.

50 The provisions of the Ordinance were nevertheless repressive, extending the minimum period of qualification for a free return passage from five to ten years; see Bridget Brereton *A History of Modern Trinidad 1783–1962* (London, Heinemann, 1981), 102.

51 *Trinidad: Its Geography, Natural Resources, Administration, Present Condition and Prospects*, 403.

## Chapter Seventeen: Intermission

1 See Minto papers, ms 21217, ff83–84, Elliot to Labouchere, 1 February 1857.

2 Minto papers, ms 13137, f259, Clara to Emma, 15 April 1857.

3 The hotel had opened in 1834 and appears to have been one of the most prestigious in Europe at the time.

4 Minto papers, ms 13136, f100, Charles to Emma, 7 June 1857.

5 Ibid., f110, Charles to Emma, 10 July 1857.

6 Minto papers, ms 13136, ff125–127, Charles to Emma, 7 September 1857. Having relocated to Wilton Crescent, Belgravia, London from Charlton following her husband's death, Emma Hislop had moved again, to 56 Chester Square, also in Belgravia. A letter from Wilton Crescent by Gibby to his Aunt Emma, who was temporarily elsewhere, before the Elliots left for Bermuda in 1846 records that 'the old house at Charlton is being pulled down and the old bricks are being used for building houses opposite Mrs. Collinses.' (Minto papers, ms 13138, ff197-198, Gibby to Emma, 2 July 1846).

7 See Minto papers, ms 13137, f266, Clara to Emma, 30 December 1857.

8 Ibid., f135, Charles to Emma, 19 November 1857.

9 *Deo volente*, God willing.

10 Minto papers, ms 13136, f139, Charles to Emma, 4 December 1857.

11 See *The Morning Post*, 20 March 1858 (British Newspaper Archive at www.britishnewspaperarchive.co.uk (accessed 1.8.2014)).

12 Harriet and Edward Southwell Russell (later Baron de Clifford), who had married in 1853, had at this time three children – Maud Clara, Edward Southwell and Charles Somerset.

13 Minto papers, ms 13138, ff205–206, Emma Clara to Emma, 8 March 1858.

14 See Minto papers, ms 13136, ff146–147, Charles to Emma, 28 July 1858.

15 Ibid., ff153–155, Charles to Emma, 10 September 1858.

16 Ibid., f114, Charles to Emma, 1 March 1859.

17 31 Kensington Park Gardens was later the home of the Llewellyn Davies family, and with the five children who lived there was the inspiration for J.M. Barrie's story *Peter Pan*.

18 In March 1860, for example, he attended a diplomatic dinner given by the Swedish and Norwegian Minister and his wife (see *The Morning Post*, 29 March 1860 (British Newspaper Archive (accessed 17.12.2013)).

19 Minto papers, ms 13136, ff223–224, Clara to Harriet. It is not clear to whom Clara's mention of her sister (whose name is not easily discernible in the letter) refers. She is known to have had at least three sisters, one of whom, Bonne Marie Jeanne Josephine, married a Charles Brown, born in London (see Hoe and Roebuck *The Taking of Hong Kong*, 258); but perhaps the word 'sister' is used here in the sense of a close female friend, rather than a blood relative.

20 Ibid., ff187–189, Gibby to Birch, 30 July 1860.

21 Ibid., Charles to Gibby, 19 September 1860.

22 See Grey papers, ms GRE/B84/10/62, Elliot to Grey, 12 June 1861.

23 See http://www.pbenyon.plus.com/RN/Pay_and_Condns/Half_Pay.htm (accessed 17.12.2015). In 2015 terms, £50,012 (illustrative – Bank of England inflation calculator (accessed 11.4.2016).

24 Minto papers, ms13138, ff164–165, Charles to Fred, 31 March 1863.

25 Ibid.

## Chapter Eighteen: Last Posting

1 *St Helena Guardian*, 9 July 1863.

2 Ibid.

3 For elaboration of this theme see Hoe and Roebuck *The Taking of Hong Kong*, 226 and passim.

4 See CO 250/4, f16, Council minutes 3 July 1863.

5 Minto papers, ms 13136, ff239–240, Clara to Emma, 28 August 1863.

6 See Philip Gosse *St Helena 1502–1938* (Oswestry, Anthony Nelson Ltd., 1990), 324.

7 CO 247/100, f47, office minute (by T.F. Elliot), 27 August 1864.

8 Minute to *Ordinance for the Better Prevention of Offences by Juvenile Persons in St Helena* (No.2, 1865), para.4, quoted in Trevor W. Hearl *St Helena Britannica, studies in South Atlantic island history*, A.H. Schulenburg (ed.) (London, Society of Friends of St Helena, 2013), Ch.28, 4.

9 CO 247/99, Layard to Rogers, August 1863.

10 Ibid., James Mundy to Rogers, 14 September 1863.

11 CO 252/32, 144, quoted in Blake *Charles Elliot RN*, 123.

12 CO 250/4, f18, Council minutes 21 September 1863.

13 CO 249/99, *St Helena Guardian* 5 March 1863.

14 Gray's appointment noted in *Crockford's Clerical Directory* for 1865, 768.

15 CO 247/104, f91, Elliot to Cardwell, 20 February 1866.

16 CO 247/104, f158, Gray to Pennell, 10 November 1866.

17 CO 247/100, Elliot to Newcastle, 14 January 1864.

18 Ibid.

19 Minto papers, ms 13138, ff282-285, Emma Clara to Emma, 27 April 1864.

20 Ibid.

21 Ibid., ms 13137, ff272-276, Clara to Emma (undated); the last sentence is presumably a reference to Charles' senior status as a Vice-Admiral.

22 Minto papers, ms 13136, ff256-261, Charles to Emma, 28 June 1864, quoted in Hoe and Roebuck *The Taking of Hong Kong*, 217–8.

23 Ibid., ms 13138, ff303–304, Emma Clara to Emma, 20 April 1865.

24 See Nigel Harris *Footnotes to History: The Personal Realm of John Wilson Croker, Secretary to the Admiralty 1809–1830, a 'Group Family'* (Eastbourne, Sussex Academic Press, 2015), 130.

25 Minto papers, ms 13136, ff324–327, Charles to Emma, 22 June 1865, quoted in Hoe and Roebuck *The Taking of Hong Kong*, 218.

26 Ibid., ff330–333, Charles to Emma, 3 August 1865, quoted in Hoe and Roebuck *The Taking of Hong Kong*, 219.

27 The third Earl was Elliot's first cousin once removed and husband of Charles's niece Nina.

28 Minto papers, ms 12256, f271, Charles to Minto, 16 February 1864.

29 See E. L. Jackson *St Helena: The Historic Island from its Discovery to the Present Date* (New York, Thomas Whittaker, 1905), 84, at https://archive. org/stream/sthelenahistoric00jackrich/sthelenahistoric00jackrich-djvu.txt (accessed 19.2.2016).

30 CO 247/111, Hooker to Sir Frederic Rogers, 31 March 1869.

31 See Gosse *St Helena 1502–1938*, 426.

32 In 2015 terms, £226,667 (illustrative – Bank of England inflation calculator at http://www.bankofengland.co.uk/education/Pages/resources/inflationtools/ calculator/flash/default.aspx (accessed 21.02 2016)

33 Minto papers, ms 13136, ff256–261, Charles to Emma, 28 June 1864, quoted in Hoe and Roebuck *The Taking of Hong Kong*, 221.

34 See Hoe and Roebuck, *The Taking of Hong Kong*, 219.

35 Minto papers, ms 21209, Clara to son Freddy and daughter-in-law Marcia, 28 November 1867, quoted in Harris *Footnotes to History…*, 130.

36 Minto papers, ms 12257, f1, Charles to Nina, 28 December 1868.

37 Taylor to Elliot, 27 March 1869 in Edward Dowden *Correspondence of Henry Taylor* ( London, Longmans, Green and Co., 1888), 289, at https://archive.org/ details/correspondenceof00tayl (accessed 26.2.2016). See also Chapter One above, Note 6.

38 Gosse *St Helena 1502-1938*, 324

39 Jackson *St Helena: The Historic Island…*, 84 (accessed 26.2.2016)

40 CO 247/110, f6, Elliot to Buckingham, 20 January 1869

41 Ibid.

42 Now Hudson R. Janisch, who would later (1873-1884) become one of St Helena's longest serving and most respected Governors. His predecessor as Colonial Secretary, Hope's other grandfather Richard Pennell, had retired in 1868.

43 CO 250/4, ff 86–87.

## Chapter Nineteen: The Final Chapter

1 *London Standard*, 23 February 1870 (British Newspaper Archive at www. britishnewspaperarchive.co.uk (accessed 1.8.2014)).

2 *Freeman's Exmouth Journal*, 7 January 1871.

3 *Exeter & Plymouth Gazette*, 11 February 1876, 6 and 20 July 1877 (British Newspaper Archive, accessed 12.2.2016).

4 Ibid.

5 1871 Census for England. The census record does not give the house any name, listing it simply as Schedule 40, Withycombe Village. Hoe and Roebuck

(*The Taking of Hong Kong*, 222) make reference to Withycourt; *Freeman's Exmouth Journal* records the Elliots as resident throughout at The Parsonage, along with others who lived there for shorter periods.

6  See Hoe and Roebuck *The Taking of Hong Kong*, 221. Freddy had married, in 1861, Marcia Ouseley. When they stayed with Charles and Clara Elliot all four grandchildren – Hugh, Ernest, Beatrice and Emily – were aged under 9.

7  Minto papers, ms 12257, ff 65-66, Fred to Nina, 19 September 1875.

8  Ibid., ff19-23, Fred to Nina, 21 September 1875.

9  1881 Census for England.

10  *Exeter and Plymouth Gazette*, 25 February 1876 (British Newspaper Archive, accessed 12.2.2016).

11  £8,000 in 2015 terms: £832,653 (illustrative – Bank of England inflation calculator at http://www.bankofengland.co.uk/education/Pages/resources/inflationtools/calculator/flash/default.aspx (accessed 9.3.2016)).

12  *Illustrated London News* quoted in *Belfast Newsletter*, 25 October 1875, (British Newspaper Archive, accessed 17.12.2013).

13  Minto papers, ms 12257, ff 65–66, Fred to Nina, 19 September 1875.

14  See Census for England of 1891, for example, where he is described as 'Living on his own means'.

15  Ibid.

16  *England, Andrews Newspaper Index Cards, 1790-1976* at http://interactive.ancestry.co.uk (accessed 11.3.2016).

17  *India List and India Office List 1905* (London, HM Government, 1905) at https://books.google.co.uk (accessed 12.3.2016).

18  1911 Census for England.

19  Ned's daughter Georgina Isabella married Henry Montagu Butler, Headmaster of Harrow School and future Master of Trinity College Cambridge, in 1861. One of the witnesses to the marriage was Emma Hislop.

20  St John in the Wilderness had been superseded as a place of regular worship by the new more conveniently located Church of St John the Evangelist, but the site continued to be used for burials.

21  *Hertford Mercury and Reformer*, 24 October 1885 (British Newspaper Archive, accessed 13.3.2016).

## Epilogue

1  Peter Burroughs *Imperial Institutions and the Government of Empire* in *The Oxford History of the British Empire, The Nineteenth Century* (Oxford, Oxford University Press, 1999), 173.

2  W. Travis Hanes III and Frank Sanello *The Opium Wars, The Addiction of One Empire and the Corruption of Another* (Naperville, Sourcebooks, Inc., 2002), 47.

3  *A Memoir* – see Chapter One Note 6.

4  *British Interests and Activities in Texas, 1838–1846*, 150.

5  Ibid., 108.

6  FO 17/12, ff59–60, Stephen to Backhouse, 23 February 1835, quoted in Hoe and Roebuck *The Taking of Hong Kong*, 228.

7  See Hoe and Roebuck, *The Taking of Hong Kong*, 226–77.

8  Henry Taylor *Autobiography*, Vol. 1, 171–2.

9  Henry Taylor *Edwin the Fair*, quoted in *Autobiography*, 168–99.

10  *Jail Journal*, 159.

11  Ibid.

12  Henry Taylor *Autiobiography*, Vol. 1, 353.

13  Edward Belcher *Narrative of a Voyage Round the World, Performed in Her Majesty's Ship Sulphur, During the Years 1836 – 1842* (London, Henry Colburn, 1843), 213-214 (Reprinted London, Forgotten Books, 2015).

14  *Macao and the British*, 216.

15  *The Opium War*, 167.

16  W. C. Hunter *An American in Canton (1825–1844)* (Hong Kong, Derwent Communications, 1994), 182, quoted in Hoe and Roebuck, *The Taking of Hong Kong*, 225.

# Bibliography

**Primary Sources**
**Manuscripts**
Aberdeen papers (British Library), ms. 43126

Grey papers (University of Durham), mss. GRE/B84, GRE/B148

Jardine Matheson Archive (University of Cambridge), James Matheson Private Letter Books Vol. 6

Minto papers (National Library of Scotland), mss. 11084, 11226, 11789, 11793, 11796, 11810, 12256, 12257, 13135, 13136, 13137, 13138, 21209, 21214, 21216A, 21217, 21218, 21219, 21220

UK Government records (National Archives, Kew):

Admiralty series ADM 1 (correspondence); 7 (ship movements); 196 (officers' service records)

Colonial Office series CO 114, 116 (British Guiana); 37, 41 (Bermuda); 152 (Leeward Islands); 295, 296 (Trinidad); 247, 250, 252 (St Helena); 325 (general)

Foreign Office series FO 17 (China); 70 (Naples, Sicily); 75 (Texas)

**Newspapers and Magazines**
*Belfast Newsletter* (British Newspaper Archive at www.britishnewspaperarchive.
    co.uk)
*Bermuda Herald*
*Bermuda Royal Gazette*
*Blackwood's Edinburgh Magazine* (London and Edinburgh, 1840) at http://
    google.co.uk
*Exeter & Plymouth Gazette* (British Newspaper Archive)
*Freeman's Exmouth Journal*
*Hertford Mercury and Reformer* (British Newspaper Archive)
*London Standard* (British Newspaper Archive)
*New York Herald* archives at fultonhistory.com
*St Helena Guardian*
*The Essequebo and Demerary Royal Gazette* at http://www.vc.id.au/edg/
    18311231rg.html
*The Gentleman's Magazine*
*The London Gazette*
*The Morning Post* (British Newspaper Archive)
*The Times* (London, England) (*The Times* Digital Archive)

**Other Contemporary Records**

Anderson, Aeneas, *An Accurate Account of Lord Macartney's Embassy to China; carefully abridged from the original work* (London, Vernor and Hood, 1798)

Anonymous, Whittingham, Ferdinand, *Bermuda, a colony, a fortress and a prison: or, Eighteen months in the Somers' Islands* (London: Longman, Brown, Green, Longmans, & Roberts, 1857), (Reprinted USA, Scholar's Choice, 2015)

Belcher, Edward, *Narrative of a Voyage Round the World, Performed in Her Majesty's Ship Sulphur, During the Years 1836 – 1842* (London, Henry Colburn, 1843) (Reprinted London, Forgotten Books, 2015)

Bernard, W. D., *Narrative of the Voyages and the Services of the Nemesis from 1840 to 1843* (London, Henry Coulburn, 1844)

de Verteuil, L. A. A., *Trinidad: Its Geography, Natural Resources, Administration, Present Condition and Prospects* (London, Ward and Lock, 1858) (Reprinted London, Forgotten Books, 2015)

Dickinson, Violet (ed.), *Miss Eden's Letters* (London, Macmillan, 1919) (Reprinted General Books LLC, Memphis, 2012)

Dowden, Edward, *Correspondence of Henry Taylor* (London, Longmans, Green and Co., 1888)

*Hansard* at http://hansard.millbanksystems.com

Hart, Daniel, *Trinidad and the Other West India Islands and Colonies* (Trinidad, The 'Chronicle' Publishing Office, 1866) (Reprinted USA, Scholar's Choice, 2015)

Mackenzie, Charles, *Notes on Haiti, made during a Residence in that Republic, Vol. 1* (London, Henry Colburn and Richard Bentley, 1830)

McPherson, Duncan MD, *Two years in China, Narrative of the Chinese Expedition from its formation in April 1840* (London, Saunders and Otley, 1843)

Mitchel, John, *Jail Journal; or, Five Years in British Prisons* (New York, The Citizen, 1854)

Ouchterlony, Lt. John, *The Chinese War: an Account of all the Operations of the British Forces from the Commencement to the Treaty of Nanking* (London, Saunders and Otley, 1844)

Parliamentary Papers, *Correspondence Relating to China*, 1840 and 1841

Taylor, Henry, *Autobiography* (London, Longmans, Green and Co., 1885)

*The Anti-Slavery Reporter* (London, London Society for the Abolition of Slavery Throughout the British Dominions, 1833)

*The Chinese Repository*, Vols. VI and VII, May 1837 to April 1839 (unabridged facsimile, Elibron Classics Replica Edition, 2005)

Thelwall, Algernon, *The Iniquities of the Opium Trade with China: Being a Development of the Main Causes which Exclude the Merchants of Great Britain from the Advantages of an Unrestricted Commercial Intercourse with that Vast Empire. With Extracts from Authentic Documents* (London, W. H. Allen and Company, 1839)

**Reference Works**

Colledge, J.J. and Warlow, Ben *Ships of the Royal Navy* (Newbury, Casemate-UK, 2010)

*Collins's Peerage of England* (Collins, London, 1812) at https://books.google.co.uk

*Crockford's Clerical Directory* for 1865

*Dictionary of Canadian Biography Online* at http://www.biographi.ca/009004-119.01.php?&id_nbr=3204

*Dod's Peerage Baronetage and Knightage of Great Britain and Ireland* (London, Whittaker & Co., 1841)

*England, Andrews Newspaper Index Cards, 1790–1976* at http://interactive.ancestry.co.uk

*India List and India Office List 1905* (London, HM Government, 1905) at https://books.google.co.uk

O'Byrne, William R. *A Naval Biographical Dictionary: comprising the Life and Services of Every Living Officer in Her Majesty's Navy, from the Rank of Admiral of the Fleet to that of Lieutenant, inclusive* (London, John Murray, 1849)

*Oxford Dictionary of National Biography* (Oxford, Oxford University Press, 2004)

*Royal Navy Pay and Conditions* at http://www.pbenyon.plus.com/RN/Pay_and_Condns/Half_Pay.htm

*William Loney RN – Background* at http://www.pdavis.nl/Background.htm

*UK Censuses* 1861, 1871, 1881, 1891, 1911

## Secondary Sources
### Books

Adams, Ephraim Douglass (ed.), *British Diplomatic Correspondence concerning the Republic of Texas, 1838–1846* (Austin, The Texas State Historical Association, 1918)

*British Interests and Activities in Texas 1838–1846* (Baltimore, The Johns Hopkins Press, 1910)

Barker, Eugene Campbell *Mexico and Texas 1821–1835: University of Texas research lectures on the causes of the Texas revolution* (New York, Russell & Russell Inc., 1965)

*The Life of Stephen F. Austin: Founder of Texas, 1793-1836* (Nashville, 1925)

Bartlett, C. J., *Great Britain and Sea Power 1815–1853* (Oxford, Clarendon Press, 1963)

Beeching, Jack, *The Chinese Opium Wars* (New York, Harcourt Brace Jovanovich, 1975)

Beeler, John Francis, *British Naval Policy in the Gladstone-Disraeli Era, 1866–1880* (Stanford, Stanford University Press, 1997)

Bennett, G. W., *A History of British Guiana, compiled from various authorities* (Georgetown, Demerara, L. M'Dermott, 1875) (published in digitised form, British Library Historical Collection)

Black, Jeremy, *British Diplomats and Diplomacy 1688–1800* (Exeter, University of Exeter Press, 2001)

Blake, Clagette, *Charles Elliot RN 1801–1875 A Servant of Britain Overseas* (London, Cleaver-Hume Press Limited, 1960)

Blake, Robert, *Jardine Matheson Traders of the Far East* (London, Weidenfeld & Nicholson, 1999)

Booth, Martin, *Opium: A History* (New York, St Martin's Griffin, 1998)

Bose, Sugata, *A Hundred Horizons. The Indian Ocean in the Age of Global Empire* (London and Cambridge Massachusetts, Harvard University Press, 2006)

Bourne, Kenneth, *The Foreign Policy of Victorian England 1830–1902* (Oxford, Clarendon Press, 1970)

Brereton, Bridget, *A History of Modern Trinidad 1783–1962* (London, Heinemann, 1981)

Buchan, John, *Lord Minto: A Memoir* (London and Edinburgh, Thomas Nelson and Sons Ltd., 1924)

Burroughs, Peter, *Imperial Institutions and the Government of Empire* in *The Oxford History of the British Empire, The Nineteenth Century* (Oxford, Oxford University Press, 1999)

Campbell, Randolph B., *An Empire for Slavery: The Peculiar Institution in Texas, 1821–1865* (Baton Rouge, Louisiana State University Press, 1991)

Chang Hsin-pao, *Commissioner Lin and the Opium War* (New York, W.W.Norton & Company Inc., 1970)

Chipman, Donald E. and Joseph, Harriett Denise, *Spanish Texas 1519–1821* (Austin, University of Texas Press, 2010)

Coates, Austin, *Macao and the British 1637-1842, Prelude to Hong Kong* (Hong Kong, Oxford University Press, 1988)

Collis, Maurice, *Foreign Mud* (London, Faber and Faber Limited, 1946)

Costin, W. C., *Great Britain and China, 1833–1860* (Oxford, The Clarendon Press, 1937)

Cundall, Frank, *Historic Jamaica* (London, The West India Committee, 1915)

da Costa, Emilia Viotti, *Crowns of Glory, Tears of Blood* (New York, Oxford University Press, 1994)

Dalton, Henry G., *The History of British Guiana* (London, Longman, Brown, Green, and Longmans, 1855)

Dickinson, Harry W., *Educating the Royal Navy: Eighteenth- and Nineteenth-Century Education for Officers* (Abingdon, Routledge, 2007)

Elliot, G. F. S., *The Border Elliots*, (Edinburgh, David Douglas, 1897)

Endacott, G. B., *A History of Hong Kong* (Hong Kong, Oxford University Press, 1964)

Evans, John, *The Victorian Elliots in Peace and War* (Stroud, Amberley Publishing, 2012)

Fay, Peter Ward, *The Opium War 1840–1842* (New York and London, W.W.Norton & Company, 1976)

Faulk, Odie B., *The Last Years of Spanish Texas 1778–1821* (The Hague, Mouton & Co., 1964)

Ferguson, Niall, *Empire: How Britain made the Modern World* (London, Penguin Books, 2003)

Gelber, Harry G., *Opium, Soldiers and Evangelicals, England's 1840–42 War with China, and its Aftermath* (Basingstoke, Palgrave Macmillan, 2004)

Gosse, Philip, *St Helena 1502–1938* (Oswestry, Anthony Nelson Ltd., 1990)

Greenberg, Michael, *British Trade and the Opening of China 1800–1842* (Cambridge, Cambridge University Press, 2008)

Hanes, W. Travis III and Sanello, Frank, *The Opium Wars, The Addiction of One Empire and the Corruption of Another* (Naperville, Sourcebooks, Inc., 2002)

Harris, Nigel, *Footnotes to History: The Personal Realm of John Wilson Croker, Secretary to the Admiralty 1809–1830, a 'Group Family'* (Eastbourne, Sussex Academic Press , 2015)

Hearl, Trevor W., *St Helena Britannica, studies in South Atlantic island history*, ed. Schulenburg, A.H. (London, Society of Friends of St Helena, 2013)

Hibbert, Christopher, *The Dragon Wakes: China and the West 1793–1911* (Harmondsworth, Penguin Books, 1984)

Hoe, Susanna and Roebuck, Derek, *The Taking of Hong Kong: Charles and Clara Elliot in China Waters* (Richmond, Curzon Press, 1999)

Holt, Edgar, *The Opium Wars in China* (London, Putnam & Company Ltd., 1964)

Inglis, Brian, *The Opium War* (London, Hodder and Stoughton, 1976)

Ishmael, Odeen, *The Guyana Story (from Earliest Times to Independence)* 2005, at http://www.guyana.org/features/guyanastory/guyana_story.html

Jackson, E. L., *St Helena: The Historic Island from its Discovery to the Present Date* (New York, Thomas Whittaker, 1905) at https://archive.org/stream/sthelenahistoric00jackrich/sthelenahistoric00jackrichdjvu.txt

James, William, *The Naval History of Great Britain 1793–1827* (London, R. Bentley, 1837), Vol. VI, at http://pbenyon.plus.com/Naval_History/Vol_VI/Contents.html

Keay, John, *The Honourable Company: A History of the East India Company* (London, Harper Collins, 1993)

Keswick, Maggie (ed.), *The Thistle and the Jade, A Celebration of 150 Years of Jardine Matheson* (London, Frances Lincoln Limited, 2008)

Kirk-Greene, Anthony, *On Crown Service* (London, I. B. Tauris & Co Ltd., 1999)

Kwarteng, Kwasi, *Ghosts of Empire: Britain's Legacies in the Modern World* (New York, Public Affairs, 2011)

Lambert, Andrew, *The Last Sailing Battlefleet: Maintaining Naval Mastery 1815–1850* (London, Conway Maritime Press 1991)

Lavery, Brian, *Empire of the Seas* (London, Conway, 2009)

Lovell, Julia, *The Opium War* (London, Picador, 2011)

Melancon, Glenn, *Britain's China Policy and the Opium Crisis: Balancing Drugs, Violence and National Honour, 1833–1840* (Aldershot, Ashgate Publishing Ltd., 2003)

Menzies, Gavin, *1421 The Year China discovered the World* (London, Bantam Press, 2002)

Merk, Frederick, *Slavery and the Annexation of Texas* (New York, Alfred A. Knopf, 1972)

Milner, Clyde A. II, O'Connor, Carol A., and Sandweiss, Martha A. (eds.), *The Oxford History of the American West* (New York and Oxford, Oxford University Press, 1994)

Minto, Countess of, *A Memoir of the Right Honourable Hugh Elliot* (Edinburgh, Edmonston and Douglas, 1868)

Morse, H. B., *International Relations of the Chinese Empire* (London, New York: Longmans, Green and Co., 1910)

Napier, Priscilla, *Barbarian Eye: Lord Napier in China, 1834, The Prelude to Hong Kong* (London, Brassey's, 1995)

Oldfellow, Oliver (Benjamin Bradney Bockett), *Our School: Or Scraps and Scrapes in Schoolboy Life* (London, John Wesley & Co., 1857, reprinted Kessinger Publishing, 2009)

Penny, F. E., *Fort St George, Madras: A Short History of Our First Possession in India* (London, Swan Sonnenschein & Co. Ltd., 1900) at http://archive.org/details/fortstgeorgemad00penngoog

Pletcher David M., *The Diplomacy of Annexation: Texas, Oregon, and the Mexican War* (Columbia, University of Missouri Press, 1975)

Pottinger, George, *Sir Henry Pottinger, First Governor of Hong Kong* (Stroud, Sutton Publishing, 1997)

Rambaud, Jacques (ed.), *Memoirs of the Comte Roger de Damas (1787–1806)* at http://archive.org/stream/memoirsofcomtero00damauoft#page/306

Rees, Sian, *Sweet Water and Bitter: The Ships that Stopped the Slave Trade* (London, Chatto & Windus, 2009)

Stranack, Ian, *The Andrew and the Onions: The Story of the Royal Navy in Bermuda 1795–1975* (Bermuda, Bermuda Maritime Press, 1990)

Studwell, Joe, *The China Dream* (London, Profile Books, 2002)

Thomas, Hugh, *The Golden Age: The Spanish Empire of Charles V* (London, Penguin Books, 2011)

Waley, Arthur, *The Opium War through Chinese Eyes* (Stanford, Stanford University Press, 1968)

Walvin, James, *The Slave Trade* (London, Thames and Hudson, 2011)

Welsh, Frank, *A History of Hong Kong* (London, Harper Collins, 1993)

Wilkinson, Henry Campbell, *Bermuda from Sail to Steam: The History of the Island from 1784 to 1901*, Vol. 2 (London, Oxford University Press, 1973)

Wood, Donald, *Trinidad in Transition: the Years after Slavery* (Oxford, Oxford University Press, 1968)

Yanne, Andrew and Heller, Gillis, *Signs of a Colonial Era* (Hong Kong, Hong Kong University Press, 2009)

### Articles, Theses, Essay and Guides

Aubrey, Philip, *Preventive Squadron – The Royal Navy and the West African Slave Trade 1811–1868,* Julian Corbett Prize Essay, University of London, 1948

Brasseaux, Carl A. and Chandler, Richard E., *The* Britain *Incident 1769–1770: Anglo-Hispanic Tensions in the Western Gulf,* Southwestern Historical Quarterly, Vol. 87, April 1984 at http://texashistory.unt.edu/ark:/67531/metapth117150/m1/425/

Cavell, Samantha, *Playing at Command: Midshipmen and Quarterdeck Boys in the Royal Navy 1793–1815,* MA thesis Louisiana State University 2006, Vol. 24 at http://etd.lsu.edu/docs/available/etd-03312006-200152/unrestricted/Cavell_thesis.pdf

Colgate, H. A., *Trincomalee and the East Indies Squadron 1746 to 1844* (unpublished MA thesis University of London 1959)

Cumpston, Mary, *Radicalism in Trinidad and Colonial Office Reactions 1855–6,* in Historical Research Vol. 36, October 2007 at onlinelibrary.wiley.com/

Davis, Robert C. *Counting European Slaves on the Barbary Coast* in Past and Present, No. 172 (Oxford University Press, August 2001)

*Exhibition information, Royal Naval Museum,* Portsmouth at http://www. royalnavalmuseum.org/visit-see-victory-cfexhibition-infosheet.htm

*Official Catalogue and Guide, Chelsea Royal Naval Exhibition, 2 May 1891,* 32 at http://www.ebooksread.com/authors-eng/1891-may-2-chelsea-royal-naval-exhibition/official-catalogue-guide-hci/page-32-official-catalogue-guide-hci.shtml

Rodwell, Dennis, *The Minto House Debacle* in Context (Magazine of the Institute of Historic Building Conservation), Vol. 36, Dec. 1992, at ihbc. org.uk/context_archive/36/minto.htm

Roebuck, Derek, *Captain Charles Elliot RN, Arbitrator: Dispute Resolution in China Waters, 1834–6* in Arbitration International (1998) at http:// arbitration.oxfordjournals.org/content

Sheridan, Richard B., *The Condition of Slaves on the sugar plantations of Sir John Gladstone in the colony of Demerara, 1812–49* in New West Indian Guide/Nieuwe West-Indische Gids, 76 (2002), Leiden, at http://www. kitlv-journals.nl/index.php/nwig/viewFile/3455/4216

Slater, Carl G., *The Problem of Purchase Abolition in the British Army 1856–1862* in Journal of the South African Military History Society, Vol. 4, No. 6, Dec. 1979, at http://samilitaryhistory.org/vol046cs.html

Tinker, Hugh, *Victorian Colonial Governors* in History Today, Vol. 40, December 1990 at http://www.historytoday.com

# Index